WELLINGTON'S ARMY, 1809-1814

NAPOLEONIC LIBRARY

PLATE I.

ARTHUR WELLESLEY, DUKE OF WELLINGTON.
From a portrait by Sir Thomas Lawrence.

WELLINGTON'S ARMY, 1809-1814

Sir Charles Oman

K.B.E. HON. D.C.L. OXFORD. HON. LL.D. CAMBRIDGE
AND EDINBURGH. F.B.A. FOR SIXTEEN YEARS
BURGESS FOR THE UNIVERSITY OF OXFORD.
CHICHELE PROFESSOR OF MODERN
HISTORY. FELLOW OF ALL SOULS
COLLEGE AND HONORARY
FELLOW OF NEW
COLLEGE. F.S.A.,
ETC.

Greenhill Books

Greenhill
Books

This edition of *Wellington's Army 1809–1814*
first published 1986 by Greenhill Books,
Lionel Leventhal Limited,
2-6 Hampstead High Street, London NW3 1QQ

ISBN 0-947898-41-7

Publishing History
Wellington's Army 1809–1814 was first
published in 1913 by Edward Arnold, London.
This edition is reproduced now exactly as
the original edition, complete and unabridged.

Greenhill Books
welcome readers' suggestions for books
that might be added to this Series.
Please write to us if there are titles
which you would like to recommend.

Printed by Antony Rowe Limited,
Chippenham, Wiltshire.

PREFACE

MUCH has been written concerning Wellington and his famous Peninsular Army in the way of formal history : this volume, however, will I think contain somewhat that is new to most students concerning its organization, its day by day life, and its psychology. To understand the exploits of Wellington's men, it does not suffice to read a mere chronicle of their marches and battles. I have endeavoured to collect in these pages notices of those aspects of their life with which no strategical or tactical work can deal, though tactics and even strategy will not be found unnoticed.

My special thanks are due to my friend Mr. C. T. Atkinson, Fellow of Exeter College, Oxford, for allowing me to use the admirable list of the brigade and divisional organization of the Peninsular Army which forms Appendix II. It is largely expanded from the article on the same topic which he printed eight years ago in the *Historical Review,* and enables the reader to find out the precise composition of every one of Wellington's units at any moment between April, 1808 and April, 1814. I have also to express my gratitude to the Hon. John Fortescue, the author of the great *History of the British Army,* for answering a good many queries which I should have found hard to solve without his aid. The index is by the same loving hand which has worked on so many of my earlier volumes.

C. OMAN.

OXFORD,
   September, 1912.

CONTENTS

LIST OF ILLUSTRATIONS

WELLINGTON'S ARMY

CHAPTER I

INTRODUCTORY—THE OLD PENINSULAR ARMY

WHILE working for the last nine years at the History of the Peninsular War, I have (as was inevitable) been compelled to accumulate many notes, and much miscellaneous information which does not bear upon the actual chronicle of events in the various campaigns that lie between 1808 and 1814, but yet possesses high interest in itself, and throws many a side-light on the general course of the war. Roughly speaking, these notes relate either to the personal characteristics of that famous old army of Wellington, which, as he himself said, " could go anywhere and do anything," or to its inner mechanism—the details of its management. I purpose to speak in these pages of the leaders and the led ; of the daily life, manners, and customs of the Peninsular Army, as much as of its composition and its organization. I shall be dealing with the rank and file no less than with the officers, and must even find space for a few pages on that curious and polyglot horde of camp followers which trailed at the heels of the army, and frequently raised problems which worried not only colonels and adjutants, but even the Great Duke himself.

There is an immense amount of interesting material to be collected, concerning the inner life of the Peninsular Army, from public documents, such as despatches, general orders, and regimental reports, and records of courts martial. But I shall be utilizing to a much greater extent non-official information, collected from the countless diaries, memoirs, and series of contemporary letters, which have come down to us from the men who took part in the great war. Nor are the controversial pamphlets to be neglected, which kept appearing for many a year, when one survivor of the old army found, in the writings of another, statements which he considered injurious to himself, his friends, his regiment, or his division. The best known and most copious of these discussions is that which centres round the publication of Napier's *Peninsular War ;* the successive appearance of its volumes led to the printing of many protests, in which some of the most prominent officers of Wellington's army took part—not only Lord Beresford, who was Napier's especial butt and *bête noir*, and replied to the historian in terms sometimes not too dignified—but Cole, Hardinge, D'Urban, and many more. This set of " strictures ", as they were called, mainly relate to the Albuera campaign. But there are smaller, but not less interesting, series of controversial pamphlets relating to the Convention of Cintra, to Moore's retreat, to the campaign of 1810 (Bussaco), the storm of Badajoz, and other topics.

The memoirs and autobiographies, of course, possess the greatest share of interest. And it may be noted as a remarkable fact that those coming from the rank and file are not very much less numerous than those which come from the commissioned ranks. If there are scores of diaries and reminiscences of colonels, captains, and subalterns, there are at least dozens of little books by sergeants, corporals, and privates. Many of these are very quaint productions indeed, printed at local presses—at Perth, Coventry, Cirencester, Louth, Ashford—even at Corfu. Very frequently some knot of military or civilian friends induced a much-travelled veteran to commit to paper the tales which had been the delight of the canteen, or of the fireside of some village inn. They are generally very good reading, but often give rather the spirit of the time and the regiment than an accurate record of its long-past exploits. One or two of these veterans' artless tales show all the characteristics of the memoirs of the prince of their tribe—the delightful but autolatrous Marbot. I have thought it worth while to give in an appendix the names and titles of the best of them. One or two, above all the little book of " Rifleman Harris " of the 95th, well deserve to be republished, but still await that honour. Perhaps regimental patriotism may some day provide us with a series of reprints of the best Soldiers' Tales.*

It is a very notable fact, which requires (but has never hitherto received) an explanation, that it is precisely with the coming in of the nineteenth century that British soldiers and officers alike began to write diaries and reminiscences on a large scale, and in great numbers. I do not, of course, mean to say that there were none such produced in the eighteenth century. Besides serious military histories like those of Kane, Stedman, or Tarleton, there do exist a certain number of narratives of personal adventure written by officers, such as Major Rogers the Scout, or the garrulous and often amusing diarist (unfortunately anonymous) who made the campaign of Culloden with the Duke of Cumberland—not to speak of the semi-apochryphal Captain Carleton. But they are few, and the writings from the ranks are fewer still, though there are certain soldiers' letters which go back as far as Marlborough's time, and one or two small books like Bristow's and Scurry's Indian reminiscences, and Sergeant Lamb's *Journal* in the American War of Independence, which are worth mentioning. But it is quite certain that there was more writing going on in the army during the ten years 1805–1815 than in the whole eighteenth century.

What was the explanation of the phenomenon ? There are, I think, two main causes to be borne in mind : the

---

* John Shipp's is the only book from the ranks which has been reprinted within the last ten years, I believe. Mr. Fitchett reproduced a few chapters of Anton and others in his rather disappointing *Wellington's Men.*

first was the glorious and inspiring character of Wellington's campaigns, which made both officers and men justifiably proud of themselves, and more anxious than any previous generation had been to put on paper the tale of their own exploits. It must have been a man of particularly cheerful disposition who cared to compile the personal narrative of his adventures during the Old American War, which was largely a record of disaster, or even in the ups and downs of the Seven Years' War, when for every Minden or Quebec there had been an evil memory like Ticonderoga or Kloster-Kampen. It is to this instinctive dislike to open up old memories of misfortune that we may attribute the fact that the first British campaigns of the French Revolutionary War, the unhappy marches and battles of the Duke of York's army in 1793, 1794, 1795 are recorded in singularly few books of reminiscences—there are only (to my knowledge) the doggerel verse of the " Officer of the Guards,'' with its valuable foot-notes, and the simple memoirs of Sergeant Stevenson of the Scots Fusilier Guards, and Corporal Brown of the Coldstream. This is an extraordinarily small output for a long series of campaigns, in which some 30,000 British troops were in the field, and where gallant exploits like those of Famars and Villers-en-Cauchies took place. But the general tale was not one on which any participant could look back with pleasure. Hence, no doubt, the want of books of reminiscences.

But I fancy that there is another and a quite distinct cause for the extraordinary outburst of interesting military literature with which the nineteenth century begins, and we may note that this outburst certainly commences a little before the Peninsular War. There exist several very good personal narratives both of the Conquest of Egypt in 1801, of the Indian Wars during the Viceroyalty of Lord Wellesley, and of the short campaign of Maida. And this cause I take to be the fact that the generation which grew up under the stress of the long Revolutionary War with France was far more serious and intelligent than that which saw it begin, and realized the supreme importance of the ends for which Great Britain was contending, and the danger which threatened her national existence. The empire had been in danger before, both in the Seven Years' War, and in the War of American Independence, but the enemy had never been so terrifying and abhorrent as the Jacobins of the Red Republic. The France of Robespierre was loathed and feared as the France of Louis XV. or Louis XVI. had never been. To the greater part of the British nation the war against the Revolution soon became a kind of Crusade against the "triple-headed monster of Republicanism, Atheism, and Sedition." The feeling that Great Britain had to fight not so much for empire as for national existence, and for all that made life worth having—religion, morality, constitution, laws, liberty—made men desperately keen for the fight, as their ancestors had never been.

Among the many aspects which their keenness took, one was most certainly the desire to record their own personal part in the great strife. It is in some such way only that I can explain the fact that the actually contemporary diaries and journals become so good as the war wears on, compared to anything that had gone before. Memoirs and reminiscences written later do not count in the argument, because they were compiled and printed long after the French war was over, and its greatness was understood. But the abundance of good material written down (and often sent to the press) during the continuance of the war is astounding. In some cases we can be sure that we owe the record to the reason that I have just suggested. For example, we certainly owe to it the long and interesting military diaries of Lord Lynedoch (the Sir Thomas Graham of Barrosa), who most decidedly went into the Revolutionary War as a Crusader and nothing less. As I shall explain when dealing with his remarkable career, he started military life at forty-four, mortgaging his estates to raise a battalion, and suddenly from a Whig M.P. of the normal type developed into a persistent and conscientious fighter against France and French ideas—whether they were expressed (as when first he drew the sword) in the frenzied antics of the Jacobins, or (as during his latter years) in the grinding despotism of Bonaparte. His diary from first to last is the record of one who feels that he is discharging the elementary duty of a good citizen, by doing his best to beat the French wherever they may be found.

I take it that the same idea was at the bottom of the heart of many a man of lesser note, who kept his pen busy during those twenty eventful years. Some frankly say that they went into the service, contrary to the original scheme of their life, because they saw the danger to the state, and were ready to take their part in meeting it. " The threat of invasion fired every loyal pair of shoulders for a red coat." *

Of the men whose memoirs and letters I have read, some would have been lawyers (like Sir Hussey Vivian), others politicians, others doctors, others civil servants, others merchants, if the Great War had not broken out. I should imagine that the proportion of officers who had taken their commission for other reasons than that they had an old family connection with the army, or loved adventure, was infinitely higher during this period than it had ever been before. A very appreciable number of them were men with a strong religious turn—a thing I imagine to have been most unusual in the army of the eighteenth century (though we must not forget Colonel Gardiner). One young diarist heads the journal of his first campaign with a long prayer.† Another starts for the front with a final letter to his relatives to the effect that " while striving to discharge his military duties he will never forget his religious ones : he who observes the former and disregards the latter is no better than a civilized brute." ‡

---

* Kincaid, *Random Shots from a Rifleman*, p. 8.
† This was Woodberry of the 18th Hussars.
‡ *Sir William Gomm's Life*, p. 31.

There were Peninsular officers who led prayer-meetings and founded religious societies—not entirely to the delight of the Duke of Wellington,* whose own very dry and official view of religion was as intolerant of "enthusiasm" as that of any Whig bishop of Mid-Georgian times. Some of the most interesting diaries of the war are those of men who like Gleig, Dallas, and Boothby, took Holy Orders when the strife came to an end. One or two of the authors from the ranks show the same tendencies. Quartermaster Surtees was undergoing the agonies of a very painful conversion, during the campaign of 1812, and found that the memories of his spiritual experiences had blunted and dulled his recollection of his regimental fortunes during that time.† A very curious book by an Irish sergeant of the 43rd devotes many more pages to religious reflections than to marches and bivouacs.‡ Another writer of the same type describes himself on his title-page as "Twenty-one years in the British Foot Guards, sixteen years a non-commissioned officer, forty years a Wesleyan class leader, once wounded, and two years a Prisoner." §

On the whole I am inclined to attribute the great improvement alike in the quantity and the quality of the information which we possess as to the inner life of the army, during the second half of the great struggle with France, not only to the fact that the danger to the empire and the great interests at stake had fired the imagination of many a participant, but still more to the other fact that the body of officers contained a much larger proportion of thoughtful and serious men than it had ever done before. And the same was the case *mutatis mutandis* with the rank and file

---

* See his curious dispatch from Cartaxo dated February 6th, 1811, concerning preaching officers.

† He describes himself as "rolling on the floor like one distracted, with the pains of hell getting hold, and hope seeming to be for ever shut out of my mind."—*Surtees*, p. 172.

‡ He calls his little book *Memoir of a Sergeant late of the 43rd Light Infantry, previously to and during the Peninsular War, including an account of his Conversion from Popery to the Protestant Religion.*

§ John Stevenson of the Scots Fusilier Guards.

also.   Not but what—of course—some of the most interesting information is supplied to us by cheerful and garrulous rattlepates of a very different type, who had been attracted into the service by the adventure of the soldier's life, and record mainly its picturesque or its humorous side.

CHAPTER II

SOURCES OF INFORMATION—THE LITERATURE OF THE
PENINSULAR WAR

IT will be well, perhaps, to give a short account of the main
sources from which our knowledge of the Peninsular Army
is derived. The official ones must be cited first. The most
important of all are, naturally enough, the Wellington
Dispatches. Of these there are two series; the first, in twelve
volumes, was published during the Duke's lifetime by
Colonel Gurwood between 1837 and 1839. The second, or
supplementary series, in fifteen volumes, was published
with copious notes by the second Duke of Wellington
between 1858 and 1872.

The series edited by Gurwood is absolutely necessary
to every student of the Peninsular War, but is most tiresome to handle, and is by no means complete. The Duke
forbade the publication of a great number of his more confidential letters, and ordered portions of others to be omitted.
He had a strong notion that a great deal of historical information could be, and ought to be, suppressed; this fact
has caused much trouble to the modern historian, who
wishes to obtain not a mere official and expurgated view of
the war, but a full and complete survey of it. To show
Wellington's attitude it may be sufficient to quote his
answer to William Napier, who asked for leave to utilize
all his papers. " He could not tell the whole truth without
hurting the feelings of many worthy men, and without
doing mischief. Expatiating on the subject, he related
many anecdotes illustrating this observation, showing errors

committed by generals and others—especially at Waterloo
—errors so materially affecting his operations that he could
not do justice to himself if he suppressed them, and yet
by giving them publicity he would ungraciously affect
the favour of many worthy men, whose only fault was
dullness." *

The Gurwood edition of the dispatches was published
some fifteen years after Napier made his application, but
numbers of the old Peninsular officers were still alive, and
the Duke adhered to his already-expressed opinion that it
would not be well to expose old quarrels and old blunders.
Paragraphs, accordingly, are often omitted in the reprint,
and in a large majority of cases, where blame was imputed
or reproofs administered to any individual, the name was
left blank. This makes the edition most tiresome to read.
It is exasperating to find that *e.g.* " nothing has given me
more concern in the late operations than the conduct of
Lieut.-Colonel —— of the —— Regt." † or that "no means
exists of punishing military disorders and irregularities of
the kind committed by Brigadier General —— and Colonel
——." Or again, when Wellington writes to the Patronage
Secretary at the Horse Guards that " I am much obliged to
you for relieving me from Major-General —— and Colonel
——. I have seen General —— and I think he will do
very well, and so will —— " ‡; or that " —— appears to be a
kind of madman," and " —— is not very wise," the reader
is reduced to despair. The only way of discovering the
names, which are often those of officers of high rank, who
figure repeatedly in any narrative of the Peninsular War,
is to go to the original dispatches at the Record Office, or,
when the communication is a private and not a public one,
to the letters at Apsley House. Meanwhile, few have the
leisure or the patience to do this, so that Wellington's
judgments on his lieutenants are still practically inaccessible.

It was, perhaps, still necessary to leave all these blanks

* *Life of Sir W. Napier,* i. 235, 236.
† *Dispatches,* vii. p. 559.   ‡ *Ibid.* vi. p. 485.

in 1837. And Gurwood was no doubt acting in strict
obedience to the Duke's orders. But nothing can excuse
his own slack editing of the massive tomes that he published.
There are no tables of contents to the volumes, nor does
the title page of each indicate the dates between which it
runs. To find out which volume will contain a letter of
November, 1810, we must take down Vols. VI. and VII.,
and see from the date of the last dispatch in one and the
first in the other, when the break comes. Supposing we
wish to discover how many communications were sent to
Graham or Spencer in 1811, there is no other way of achieving our object than running through every page of the two
volumes in which the correspondence of that year is contained ! There is a so-called index to the whole series,
but it is practically useless, from the small number of
headings given. The reader will look in it vainly for obvious
places-names such as Chaves, Casal Novo, Castello Branco,
Vera, St. Pierre, for personal names such as Lapisse, Latour
Maubourg, Bonnet, Montbrun, Abadia, Penne-Villemur,
O'Donnell, Del Parque, Erskine, Anson, Victor Alten,
Barnard, Beckwith. On the other hand he will find silly
headings such as under L, "Lies, encouragement of," or
under I, "Invincibility of British Troops." Perhaps the
most ridiculous entry in this absurd compilation is that of
" Light Division," to which there is annexed just one
note, " satisfactory conduct of, on April 6, 1811," as if that
was the sole occasion on which it was necessary to mention
that distinguished unit of the British army. There are no
headings under regiments at all, so that if one wishes to
see what the Duke said about the 52nd or the Black Watch,
one simply gets no help.

But there is another trick of Gurwood's which is even
worse than his want of tables of contents or adequate
index-entries. He omitted all the elaborate statistics
which used to accompany the Duke's dispatches, without
exception. The beautiful tables of casualties which
explain the distribution of losses between regiments and

divisions, are in every case boiled down into three bald totals of " killed, wounded, and missing," for the whole army, no indication of units being left.   Even Lord Londonderry's modest two volumes, the first attempt at a general history of the Peninsular War, give far more useful information on the all-important topics of strengths and losses than all Gurwood's tomes.   For that sensible author rightly saw that nothing could be more serviceable to the reader than an occasional table of the organization and numbers of the whole allied army, and that the detailed casualty-list of such a fight as Talavera or Albuera is indispensable.   The purblind Gurwood preferred to put in a note, " the detail of divisions, regiments, and battalions has been omitted, being too voluminous," * when he was dealing with an important return.   The historian owes him small thanks for his precious opinion.

It is an immense relief to pass from Gurwood's ill-arranged work to the volumes of the *Wellington Supplementary Dispatches*, which were published by the second Duke between 1858 and 1872.   Though the mass of Peninsular material contained in this series is comparatively small, it comprises a great quantity of familiar and private correspondence, which had been deliberately omitted from the earlier publication.   And, moreover, it is admirably edited ; the second Duke knew what was important and what required explanation, appended valuable and copious notes, and was able (since the elder generation was now practically extinct) to abandon the exasperating reticence used by Gurwood.   Moreover, he added a vast quantity of letters written not by, but to, his father, which serve to explain the old Duke's sometime cryptic replies to his correspondents.   Even a few necessary French documents have been added.   Altogether these volumes are excellent, and make one wish that the editing of the whole of the Wellington papers had fallen into the same hands.

* This preposterous remark may be found on p. 28 of vol. vi.

There is a third series of Official publications which though not so " generally necessary for salvation " as the Dispatches, for any student of the Peninsular War, is very valuable and needs continually to be worked up. This is the seven volumes of *General Orders*, from 1809 to 1815, which are strictly contemporary documents, as they were collected and issued while the war was in progress—the 1809–10 volumes were printed in 1811, the 1811 volume in 1812, and so on. The last, or Waterloo volume, had the distinction of being issued by the British Military Press in Paris, " by Sergeant Buchan, 3rd Guards," as printer. The *General Orders* contain not only all the documents strictly so called, the notices issued by the commander-in-chief for the army, but an invaluable *précis* of all courts-martial other than regimental ones, and a record of promotions, gazettings of officers to regiments, rules as to issue of pay and rations, and directions as to all matters of detail relating to organization, hospitals, depôts, stores, routes, etc. If any one wishes to know on what day the 42nd was moved from the first to the second division, when precisely General Craufurd got leave to go home on private business, what was the accepted value of the Spanish dollar or the Portuguese Cruzado Novo at different dates, when expressed in English money, or what was the bounty given when a time-expired man consented to renew his service for a limited period, these are the volumes in which he will find his curiosity satisfied. They cannot be called interesting reading—but they contain facts not elsewhere to be found.

There is an exactly corresponding series of General Orders for the Portuguese Army, in six yearly volumes, called *Ordens do Dia* : it was issued by Marshal Beresford, and contains all the documents signed by him. Whenever a student is interested in the career of one of the numerous British officers in the Portuguese service, he must seek out the records of his doings in these volumes. They are not easy to work in, as they have no yearly indices, and much patience is required to discover isolated notices of individuals. These volumes are practically inaccessible in England. It was with the greatest difficulty that a Lisbon friend hunted me up a copy after long search, and I am not aware that there is another on this side of the sea. But by its use only can we trace the service of any Anglo-Portuguese officer. There was supposed to be an "Ordem" every morning, and when nothing was forthcoming in the way of promotions, court-martial reports, or decrees, Beresford's chief of the staff used to publish a solemn statement that there was no news, as thus—

Quartel-General de Chamusca, 7. 1. 1811.
Nada de novo.
Adjudante-General Mosinho.

This happened on an average about twice a week.

In addition to these printed series there is an immense amount of unprinted official correspondence in the Record Office which bears on the Peninsular War. It will be found not only in the War Office section, but in those belonging to the Foreign Office and the Admiralty. As an example of the mysteries of official classification, I may mention that all documents relating to French prisoners will have to be looked for among the Admiralty records, under the sub-headings *Transport* and *Medical*. If, as occasionally happens, one wishes to find out the names and regiments of French officers captured on some particular occasion, *e.g.* Soult's retreat from Oporto, or the storm of Badajoz, it is to the Admiralty records that one must go! Officers can always be identified, but it is a herculean task to deal with the rank and file, for they used to be shot into one of the great prisons, Norman's Cross, Porchester, Stapleton, etc., in arbitrary batches, with no regard to their regimental numbers. It would take a week to hunt through the prison records with the object of identifying the number of privates of the 34th Léger captured at Rodrigo, since they may have gone in small parties to any one of a dozen destinations. Many of the prison registers have lost one or other of their outer-boards, and the handling of them is a grimy business for the fingers, since they are practically never consulted.

While nearly the whole of the Wellington dispatches have been printed, it is only a small part of the Duke's " enclosures ", added to each dispatch, that have had the same good fortune. These always repay a cursory inspection, and are often highly important. The greater part of Sir John Moore's correspondence with Lord Castlereagh, and many dispatches of Moore's subordinates—Baird, Leith, and Lord W. Bentinck—with a number of valuable returns and statistics,—are printed in a large volume entitled *Papers Relative to Spain and Portugal, Presented to Parliament in* 1809." There are, to the best of my knowledge, no similar volumes relating to Graham's campaign from Cadiz in 1811, or Maitland's and Murray's operations on the east side of Spain in 1813–14. A good deal of information about the latter, however, may be got from the enormous report of the court-martial on Murray, for his wretched *fiasco* at the siege of Tarragona, which is full of valuable facts. The details of the other minor British enterprises in the Peninsula—such as those of Doyle, Skerret, Sir Home Popham, and Lord Blayney, all remain in manuscript, —readily accessible to the searcher, but not too often consulted. The Foreign Office section at the Record Office is highly valuable not only to the historian of diplomacy, but to the purely military historian, because Stuart, Vaughan, Henry Wellesley, and the other representatives of the British Government at Madrid, Seville, and Cadiz, used to send home, along with their own dispatches, numberless Spanish documents. These include not only official papers from the Regency, but private documents of great value, letters from generals and statesmen who wish to keep the British agent informed as to their views, when they have clashed with the resolves of their own government. There are quite a number of military narratives by Spanish

officers, who are set on excusing themselves from responsibility for the disasters of their colleagues. And the
politicians sometimes propose, in private and confidential
minutes, very curious plans and intrigues. Sir Charles
Vaughan kept a certain number of these confidential papers
in his own possession when he left Cadiz, and did not turn
them over to the Foreign Office. They lie, along with
his private correspondence, in the Library of All Souls'
College, Oxford.

Since we are dealing with the British army, not with
the general history of the Peninsular War, I need only
mention that unpublished documents by the thousand,
relating to the French, Spanish, and Portuguese armies,
may be found at Paris, Madrid, and Lisbon, and that the
researcher is invariably welcomed and courteously treated.
It may be worth while to make a note, for the benefit of
beginners, to the effect that the French military documents
are not concentrated in one mass, but are divided between
the *Archives Nationales*, and the *Archives de la Guerre* at
the Ministry of War. If a return or a dispatch is not to
be found in one of these repositories, it may yet turn up
in the other. The Spanish records are very "patchy,"
full on some campaigns, almost non-existent on others.
For example, the documents on the luckless Ocaña campaign of 1809 are marvellously few ; there does not exist
a single complete "morning state", by regiments and
divisions, of Areizaga's unhappy army. I fancy that the
whole of the official papers of his staff were captured in the
rout, and destroyed by ignorant plunderers—they did not
get into the French collections. Hence there have only
survived the few dispatches which Areizaga and some of
his subordinates sent to the Spanish Ministry of War.

So much for Official Records. Passing on to the publications of individual actors in the war, we must draw a
sharp line between those which were issued during or immediately after the campaigns with which they deal, and those

which were written down, with or without the aid of contemporary notes or journals, many years after. The former,
of course, possess a peculiar interest, because the writers'
narrative is not coloured by any knowledge of what is yet
to come. An officer writing of Corunna or Talavera with
the memory of Vittoria and Waterloo upon him, necessarily
took up a different view of the war from the man who set
down his early campaign without any idea of what was to
follow. Early checks and hardships loom larger in the
hour of doubt and disappointment, than when the recollection of them has been dimmed by subsequent hours of
triumph. The early material, therefore, is very valuable,
but it is not so copious as that which was written down
later, and it largely exists in the form of letters and diaries,
both of which are less readable than formal narratives.
As good types of this sort of material we may name Ormsby's
and Ker-Porter's *Journals of the Campaign of 1808–09*,
Hawkers' *Journal of the Talavera Campaign*, Stothert's
Diary of 1809–11, and General MacKinnon's Journal of
the same three years, all of which were published within a
few months of the last entry which each contains. Next
to these come the books which consist of contemporary
material, published without alteration from the original
manuscripts, but only many years after they had been
written. The best of these for hard facts, often facts not
to be found elsewhere, is the diary of Tomkinson of the
16th Light Dragoons : * with it may be mentioned the
Journal of George Simmons of the 95th, published in 1899
with the title, " A British Rifle Man," † the Journals of Sir
William Gomm, 1808–15,‡ Sir George Warre's Letters
of 1808–12,§ which only saw the light two years ago, and
Larpent's *Private Journal*, printed in 1852.|| These volumes

---

* Only printed in 1894.
† Edited by Col. Willoughby Verner.
‡ Published 1881. Invaluable as a private record for the staff.
§ Edited by his kinsman, the present Provost of Eton.
|| Larpent was a lawyer who acted as Wellington's Judge Advo-
cate.

all have short notes by the editors, but the text is the writing of the Peninsular time, untampered with and unaltered.

These books and their minor contemporaries stand in a class by themselves, as contemporary material reflecting accurately the spirit of the times. Much more numerous, however, are the books which, though produced by actors in the Great War, appeared at dates more or less remote from the years whose events they narrate. The formal histories are comparatively few, the reason being that Napier's magnificent (if somewhat prejudiced and biassed) volumes completely put off other possible authors, who felt that they lacked his genius and his power of expression, from the idea of writing a long narrative of the war as a whole. This was a misfortune, since the one book which all students of military history are thereby driven to read, was composed by a bitter political partisan, who is set on maligning the Tory government, has an altogether exaggerated admiration for Napoleon, and owned many personal enemies in the British army, who receive scant justice at his hands. At the same time we must be grateful that the work was written by one who was an actual witness of many of the campaigns that he relates, conscientiously strove to get at all other first-hand witnesses, and ransacked the French as well as the British official papers, so far as he could obtain access to them. The merits of his style are all his own, and will cause the *History of the Peninsular War* to be read as an English classic, as Clarendon's *History of the Great Rebellion* is read, even when research has shown (as in Clarendon's case) that much of the narrative needs reconstruction, and that the general thesis on which it is constructed lacks impartiality.

The only other general histories of the war which appeared were Southey's (three vols. published 1832) and Lord Londonderry's.* The former was written by a literary man without any military experience, who had seen nothing

* It is hardly necessary to mention Jones's slight Sketch (1818) or Goddard's mass of undigested contemporary material (1814).

of the Peninsula during the years of the struggle, and had as almost his only merit, a good knowledge of the Spanish sources, of which he was too uncritical. The book fell dead, being unable to compete with Napier, and lacking all the authority of personal knowledge which was the latter's strong point. The smaller book of Lord Londonderry (two volumes, published 1829) is by no means without merit, but has many faults, always hovering on the edge between formal history and personal reminiscences. Wherever Charles Stewart had not been present, he passes lightly over the episodes of war, and obviously had taken no very great pains to collect first-hand material. At the same time the book has value, as giving the views of a highly-placed staff officer, who had the opportunity of seeing every episode from the point of view of Head Quarters, and had strong convictions and theories of his own. He had also the saving grace of loving statistics, and printed many valuable appendices of "morning states" and casualty-lists, things of which Napier was far too sparing, and which Gurwood suppressed altogether. As a general record the book could not cope with Napier, and has been forgotten—somewhat undeservedly—no less than Southey's vast quartos. There is absolutely no other general history by a contemporary which needs mention. Of course I omit foreign sources, which help us little with regard to the British army, though they are indispensable for a general study of the war. Foy's unfinished *Guerre de la Peninsule*, if we may judge from the volumes which appeared before his death, would have been a very prejudiced affair—his account of the British troops in Vol. I. is a bitter satire, contrasting oddly enough with his confessions concerning their merits in his *Journal*, of which a large portion was published a few years ago by Girod de l'Ain under the title *Vie Militaire du Général Foy*. After all the detraction in his formal history, it is interesting to read the frank letter which says, in 1811, that for a set battle on a limited front he acknowledges the superiority of the English infantry to the French, " I keep this opinion

to myself," he adds, " and have never divulged it, for it
is necessary that the soldier in the ranks should not only
hate his enemy, but also despise him." * Foy kept the
opinion so closely to himself, that no one would have
suspected it who had read only his formal history of the
Peninsular War.

Another French general history is Marshal Jourdan's
Guerre d'Espagne, issued only ten years ago by the Vicomte
de Grouchy, though large parts of it had been utilized in
Ducasse's *Life and Correspondence of King Joseph Bonaparte*. This covers the whole war down to Vittoria, and
is notable for its acute and often unanswerable criticism of
Soult and Masséna, Marmont, and, not least, of Napoleon
himself. It is less satisfactory as a vindication of Jourdan's
own doings. Marmont's autobiography only covers his fifteen
months of command from May, 1811, to July, 1812 : while
St. Cyr's and Suchet's very interesting accounts of their
own periods of activity relate entirely to Catalonia and the
eastern side of the Peninsula. St. Cyr does not touch
British affairs at all ; Suchet treats his campaigns against
Maitland and Murray in a much more cursory style than
his previous successes against the Spanish armies.† The
other French formal narratives by contemporaries and
eye-witnesses are for the most part monographs on particular
campaigns in which the writers took part—such as Thiébault's work on Junot in Portugal—full of deliberate
inaccuracies—which was published in 1817, and Lapène's
Conquête d'Andalousie, en 1810-12, and *Campagnes de
1813-14* (both published in 1823 in volumes of different
size) which deal only with the army of Soult. There are,
however, two general histories by German officers—Schepeler
(who served with the Spaniards), and Riegel (who served
with the French)—which both require mention. The former
is especially valuable.‡

* *Journal* in Girod de l'Ain, p. 98.
† His well-written two volumes (issued 1829) are said to have
been very largely the work of his aide-de-camp, St. Cyr-Nugues.
‡ Vacani's Italian general history of the war is very slight on the

Among Peninsular historians two deserve special notice. The Conde de Toreno, a Spanish statesman who had taken part in the war as a young man, produced in 1838 three massive volumes which are, next to Napier, the greatest book that makes this war its subject. He is a first-hand authority of great merit, and should always be consulted for the Spanish version of events. He was a great master of detail, and yet could paint with a broad brush. It is sometimes necessary to remember that he is a partisan, and has his favourites and his enemies (especially La Romana) among the generals and statesmen of Spain. But on the whole he is a historian of high merit and judgment. With Toreno's work must be mentioned the five small volumes of the Portuguese José Accursio das Neves, published in 1811, when Masséna had but just retreated from before the Lines of Torres Vedras. This is a very full and interesting description of Junot's invasion of Portugal, and of the sufferings of that realm which came to an end with the Convention of Cintra. It is the only detailed picture of Portugal in 1808. Unfortunately the author did not complete the story of 1809-10.

At the end of this note on historical works, as distinguished from memoirs or diaries of adventure, we must name two excellent books, one English and one French, on the special subject of siege operations. These two monographs by specialists, both distinguished engineer officers—Sir John Jones' *Journal of the Sieges in Spain 1811-13*, and Colonel Belmas' *Journaux des Sièges dans la Peninsule 1808-13*, published respectively in 1827 and 1837—are among the most valuable books dealing with the Peninsular War, both containing a wealth of detail and explanatory notes. The work of Belmas is especially rich in reprints of original documents bearing on the sieges, and in statistics of garrisons, losses, ammunition expended, etc. They were so complete, and supplemented each other so

English side, being mainly devoted to the doings of the Italians in Catalonia.

well, that little was done to add to the information that they give, till Major J. Leslie's admirable edition of the *Dickson Papers* began to appear a few years ago, and appreciably increased our knowledge of the English side of the siege operations.

Having made an end of the formal histories written by contemporaries and eye-witnesses, it remains that we should speak of a class of literature much larger in bulk, and generally much more interesting, considered in the light of reading for the general student—the books of autobiographies and personal reminiscences which were written by participants in the war some time after it had come to an end—at any time from ten to forty years after 1814. Their name is legion. I am continually discovering more of them, many of them printed obscurely in small editions and from local presses, so that the very knowledge of their existence has perished. And so many unpublished manuscripts of the sort exist, in France no less than in England, that it is clear that we have not even yet got to the end of the stock of original material bearing on the war. Some of the most interesting, *e.g.* the lively autobiography of Blakeney of the 28th,* and that of Ney's aide-de-camp Sprünglin,† have only appeared during the last few years.

These volumes of personal adventures differ greatly in value : some were written up conscientiously from contemporary diaries : others contain only fragments, the most striking or the most typical incidents of campaigns whose less interesting every-day work had been forgotten, or at least had grown dim. Unfortunately in old age the memory often finds it hard to distinguish between things seen and things heard. It is not uncommon to find a writer who represents himself as having been present at scenes where he cannot have been assisting, and still more frequent to

---

* Published under the rather romantic title of *A Boy in the Peninsular War* (which suggests a work of fiction), by Julian Corbett, in 1899.

† Published in the *Revue Hispanique* in 1907.

detect him applying to one date perfectly genuine anecdotes which belong to another. One or two of the most readable narratives frankly mix up the sequence of events, with a note that the exact dating can not be reconstructed. This is notoriously the case with the most vivid of all the books of reminiscences from the ranks—the little volume of "Rifleman Harris," whose tales about General Robert Craufurd and the Light Division flow on in a string, in which chronology has to take its chance, and often fails to find it.

Another source of blurred or falsified reminiscences is that an author, writing many years after the events which he has to record, has generally read printed books about them, and mixes up this secondary knowledge with the first-hand tale of his adventures. Napier's Peninsular War came out so comparatively early, and was so universally read, that screeds from it have crept into a very great number of the books written after 1830. Indeed, some simple veterans betray the source of their tales, concerning events which they cannot possibly have witnessed themselves, by repeating phrases or epigrams of Napier's which are unmistakeable. Some even fill up a blank patch in their own memory by a *précis* of a page or a chapter from the great history. It is always necessary to take care that we are not accepting as a corroboration of some tale, that which is really only a repetition of it. The diary of a sergeant of the 43rd mentioned above,* contains an intolerable amount of boiled-down Napier. It is far more curious to find traces of him in the famous Marbot, who had clearly read Mathieu Dumas' translation when it came out in French.

The books of personal adventure, as we may call the whole class, may roughly be divided into three sections, of decreasing value in the way of authority. The first and most important consists of works written upon the base of an old diary or journal, where the memory is kept straight as to the sequence of events by the contemporary record,

* See p. 7.

and the author is amplifying and writing up real first-hand material. Favourable examples of this are Leach's *Rough Sketches of the Life of an Old Soldier*,* Leslie of Balquhain's *Military Journal*,† which in spite of its title is not in journal shape, but reads as a continuous narrative, and Sir George Bell's *Rough Notes of Fifty Years' Service*,‡ all of which are definitely stated by the authors to have been founded on their note-books of the war time, and therefore can as a rule be treated as first-hand evidence. They can generally be trusted as authorities against any divergent tales based on the narratives of writers who wrote their reminiscences without any such foundation, and where they get off the lines of contemporary evidence they usually give the reader warning. For example, Leach gives valuable material to show the inaccuracy of Napier's exaggerated estimate of the length and pace of the Light Division's march to Talavera, whose erroneous figures have been repeated in so many subsequent books. And yet Leach was not conscious of the fact that the data which he gives were incompatible with Napier's story, and repeats it in a general way— because he published his book several years after the appearance of Napier's second volume, and had (like many other members of the Light Division) absorbed the legend as a matter of faith on Napier's authority. It was reserved for Sir John Bell,§ who had served under Craufurd but joined too late for Talavera, to explode the story. But his demonstration of its inaccuracy has not travelled far, while the original legend has gone all round the world, and is still reproduced, as an example of unparalleled rapidity of movement, in serious military works.

Infinitely less valuable than the books founded on private diaries or letters of contemporary date, are those which were written down long after the war, from unaided

* Published 1831. A first-rate authority for Rifle Brigade and Light Division matters.
† Of the 29th Regt. Published only in 1887.
‡ Published 1867.
§ Not to be confused with Sir *George* Bell.

memory only. They are, of course, progressively less valuable for evidence according as the date at which they were indited recedes from the period with which they deal. Gleig's charming *The Subaltern*, printed as early as 1825, may be better trusted for matters of detail than Blakeney's equally vivid narrative written in the remote island of Paxos about 1835, and Blakeney is more valuable than Hennegan's highly romantic *Seven Years of Campaigning*, published only in 1847, when thirty winters had blurred reminiscence, and allowed of the accretion of much second-hand and doubtful material round the original story. The strength of men's memories differs, so does their appreciation of the relative value of a dramatic narrative as compared with a photographic record of personal experiences. But in a general way we must allow that every year that elapses between the event and the setting down of its narrative on paper decreases progressively the value of the record. As an example of the way in which the failing powers of old age can confuse even a powerful memory, we may mention the curious fact that Wellington himself, twenty years after his last campaign, seems to have told two auditors that he had visited Blücher's camp on the very eve of Waterloo, the night between the 17th and 18th of June, 1815, a statement quite incredible.* It was apparently a blurred memory of his real visit to the Prussian headquarters on the early afternoon of the 16th, of which ample details are known.

Failing memory, the love of a well-rounded tale, a spice of autolatry, and an appreciation of the picturesque, have impaired the value of many a veteran's reminiscences. Especially if he is a well-known *raconteur*, and has repeated his narrative many times before he sets it down on paper, does it tend to assume a romantic form. The classical example, of course, is Marbot, whose memoirs contain

---

* See for a dissection and disproof of this story Ropes's *Waterloo*, pp. 238–242, 3rd edition. Mr. Horsburgh (p. 138) and others accept the story. But despite Lady Shelley's note it is really incredible.

many things demonstrably false, *e.g.* that he brought the
news of the *Dos Mayo* insurrection at Madrid to Napoleon,
or that in 1812 he took his regiment from Moscow to the
neighbourhood of Poltava, and brought it back (400 miles !)
in less than a fortnight with a convoy of provisions, or that
he saw 6000 men drowned on the broken ice of the lake of
Satschan at the end of the battle of Austerlitz.* Marbot
is, of course, an extreme example of amusing egotism, but
parallels on a minor scale could be quoted from many of
his contemporaries, who wrote their tale too late. We
may mention Thiébault's account of the combat of Aldea
da Ponte, when he declares that he fought 17,000 Anglo-
Portuguese and produced 500 casualties in their ranks,
when he was really opposed by one British brigade and two
Portuguese battalions, who lost precisely 100 men between
them. Yet the account is so lengthy and detailed, that if
we had not the British sources before us, we should be
inclined to think that we were reading an accurate narrative
of a real fight, instead of a romantic invention reconstructed from a blurred memory. It was the only Peninsular fight in which Thiébault exercised an independent
command—and every year added to its beauties as the
general grew old.

While, therefore, we read the later-written Peninsular
narratives with interest, and often with profit, as reflections
of the spirit of the time and the army, we must always be
cautious in accepting their evidence. And we must begin
by trying to obtain a judgment on the " personal equation "
—was the author a hard-headed observer, or a lover of
romantic anecdotes ? What proportion, if any, of the facts
which he gives can be proved incompatible with contemporary records ? Or again, what proportion (though not demonstrably false) seem unlikely, in face of other authorities ?
Had he been reading other men's books on a large scale ?
Of this the usual proof is elaborate narrative concerning

---

* For a dissection of Marbot's blunders see the essay on his
methods in Holland Rose's *Pitt and Napoleon*, pp. 156–166.

events at which he cannot possibly have been present,
with or without citation of the source from which he has
obtained the information.   It is only when the author has
passed his examination with credit on these points, that we
can begin to treat him as a serious authority, and to trust
him as evidence for scenes at which we know that he was
actually present. Many a writer of personal adventures
may finally be given his certificate as good authority for
the annals of his own battalion, but for nothing more.
It is even possible that we may have to make the further
restriction that he may be trusted on the lucky days, but not
on the less happy ones, in the history of his own beloved
corps.   Reticence as to " untoward incidents " is not uncommon. As to things outside the regiment, there was
often a good deal of untrustworthy gossip abroad, which
stuck in the memory even after long years had passed.

Among all the books of regimental adventure, I should
give the first place for interest and good writing to Lieut.
Grattan's *With the Connaught Rangers*.   It is not too much
to say that if the author had taken to formal history, his
style, which is vivid without exaggeration, and often
dignified without pomposity, would have made him a
worthy rival of Napier as an English classic.   His descriptions of the aspect and psychology of the stormers marching
down to the advanced trenches at Ciudad Rodrigo, and of
the crisis of the battle of Salamanca, are as good as anything
that Napier ever wrote.   A reader presented with many of
his paragraphs would say without hesitation that they were
excerpts from the great historian.   Unfortunately Grattan
suffered from one of the faults which I have named above
—he *will* give untrustworthy information about episodes
at which he was not present—it is at best superfluous and
sometimes misleading.   But for what the 88th did at
Bussaco and Fuentes, at Badajoz and Salamanca, he is
very good authority.   And he is always a pleasure to read.
Two good books—Gleig's *The Subaltern,* and Moyle Sherer's
Recollections of the Peninsula—have a share of the literary

merit of Grattan's work, but lack his power. They give respectively the day-by-day camp life of the 85th in 1813–14, and of the 48th in 1811–13, in a pleasant and life-like fashion, and since both were published within ten years of the end of the war—Gleig's in 1825, Sherer's in 1824—the writers' memories were still strong, and their statements of fact may be relied upon. Both have the merit of sticking closely to personal experience, and of avoiding second-hand stories.

Those lively tales of adventure—Kincaid's *Adventures in the Rifle Brigade*, Sir Harry Smith's *Autobiography*, and Blakeney's memoir (which its editor called *A Boy in the Peninsular War*) *—were all written at a much later date, from twenty to thirty years after Waterloo, and show their remoteness from the time that they describe not so much by want of detail, nor of picturesque power of description, —all three authors were good wielders of the pen—as by the selection of the facts that they record. Much of the every-day life of the regiment has been forgotten or grown dim, and only the great days, or the most striking personal experiences, or quaint and grotesque incidents, are recorded. This very fact makes them all very good reading—they contain (so to speak) all the plums of the cake and comparatively little of the less appetizing crust. Harry Smith's chapters are practically the tale of his Odyssey in the campaigns of 1812–13 along with the heroic little Spanish wife whom he had picked up and married at the storm of Badajoz. Kincaid is a humourist—he remembers all the grotesque incidents, ludicrous situations, practical jokes, and misadventures, in which he and his comrades were concerned, and pours them out in a string of anecdotes, loosely connected by a narrative of which he says that he refuses to be responsible for the exact sequence or dating. It is very amusing, and some of the more striking stories can be verified from other and better authorities. But

* Blakeney wrote about 1835, at Paxos in the Ionian Isles; Smith in 1844, in India; Kincaid in 1847.

the general effect is often as if we were reading a chapter out of Lever's *Charles O'Malley*, or some such old-fashioned Pensinsular romance. Blakeney's book gives a better impression for solidity, and he fills up many an incident, otherwise known to us only in outline, with picturesque detail which bears every appearance of truth. But I have once or twice found his narrative refusing to square in with contemporary documents, and when this is the case the story written twenty-five years after the event must go to the wall.* He must be used with caution, though he is giving a genuine record to the best of his ability.

Nearly all the reminiscences from the ranks are subject to these same disabilities. With hardly an exception they were written down long years after the events recorded. Usually the narrator had no books or notes to help him, and we get a genuine tale, uninfluenced by outer sources, but blurred and foreshortened by the lapse of time. The details of personal adventure are perfectly authentic to the best of the veteran's memory ; incidents of battle, of camp hardships, of some famous court-martial and subsequent punishment-parade, come out in a clear-cut fashion. But there are long gaps of forgotten months, frequent errors of dating, and often mistakes in the persons to whom an exploit, an epigram, or a misadventure are attributed. Yet these little volumes give the spirit of the rank and file in the most admirable fashion, and enable us to realize the inner life of the battalion as no official document can do. There are a few cases where the author has got hold of a book, generally Napier's great history, and to a great extent spoils his work by letting in passages of incongruous eloquence, or strategical disquisition, into the homely stuff of his real reminiscences.†

* His extraordinarily vivid narrative of the fortunes of Browne's provisional battalion at Barrosa conflicts in detail with contemporary evidence which there is no reason to doubt, *e.g.* as to the numbers of the battalion, and as to the exact behaviour of General Whittingham.

† A strong case is that of the sergeant of the 43rd, mentioned above, on p. 7, who lets in scraps of Napier into his patchwork with the most unhappy effect.

One soldier's little volume stands out from all the rest for its literary merit—it is the work of a man of superior education, who had enlisted in a moment of pique and humiliation to avoid facing at home the consequences of his own conceit and folly. This short story of 150 pages called *Journal of T. S., a Soldier of the 71st Highland Light Infantry, 1806–15*, was written down as early as 1818,* when memory was still fresh. Its value lies in the fact that the author wrote from the ranks, yet was so different in education and mental equipment from his comrades, that he does not take their views and habits for granted, but proceeds to explain and comment on them. " I could get," as he notes, " no pleasure from their amusements, but found it necessary to humour them in many things, and to be obliging to all. I was thought saucy, and little courted by them, they not liking my dry manner as they called it." His narrative is that of an intelligent observer of the behaviour of the regiment, in whose psychology he is deeply interested, rather than that of a typical soldier. Having a ready pen and a keen observant eye, he produced a little book of extraordinary interest. The chronicle of his marches, and the details of the actions which he relates, seem very accurate when compared with official documents.

Sergeant Donaldson of the 94th was another notable Scot whose book, *The Eventful Life of a Soldier*, is well worth reading. He was not so well educated as T. S., nor had he the same vivid literary style. But he was an intelligent man, and possessed a wider set of interests than was common in the ranks, so that it is always worth while to look up his notes and observations. His description of the horrors of Masséna's retreat from Portugal in 1811 is a very striking piece of lurid writing. After him may be mentioned a quartermaster and a sergeant—Surtees and Costello—both of the Rifle Brigade,—whose reminiscences are full of typical stories reflecting the virtues and failings

* But only published by Constable & Co. in 1828. For more of his story, see the chapter on " The Rank and File."

of the famous Light Division. For the views and ways of thought of the ordinary private of the better sort, the little books of " Rifleman Harris," already cited above, Lawrence of the 40th, and Cooper of the 7th Fusiliers,* are valuable authority. They are admirable evidence for the way in which the rank and file looked on a battle, a forced march, or a prolonged shortage of rations. But we must not trust them overmuch as authorities on the greater matter of war.

There is a considerable bulk of French reminiscences dealing with the purely British side of the Peninsular War. Beside Marbot's and Thiébault's memoirs, of which I have already made mention, three or four more must not be neglected by any one who wishes to see Wellington's army from the outside. By far the most vivid and lively of them is Lemonnier-Delafosse of the 31st Léger, whose *Souvenirs Militaires* were published at Havre in 1850. He is a bitter enemy, and wants to prove that Wellington was a mediocre general, and ought always to have been beaten. But he does his best to tell a true tale, and acknowledges his defeats handsomely—though he thinks that with better luck they might have been victories. Failing memory can be detected in one or two places, where he makes an officer fall at the wrong battle, or misnames a village. Fantin des Odoards, also (oddly enough) of the 31st Léger, kept a journal, so that his reminiscences of 1808–11 are very accurate. He is specially valuable for Moore's retreat and Soult's Oporto campaign. A far more fair-minded man than Delafosse, he is full of acknowledgments of the merit of his British adversaries, and makes no secret of his disgust for the Spanish war,—a nightmare of plunder and military executions naturally resulting from an unjust aggression. A third valuable author is Colonel St. Chamans, an aide-de-camp of Soult, whom he cordially

* Sergeant Lawrence's *Autobiography* was not published till 1886.   Cooper's *Seven Campaigns in Portugal*, etc., came out in 1869.

detested, and whose meanness and spirit of intrigue he is
fond of exposing.   He is of a light and humorous spirit—
very different from another aide-de-camp, Ney's Swiss
follower, Sprünglin, whose journal * is a most solid and heavy
production, of value for minute facts and figures but not
lively.   Unlike St. Chamans in another respect, he is devoted
to his chief, the Marshal, of whom he was the most loyal
admirer.   But I imagine that Ney was a much more
generous and loveable master than the wily Soult.

Other useful French volumes of reminiscences are those
of Guingret of the 6th corps, full of horrible details of
Masséna's Portuguese misfortunes; of D'Illens, a cavalry
officer who served against Moore and Wellesley in 1808–09 ;
and of Vigo-Roussillon, of the 8th Line, who gives the only
good French narrative of Barrosa.   Parquin is a mere
sabreur, who wrote his memoir too late, and whose anecdotes
cannot be trusted.   He survived to be one of the followers
of Napoleon III. in his early and unhappy adventures at
Boulogne and elsewhere.   Other French writers, such as
Rocca and Gonneville, were long in Spain, but little in contact with the British, being employed on the Catalan coast,
or with the army of the South on the Granada side.   So
much for the works of actors in the Great War, who relate
what they have themselves seen.   We need spend but a
much smaller space on the books of the later generations,
which are but second-hand information, however carefully
they may have been compiled.

The British regimental histories ought to be of great
value, since the series compiled by the order of the Horse
Guards, under the general editorship of Richard Cannon, in
the 1830's, might have been enriched by the information
obtainable from hundreds of Peninsular veterans, who were
still surviving.   Unfortunately nearly every volume of it
is no more than bad hack-work.   In the majority of the
volumes we find nothing more than copious extracts from
Napier, eked out with reprints of the formal reports

* Only printed quite lately in the *Revue Hispanique* for 1907.

taken from the *London Gazette*. It is quite exceptional to
find even regimental statistics, such as might have been
obtained with ease from the pay-lists and other documents
in possession of the battalion, or stored at the Record Office.
Details obtained through enquiry from veteran officers who
had served through the war are quite exceptional. Some
of his volumes are less arid and jejune than others—and
this is about all that can be said in favour of even the best
of them.

All the good regimental histories, without exception,
are outside the official " Cannon " series. Some are excellent; it may be said that, as a general rule, those written
latest are the best : the standard of accuracy and original
research has been rising ever since 1860. Among those
which deserve a special word of praise are Colonel Gardyne's
admirable *The Life of a Regiment* (the Gordon Highlanders),
published in 1901 ; Cope's *History of the Rifle Brigade*
(full of excerpts from first-hand authorities) which came out
in 1877 ; Moorsom's *History of the 52nd Oxfordshire Light
Infantry* (the first really good regimental history which was
written), published in 1860 ; Davis's *History of the 2nd Foot*
(Queen's West Surrey), and Colonel Hamilton's *14th Hussars*.
By the time that these began to appear, the level of research
was beginning to rise, and it was no longer considered
superfluous to visit the Record Office, or to make enquiries
for unpublished papers among the families of old officers.
All those mentioned above are large volumes, but even the
smaller histories are now compiled with care, and their
size is generally the result not of scamped work (as of old),
but of the fact that some regiments have, by the chance of
their stations, seen less service than others, and therefore
have less to record. I may mention as books on the smaller
scale which have proved useful to me, Hayden's history
of the 76th, Smyth's of the 20th, and Purdon's of the 47th.
A rare example of the annals of a smaller unit, a battery
not a battalion, is Colonel Whinyates' story of C Troop,
R.H.A., which he called *From Corunna to Sebastopol*, in

which much loyal and conscientious work may be found.
But the history of the whole of the Artillery of the Peninsular
Army, Portuguese as well as English, is now being worked
out in admirable detail in the *Dickson Papers*, edited by
Major John Leslie, R.A., who knows everything that can
be known about the units of his corps which served under
Wellington.   Sir Alexander Dickson, it may be remarked,
was Commanding Officer of the Artillery in the later
campaigns of 1813 and in 1814, and before he obtained that
post had been in charge of all the three sieges of Badajoz
as well as those of Olivenza and Ciudad Rodrigo.   Since he
had been lent to the Portuguese artillery, his papers give
copious information as to the auxiliary batteries of that
nation which were attached to the Peninsular Army.   It
is devoutly to be wished that some officer would take up
a corresponding task by compiling the annals of the Royal
Engineers in the Peninsular War.   Connolly's *History of
the Royal Sappers and Miners* (published so far back as
1857), has much good information, but infinitely more
could be compiled by searching the Record Office, and
collating the memoirs of Boothby, Burgoyne, Landmann,
and other engineer officers who have left journals or
reminiscences.

Along with the British regimental histories should be
named two sets of volumes which are of the same type,
though they relate to larger units than a regiment, and do
not deal with our own troops.   The first class deals with
our German auxiliaries, and is headed by Major Ludlow
Beamish's valuable and conscientious *History of the King's
German Legion*.   This was written in 1832, but is a very
favourable example of research for a book of the date, when
Cannon's miserable series represented the level of English
regimental history.   The two volumes contain many original
letters and documents, and some excellent plates of uniforms.   In 1907 Captain Schwertfeger went over the same
ground in his *Geschichte der Königlich Deutschen Legion,**

* Hanover, 1907, 2 vols.

and added appreciably to Beamish's store of facts. The Brunswick Oels regiment, which served Wellington from 1811 to 1814, has also a German biographer in Colonel Kortfleisch, who has served in the 88th German Infantry, which now represents that ancient corps. There is no similar history for the *Chasseurs Brittaniques*, the last of the old Peninsular foreign corps.

For the Portuguese Army a good description of the state of affairs in 1810, when it had just been reorganized, is contained in Halliday's *Present State of Portugal*, published in 1812. Chaby's *Excerptos Historicos* * contains a good deal of valuable material for its subsequent history, but is sadly ill-arranged and patchy. Only the Portuguese artillery in the Peninsular War has been dealt with in Major Teixeira Botelho's *Subsidios para a Historia da Artilheria Portegueza*, which is very full and well documented. The life of a British officer serving with a Portuguese regiment can be studied in the *Memoirs of Bunbury* (20th Line),† and Blakiston (5th Caçadores).‡

After regimental histories, the next most important source of information, in the way of books not written by those who served under Wellington, is personal biographies. Captain Delavoye's *Life of Lord Lynedoch* (Sir Thomas Graham) § is perhaps the most useful among them, not so much for any merit of style or arrangement, as for the excellent use of contemporary documents not available elsewhere. A large portion of the volume consists of excerpts from Graham's long and interesting military journal, and letters from and to him are printed *in extenso*. Thus we get first-hand information on many events at which no other British witness was present, *e.g.* Castaños' campaign on the Ebro in 1808, as well as comments on better known operations, such as Sir John Moore's Corunna

* Published at Lisbon in 4 vols., 1862–80.
† His book is called *Reminiscences of a Veteran*, and was published so late as 1861.
‡ *Twelve Years of Military Adventure*, published 1829.
§ Published in 1880.

retreat, and the Barrosa expedition of 1811. Unfortunately both journal and letters fail for the campaign of 1813, in which Graham took such a distinguished part.

H. B. Robinson's *Memoirs of Sir Thomas Picton* * was a book of which Napier fell foul—there are many caustic comments on it in his controversial appendices. But it is not nearly so bad a work as might have been expected from his way of treating it. Indeed I fancy that Napier was paying off an old Light Division grudge against Picton himself, whom he personally disliked. The narrative is fair, and the quantity of contemporary letters inserted give the compilation some value. Sidney's *Life of Lord Hill* † is far inferior to Robinson's book : the author did not know his Peninsular War well enough to justify the task which he took in hand, and the letters, of which he fortunately prints a good many, are the only valuable material in it. It is curious that both Picton and Hill had their lives written by clergymen, when there were still a good many old Peninsular officers surviving who might have undertaken the task.

Of the other chief lieutenants of Wellington, Beresford has never found a biographer, though the part which he played in the war was so important. There must be an immense accumulation of his papers somewhere, in private hands, but I do not know where they lie. The only account of him consists of a few pages in a useful but rather formal and patchy little book by J. W. Cole, entitled, *Memoirs of British Generals Distinguished during the Peninsular War.*‡ Lord Combermere (Stapleton Cotton) was in high command throughout Wellington's campaigns, but was hardly up to his position, though he earned his chief's tolerance by strict obedience to orders, a greater merit in the Duke's eyes than military genius or initiative. There is a biography of him by Lady Combermere and Captain W. Knollys (1866) but the Peninsular chapters are short. Of Sir Lowry Cole, Sir

---

* Published 1835, 2 vols.   † Published 1845.
‡ Two vols., published 1856.

John Gaspard Le Marchant, and several other prominent divisional generals and brigadiers, the only biographies are those in J. W. Cole's book mentioned above. Sir James Leith, more fortunate, had a small volume dedicated to his memory by an anonymous admirer in 1818, but it was written without sufficient material, Leith's private correspondence not (as it seems) being in the author's hands, while official documents were not for the most part available at such an early date. There is a good deal, however, concerning this hard-fighting general's personality and adventures to be gleaned from the memoirs of his nephew and aide-de-camp, Leith Hay.

Of officers who did not attain to the highest rank under Wellington, but who in later years made a great career for themselves, there are two biographies which devote a large section to Peninsular matters, those of Lord Gough by R. S. Rait (two vols., 1903), and of Lord Seaton (Colborne of the 52nd) by Moore Smith. These are both excellent productions, which give much private correspondence of the time, and have been constructed on modern lines, with full attention to all possible sources first- and second-hand. They are both indispensable for any one who wishes to make a detailed study of the Peninsular campaigns. There are also short memoirs of Sir Denis Pack * and Lord Vivian,† each produced by a grandson of the general, and giving useful extracts from journals and correspondence. The campaign of Sir John Moore can, perhaps, hardly be considered as falling into the story of Wellington's army, but it is impossible to avoid mentioning the full (and highly controversial) biography of the hero of Corunna by Sir J. F. Maurice,‡ which contains an invaluable diary, and much correspondence. It is an indispensable volume, at any rate, for those who wish to study the first year of the Peninsular War, and to mark the difference between the personalities and military theories of Moore and Wellington.

* By D. Beresford-Pack, 1905.
† By Hon. Claud Vivian, 1897.   ‡ Two vols., 1904.

Of formal and detailed histories of the Peninsular War written in recent years there is one in Spanish by General Arteche, a very conscientious and thorough-going worker at original documents, who got up a good many English authorities, but by no means all. For the Spanish version of the whole war he is absolutely necessary. So, for the Portuguese version, is the immense work of Soriano da Luz, which is largely founded on Napier, but often differs from him, and brings many unpublished documents to light. Colonel Balagny has started a history of the war in French on a very large scale, delightfully documented, and showing admirable research. In five volumes he has only just got into 1809, so the whole book will be a large one. Mr. Fortescue's fine history of the British Army has just started on the Peninsular campaign in its last volume. To my own four volumes, soon I hope to be five, I need only allude in passing. There is one immense monograph on Dupont's Campaign by a French author, Colonel Titeux, which does not touch English military affairs at all. Two smaller but good works of the same type by Colonel Dumas and Commandant Clerc are both, oddly enough, dedicated to the same campaign,—Soult's defence of the Pyrenean frontier in 1813–14 : the former is the better of the two : both have endeavoured, in the modern fashion, to use the reports of both sides, not to write from the documents of one only ; but Dumas has a better knowledge of his English sources than Clerc.

It is beyond my power to guess why similar monographs on separate campaigns of the war do not appear in English also. But the few *brochures* purporting to treat of such which have appeared of late on this side of the channel, are mostly cram-books for examinations, resting on no wide knowledge of sources, and often consisting of little more than an analysis of Napier, with some supplementary comments hazarded. They contrast very unfavourably with a book such as that of Colonel Dumas.

CHAPTER III

So much for our sources. We may now proceed to discover what we can deduce from them. And we must inevitably begin with a consideration of the great leader of the British army. I am not writing a life of Wellington, still less a commentary on his campaigns—with which I am trying to deal elsewhere. My object is rather to paint him as he appeared to his own army, and as his acts and his writings reveal him during the course of his Peninsular campaigns. The Arthur Wellesley of 1809 is difficult to disentangle in our own memories from the familiar figure of Victorian reminiscences. We think of him as the "Great Duke," the first and most honoured subject of the crown, round whom centre so many stories, more or less well founded, illustrating his disinterestedness, his hatred of phrases, insincerities, sentiment, and humbug generally, his punctiliousness, his bleak frugality, and his occasional scathing directness of speech—for he could never "suffer fools gladly." He had become a legend long before he died, and it takes an effort of mind to differentiate the old man of 1850 from the general of 1809, who had still, in the eyes of most men, his reputation to make. For those who understood the greatness of his Indian exploits were few. It was not Napoleon only who thought that to call Wellesley a "sepoy general" was sufficient to reduce his reputation to that of a facile victor over contemptible enemies.

When he took command of the Peninsular Army in the April of that year, Arthur Wellesley was thirty-nine: he

had just reached early middle age.   He was a slight but
wiry man of middle stature, well built and erect, with a
long face, an aquiline nose, and a keen but cold grey eye.
His reputation as a soldier was already high ; but few save
those who had served under him in India understood the
full scope of his abilities.   Many undervalued him, because
he was a member of a well-known, but ill-loved family
and political group, and had owed his early promotion and
opportunities of distinguishing himself to that fact.   It
was still open to critics to say that the man who had commanded a battalion in the old Revolutionary War at the
age of twenty-three, and who had headed an army in India
before he was quite thirty, had got further to the front
than he deserved by political influence.   And it was true
(though the fact is so often forgotten), that in his early
years he had got much help from his connections, that he
had obtained his unique chance in India because he was
the brother of a viceroy, and that since his return from the
East he had been more of a politician than a general.   Was
he not, even when he won Vimeiro, Secretary for Ireland in
the Tory government of the day ?   It was a post whose
holder had to dabble in much dirty work, when dealing
with the needy peers, the grovelling place-mongers, and
the intriguing lawyers of Dublin.   Wellesley went through
with it all, and not by any means in a conciliatory way.
He passed the necessary jobs, but did not hide from the
jobbers his scorn for them.   When the Secretary for Ireland
had to deal with any one whom he disliked, he showed a
happy mixture of aristocratic hauteur and cold intellectual
contempt, which sent the petitioner away in a bitter frame
of mind, whether his petition had been granted or no.
Unfortunately, he carried this manner from the Irish
Secretaryship on to the Headquarters of the Peninsular
Army.   It did not tend to make him loved.

Fortunately for Great Britain, it does not always follow
that, because a man has been pushed rapidly to the front
by political influence, he is therefore incompetent or

unworthy of the place given him. Every one who came into
personal contact with Arthur Wellesley soon recognized
that Castlereagh and the other ministers had not erred
when they sent the " Sepoy General " to Portugal in 1808,
and when they, despite of all the clamour following the
Convention of Cintra, despatched him a second time to
Lisbon in 1809, this time with full control of the Peninsular
Army. From the first opening of his Vimeiro campaign
the troops that he led had the firmest confidence in him—
they saw the skill with which he handled them, and criticism
very soon died away. It was left for Whig politicians at
home, carpers with not the slightest knowledge of war, to
go on asserting for a couple of years more that he was an
over-rated officer, that he was rash and reckless, and that
his leadership would end, on some not very distant day,
with the expulsion of the British army from the Peninsula.
At the front there were very few such doubters—though
contemporary letters have proved to me that one or two
were to be found.*

To say that Wellington from the first was trusted alike
by his officers and his men, is by no means to say that he
was loved by them. He did everything that could win
confidence, but little that could attract affection. They
recognized that he was marvellously capable, but that he
was without the supreme gift of sympathy for others.
" The sight of his long nose among us," wrote one of his
veterans, " was worth ten thousand men any day of the
week. I will venture to say that there was not a heart in
the army which did not beat more lightly when we heard
the joyful news of his arrival." † But this does not mean
that he was regarded with an enthusiasm of the emotional

---

* *E.g.* the cavalry general Long, who was writing in the spring
of 1810 that " the next campaign in the Peninsula will close the
eventful scene in the Peninsula, as far as we are concerned. I am
strongly of opinion that neither ' Marshal ' Wellington nor ' Marshal '
Beresford will prevent the approaching subjugation of Portugal."
And, again, " Wellington, I suspect, feels himself tottering on his
throne, and wishes to conciliate at any sacrifice."

† Kincaid, chap. v., May, 1811.

and affectionate sort. Another Light Division officer sums up the position in the coldest words that I have ever seen applied to the relations of a great general with his victorious army. " I know that it has been said that Wellington was unpopular with the army. Now I can assert with respect to the Light Division that the troops *rather liked him than otherwise*. . . . Although Wellington was not what may be called popular, still the troops possessed great confidence in him, nor did I ever hear a single individual express an opinion to the contrary." *

There must, indeed, have been something to repel enthusiasm and affection in the leader of whom, after five years of victories won and hardships suffered in common, it could be said that his troops " rather liked him than otherwise." But they found that he was a hard master, slow to praise and swift to blame and to punish. Though he knew the military virtues of his rank and file, and acknowledged that they had more than once " got him out of a scrape " by performing the almost impossible, he did not love them. He has left on record unpardonable words concerning his men. " They are the scum of the earth. English soldiers are fellows who have enlisted for drink— that is the plain fact : they have *all* enlisted for drink." †
Quite as bad in spirit is one of his sayings before a Royal Commission on the Army. " I have no idea of any great effect being produced on British soldiers by anything but the fear of immediate corporal punishment." Naturally enough a leader with such views never appealed to the better side of his men : he never spoke or wrote about honour or patriotism to them, but frequently reminded them of the lash and the firing-party, that were the inevitable penalty for the straggler, the drunkard, the plunderer, and the deserter. Nothing cooled the spirits of officers and men alike more than the strength and vigour of his rebukes, as compared with the official formality of

* Cooke's *Narrative of events in the South of France*, pp. 47, 48.
† Stanhope's *Conversations with the Duke of Wellington*, p. 14.

his terms of praise. It was possible to have a full appreciation of his marvellous powers of brain, and a complete confidence in him as a leader, without feeling the least touch of affection for this hard and unsympathetic figure.

The distressing point in all this is that the Peninsular Army, though it had its proportion of hardened sots and criminals, was full of good soldiers who knew what honour and loyalty meant, and were perfectly capable of answering any stirring appeal to their heart or their brain. There are dozens of diaries and autobiographies written in the ranks which show the existence of a vast class of well-conditioned intelligent, sober, even religious men, who were doing their work conscientiously, and would have valued a word of praise—they often got it from their regimental officers—seldom from their commander-in-chief. And we may add that if anything was calculated to brutalize an army it was the wicked cruelty of the British military punishment code, which Wellington to the end of his life supported. There is plenty of authority for the fact that the man who had once received his 500 lashes for a fault which was small, or which involved no moral guilt, was often turned thereby from a good into a bad soldier, by losing his self-respect and having his sense of justice seared out. Good officers knew this well enough, and did their best to avoid the cat-of-nine-tails, and to try more rational means—more often than not with success.*

It might have been expected that Wellington would at least show more regard for the feelings of his officers, however much he might contemn his rank and file. As a rule he did not. He had some few intimates whom he treated with a certain familiarity, and it is clear that he showed consideration and even kindness to his aides-de-camp and other personal retainers. But to the great majority of his officers, even to many of his generals and heads of

---

* For a curious instance of this sort in the 92nd, see Hope's *Military Memoirs of an Infantry Officer*, pp. 449–451. Cf. Sir George Napier's *Autobiography*, pp. 125–128.

departments, he bore himself very stiffly : he would administer to them humiliating snubs or reproofs before others, and ignore their remarks or proffered counsel in the most marked way. A few examples may serve. Sir Thomas Picton was one of his most distinguished lieutenants, and was specially summoned by him to come over to Brussels to take his part in the campaign of 1815. The moment that he arrived in the Belgian capital he sought the Duke, who was walking in the Great Park. We have the witness of Picton's aide-de-camp for the following reception. " The general's manner was always more familiar than the Duke liked in his lieutenants, and on this occasion he approached him in a careless sort of way, just as he might have greeted an equal. The Duke bowed coldly to him, and said, ' I am glad you are come, Sir Thomas. The sooner you get on horseback the better : no time to be lost. You will take the command of the troops in advance.' That was all. Picton appeared not to like the Duke's manner, and when he had bowed and left, he muttered words which convinced those who were with him that he was not much pleased with his interview." * Such was the welcome vouchsafed to one of the best officers in the army, whom Wellington had specially sent for, and whom he had not seen for a long space of time. Another picture of Wellington's manners may be taken from the memoir of one of his departmental chiefs, Sir James McGrigor. " One morning I was in his lordship's small room, when two officers came to request leave to go home to England. An engineer captain first made his request : he had received letters informing him that his wife was dangerously ill, and that the whole of his family were sick. His lordship quickly replied, ' No, no, sir. I cannot spare you at this moment.' The captain, with a mournful face, drew back. Then a general officer, of noble family, commanding a brigade, advanced saying, ' My lord, I have lately been suffering much from rheumatism —— '. Without allowing him time to complete his sentence,

* Gronow's *Recollections*, p. 66.

Lord Wellington rapidly said, 'and you want to go to England to be cured. By all means. Go there immediately.' The general, surprised at his lordship's tone and manner, looked abashed, but to prevent his saying anything more, his lordship turned and began to address me, enquiring about the casualty-returns of the preceding night, and the nature of them." * An interview with the commander-in-chief was such a trying thing for the nerves that some officers went away from it in a flood of tears—as did Charles Stewart after one famous reproof—and others suffocating from suppressed maledictions.

Wellington's temper was tried by having to deal with some inefficient and slack officers—foisted upon him from home—for never till the end of the war (as he bitterly complained) was he allowed complete liberty in choosing his subordinates. But it was not on them alone that his thunders fell. He often raged at zealous and capable subordinates, who had done no more than think for themselves in an urgent crisis, when the orders that they had received seemed no longer applicable. Sir James McGrigori whom I have just quoted above, once moved some commissariat stores to Salamanca, where there was a great accumulation of sick and wounded. " When I came to inform him his lordship started up, and in a violent manner began to repudiate what I had done. 'I shall be glad to know,' he asked, ' who commands this army—I or you ? I establish one route, one line of communication—you establish another by ordering up supplies by it. As long as you live, sir, never do that again. Never do *anything* without my orders.' I pleaded that there had been no time to consult him, and that I had to save lives. He peremptorily desired me ' never again to act without his orders.' " Three months afterwards McGrigor ventured to say, " My lord, you will remember how much you blamed me at Madrid, for the steps that I took when I could not consult your lordship, and acted for myself. Now, if I

* McGrigor's *Autobiography*, pp. 304, 305.

had not, what would the consequences have been ? " He answered, " It is all right as it has turned out, but still I recommend you to *have my orders for what you do.*" This was a singular feature in his lordship's character.'

Anything that seemed to Wellington to partake of the nature of thinking for oneself was an unpardonable sin in a subordinate. This is why he preferred blind obedience in his lieutenants to zeal and energy which might lead to some contravention of his own intention. Thus it came that he preferred as lieutenants not only Hill, who was a man of first-class brain-power notwithstanding his docility, but Spencer and Beresford, who most certainly were not. Hence, too, his commission of the cavalry arm throughout the war to such a mediocre personage as Stapleton Cotton (of whom he used the most unflattering language).* These men could be trusted to obey without reasoning, while Robert Craufurd, the ablest general in the Peninsula, or Picton, could not, but were liable to think for themselves. It may be noted that Hill, Beresford, Graham and Crau-furd, were the only officers to whom Wellington ever con-descended in his correspondence to give the why and wherefore of a command that he issued : the others simply received orders without any commentary. There are instances known in which a word of reasonable explanation to a subordinate would have enabled him to understand a situation, and to comprehend why directions otherwise incomprehensible were given him. Tiresome results occa-sionally followed. This foible of refusing information to subordinates for no adequate reason has been shared by other great generals—*e.g.* by Stonewall Jackson, as Colonel Henderson's biography of that strange genius sufficiently shows. It is a trick of the autocratic mind.

It hardly requires to be pointed out that this determina-tion to allow no liberty of action to his lieutenants, and to keep even small decisions in his own hands, effectually pre-vented Wellington from forming a school of generals capable

* When sending him to command in India.

of carrying out large independent operations. He trained admirable divisional commanders, but not leaders of armies. The springs of self-confidence were drained out of men who had for long been subjected to his *régime*.

Probably the thing which irritated Wellington's subordinates most was his habit of making his official mention of names in dispatches little more than a formal recital in order of the senior officers present. Where grave mistakes had been committed, he still stuck the names of the misdemeanants in the list, among those of the men who had really done the work. A complete mystification as to their relative merits would be produced, if we had only the dispatches to read, and no external commentary on them. He honourably mentioned Murray in his Oporto dispatch, Erskine in his dispatch concerning the actions during Masséna's retreat in 1811, Trip in his Waterloo dispatch, though each of these officers had done his best to spoil the operations in which he was concerned. On the other hand, he would make the most unaccountable omissions: his Fuentes de Oñoro dispatch makes no mention of the British artillery, which had done most brilliant service in that battle, not merely in the matter of Norman Ramsay's well-known exploit, which Wellington might have thought too small a matter to mention, but in the decisive checking of the main French attack. There are extant heart-rending letters from the senior officers commanding the artillery, deploring the way in which they have been completely ignored: "to read the dispatch, there might have been no British artillery present at all." A similar inexplicable omission of any record of zealous service occurs in Wellington's dispatch recording the fall of Badajoz, where no special praise of the services of his engineer officers is made, though 50 per cent. of them had been killed or wounded during the siege. "You may suppose we all feel hurt at finding our exertions have not been deemed worthy of any sort of eulogium," writes John Jones, the historian of the sieges of the Peninsula, to one of his colleagues. And

Fletcher, the commanding engineer, writes to a friend : " You will observe that Lord W. has not mentioned the engineers in the late actions : how I hate such capriciousness ! " * The cold phrase in which their desperate service was acknowledged is " the officers and men of the corps of engineers and artillery were equally distinguished during the operations of the siege and its close." Fletcher would gladly have exchanged the personal honour of a decoration, which was given him along with other senior officers, for three lines of warm praise of the exertions of his subordinates.

Perhaps, however, the most astounding instance of Wellington's ungracious omissions is that his famous Waterloo dispatch contains no mention whatever of the services of Colborne and the 52nd, the battalion which gave the decisive stroke against the flank of the Imperial Guard, during Napoleon's last desperate assault on the British line. Colborne, the most unselfish and generous of men, could never forget this slight. He tried to excuse it, saying, " dispatches are written in haste, and it is impossible for a general to do justice to his army." And when he heard his officers complaining that the British Guards had been given all the credit for the final repulse of the French column, he said, " For shame, gentlemen ! One would think that you forgot that the 52nd had ever been in battle before." But there was a bitter comment in the table talk of his later years. " The Duke was occasionally not above writing in his dispatches to please the aristocracy. . . . I don't mean to say that this was peculiar to him. It used to be a common thing with general officers." † Enough, however, of these illustrative anecdotes of the limitations of a very great soldier and a very honourable man. They have

* These two letters are in the Rice-Jones Correspondence (this R.E. officer is not to be confounded with Sir John Jones, the historian), lent to me by Hon. Henry Shore of Mount Elton, Clevedon.

† See *Colborne's Life and Letters*, ed. Moore Smith, pp. 126, 127 ; 235, 236.

to be mentioned in order to explain how it came to pass
that Wellington was implicitly trusted, and never loved.
But they compel me to acquiesce in the hard judgment
which Lord Roberts wrote in his *Rise of Wellington*—"the
more we go into his actions and his writings in detail,
the more do we respect and admire him as a general, and the
less do we like him as a man." I conclude this paragraph
with two quotations from two eloquent writers who served
through long years of the Peninsular campaigns. "Thus
terminated the war, and with it all remembrances of the
veteran's services" are the last words of William Napier's
penultimate chapter.* Grattan of the 88th, a forgotten
writer now, but one who wielded a descriptive pen no less
vivid than Napier's, puts the complaint more bitterly.
"In his parting General Order to the Peninsular Army he
told us that he would never cease to feel the warmest
interest for our welfare and honour. How that promise
has been kept every one knows. That the Duke of Wellington is one of the most remarkable (perhaps the greatest)
men of the present age, few will deny. But that he
neglected the interests and feelings of his Peninsular army,
as a body, is beyond all question. And were he in his grave
to-morrow, hundreds of voices that now are silent would
echo what I write." †

If I have dwelt perhaps at over-great length on the
limitations of Wellington's heart, it is only fair that full credit
should be given to his wonderful powers of brain. To comprehend the actual merit of his military career, it is not
sufficient to possess a mere knowledge of the details of his
tactics and his strategy. The conditions under which he
had to exercise his talents were exceptionally trying and
difficult. When he assumed command at Lisbon on April
22, 1809, the French were in possession of all Northern and
Central Spain, and of no inconsiderable part of Northern
Portugal also. The Spanish armies had all been dashed to
pieces—there was no single one of them which had not

* *Napier*, vi. p. 175.   † *Grattan*, p. 332.

suffered a crushing defeat, and some of them (such as Cuesta's army of Estremadura, and La Romana's army of Galicia) were at the moment little better than wandering bands of fugitives. The British army of which Wellesley took command when he landed at Lisbon, though it only mustered 19,000 men present, or 21,000 including men in hospital, was the only solid force, in good order and intact in *morale*, on which the allies could count in the Iberian Peninsula. The task set before Wellesley was to see if he could defend Portugal, and co-operate in the protection of Southern Spain, it being obvious that the French were in vastly superior numbers, and well able to take the offensive if they should chose to do so. There were two armies threatening Lisbon. The one under Soult had already captured Oporto and overrun two Portuguese provinces, shortly before Wellesley's landing. The other, under Victor, lay in Estremadura close to the Portuguese border, and had recently destroyed the largest surviving Spanish army at the battle of Medellin on March 28. Was it possible that 19,000 British troops could save the Peninsula from conquest, or even that they could keep up the war in Central Portugal ? Never was a more unpromising task set to the commander of a small army.

Fortunately we possess three documents from Wellesley's own hand, which show us the way in which he surveyed the position that was before him, and stated his views as to the future course of the Peninsular War. He recognized that it was about to be a very long business, and that his task was simply to keep the war going as long as possible, with the limited resources at his disposition. Ambitious schemes for the expulsion of the French from the whole Peninsula were in 1809 perfectly futile. The hypothesis which he sets forth in the first of the three documents to which I allude, his *Memorandum on the Defence of Portugal*, laid before Castlereagh on March 7, before he had taken ship for Lisbon, is a marvel of prophetic genius. No more prescient document was ever written. Rejecting the decision of Sir John Moore, who had declared that Portugal was quite indefensible, Wellesley states that a British army of not less than 30,000 men, backed by the levies of Portugal, ought to be able to maintain itself for an almost indefinite period on the flank of the French army in Spain. Its presence on the Tagus would paralyse all offensive movements of the enemy, and enable the Spaniards to make head in the unsubdued provinces of their realm, so long as Portugal should remain intact. The French ought, if they were wise, to turn all their disposable forces against the British army and Portugal, but he believed that even then, when the geography of the country was taken into consideration, they would fail in their attempt to overrun it. They could not succeed, as he held, unless they were able to set aside 100,000 men for the task, and he did not see how in the spring of 1809 they could spare such a large detachment, out of the forces which they then possessed in the Peninsula. If they tried it with a smaller army, he thought that he could undertake to foil them. He believed that he could cope with Soult and Victor, the two enemies who immediately threatened Portugal.*

Further forward it was impossible to look. If a war should break out between Napoleon and Austria, as seemed likely at the moment in March, 1809, to one who (like himself) was in the secrets of the British Cabinet, the Emperor would not be able to send reinforcements to Spain for many a day. But, even so, the position of the French in the Peninsula was so strong that it could only be endangered if a very large allied force, acting in unison under the guidance of a single general, should be brought to bear upon them. Of the collection of such a force, and still more of the possibility of its being entrusted to his own command, there was as yet no question. Wellesley was aware of the jealousy of foreign interference which the Spanish Junta nurtured : there was little probability that

* The memorandum is on pp. 261–263 of vol. iv. of Wellington's Dispatches.

they would entrust him with the supreme control over their armies. It was, indeed, only in 1812, when he had acquired for himself a much greater reputation than he owned in 1809, and when the Spanish Government had drunk the cup of humiliation to the dregs, that he was finally given the position of commander-in-chief of the Spanish armies.

This memorandum is a truly inspired document, which shows Wellesley at his best. It is not too much to say that it predicts the whole course of the Peninsular War—whose central point was to be invasion of Portugal in 1810 by a French army of 65,000 instead of the required 100,000 men, and that army, as-he had foreseen, Wellesley was able to check and foil.

The second document of a prophetic sort that we have to notice is Wellesley's reply to Mr. Canning's question to him as regards the future general policy of the war, written on September 5, 1809. The whole aspect of affairs had been much changed since March, by the fact that Austria had tried her luck in a war against Napoleon, and had been beaten at Wagram and forced to make peace. It was therefore certain that the Emperor would now have his hands free again, and be able to reinforce his armies in the Peninsula. Wellesley replies that it is hopeless to attempt to defend both Southern Spain and Portugal also, even if the British army were raised to 40,000 men. But Portugal can still be defended.* He expresses the strongest objection to any attempt to cover Andalusia and Seville, for to endeavour to do so must mean that Lisbon would have to be given up.

The third great prophetic despatch is the Memorandum of October 26, 1809, ordering the construction of the Lines of Torres Vedras. Wellesley looks a full year ahead. He sees that Napoleon can now reinforce his Spanish armies, but that the new troops cannot get up till the next spring. When they appear, the British army will have to retreat

* *Dispatches,* vol. v. pp. 123, 124.

on Lisbon, where lines of such strength can be planned that there is a good prospect of bringing the invaders to a stand. Meanwhile the countryside shall be cleared of population and provisions, so that the French, if they keep concentrated, must starve, and the allied army shall so conduct its operations that the enemy will be compelled to remain *en masse*. Then follow directions to Colonel Fletcher (commanding the engineers) to make his plans for an immense line of redoubts covering the Lisbon peninsula from sea to sea. What was foreseen came to pass : the French reinforcements arrived : the invasion of Portugal under Masséna took place in 1810. But the whole countryside was swept clear of food, and when the marshal reached the Lines with his half-starved army, he was completely blocked, refused to attack the formidable positions, and, after a few weeks of endurance in front of them, withdrew with his famished troops. It was on October 26, 1809, that Wellington ordered the Lines to be laid out. On October 14, 1910, Masséna appeared in front of them and was foiled : Wellington had made his preparations exactly a year ahead !

Careful long-sighted calculation was perhaps the Duke's strongest point. He had an immense grasp of detail, kept intelligence officers of picked ability out on every front, and had compiled an almost exactly correct muster-roll of the forces opposed to him. Seldom had a general of his time such a complete knowledge of his adversaries, and this he owed to the pains that he took to obtain it. His great scouts Colquhoun Grant,* Waters, and Rumann were always far out to the front, often within the French lines, sending him daily information, which he filed and dissected. In addition he had many Spanish and Portuguese correspondents, whose information would have been more valuable if it had not contained too much hearsay, and if they had been able to judge numbers with the trained

* For an interesting chapter on the adventures of Colquhoun Grant see the autobiography of his brother-in-law, Sir J. McGrigor.

eye of a soldier.   Once he complained that he and Marmont
were almost equally handicapped as regards information
from the natives—for if the Frenchmen got none, he himself
got too much : the proportion of it which was inaccurate
spoiled the value of the rest.   But Grant or Waters never
made mistakes.   Part of his system was the cross-ques-
tioning of every deserter and prisoner as to the number
and brigading of his regiment, and the amount of battalions
that it contained.   By constant comparison of these reports
he got to know the exact number of units in every French
corps, and their average strength.

But this was less important than his faculty for judging
the individual characters of his opponents.   After a few
weeks he got his fixed opinion on Masséna or Victor, Soult
or Marmont, and would lay his plans with careful reference
to their particular foibles.   I think that this is what he
meant when he once observed that his own merit was, perhaps, that he knew more of " what was going on upon
the other side of the hill,"—in the invisible ground occupied
by the enemy and hidden by the fog of war—than most
men.

This insight into the enemy's probable move, when their
strength, their object, and the personal tendencies of their
leader were known, was a most valuable part of Wellesley's
mental equipment.   The best known instance where it
came into play was on the day of Sorauren.   In the midst
of the battles of the Pyrenees, when the British army had
taken up its fighting position, though its numbers were as
yet by no means complete, and two divisions were still
marching up, Wellington arrived from the west to assume
command.   He could see Soult on the opposite hill surrounded by his staff, and it was equally certain that Soult
could see him, and knew the reason of the cheer which ran
along the front of the allied army as he rode up.   Wellington
judged, and rightly, that the news of his arrival, and the
sight of him in position, would cause the marshal to delay
his attack till the last of the French reserves had come on

the field. "I had an excellent glass: I saw him spying at us—then write and send off a letter : *I knew what he would be writing*, and gave my orders accordingly." * Wellington judged Soult a cautious general, knew that his own presence would redouble his caution, and so judged that the order given by the marshal would be for the checking of a threatened attack, which would have been very dangerous at the moment, if it had been pressed. "The 6th Division will have time to come up, and we shall beat him," is said to have been his comment, when he saw Soult hurriedly write and dispatch an order to his front line.

Wellington played off a similar piece of bluff on Marmont at Fuente Guinaldo in September, 1811, when he drew up in a position strong indeed, but over-great for the numbers that he had in hand, and seemed to offer battle. He was aware that his own reputation for caution was so great that, if the enemy saw him halt and take up his ground, they would judge that he had concentrated his whole force, and would not attack him till their own reserves were near. He absconded unmolested in the night, while Marmont's rear columns were toiling up for the expected battle of the next day.

For a long time in 1809–10 Wellesley had to assume a defensive attitude. It was not till 1811 that it at last became possible for him to think of taking the offensive, nor was it till 1812, the glorious year of Ciudad Rodrigo, Badajoz, and Salamanca, that the dream reached its realization, Hence came it that for a long time he was regarded only as a cautious and calculating general, a master of defensive warfare. This conception of him was wrong ; as events showed, in 1812–1813, that he could be a very thunderbolt of war, when propitious chance gave him the opportunity, could strike the boldest blows, and launch his army upon the enemy with the most ruthless energy. But, in the earlier years of his command, he was always hopelessly outnumbered, and forced to parry rather than to strike.

* Stanhope's *Conversations with the Duke of Wellington*, p. 19.

He had to run no risks with his precious little army, the 30,000 British troops on whom the whole defence of the Peninsula really depended : because if it were destroyed it could not be replaced. With these 30,000 men he had covenanted, in his agreement with Castlereagh, when first he sailed to take command at Lisbon, that he would keep up the war indefinitely. If by taking some great risk he had lost 15,000 or even 10,000 men, the government would have called him home, and would have given up the struggle. Thus he had to fight with the consciousness that a single disaster might ruin not only his own plans, but the whole cause of the allies in Spain. No wonder that his actions seem cautious ! Yet even in 1810–1811 he took some serious risks, such as the offering of battle at Bussaco and Fuentes de Oñoro. When even a partial defeat would mean his own recall, and the evacuation of Portugal, it required no small resolution even to face such chances as these. But his serene and equable temper could draw the exact line between legitimate and over-rash enterprise, and never betrayed him.

All the more striking, therefore, was the sudden development into a bold offensive policy which marked the commencement of that year of victories 1812. The chance had at last come : Napoleon was ceasing to pour reinforcements into Spain—the Russian War was beginning to loom near at hand. The French no longer possessed their former overwhelming superiority : in order to hold in check Wellington's army, now at last increased by troops from home to 40,000 British sabres and bayonets, they had to concentrate from every quarter, and risk their hold on many provinces in order to collect a force so large that the British general could not dare to face it. At last, in the winter of 1811–1812, Napoleon himself intervened as Wellington's helper, by dispersing his armies too broadcast. The actually fatal move was the sending of 15,000 of Marmont's " Army of Portugal," the immediate adversary of the Anglo-Portuguese host, for a distant expedition to the coast of the

Mediterranean in aid of Marshal Suchet. It was the absence of this great detachment, which could not return for many weeks, that emboldened Wellington to make his first great offensive stroke, the storming of Ciudad Rodrigo on January 19, 1812, after a siege of only twelve days.

Following on this first success came the dear-bought but decisive success of the storming of Badajoz on April 7 ; this was a costly business, because Wellington had to operate " against time," since, if he lingered over-long, the French armies from north and south would combine, outnumber him, and drive him back into Portugal. Badajoz had to be stormed by sheer force, before all the arts of the engineer and artillerist had worked their full effect. The fire of the besieged had not been subdued, nor had the approaches of the assailants been pushed close up to the walls, as science would have dictated. But by making three simultaneous attacks on different points of the fortress, and succeeding at two of them, Wellington achieved his object and solved his "time problem." He showed here, for the first time, that he could, if it was necessary, spend the lives of his men remorselessly, in order to finish in a few days a task which, if much longer delayed, would have had to be abandoned. This was to his French enemies a revelation of a new side of his character. He had been esteemed one who refused risks and would not accept losses. If they had known of the details of his old Indian victory of Assaye, they would have judged his character more truly.

But Salamanca was the real revelation of Wellington's full powers. It was a lightning stroke, a sudden offensive movement made at a crisis of momentary opportunity, which would have ceased if the hour had not been seized with all promptitude. Wellington hurled his army unexpectedly at the enemy, who was manœuvring in full confidence and tranquillity in front of his line, thinking that he had to deal with an adversary who might accept a battle (as at Vimeiro, Talavera, or Bussaco), but might be trusted not to force one on. Salamanca surprised and dismayed the more sagacious of the French officers. Foy, the most intelligent observer among them, put down in his diary six days later, "This battle is the most cleverly fought, the largest in scale, the most important in results, of any that the English have won in recent times. It brings up Lord Wellington's reputation almost to the level of that of Marlborough. Up to this day we knew his prudence, his eye for choosing good positions, and the skill with which he used them. But at Salamanca he has shown himself a great and able master of manœuvring. He kept his dispositions hidden nearly the whole day : he allowed us to develop our movement before he pronounced his own : he played a close game ; he utilized the " oblique order " in the style of Frederick the Great. . . . The catastrophe of the Spanish War has come—for six months we ought to have seen that it was quite probable " *

This is one of the most striking and handsome compliments ever paid by a general of a beaten army to the commander of the victorious adversaries. It is perfectly true, and it reflects the greatest credit on Foy's fair-mindedness and readiness to see facts as they were. The conqueror of Salamanca was for the future a much more terrifying enemy than the victor of Bussaco or Talavera had been. It is one thing to be repulsed—that had often happened to the French before—another to be suddenly assailed, scattered, and driven off the field with crushing losses and in hopeless disorder, as happened to Wellington's enemies under the shadow of the Arapiles on July 22, 1812.

Wellington as a great master of the offensive came into prominence in 1812, and for the rest of the war it is this side of him which is most frequently visible, though the retreat from Burgos shows that his prudence was as much alive as ever. During the few days that preceded that retreat there was very great temptation to try a hard stroke at one of the French armies that were converging on the two halves of his own force. Napoleon would undoubtedly

* Foy's diary in Girod de l'Ain, p. 173.

have made the attempt. But, Wellington, knowing that his own total numbers were much inferior to those of the enemy, and that to concentrate in front of either Soult or Souham would be to take a terrible risk on the other flank, preferred a concentric retreat towards his base on the frontier of Portugal, to a battle in the plains of Castille, where he was far from home and support, and where a defeat might lead to absolute ruin.

This was the last time that he was outnumbered and forced back upon his old methods. In 1813, owing to Napoleon's drafts from the army of Spain, which were called off to replace the troops lost in the Moscow campaign, the allies had at last a superiority in numbers, though that superiority consisted entirely in Spanish troops of doubtful solidity. But even these were conditions far more favourable than Wellington had ever enjoyed before—he knew how to use his newly joined Spanish divisions in a useful fashion, without placing them in the more dangerous and responsible positions. The campaigns of 1813 and 1814 are both essentially offensive in character, though they contain one or two episodes when Wellington was, for the moment, on the defensive in his old style, notably the early part of the battles of the Pyrenees, where, till his reserves came up, he was fending off Soult by the use of his more advanced divisions. But the moment that his army was assembled he struck hard, and chased the enemy over the frontier, again in the series of operations that begun on the last day of Sorauren. There was a very similar episode during the operations that are generally known as the battle of the Nive, where Wellington had twice to stand for a movement in position, while one of his wings was assailed by Soult's main body. But this was distinctly what we may call defensive tactical detail, in a campaign that was essentially offensive on the whole. The main character of the operations of 1813–14 may be described as the clearing out of the enemy from a series of positions—generally heavily fortified—by successful breaking through of the lines which Soult on each occasion failed to hold. Invariably the French army was nailed down to the position which it had taken up, by demonstrations all along its front, while the decisive blow was given at selected points by a mass of troops collected for the main stroke.

CHAPTER IV

WELLINGTON'S INFANTRY TACTICS—LINE *VERSUS* COLUMN

EVERYONE who takes a serious interest in military history is aware that, in a general way, the victories of Wellington over his French adversaries were due to a skilful use of the two-deep line against the massive column, which had become the usual fighting-formation for a French army acting on the offensive, during the later years of the great war that raged from 1792 till 1814. But I am not sure that the methods and limitations of Wellington's system are fully appreciated, and they are well worth explaining. And on the other hand it would not be true to imagine that all French fighting, without exception, was conducted in column, or that blows delivered by the solid masses whose aspect the English knew so well, were the only ideal of the Napoleonic generals. It is not sufficient to lay down the general thesis that Wellington found himself opposed by troops who invariably worked in column, and that he beat those troops by the simple expedient of meeting them, front to front, with other troops who as invariably fought in the two-deep battle line. The statement is true in a general way, but needs explanation and modification.

The use of infantry in line was, of course, no invention of Wellington's, nor is it a universal panacea for all crises of war. During the eighteenth century, from Marlborough to Frederic the Great, all European infantry was normally fighting in line, three or four deep, and looking for success in battle to the rapidity and accuracy of its fire, not to the impetus of advances in heavy masses such as had been

pikemen of the sixteenth or seventeenth
and were to be introduced again by the French
...als of the Revolutionary period.   Everyone knows
now the victories of Frederic the Great were in part to be
attributed to the careful fire-drill of his infantry, who, with
their iron ramrods and rapid manual exercise, used to put
in a far larger and more effective discharge of musket-balls
per minute than their adversaries.   But both parties were
as a rule fighting in three-deep line, Austrians no less than
Prussians.   Armies had a stereotyped array, with infantry
battalions deployed in long lines in the centre, and heavy
masses of cavalry covering the wings.   A glance at the
battle-plans of the War of the Austrian Succession, or of
the Seven Years' War, shows a marvellous similarity in the
general tactical arrangements of the rival hosts, and front-
to-front collisions of long parallel lines were quite common,
though commanders of genius had their own ways of varying
the tactics of the day.   Frederic the Great's famous
"oblique order," or advance in *échelon*, with the strong
striking-wing brought forward, and the weaker " containing-
wing" held back and refused, is sufficiently well known.
Occasionally he was able to vary it, as at Rossbach and
Leuthen, and to throw the greater part of his troops across
the enemy's flank at right angles, so as to roll him up in
detail.   But these were " uncovenanted mercies " obtained
owing to the abnormal sloth or unskilfulness of the opposing
general.   Torgau needs a special word of mention, as
Frederic's only battle fought of choice in a thoroughly
irregular formation.

There were one or two cases in the old eighteenth-
century wars of engagements won by the piercing of a
hostile centre, such as Marshal Saxe's victory of Roucoux
(1746), and we may find, in other operations of that great
general, instances of the use of deep masses, battalion deployed behind battalion, for the attack of a chosen section
of the hostile position, and others where a line of deployed
infantry was flanked or supported by units practically in

column. But this was exceptional—as exceptional as the somewhat similar formation of Cumberland's mass of British and Hanoverian infantry at Fontenoy, which, though often described as a column, had originally consisted of three successive lines of deployed battalions, which were ultimately constricted into a mass by lateral pressure. Some of Marshal Broglie's and Ferdinand of Brunswick's fights during the Seven Years' War were also fought in a looser order of battle than was normal.

Normally the tactics of the eighteenth century were directed to the smashing up of one of the enemy's wings, either by outflanking it, or by assailing it with very superior forces, while the rest of the enemy's army was " contained " by equal or inferior numbers, according as the assailant had more or less troops than his enemy. The decisive blow was very frequently delivered by a superior force of cavalry concentrated upon the striking wing, which commenced the action by breaking down the inferior hostile cavalry, and then turned in upon the flank of the infantry of the wing which it had assailed. Such a type of battle may sometimes be found much later, even in the Peninsular War, where Ocaña was a perfect example of it.

Speaking roughly, however, the period of set battles fought by enemies advancing against each other in more or less parallel lines ended with the outbreak of the war of the French Revolution. There had been a fierce controversy in France from 1775 to 1791 between the advocates of the linear, or Frederician, battle-order—headed by General Guibert, and the officers who wished to introduce a deeper formation, which they claimed to have learnt from the instructions of Marshal Saxe—of whom the chief was General Menil-Durand. The former school had triumphed just before the war began, and the *Réglement d'Infanterie* of 1791 accepted all their views. It was on this drill-book that the French infantry stood to fight in the following year, when the war on the Rhine and in Belgium began.*

* For an analysis of the controversy, see Dumolin's preface to his

But the attempt of the first generals of Revolutionary France to fight on the old linear system was a failure. The troops of the Republic had been demoralized by the removal or desertion of the greater proportion of their commissioned officers, and their *cadres* had been hastily filled with half-trained recruits. At the same time hundreds of new units, the battalions of volunteers, had been formed on no old *cadre* at all, but, with officers and men alike little better than untrained civilians, took the field along with the reorganized remains of the old royal army. It is hardly necessary to remark, that these raw armies suffered a series of disgraceful defeats at the hands of the Austrian and other allied troops in 1792–93. They were beaten both in tactics, in manœuvring, and in fire-discipline by the well-drilled veteran battalions to which they were opposed.

The French Republic, when it came under the control of the Jacobins, tried to set matters right by accusing its generals of treason, and arrested and guillotined a considerable proportion of the unfortunate commanders-in-chief to whom its armies had been entrusted. But neither this heroic device, nor the sending to the armies of the well known " representatives *en mission* " from the National Assembly, who were to stimulate the energy of the generals, had satisfactory results. As the representatives were generally as ignorant of military affairs as they were self-important and autocratic, they did no more than confuse and harass the unhappy generals on whom they were inflicted.

One thing, however, the Jacobin government did accomplish : it pushed into the field reinforcements in such myriads that the armies of the allies were hopelessly outnumbered on every frontier. The first successes of the Republican armies in the North were won by brute force, by heaping double and triple numbers upon the enemy. And the new tactics of the Revolutionary leaders were

Précis des Guerres de la Révolution, and compare Colin's *Education Militaire de Napoleon.*

evolved from a consciousness of superiority in this respect, a determination to swamp troops that manœuvred better than their own, by hurling preponderant masses upon them, regardless of the losses that must necessarily be suffered. For they had inexhaustible reserves behind them, from the newly-decreed levies *en masse*, while the bases of the allies were far off, and their trained men, when destroyed, could only be replaced slowly and with difficulty.

When the generals of the Revolution threw away the old linear tactics learned in the school of Frederic the Great, as inapplicable to troops that could not manœuvre with the same speed and accuracy as their enemies, the improvised system that succeeded was a brutal and wasteful one, but had the merit of allowing them to utilize their superiority of numbers. It is possible that those of them who reasoned at all upon the topic—and reasoning was not easy in that strenuous time, when a commander's head sat lightly on his shoulders—saw that they were in a manner utilizing the idea that had been tried in a tentative way by Maurice de Saxe, and by one or two other generals of the old wars—the idea that for collision in long line on a parallel front, partial attacks in heavy masses on designated points might be substituted. But it is probable that there was more of improvisation than of deliberate tactical theory in the manœuvres of even the best of them.

The usual method was to throw at the hostile front a very thick skirmishing line, which sheathed and concealed a mass of heavy columns, concentrated upon one or two critical points of the field. The idea was that the front line of *tirailleurs* would so engage the enemy, and keep him occupied all along his front, that at the crucial section of the combat the supporting columns would get up to striking distance with practically no loss, and could be hurled, while still intact, upon those points of the hostile array which it was intended to pierce ; they would go through by their mere impetus and weight, since they were only exposed to fire for a few minutes, and could endure the loss suffered in that time without losing their *élan* or their pace. The essential part of the system was the enormously thick and powerful skirmishing line : whole battalions were dispersed in chains of *tirailleurs*, who frankly abandoned any attempt at ordered movement, took refuge behind cover of all sorts, and were so numerous that they could always drive in the weak skirmishing line of the enemy, and get closely engaged with his whole front. The orderly battalion-volleys of the Austrian, or other allied troops opposed to them, did comparatively little harm to these swarms, who were taking cover as much as possible, and presented no closed body or solid mark for the musketry fire poured upon them. It looks as if the proper antidote against such a swarm-attack would have been local and partial cavalry charges, by squadrons judiciously inserted in the hostile line, for nothing could have been more vulnerable to a sudden cavalry onslaught than a disorderly chain of light troops.   On many occasions in the campaigns of 1792–93 the French infantry had shown itself very helpless against horsemen who pushed their charge home, not only in cases where it was caught unprepared, but even when it had succeeded in forming square with more or less promptitude.*   But this particular remedy against the swarm-attack does not seem to have been duly employed, and indeed many parts of Flanders are so cut up by small enclosures, that the use of cavalry as a universal panacea might often have proved impossible.

The masses which supported the thick lines of *tirailleurs* were formed either in columns of companies or columns of " divisions," *i.e.* double companies.†   In the former case the eight companies, each three deep, were drawn up behind each other. In the latter the front was formed by a " division," and the depth was only twelve men. In either

* See especially the record of the great English and Austrian charges against French infantry at Villers-en-Cauchies, Beaumont, and Willems (Fortescue's *British Army*, lv. 240–56).

† The French battalion then comprising nine companies, of which one, the Voltigeur company, would not be in the column.

case none but the two front ranks could use their firearms
properly, and the rest were useless save for the impetus
that they gave the rolling mass. But such a column, when
properly sheathed by the skirmishing line till the last
moment, generally came with a very effective rush against
the allied line opposed to it, which would have been already
engaged with the *tirailleurs* for some time, and had probably been much depleted by their fire. It is equally
clear that, without its protective sheath of skirmishers,
such a heavy column would have been a very clumsy
instrument of war, since it combined the minimum of
shooting power with the maximum of vulnerability. But
when so shielded, the columns which attacked in masses at
a decisive spot, leaving the rest of the hostile line " contained " by an adequate force, had a fair chance of pene-
trating, though the process of penetration might during the
last two or three minutes be very costly to the troops
forming the head of the column.

The best early summary of this change in French tactics
which I know occurs in an anonymous English pamphlet
published in 1802, which puts the matter in a nutshell.
" The French army was composed of troops of the line
without order, and of raw and undisciplined volunteers.
They experienced defeats in the beginning, but in the
meantime war was forming both officers and soldiers. In an
open country they took to forming their armies in columns
instead of lines, which they could not preserve without
difficulty. They reduced battles to attacks on certain
points, where brigade succeeded brigade, and fresh troops
supplied the places of those who were driven back, till they
were enabled to force the post, and make the enemy give
way. They were fully aware that they could not give
battle in regular order, and sought to reduce engagements
to important affairs of posts : this plan has succeeded.
They look upon losses as nothing, provided they attain
their end ; they set little store by their men, because they
have the certainty of being able to replace them, and the

customary superiority of their numbers affords them an
advantage which can only be counterbalanced by great
skill, conduct, and activity." *

After 1794, when the Republican armies had won their
first series of great successes, and had driven their enemies
behind their own frontiers, there is a distinct change in
the tactical conceptions of the French. The troops had im-
proved immensely in morale and self-confidence : a new race
of generals had appeared, who were neither obsessed by
reminiscences of the system of Frederic the Great, like some
of their predecessors, nor spurred to blind violence and the
brutal expenditure of vast numbers of men like certain others.
The new generals modified the gross and unscientific methods
of the Jacobin armies of 1793–94, which had won victory
indeed, but only by the force of numbers and with reckless
loss of life. There remained as a permanent lesson, however, from the earlier campaigns two principles—the
avoidance of dispersion and extension, by which armies
" cover everything and protect nothing," and the necessity
of striking at crucial points rather than delivering " linear "
battles, fought out at equal intensity along the whole front.
In general French tactics became very supple, the units
manœuvring with a freedom which had been unknown to
earlier generations. The system of parting an army into
divisions, now introduced as a regular organization,† gave
to the whole army a power of independent movement
unknown in the days when a line of battle was considered
a rigid thing, formed of brigades ranged elbow to elbow,
none of which ought to move without the direct orders of
the general-in-chief. A front might be composed of separate
divisions coming on the field by different roads, and each
adopting its own formation, the only necessity being that

---

* From an essay entitled *Character of the Armies of the various
European Powers*, in a collection called *Essays on the Theory and
Practice of the Art of War*. 3 vols. London : Philips & Co.

† Though Marshal Broglie had used something like an approach
to permanent divisions in the Seven Years' War : see Colin's *Transformations de la Guerre*, p. 97.

there should be no great gaps left between them. As a matter of fact this last necessary precaution was by no means always observed, and there are cases in the middle, and even the later, years of the Revolutionary War, in which French generals brought their armies upon the field in such disconnected bodies, and with such want of co-operation and good timing, that they were deservedly defeated in detail.* Bonaparte himself is liable to this charge for his order of attack at Marengo, where he committed himself to a general action before the column of Desaix was near enough to the field, and as nearly as possible suffered a crushing reverse for the want of a mass of troops whose action was absolutely necessary to him. Hoche, Jourdan, and Moreau (the last especially), all committed similar mistakes from time to time. But these errors were at least better than an adhesion to the stereotyped tactics of the older generation, where formal set orders of battle had been thought absolutely necessary.

As a rule we find the French operating in the later years of the Republic with methods very different from those of 1793, with skill and swiftness, no longer with the mere brute force of numerical superiority, winning by brilliant manœuvring rather than by mere bludgeon work. Yet, oddly enough, there was no formal revision of official tactics ; the *Reglement d'Infanterie* which had been drawn up in 1791, whose base was the old three-deep line of Frederic the Great, had never been disowned, even when it was for the most part disregarded, in the period when swarm-attacks of *tirailleurs*, supported by monstrous heavy columns, had become, perforce, the practical method of the French armies. When that unsatisfactory time passed by, the same old drill-book continued to be used, and was no longer so remote from actual practice as it had been. For

---

* Colin quotes as bad examples of French armies coming on the field dispersedly, without the proper timing and co-operation, Wattignies, Neresheim (1796), and all Moreau's operations beyond the Rhine in that year from Rastadt to Ettlingen (*Transformations de la Guerre*, p. 99).

the use of the deployed battalion began to come up again, as the handiness of the troops increased, and their self-reliance was restored.   Only the early Revolutionary War had left two marks upon French tactics—for hard and heavy work, such as the forcing of passes, or bridges, or defiles, or the breaking of a crucial point in the enemy's line, the deep column remained habitually employed : while the old idea of the orderly continuous line of battle was gone for ever, or almost gone, for (oddly enough) in Napoleon's last and least lucky fight, Waterloo, the order of the imperial host was more like the trim and symmetrical array of a Frederician army than any French line of battle that had been seen for many a year.   Certainly it would have pleased the eye of the Prussian king much better than the apparently irregular, though carefully thought out, plans of battle on which Jena or Wagram, Borodino or Bautzen were won.

It would be doing injustice to Napoleon to represent him as a general whose main tactical method rested solely on the employment of massive columns for the critical operation on each battlefield.   He was quite aware that infantry ought to operate by its fire, and that every man in the rear ranks is a musket wasted.   If the Emperor had any favourite formation it was the *ordre mixte*, recommended by Guibert far back before his own day, in which a certain combination of the advantages of line and column was obtained, by drawing up the brigade or regiment with alternate battalions in line three-deep and in column.   This formation gave a fair amount of frontal fire from the alternate deployed battalions, while the columns dispersed among them gave solidity, and immunity from a flank attack by cavalry, which might otherwise roll up the line. If, for example, a regiment of three battalions of 900 men each were drawn up in the *ordre mixte*, with one deployed battalion flanked by two battalions in column, it had about 730 men in the firing line, while if arranged in three columns, it would only have had about 200 able to use their muskets freely. Still, at the best, this formation was heavy, since all the serried back-ranks of the flanking battalions had no power to join in the fusillade. For simple fire-effect it was as inferior to the line as it was superior to the mere column.

Napoleon, however, was certainly fond of it. From the crossing of the Tagliamento (1797), when he is first recorded to have used it, he made very frequent employment of it. In a dispatch to Soult, sent him just before Austerlitz, he directed him to use it "*autant que faire se pourra.*" It is curious, however, to note that the marshal, less than a week after, having to strike the decisive blow in that battle, did not, after all, use the *ordre mixte*, but fought in lines of battalions in "columns of divisions," as he particularly mentions in his report to the Emperor.*

But the *ordre mixte* was certainly employed again and again, not only in those parts of the battle where Napoleon was simply "containing" his enemy, and where he was merely keeping up the fight and pinning the adversary to his position, but also on the crucial points, where he was endeavouring to deal his main blow. We have notes to the effect that Lannes' Corps at Jena, Augereau's at Eylau, and Victor's at Friedland, which were all "striking forces," not "containing forces," used this formation. Its supposed solidity did not always save it from disaster, as was seen in the second of the cases quoted above, where Augereau's whole corps, despite of its battalions in column, was ridden down by a flank attack of Russian cavalry, charging covered by a snowstorm.

In spite, however, of Napoleon's theoretical preference for the *ordre mixte*, and his knowledge that the column was a costly formation to employ against an enemy whose fire was not subdued, it is certain that he used it frequently, not only for the forcing of bridges or defiles (as at Arcola

---

* See Dumolin's *Précis d'Histoire Militaire*, x. p. 263, and Colin's *Tactique et Discipline*, p. lxxxv.

and Ebersberg *), but for giving the final blow at a point where he was determined to break through, and where the enemy was holding on with tiresome persistence. At Wagram the flank-guards of Macdonald's conquering advance were formed by 13 battalions in solid column, one behind the other, though its front consisted of eight deployed battalions. Friant's division on the right wing also attacked with three regiments formed " *en colonne serrée par bataillons.*" At Friedland, Ney's right division (Marchand) came to the front in a single file of ten battalions one behind the other, and never got deployed, but attacked in mass and was checked. In 1812 and 1813 advance in heavy masses was usual—whole regiments formed in " column of divisions," battalion behind battalion,† with only 200 yards' distance between regiment and regiment.

Napoleon was quite aware of the disadvantages of such formations, " même en plaine," he observed in a celebrated interview with Foy, " les colonnes n'enfoncent les lignes qu'autant qu'elles sont appuyées par le feu d'une artillerie très supérieure, qui prépare l'attaque." ‡ And his advances in column were habitually prepared by a crushing artillery fire on the point which he was about to assail, a fire which he himself, as an old artillery officer, knew how to direct with the greatest accuracy and efficiency. It seems that he relied much more on such preparation by concentrated batteries for the shielding of his columns, than on sheathing them by a thick skirmishing line, the old device of the generals of the Republic. An enemy's firing line might be occupied and demoralized by shot and shell, as well as by a screen of skirmishers. Jena, indeed, seems to be about the only one of his battles in which a hostile line was

---

* At Arcola Augereau's division attacked the bridge over a raised road passing over a dyke only 30 feet broad, with marshes on each side. There were three regiments, one behind the other. Cohorn's column at Ebersburg was not so deep, only a brigade. But it had to defile over a bridge 200 yards long.

† *E.g.* : this was the formation of the 3rd corps at Lützen, see Fabry, *Journal des 3me et 5me Corps en 1813*, p. 7.

‡ Foy's *Vie Militaire*, ed. Girod de l'Ain, p. 107.

masked and depleted by a heavy *tirailleur* attack, before the columns in support charged and routed it. Often the light infantry seems to have been practically non-existent, and it was artillery and formed battalions alone which fought out the engagement. French generals in the imperial campaigns appear habitually to have used for the skirmishing line no more than the *Voltigeur* company of each battalion,* a force making one-ninth of the whole unit only, till the number of companies was cut down in 1808 from nine to six, when the *Voltigeurs* became one-sixth of the total. We are very far, by 1805 or 1809, from the day of the great " swarm-attacks " of the early Republic.

It was the tactics of the Empire, not those of the Republic, which Wellington had to face, when he took command of the allied army in the Peninsula in 1809. He had to take into consideration an enemy whose methods were essentially offensive, whose order of infantry fighting was at the best— in the *ordre mixte*—rather heavy, and in many cases, when the column of the battalion or the regiment was used, exceptionally gross and crowded. He knew that the enemy would have a far more numerous cavalry than was at his own disposition, and that it would be used with reckless boldness—the cavalry stroke in the Napoleonic battle accompanied, if it did not precede, the infantry stroke. Moreover, the French army would have a very powerful and effective artillery, trained to prepare the way for infantry attacks by the greatest artillerist in the world. His own proportion of guns to infantry was ridiculously low : there was not even one battery per division in 1809.

What was there to oppose to this dangerous enemy in the way of tactical efficiency ? Roughly speaking we may say that the one point of superiority on which Wellesley counted, and counted rightly, was the superiority of the English formation for infantry in the two-deep line to the heavier order of the enemy's battalions. For this

---

* Habitually but not invariably : *e.g.* for a use of eight skirmishing companies from five battalions at Villamuriel in Oct. 12, by Maucune, see Béchaud's *Journal*, pp. 406-7, in *Études Napoléoniemes* I.

formation he was, of course, not responsible himself : he took it over as an accepted thing, and thought that he knew how to turn it to the best account.

The effects of the French War on British tactics had been notable and interesting. The first reflections published on the new type of war on this side of the Channel seem to have been mainly inspired by the experience of the Duke of York's army in 1793–94, when the thick chains of *tirailleurs*, which formed the protective screen, or first line, of the Republican armies, had done so much damage to troops which fought them in the old three-deep order, adopted from Frederic the Great, without any sufficient counter-provision of skirmishers. We find early in the war complaints that the British forces had no adequate proportion of light troops—that the one light company per battalion, normally used, was wholly unable to prevent the French *tirailleur* swarm from pressing up to the main line, and doing it much harm before the real attack was delivered. Two remedies were proposed—the first was that the proportion of light companies in a battalion should be increased from one to two,* or that in each regiment a certain number of men should be selected for good marksmanship, and taught light infantry drill, while still remaining attached to their companies. Of these proposals the first was never tried : the second was actually practised by certain colonels, who trained fifteen or twenty men per company as skirmishers : they were called " flankers," and were to go out along with the light company. The only British battle where I have found them specially mentioned is Maida, where their mention illustrates the danger of the system. Generals wanting more light troops habitually purloined the light companies of regiments to make " light battalions "; but not only did they do this, but they sometimes even stole the " flankers " also from the centre companies.

* Sir James Sinclair in his *Observations on the Military System of Great Britain, so far as respects the formation of Infantry*, deals with this idea at great length, and proposes to have 160 skirmishers to each battalion of 640 men.

Stuart had at Maida not only the light companies, but also the "flankers" of regiments left behind in Sicily, which had therefore been deprived of every marksman that they possessed—an execrable device. The system, however, was only tentative ; it soon disappeared ; Wellington never skimmed the centre companies of their good shots, though he did occasionally create a light battalion of light companies—even this was exceptional.

But there was a second alternative course open to the British : instead of developing more skirmishers in each battalion, they might create new light-infantry corps, or turn whole units of the line into light troops. For the former there was good precedent : in the War of the American Revolution the British generals had of necessity embodied corps of riflemen, to oppose to the deadly marksmen from the backwoods who formed the most efficient part of the American armies. Such were Simcoe's Rangers, and the dismounted part of Tarleton's famous Legion— whose remainder consisted of veritable mounted infantry— the first of their sort in the British army, since dragoons had forgotten their old trade and become cavalry of the line. But all the Rangers, etc., had been disbanded in 1783, and their use seems to have been forgotten before the French War began ; the system had to begin again *de novo*. It was not till 1798 that the first British rifle battalion was created, to wit the 5th Battalion of the 60th Regiment, or Royal Americans, which was formed as a Jäger unit out of the remains of many defunct foreign light corps in British pay : it remained mainly German in composition even during the Peninsular War. This was the first green-coated battalion ; the second was Coote Manningham's "Experimental Rifle Corps," formed in January, 1800, and finally taken into the service after some vicissitudes, as the 95th—a name famous in Peninsular annals, though now almost obliterated by its new title of the "Rifle Brigade." The regiment was enlarged to three battalions before it came into Wellington's hands. Later on, though

the number of rifle corps was not increased, yet an addition
was made to the light troops of the British army by turning
certain picked battalions into light infantry. They were
armed with a special musket of light weight, not with a
rifle, and all the companies equally were instructed in
skirmishing work. The first corps so treated was the 90th
or Perthshire Light Infantry, which received the title in
1794. The precedent was not, however, acted on again
till in 1803, the 43rd and 52nd, the famous regiments of the
Peninsular Light Division, were honoured with the same
designation. The last additions during the period of the
Napoleonic wars were the 68th and 85th in 1808, and the
51st and 71st in 1809. Most of these corps had two battalions, but, even so, the provision of light infantry was not
large for an army which had then nearly 200 battalions
embodied. There were also some foreign corps to be taken
into consideration, which stood on the British muster-rolls,
such as the two Light Battalions of the King's German
Legion, the Brunswick Oels Jägers, and the Chasseurs
Britanniques, who all four served in the Peninsula. All
these save the last were created after 1803 : but at least
during the second period of the great French War, our
armies were not practically destitute of light troops, as they
were in 1793. We shall see that this had no small importance in Wellington's tactical devices.

The other lesson that might possibly have been deduced
from the campaigns of the earlier years of the great war
was the efficacy of columns for striking at the critical
points of an enemy's line. The continental enemies of
France were affected by what they had seen of this sort of
success, and often copied the formation of their adversaries.
But it is notable that the old and wholesome prejudice of
the British in favour of the line was in no way disturbed
by what had happened of late. The idea that the column
was a clumsy and expensive formation was not shaken,
and the theory that infantry ought to win by the rapidity
and accuracy of its shooting, and that every musket not

in the firing-line was wasted, continued to prevail. The reply of the British to the *ordre mixte* was to reduce the depth of the deployed battalion from three ranks to two, because it had been discovered that the fire of the third rank was difficult, dangerous to those in front, and practically ineffective. Sir David Dundas's drill-book of 1788 with its Prussian three ranks, which had been the official guide of the British infantry of late, was not formally cancelled at first, but it was practically disregarded, and the army went back to the two-rank array, which it had habitually used in the American War, and had abandoned with regret. Apparently the Duke of York did not altogether approve this change : he at least once issued a General Order, to remind colonels that the formation in three ranks was still officially recognized and ought not to be forgotten. But the permission given by an order in 1801, that inspecting officers might allow regiments to appear " even at reviews " in the two ranks, probably marked the practical end of the Prussian system.* It had certainly been disused by many officers long before that date, and it is certain that in Abercrombie's Egyptian campaign the double instead of the triple rank was in general use.† British military opinion had decided that fire was everything, and that the correct answer to the French columnar attack was to put more men into the firing line.

A conclusive proof of the efficacy of the double when opposed to the triple rank was very clearly given at the half-forgotten Calabrian battle of Maida, three years after the commencement of the second half of the great French War. At this fight the French General Reynier had deployed the whole, or the greater part, of his battalions, who

---

* See Fortescue, *British Army*, iv. p. 921.
† See the anecdote of the 28th regiment at Alexandria, whose rear rank faced about, and fought back-to-back with the front rank, when unexpectedly assailed from behind by French cavalry which had passed through a gap in the line. Hence the grant of the double shako-plate, before and behind, made to the regiment.

were not as usual fighting either in *ordre mixte* or in battalion column. The result was very decisive—5000 British infantry in the thinner formation received the attack of 6000 French in the heavier, and inflicted on them, purely by superior fire-efficiency, one of the most crushing defeats on a small scale that was ever seen, disabling or taking 2000 men, with a total loss to themselves of only 320.* It is worth while remembering that some of the officers who were afterwards to be Wellington's trusted lieutenants were present at Maida, including Cole, Kempt, Oswald, and Colborne.* This was about the only instance that I know where English and French came into action both deployed, and on a more or less parallel front. Usually it was a case of " column against line."

Sir Arthur Wellesley had been nine years absent in India before he returned to England in 1805, so that he had to learn the difference between the Republican and the Imperial armies by new experience. The problem had long been interesting him. Before he left Calcutta he is said to have remarked to his confidants that the French were sweeping everything before them in Europe by the use of column formations, but that he was convinced that the column could, and would, be beaten by the line. What he heard after his return to England evidently confirmed him in this opinion. A conversation which he had with Croker, just before he set sail on the expedition which was to end at Vimeiro, chances to have been preserved in the latter's papers, under the date, June 14, 1808. Sitting silent, lost in reverie for a long time, he was asked by Croker the subject of his thoughts. " To say the truth," he replied, " I am thinking of the French I am going to fight. I have not seen them since the campaigns in Flanders [1793-94]

---

* Till lately I had supposed that Reynier had at least his left wing, or striking *échelon*, in columns of battalions, but evidence shown me by Col. James proves that, despite of the fact that the French narratives do not show it, the majority at least of Reynier's men were deployed. This is borne out by Bunbury's narrative, p. 244, where it is definitely stated, as well as by Boothby's, p. 78.

when they were capital soldiers, and a dozen years of
victory under Bonaparte must have made them better still.
'Tis enough to make one thoughtful. But though they
may overwhelm me, I don't think that they will out-
manœuvre me. First, because I am not afraid of them,
as every one else seems to be, and secondly, because (if all
I hear about their system is true) I think it a false one
against steady troops. I suspect all the continental armies
are half-beaten before the battle begins. I at least will
not be frightened beforehand."

Wellesley went out to Portugal, there to try what could
be done with steady troops against the " French system."
But it would be to convey a false impression of his meaning
if we were to state that he simply went out to beat column
with line—though the essential fact is sufficiently true.
He went out to try his own conception of the proper way
to use the line formation, which had its peculiarities and
its limitations. The chief of these were that—

(1) The line must not be exposed before the moment
of actual conflict : *i.e.* it must be kept under cover as much
as possible.

(2) That till the critical moment it must be screened
by a line of skirmishers impenetrable to the enemy's
tirailleurs.

(3) That it must be properly covered on its flanks,
either by the nature of the ground, or by cavalry and
artillery.

When we investigate all his earlier pitched battles, we
shall see that each of these three requisites was as far as
possible secured.

(1) It was necessary for success that the line should be
kept concealed from the enemy's distant fire of artillery
and infantry as long as possible. Hence we find that one
of the most marked features of Wellesley's many defensive
battles was that he took up, whenever it was feasible, a
position which would mask his main line, and show nothing
to the enemy but his skirmishers and possibly his artillery,

for the latter having to operate before the infantry fighting began, and being obliged to take up positions which would command the ground over which the enemy must advance, were often visible from the first. At Vimeiro, Wellesley so concealed his army that Junot, thinking to turn his left flank, found his turning column itself outflanked by troops moved under cover behind a skyline. At Bussaco, Masséna, no mean general, mistook Wellington's centre for his extreme right, and found his attacking columns * well outflanked when the attack had been pressed to its issue. At Salamanca it was much the same ; the main part of the British line was well concealed behind a low ridge of hills, while Pakenham's division and its attendant cavalry, the force which executed the great stroke, were concealed in a wooded tract, far outside the French marching column that vainly thought to get round the allied right wing. At Waterloo, the clearest case of all, the whole of Wellington's infantry of the front line was so far drawn back from the edge of the slope that it was invisible, till the enemy had climbed to the brow of the plateau on which it was arrayed. Only the artillery, the skirmishing line, and the troops in the outlying posts of Hougoumont and La Haye Sainte could be made out by Napoleon's eye. Talavera, as I shall mention below, is the only exception to this general rule in the Duke's defensive battles.

Wellington's ideal position was a rising ground with a long *glacis* of slope in front, and a plateau or a dip behind it. The infantry was drawn back from the skyline, and placed behind the crest, if the hill were saddle-backed, or some hundreds of yards away from the edge, if it were flat-topped. There they stood or lay till they were wanted, secure from artillery fire : they moved forward to their actual fighting ground only when the fire-combat of infantry was to begin. Every one will remember Wellington's caustic comment on the Prussian order of battle at Ligny, where Blücher had drawn out his army in a chequered

* Those of Reynier. See my *Peninsular War*, Bussaco chapter.

array all along the declivity of a descending slope. " Damnably mauled these fellows will be—every man visible to the enemy." * Or in more solemn phrase, as he afterwards consigned it to paper : " I told the Prussian officers, in the presence of Colonel Hardinge, that according to my judgment, the exposure of the advanced columns, and indeed of the army, to cannonade, standing as they did displayed to the aim of the enemy's fire, was not prudent." †

By the end of the Peninsular War, as I have already had occasion to observe, it had become so well known to the French that Wellington's army, ready for a battle, would be under cover, that he was able, as at Fuente Guinaldo in 1811, and at Sorauren in 1813, to play off on them the trick of offering to fight in a half-manned position, because he knew that they would take it for granted that the ground invisible to them was held by an adequate force. There is an interesting testimony to the same effect in the Waterloo campaign. On the morning before the battle of Quatre Bras began, General Reille, a veteran of the Spanish war, remained halted for some time before a position held by nothing but a single Dutch-Belgian division, because (as he expressed it), " Ce pourrait bien être une bataille d'Espagne—les troupes Anglaises se montreraient quand il en serait temps." ‡ This was the lesson taught by many years of Peninsular experience—but on this occasion it chanced to be singularly ill applied—since a vigorous push would have shown Reille that there were as yet no red-coats concealed behind the trees of the Bois de Bossu.

It was only when absolute necessity compelled, owing to there being no cover available in some parts of his chosen position, that Wellington very occasionally left troops in his battle-front visible to the enemy, and exposed to artillery

* See Stanhope's *Conversations with the Duke of Wellington*, p. 109.
† The phrase comes from the *De Ros Manuscript*, quoted in Maxwell's *Life of Wellington*, ii. p. 20.
‡ Foy's *Vie Militaire*, ed. Girod de l'Ain, pp. 270, 271.

fire from a distance. The best known instance of this occurred with his centre brigades at Talavera, who were unmasked perforce, because between the strong hill which protected his left, and the olive groves which covered his right, there were many hundred yards of open ground, without any serviceable dips or undulations to conceal the line. And this was almost the only battle in which we find record of his troops having suffered heavily by artillery fire before the clash of infantry fighting began.*

(2) The second postulate of Wellington's system was, as I have remarked above, that the infantry of his battle-line must be covered by such a powerful screen of skirmishers, that the enemy's advanced line of *tirailleurs* should never be able to get near enough to it to cause any real molestation, and that it should not be seriously engaged before the French supporting columns came up to deliver the main attack. His old experience in Flanders in 1794 had taught him that the line cannot contend at advantage with a swarm of light troops, who yield when charged, but return the moment that the charge has stopped and the line has drawn back to its original position. There were evil memories of this sort not only from Flanders, but from the Egyptian Expedition of 1801, when Abercrombie's less engaged brigades suffered severely at the battle of Alexandria from the incessant fire of skirmishers at long range, to whom no proper opposition was made.†

The device which Wellesley practised was to make sure that he should always have a skirmishing screen of his own, so strong that the French *tirailleurs* should never be able to force it in and to get close to the main line. The moment that he had assumed command in April, 1809, he set to work to secure this *desideratum*. His first measure was to add to every brigade in his army an extra company of

---

* Donkin's Brigade, Wellington's last reserve, which was never engaged with infantry all day, lost 195 men without firing a shot—save by its skirmishers.

† See Fortescue, iv. p. 841.

trained riflemen, to reinforce the three light companies of
the brigade.* In April, 1809, he broke up the oldest rifle
battalion in the British army, the fifth of the 60th regiment,
and began to distribute a company of it to each of his
brigades, save to those of the King's German Legion, which
were served by special rifle companies of their own.† Thus
each of the brigades which fought at Talavera had a special
extra provision of light troops. Furthermore, when the
new Light Division was instituted on the 1st of March, 1810,
each of its two brigades was given a number of companies
of the 95th rifles : and of the other brigades formed in 1810–11
most were provided with an extra light company by means
of taking fractions from the 95th or the newly arrived
Brunswick Oels Jägers, and those which were not, had light-
infantry corps of their own inside them. But this was
not all.‡

In the summer of 1810, Wellington began the system
of incorporating a Portuguese brigade of five battalions in
each British division. Of these five one was always § a
Caçador or light battalion, specially trained for skirmishing.

---

* The interesting circular to Brigadiers conveying this information runs, " The Commander of the Forces recommends the companies of the 5/60th regiment to the particular care of the officers
commanding the brigades to which they are attached : they will
find them to be most useful, active, and brave troops in the field,
and they will add essentially to the strength of their brigades."—
General Orders, p. 262.

† These " independent rifle companies " of the K.G.L., which
appear in so many " morning states," were isolated men left behind
(mainly, no doubt, in hospital) by the two " Light Battalions " of
the K.G.L. when they left Portugal in company with Sir John Moore.

‡ To descend into detail, in May, 1811, the 5/60th supplied light
companies to Stopford's, Nightingale's, Mackinnon's (3 companies),
Myers', Hulse's, Colborne's, Hoghton's, and Abercrombie's brigades.
The Brunswick Oels Jägers supplied the extra company to Hay's
and Dunlop's brigades, while the rest of the battalion was in Sontag's
brigade. The 3/95th gave a company to Howard's brigade, while the
other battalions of this famous rifle corps were in the two brigades of
the Light Division. The German brigade of Löwe had its own "independent light companies." Only Colville's and Burne's brigades had
no such provision in the whole army.

§ Save in Hamilton's Portuguese division, which did not get
its Caçador battalions till 1812.

The old Portuguese army had not included such battalions, which were all newly raised corps, intended entirely for light infantry work. There were originally only six of them, but Wellington ordered a second six to be raised in 1811, utilizing as the cadre of the 7th, 8th, 9th the old Loyal Lusitanian Legion, which Sir Robert Wilson had formed early in the war. As the Portuguese army contained just twenty-four regiments of the line, in twelve brigades, the Caçador battalion gave precisely one unit to each brigade, save that two were incorporated in the Light Division, while none was left with the two regiments which remained behind in garrison at Abrantes and at Cadiz respectively.

As the Caçador battalions were essentially light troops, and used wholly for skirmishing, it resulted that when an Anglo-Portuguese division of the normal strength of six British and five Portuguese battalions set itself in battle array, it sent out a skirmishing line of no less than eight British and ten Portuguese companies, viz. one each from the line battalions, two of British rifles, six of Caçadores, or a total of from 1200 to 1500 men to a total strength of 5000 to 5500. This, as will be obvious, was a very powerful protective sheath to cover the front of the division. It was not always required—the French did not invariably send out a skirmishing line in advance of their main attack : but when they did, it would always be restrained and kept off from the main front of the divisional line. If the enemy wished to push it in, he had to bring up his formed battalions through his *tirailleurs*, and thus only could he reach the front of battle. The French regiments, whether formed in *ordre mixte* or (as was more common) in column, had to come to the front, and only so could reach the hitherto intact British line. It may be noted that the enemy rarely used for his skirmishing line more than the *voltigeur* company of each battalion ; as his divisions averaged ten to twelve battalions * and the unit was a

* In 1811 of the armies opposed to Wellington (Soult's and Marmont's) there was one division of 6 battalions, one of 9, two of

six-company battalion of 600 men or under, with only one *voltigeur* company, a French division would send out 1000 to 1200 skirmishers, a force appreciably less than the light troops of a British division of approximately equal force. Hence Wellington never seems to have been seriously incommoded by the French skirmishers.

So considerable was the British screen of light troops that the French not unfrequently mistook it for a front line, and speak of their column as piercing or thrusting back the first line of their opponents, when all that they had done was to drive in a powerful and obstinate body of skirmishers bickering in front of the real fighting formation.* Invariably, we may say, they had to use their columns to attack the two-deep line while the latter was still intact, while their own masses had already been under fire for some time and were no longer fresh.

It will be asked, perhaps, why the marshals and generals of Napoleon did not deploy their columns before the moment of contact. Why do we so seldom read of even the *ordre mixte* in use—Albuera is the only battle where we distinctly find it mentioned ? The answer to this objection is, firstly, that they were strongly convinced that the column was the better striking force to carry a given point, and that they were normally attacking not the whole British line but the particular section or sections where they intended to break through. But, secondly, we may add that they frequently did attempt to deploy, but always too late, since they waited till they had driven in the British skirmishing line, and tried to assume the thinner formation when

10, one of 11, seven of 12, one of 13. The battalions varied from 400 apiece in the 5th corps to over 600 in the 1st corps. The average was about 500, not including men detached or in hospital. A *voltigeur* company would have varied between 80 and 110 men.

* Note especially Vigo-Roussillon's account of Barrosa, where he speaks of his regiment having pierced the first British line, when all that it really did was to thrust back four companies of the 95th rifles, and two of the 20th Portuguese. Similarly Reynier's report on Bussaco says that Merle's division broke the front line of Picton, and only failed before his second. But the " front line " was only five light companies.

they were already under fire and heavily engaged. It was not always that the British noted this endeavour—so late was it begun, so instant was its failure. But there is evidence that it was tried by Kellermann's grenadiers at Vimeiro, by part at least of Leval's division at Barrosa, by Merle's column at Bussaco, when it had already reached the summit of the Serra, and was closely engaged with Picton's troops. At Albuera we have a good description of it from the British side. When Myers' fusilier brigade marched against the flank of the 5th Corps, in the crisis of that battle, Soult launched against them his reserve, the three regiments of Werlé, which became at once locked in combat at very short range with the fusiliers. "During the close action," writes a British officer (Blakeney of the 7th), "I saw their officers endeavouring to deploy their columns, but all to no purpose. For as soon as the third of a company got out, they would immediately run back in order to be covered by the front of their column." The fact was, that the effect of the fire of a British regiment far exceeded anything that the enemy had been wont to cope with when engaged with continental troops, and was altogether devastating. Again and again French officers who came under it for the first time, made the miscalculation of trying the impossible. Nothing could be more inevitably productive of confusion and disorder than to attempt deployment under such a heavy fire. Wherefore many French commanders never tried it at all, and thought it more safe to go on to the final shock with their battalions in the usual "column of divisions," in which they had begun their attack. This was little better, and quite as costly in the end. "Really," wrote Wellington, in a moment of unwonted exhilaration, after the combat of Sabugal, "these attacks in column against our lines are very contemptible." * This was after he had viewed from the other bank of the Coa, "where I could see every movement on both sides," the 43rd regiment repulse in succession three attacks by

* Wellington to Beresford, *Dispatches*, vii. p. 427.

French columns which came up against it, one after the other.

(3) We now come to the third postulate of Wellington's system—the two-deep fighting line must be covered on its flanks, either by the ground, or by cavalry and artillery support, or by infantry prolonging the front beyond the enemy's immediate point of action. At Talavera one of his flanks was covered by a precipitous hill, the other by thick olive plantations. At Bussaco both the French attacks were hopelessly outflanked by troops posted on high and inaccessible ground, and could only be pushed frontally. At Fuentes de Oñoro the final fighting position rested on a heavily occupied village at one end, and on the ravine of the Turon river upon the other. At Salamanca the 3rd Division, the striking-force which won the battle, had its line covered on its outer flank by a British and a Portuguese brigade of cavalry. At Vittoria the whole French army was enveloped by the concentric and converging attack of the much longer British line. At Waterloo flank protection was secured by the advanced post of Hougoumont and a "refused" right wing at one end of the position: by the group of fortified farms (Papelotte, La Haye, etc.), and a mass of cavalry at the other. Wellington, in short, was very careful of his flanks. Only once indeed, so far as I remember, did the French get round the outlying end of his army and cause him trouble. This was in the first episode of Fuentes de Oñoro, where the 7th Division, placed some way out, as a flank-guard, suffered some loss by being taken in rear by French cavalry which had made a great circuit, and only escaped worse disaster because two of its battalions, the 51st and *Chasseurs Britanniques*, had time to form front to flank, and adapt themselves to the situation, and because a few British squadrons sacrificed themselves in checking, so long as was possible, the enemy's superior horse.

There was one universally remembered instance during the war which demonstrated the terrible risk that the line might run if it were not properly protected on the flanks. At Albuera Colborne's brigade of the 2nd Division was thrown into the fight with its flank absolutely bare—there was no support within half a mile—by the recklessness of its divisional general, William Stewart. It was caught unprepared by two regiments of French cavalry, charging in at an angle, almost on its rear, and three battalions were literally cut to pieces, with a loss of 1200 men out of 1600 present, and five colours. Wellington would never have sent it forward without the proper support on its wings, and it is noteworthy that, later on the same day, Cole took the 4th Division into action on the same hill, and against the same enemy, with perfect success, because he had guarded one flank with a battalion in column, and the other (the outer and more exposed one) with a battalion in square and a brigade of cavalry.

These, then, were the necessary postulates required for the successful use of line against column, and when they were duly borne in mind, victory was secure with any reasonable balance in numbers. The essential fact that lay behind the oft-observed conclusion was simply that the two-deep line enabled a force to use every musket with effect, while the " column of divisions " put seven-ninths of the men forming it in a position where they could not shoot at all, and even the *ordre mixte* praised by Napoleon placed from seven-twelfths to two-thirds of the rank and file in the same unhappy condition.* But Albuera is the only fight in the war in which there is definite proof that the enemy fought in the *ordre mixte* with deployed battalions and battalions in column ranged alternately in his front.†

* If the *ordre mixte* was formed by a regiment of three battalions of 600 men each, only 634 men out of 1800 were in the front two ranks. If by a regiment of four battalions (two deployed, two in column in the flanks), the slightly better result of 1034 men out of 2400 able to use their muskets would be produced.

† This I have from a document in the archives of the Ministry of War at Paris, which says that " the line of attack was formed by a brigade in column of attack. To its right and left the front line was in a mixed formation ; that is to say, on each side of the central column

Usually he came on with his units all in columns of divisions, and very frequently (as at Bussaco and in certain episodes at Talavera) he had battalion behind battalion in each regiment. It was a gross order of fighting, but D'Erlon invented a worse and a more clumsy formation at Waterloo, where he sent forward whole divisions with eight or nine battalions deployed one behind the other, so as to produce a front of only 200 men and a depth of twenty-four—with only one man in twelve able to use his musket.

Clearly, however, the column of divisions (double companies) was the normal French order, *i.e.* in a battalion of 600 men in six companies, we should get a front of 66 muskets and 132 men able to fire, while 468 were in the rear ranks, able to be shot but not to shoot. If an English battalion of equal strength lay in front, in its two-deep line, it could give a discharge of 600 muskets against one of 132, and this was not all. Its front was nearly five times that of the French battalion, so that its fire lapped round the flanks of the advancing mass, demoralizing it because there was no proper power to reply. Often the British line, during the moments of fire-combat, somewhat threw forward its wings in a shallow crescent, and blazed with three sides of the column at once. This was done by the 43rd and 52nd at Bussaco, with great effect, against the French brigade, that of Simon, which came up the slope in front of them, with its leading regiment ranged three battalions deep, in a most vulnerable array. How could it be expected that the column would prevail ? Effective against an enemy who allowed himself to be cowed and beaten by the sight of the formidable advancing mass, it was helpless against steady troops, who stood their ground and emptied their muskets, as fast as they could load, into a mark which it was impossible to miss. This, probably,

was a battalion deployed in line, and on each of the outer sides of the deployed battalions was a battalion or regiment in column, so that at each end the line was composed of a column ready to form square, in case hostile cavalry should attempt to fall upon one of our flanks."

is what Wellington meant when (as mentioned above) he stated to Croker, ere ever he sailed for Portugal, that " if all I hear about their system is true, I think it a false one against steady troops. I suspect all the continental armies are half-beaten before the battle begins." That is to say, the column might win by the terror that its massive weight and impetus inspired ; but if the enemy refused to be terrorized, he would be able to hold his own, and to inflict enormous losses on the crowded formation.

It only remains to be said that, with the battalion in column of divisions as unit, the French had two ways of drawing up their attacking line. They might either draw up the battalions of each regiment in a line of columns, or they might place them one behind the other, making the whole regiment into a single column. Both methods were from time to time employed. It was not details of arrangement like this which made the difference—the essential weakness was the " column of divisions " which formed the base of all the array—it was too helpless in fire-contest against the line.

The physical aspect of the contest between line and column we have now sufficiently dealt with. What was the moral aspect ? Fortunately we can explain it with accuracy, because one of the many thousands of French officers who went through the Peninsular War has left us, not personal anecdotes or confused impressions like so many of his fellows, but a real account of the mental state of a battalion going forward in column to attack the British line. I make no excuse for quoting in full the paragraphs of Bugeaud, a *chef de bataillon* in 1812—a marshal of African fame thirty years later—because they give us exactly what we want to know. It should be premised, however, that Bugeaud did not serve in the Army of Portugal, nor face Wellington's own troops. He served in Suchet's army, along the Mediterranean Coast of the Peninsula, and his personal observations must have been made at Castalla and other combats in the East. It is to be noted also that he gives no account of the clash of skirmishers which so often took place, and describes his column as going forward unsheathed to the main clash of battle.

"I served seven years in the Peninsula," he says; "during that time we sometimes beat the English in isolated encounters and raids [*e.g.* Ordal] which as a field officer detached I was able to prepare and direct. But during that long period of war, it was my sorrow to see that only in a very small number of general actions did the British army fail to get the better of us. We almost invariably attacked our adversaries, without either taking into account our own past experience, or bearing in mind that the tactics which answered well enough when we had only Spaniards to deal with, almost invariably failed when an English force was in our front.

"The English generally held good defensive positions, carefully selected and usually on rising ground, behind the crest of which they found cover for a good part of their men. The usual obligatory cannonade would commence the operation, then, in haste, without duly reconnoitring the position, without ascertaining whether the ground afforded any facilities for lateral or turning movements, we marched straight forward, 'taking the bull by the horns.' *

"When we got to about a thousand yards from the English line the men would begin to get restless and excited : they exchanged ideas with one another, their march began to be somewhat precipitate, and was already growing a little disorderly. Meanwhile the English, silent and impassive, with grounded arms, loomed like a long red wall ; their aspect was imposing—it impressed novices not a little. Soon the distance began to grow shorter : cries of ' *Vive l'Empereur*,' ' *en avant à la baïonnette*,' broke from our mass. Some men hoisted their shakos on their muskets, the quick-step became a run : the ranks began to be mixed up : the men's agitation became tumultuous, many soldiers

* A phrase used by a French marshal at Bussaco !

began to fire as they ran. And all the while the red English line, still silent and motionless, even when we were only 300 yards away, seemed to take no notice of the storm which was about to beat upon it.

"The contrast was striking. More than one among us began to reflect that the enemy's fire, so long reserved, would be very unpleasant when it did break forth. Our ardour began to cool : the moral influence (irresistible in action) of a calm which seems undisturbed as opposed to disorder which strives to make up by noise what it lacks in firmness, weighed heavily on our hearts.

"At this moment of painful expectation the English line would make a quarter-turn—the muskets were going up to the 'ready.' An indefinable sensation nailed to the spot many of our men, who halted and opened a wavering fire. The enemy's return, a volley of simultaneous precision and deadly effect, crashed in upon us like a thunderbolt. Decimated by it we reeled together, staggering under the blow and trying to recover our equilibrium. Then three formidable *Hurrahs* termined the long silence of our adversaries. With the third they were down upon us, pressing us into a disorderly retreat. But to our great surprise, they did not pursue their advantage for more than some hundred yards, and went back with calm to their former lines, to await another attack. We rarely failed to deliver it when our reinforcements came up—with the same want of success and heavier losses." *

This is the picture that we need to complete our study of the conflict of column with line. The psychology of the huddled mass going forward to inevitable defeat could not be better portrayed. The only thing that is hard for us to understand is the reason which induced capable men like Soult, D'Erlon, or Foy to continue to use the columnar formation all through the dark days of 1813–14, and even in the final campaign of Waterloo. All honour must be

* Reprinted by General Trochu in his *Armée française en 1867*, pp. 239, 240.

paid, however, to the rank and file who, with five years of such experience behind them, were still steadfast and courageous enough to put up a good fight even in their last offensive battles in the Pyrenees, as well as in the defensive actions of Orthez and Toulouse.

CHAPTER V

WELLINGTON'S TACTICS—THE CAVALRY AND ARTILLERY

HITHERTO we have been confining our outlook on Wellington's tactics to his use of infantry. But a few words must be added as to his methods of handling the other two arms—cavalry and artillery. There are fortunately one or two *memoranda* of his own which enable us to interpret his views on the use of these arms, which were to him mainly auxiliary ; for the epigram that he was " essentially an infantry general " is in the main correct, though it needs some comment and explanation. In the early part of his Peninsular campaigning he was forced to be an " infantry general," since the home government kept him unreasonably short in the matter of horsemen and guns till the year 1811 was far spent. Moreover, the ground over which he had to fight in 1809–10–11 must be considered.

The Iberian Peninsula may from the point of view of the cavalry tactician be divided into two sets of regions, in the one of which the mounted arm is all-important, while in the other it may, almost without exaggeration, be described as well-nigh negligible as an element of military strength, being only usable on a small scale, for exploration and observation, and not being able to be employed effectively in mass.

To the first-named class of regions, the tracts eminently suitable for the employment of cavalry, belong the great plateau of Central Spain, the broad arable plains of Old Castile and Leon, from Burgos to Ciudad Rodrigo and from Astorga to Aranda. Here, in a gently undulating upland, little enclosed, and mainly laid out in great common-fields, cavalry has one of the suitable terrains that can be found for it in Europe—as favourable as Champagne, or the lowlands of Northern Germany. This is also, almost to the same extent, the case with the loftier and less culti-vated plateau of New Castile, and with the melancholy thinly peopled moors of La Mancha and Estremadura, where the horseman may ride ahead for twenty or thirty miles without meeting any serious natural obstacle, save at long intervals the steep cleft of a ravine, dry in summer, full of a fierce stream in winter. Nor are the great central uplands the only tracts of Spain where cavalry finds an admirable field for operations : the central valley of the Ebro in Aragon, and the whole of the broad plain of the Guadalquivir in Andalusia, are equally suited for the employment of the mounted arm, on the largest scale. Napoleon, therefore, was entirely justified when he attached a very large proportion of horse to his Army of Spain, and when he uttered his *dictum* that great portions of it must inevitably be the possession of the general who owned the larger and the more efficient mass of squadrons.

On the other hand, there are large tracts of the Peninsula where cavalry is almost as useless as in Switzerland or Calabria. Such are the whole Pyrenean tract on the north, extending from Catalonia, by Aragon and Navarre, to the Asturian and Galician lands along the southern shore of the Bay of Biscay. It will be remembered that, during the Pyrenean Campaign of 1813, Wellington sent back very nearly all his cavalry to the plain of the Ebro, while Soult left his in the plain of the Adour. Sir John Moore's small but fine cavalry force was useless to him in the Corunna retreat, when once Astorga had been passed, and the Galician mountains entered. He sent it on before him, with the exception of a squadron or two kept with the rear-guard. Soult's more numerous mounted force, in that same campaign, was only useful in picking up Moore's stragglers, and keeping the British continuously on the march—it was brought to a dead stop every time that the retreating army showed an infantry rear-guard, and stood at bay in one of the innumerable Galician defiles.

There is another tract of the Peninsula almost as unsuited as the Pyrenean and Galician highlands for the use of cavalry—and that is Portugal, where so much of Wellington's earlier campaigning took place. Deducting some coast plains of comparatively small extent, all Northern and Central Portugal is mountainous—not for the most part mountainous on a large scale, with high summits and broad valleys, but mountainous on a small scale with rugged hills of 2000 or 3000 feet, between which flow deeply-sunk torrents in narrow ravines—where roads are all uphill and downhill and a defile occurs every few miles. It was the character of this country-side which made Wellington's army of 1810–11, with its very small cavalry force—only seven British and four or five Portuguese regiments—safe against Masséna's immensely preponderant number of squadrons. All through the long retreat from Almeida to the lines of Torres Vedras the allied army could never be caught, turned, or molested ; the cavalry on both sides was only employed in petty rear-guard actions, in which the small force brought the larger to a check in defiles, and generally gave back only when the invader brought up infantry to support his attack. For all the good that it did him, Masséna might have left his 7000 cavalry behind him when he entered Portugal—a few squadrons for exploration was all that he needed. Jammed in narrow defiles, where they were helpless, his mounted men were often more of an incumbrance than a help to him.

On the other hand, when the slopes of the Portuguese mountains were once left behind, Wellington was forced to be most cautious, and to restrict his action to favourable ground (as at Talavera, and Fuentes d'Oñoro) so long as the enemy was hopelessly superior in his number of squadrons. It was only after 1811, when his cavalry regiments were about doubled in numbers, that he could venture down

into the plains, and deliver great battles in the open like
Salamanca—the first engagement which he ever fought
in the Peninsula where his cavalry was not inferior by a
third or even a half to that of the French.

Beside the Pyrenean regions and Portugal, there are
other districts of the Peninsula where the cavalry arm is
handicapped by the terrain—Catalonia for example, where
the inland is one mass of rugged valleys, the coastland of
the kingdom of Granada, and the great ganglion of mountain
lands where Aragon, Valencia, and New Castile meet.   But
as these were tracts where the British army was little
engaged, I pass them over with a mention.   But it must
also be remembered that each of the great upland plateaux
of Spain—Leon, New Castile, La Mancha, and Estremadura,
is separated from the others by broad mountain belts,
where the Spanish guerillero bands made their headquarters,
and rendered communication between plain and plain
difficult and perilous.

In such a country of contrasts, how did the various
combatants use their mounted men during the six long
years between Vimeiro and Toulouse ?   What was the
relative value of the different national cavalry, and what
were its tactics for battle and for the equally important
work of exploration, and of the covering and concealing
the movements of the other arms ?

French cavalry tactics had, by 1808, when the war
began, developed into as definite a system as those of the
infantry.   Napoleon was fond of massing his horsemen in
very large bodies, and launching them at the centre no
less than at the flank of the army opposed to him.   In the
times of Marlborough and of Frederic the Great cavalry
was almost always drawn up in long lines on the wings,
and used first for the beating of the hostile containing
cavalry, and then for turning against the unprotected flank
of the enemy's infantry in the centre.   A cavalry dash at
a weak point in the middle of the hostile front was very
rare indeed, and only tried by the very few generals of first

rate intelligence, who had emancipated themselves from
the old routine which prescribed the regular drawing up of
an army. Marlborough's cavalry charge at the French
right-centre at Blenheim is almost the only first-rate
example of such a stroke in the old wars of the eighteenth
century. Frederic's great cavalry charge at Rossbach,
which is sometimes quoted as a parallel, was after all no
more than a sudden rush of the Prussian flank-cavalry at
the exposed wing of an army which was unwisely trying to
march around the position of its adversary. But Napoleon
was the exponent of great frontal attacks of cavalry on
chosen weak spots of the enemy's line, which had already
been well pounded by artillery or weakened in some other
way. He would use 6000, 8000, or (as at Waterloo) even
12,000 men for one of these great strokes. At Austerlitz
and Borodino these charges were made straight at the
enemy's front : Marengo and Dresden were won by such
rushes : Eylau was only saved from falling into a disaster
by a blow of the same kind. But cavalry had to be used
at precisely the right moment, to be most skilfully led,
and to be pushed home without remorse and despite of all
losses, if it was to be successful. Even then it might be
beaten off by thoroughly cool and unshaken infantry, as
at Waterloo. It was only against exhausted, distracted,
or untrained battalions that it could count with a reasonable
certainty of success.

All through the war the raw and badly-drilled Spanish
armies supplied the French squadrons with exactly this
sort of opportunities. They were always being surprised
before they had been formed by their generals in line of
battle, or caught in confusion while they were executing
some complicated manœuvre. If attacked while they were
in line or in column of march, they always fell victims to a
cavalry charge, being from want of discipline extraordinarily
slow to form square. As if this was not enough, they were
often weak enough in morale to allow themselves to be
broken even when they had time to form their squares.

The battles of Medellin, Ocaña, the Gebora, and Saguntum, were good examples of the power of a comparatively small mass of cavalry skilfully handled, over a numerous but ill-disciplined infantry. But the little-mentioned combat of Margalef in 1810 is perhaps the strongest example of the kind, for there six squadrons of Suchet's cavalry (the 13th Cuirassiers supported by two squadrons of the 3rd Hussars) actually rode down in succession, a whole division of some 4000 men, whom they caught while forming line of battle from column of march. This was done, too, despite of the fact that the Spanish infantry was accompanied by three squadrons of cavalry (who made the usual bolt at the commencement of the action), as well as by a half-battery of artillery.

It was of course a very different matter when the French cavalry had to face the steady battalions of the British army. Looking down all the record of battles and skirmishes from 1808 down to 1814, I can only remember two occasions when the enemy's cavalry really achieved a notable tactical success. Oddly enough both fell within the month of May, 1811. At Albuera there occurred that complete disaster to a British infantry brigade which has already been described in the preceding chapter. The other, and much smaller, success achieved by French cavalry over British infantry at Fuentes de Oñoro, a few days before the greater disaster at Albuera, has also been alluded to.* These two disasters were wholly exceptional; usually the British infantry held its own, unless it was absolutely taken by surprise, and this even when attacked frontally by cavalry while it was deployed in the two deep line, without forming square. If the British had their flanks covered, they were perfectly safe, and turned back any charge with ease.

Indeed the repulse of cavalry by British troops in line, who did not take the trouble to form square because their flanks were covered, was not infrequent in the Peninsular

* See page 87 above.

War. The classic instance is that of the 5th Northumberland Fusiliers at El Bodon in 1811, who advanced in line firing against two French cavalry regiments and drove them off the heights, being able to do so because they had a squadron or two of British horse to protect them from being turned. A very similar feat was performed by the 52nd at Sabugal in 1811 : and Harvey's Portuguese brigade did as much at Albuera.

Much more, of course, was the square impregnable. When once safely placed in that formation, British troops habitually not only withstood cavalry charges at a standstill, but made long movements over a battlefield inundated by the hostile cavalry. At Fuentes de Oñoro the Light Division, three British and two Portuguese squares, retreated at leisure for *two miles* while beset by four brigades of French cavalry, and reached the ground which they had been ordered to take up with a total loss of one killed and thirty-four wounded. Similarly at El Bodon the square composed of the 5th and 77th retreated for six miles, in the face of two cavalry brigades which could never break into them.*

Indeed it may be stated, as a rule almost without exception, that troops in square, whether British or French, were never broken during the Peninsular War even by very desperate and gallant charges. One of the best instances of this general rule was the case of the combat of Barquilla, where two grenadier companies of the French 22nd, surprised while covering a foraging party by five squadrons of British cavalry, got away in a level country after having been charged successively by three squadrons of the 1st Hussars of the German Legion, the 16th and the 14th Light Dragoons. One of these three squadron-charges, at least (that of the 14th), had been pushed home so handsomely that an officer and nine men fell actually among the French front rank, and a French observer noted bayonets

* For details see below, in the chapter dealing with General Picton, p. 134.

broken, and musket barrels deeply cut into by the sweeping blows of the light dragoons, who yet failed entirely to break in.

There was indeed only one extraordinary case of properly formed squares being broken during the whole war, a case as exceptional in one way as the disaster to Colborne's brigade at Albuera was in the other. This was at the combat of Garcia Hernandez, on the morning after the battle of Salamanca, where the heavy dragoons of the K. G. L. delivered what Foy (the French historian of the war) called the best charge that he had ever seen. The rear-guard of Marmont's army had been formed of the one division which had not been seriously engaged in the battle, so that it could not be said to have been composed of shaken or demoralized troops. Nevertheless, two of its squares were actually broken by the legionary dragoons, though drawn up without haste or hurry on a hillside favourable for defensive action. According to Beamish's *History of the German Legion*, a work composed a few years later from the testimony of eyewitnesses, the first square was broken by a mortally wounded horse, carrying a dead rider, leaping right upon the kneeling front rank of the square, and bearing down half a dozen men by its struggles and kicking. An officer, Captain Gleichen, spurred his horse into the gap thus created, his men followed, a wedge was thrust into the square, and it broke up, the large majority of the men surrendering. The second square, belonging to the same regiment, the 6th Léger, was a little higher up the hillside than the first : it was a witness of the destruction of the sister-battalion, and seems to have been shaken by the sight : at any rate, when assailed a few minutes later by another squadron of the German Dragoons, it gave a rather wild though destructive volley, and wavered at the moment of receiving the attack, bulging in at the first charge. This was, of course, fatal. The broken squares lost 1400 prisoners, beside some 200 killed and wounded. The victorious dragoons paid a fairly high price for their success, losing 4 officers and 50 men killed, and 2 officers, and 60 men wounded out of 700 present ; the extraordinary proportion of killed to wounded, 54 to 62 marking the deadly effect of musketry at the closest possible quarters.

This (as I said before) was the exception that proved the rule : the invulnerability of a steady square was such a commonplace, that Foy and the other old officers of the Army of Spain, looked with dismay upon Napoleon's great attempt at Waterloo to break down the long line of British squares between La Haye Sainte and Hougoumont, by the charges of some ten or twelve thousand cavalry massed on a short front of less than a mile. The Emperor had not allowed for the superior resisting power of a thoroughly good infantry.

Of fights between cavalry and cavalry, when the two sides were present in numbers so fairly equal as to make the struggle a fair test of their relative efficiency, there were comparatively few in the Peninsular War. In the early days of the war Wellington was too scantily provided with horsemen, and could never afford to engage in a cavalry battle on a large scale. He had only six regiments at Talavera in 1809, only seven in the Bussaco campaign of 1810. When he divided his army for the simultaneous campaign in Beira and in Estremadura in March, 1811, he could only give Beresford three regiments, and keep four for himself. Nor could the deficiency be supplied (as was done in the artillery arm) by using Portuguese auxiliaries. The cavalry of that nation was so weak and so badly mounted that it is doubtful whether there were ever so many as 2000 of them in the field at once. Many of the twelve regiments were never mounted, and did garrison duty as infantry throughout the war.

It was not till the summer and autumn of 1811 that Wellington at last began to get large reinforcements of the mounted arm from England, which more than doubled his strength, for in the campaign of 1812 he had no less than fifteen regiments instead of seven. In the winter of 1812–13 further reinforcements came out, and in the Vittoria campaign he had at last a powerful cavalry equal or superior to that of the French.*

Yet even allowing for the weakness of Wellington's mounted strength in his earlier campaigns, we must acknowledge that they played a comparatively small part in his scheme of operations. Though his dragoons did good service in keeping his front covered, and performed many gallant exploits (we need only mention Talavera and Fuentes de Oñoro to instance good self-sacrificing work done), they were seldom used as part of the main striking force that won a victory. Indeed, the charge of Le Marchant's heavy brigade at Salamanca is about the only instance that can be cited of really decisive action by cavalry in any of the Duke's battles. There were other notable successes to be remembered, but they were in side issues, and often not under the chief's own eye—as, for example, Bock's breaking of the squares at Garcia Hernandez on the day after Salamanca, and Lumley's very creditable victory over Latour Maubourg at Usagre on May 25, 1811.

Even when Wellington had at last a large cavalry force in 1812–14, it was seldom found massed, and I believe that more than three brigades were never found acting together. Such a force as six regiments was seldom seen in line and engaged. For the use of cavalry as a screen we may mention the combat of Venta del Pozo, during the retreat from Burgos in 1812. This was a skirmish fought by two brigades to cover the withdrawal of the infantry, which had to hurry hard on the way toward Salamanca and safety.

Something, no doubt, must be allowed for the fact that Wellington never, till the Waterloo campaign, had an officer of proved ability in chief command of his cavalry.

---

* Though a few depleted regiments also went home, so that the total strength never was over 18 regiments, 9000 horse or under, to 70,000 men in all. See pages 192–3.

Stapleton Cotton, who served so long in that capacity, was not a man of mark. Lumley, who had a short but distinguished career as a divisional commander, went home sick in 1811, and Le Marchant, who came out from home with a high reputation, was most unfortunately killed in his first battle, Salamanca, where his brigade did so much to settle the fortunes of the day. But allowing for all this, it remains clear that Wellington made comparatively little use of the cavalry arm—which could hardly have been expected when we remember how effectively he had used his horse at Assaye, quite early in his career. Possibly the fact that he was so hopelessly outmatched in this arm in 1809–11 sunk so much into his soul, that when he got his chance, later on, he was not ready to use it. Certainly several cases can be cited where it was not duly used to press a completed victory—most particularly after Vittoria and Orthez. There is no concealing the fact that Wellington's reluctance to use great cavalry attacks was, at bottom, due to his doubts as to the tactical skill of his senior officers, and the power of his regiments to manœuvre. He divulged his views on the subject, twelve years after the war was over, in a letter to Lord John Russell, dated July 31, 1826. " I considered our cavalry," he wrote, " so inferior to the French from want of order, that although I considered one of our squadrons a match for two French, yet I did not care to see four British opposed to four French, and still more so as the numbers increased, and order (of course) became more necessary. They could gallop, but could not preserve their order."

This seems a very hard judgment, when we examine in detail the cavalry annals of the Peninsular War. There were cases, no doubt, where English regiments threw away their chances by their blind fury in charging, and either got cut up from pursuing an original advantage to a reckless length, or at any rate missed an opportunity by over-great dispersion or riding off the field. The earliest case was seen at Vimeiro just after Wellington's first

landing in the Peninsula, when two squadrons of the 20th
Light Dragoons, after successfully cutting up a beaten
column of infantry, pushed on for half a mile in great disorder, to charge Junot's cavalry reserves, and were horribly
maltreated—losing about one man in four. An equally
irrational exploit took place at Talavera, where the 23rd
Light Dragoons, beaten off in a charge against a square
which they had been ordered to attack, rushed on beyond
it, against three successive lines of French cavalry, pierced
the first, were stopped by the second, and had to cut their
way back with a loss of 105 prisoners and 102 killed and
wounded—nearly half their strength. An equally headlong
business was the charge of the 13th Light Dragoons at
Campo Mayor on March 25, 1811, when that regiment, having
beaten in fair fight the French 26th Dragoons, and captured
eighteen siege-guns which were retreating on the road,
galloped on for more than six miles, sabring the scattered
fugitives, till they were actually brought up by the fire of
the fortress of Badajoz, on to whose very glacis they had
made their way. The captured guns, meanwhile, were
picked up by the French infantry who had been retreating
along the high-road behind their routed cavalry, and
brought off in safety—the 13th not having left a single
man to secure them. Here, at any rate, not much loss was
suffered, though a great capture was missed, but similar
galloping tactics on June 11, 1812, at the combat of Maguilla,
led to a complete disaster. Slade's heavy brigade (1st
Royals and 3rd Dragoon Guards) fell in with L'Allemand's
French brigade, the 17th and 27th Dragoons. Each drew
up, but L'Allemand had placed one squadron in reserve far
beyond the sky line, and out of sight. Slade charged, beat
the five squadrons immediately opposed to him, and then
(without reforming or setting aside any supports) galloped
after the broken French brigade in complete disorder for
a mile, till he came parallel to the unperceived reserve
squadron, which charged him in flank and rear : the rest
of the French halted and turned ; Slade could not stand, and

was routed, having 40 casualties and 118 prisoners. Wellington wrote about this to Hill : " I have never been more annoyed than by Slade's affair. Our officers of cavalry have acquired a trick of galloping at everything. They never consider the situation, never think of manœuvring before an enemy, and never keep back or provide for a reserve. All cavalry should charge in two lines, and at least one-third should be ordered beforehand to pull up and reform, as soon as the charge has been delivered, and the enemy been broken." *

In the first three of the cases mentioned above, the discredit of the rash and inconsiderate pressing on of the charge falls on the regimental officers—in the last on the brigadier, Slade. It must be confessed that Wellington was not very happy in his senior cavalry officers—Erskine, Long, and Slade have all some bad marks against them— especially the last-named, whose proceedings seem nearly to have broken the heart of the lively and intelligent diarist Tomkinson, of the 16th Light Dragoons, who had the misfortune to serve long under him. Stapleton Cotton, the commander of the whole cavalry, was but a mediocrity ; every one will remember his old chief's uncomplimentary remarks about him *àpropos* of the siege of Bhurtpore. The man who ought to have been in charge of the British horse during the whole war was Lord Paget, who had handled Sir John Moore's five cavalry regiments with such admirable skill and daring during the Corunna campaign : his two little fights of Sahagun and Benevente were models in their way. But he was unhappily never employed again till Waterloo—where his doings, under his new name of Lord Uxbridge, are sufficiently well known. But a question of seniority, and an unhappy family quarrel with the Wellesleys (having absconded with the wife of Wellington's brother Henry, he fought a duel with her brother in consequence) prevented him from seeing service under the Duke in the eventful years 1809–14. Of the cavalry generals who took

* See *Dispatches*, vol. viii. p. 112.

part in the great campaigns, after Paget the most successful
was Lumley, who has two very fine achievements to his
credit—the containing of Soult's superior cavalry during
the crisis of the battle of Albuera, and the combat of Usagre,
of May 25, 1811, noted above.   This was considered such an
admirable piece of work by the enemy, that it is related at
great length in Picard's *Histoire de la Cavalerie*, alone
among all British successes of the Peninsular War.

It needs a word of notice, as it is hardly mentioned in the
Wellington dispatches, and very briefly by Napier.   Latour-
Maubourg had been sent by Soult to push back Beresford's
advanced posts, and discover his position.   He had a very
large force—two brigades of dragoons and four regiments
of light cavalry, in all 3500 sabres.   Lumley, who was
screening Beresford's movements, had only three British
regiments (3rd Dragoon Guards, 4th Dragoons, 13th Light
Dragoons), 980 sabres, and Madden's and Otway's Portuguese
brigades, 1000 sabres, with 300 of Penne Villemur's Spanish
horse.   Wishing to contain the French advance as long as
possible, he took up a position behind the bridge and village
of Usagre, a defile through which the French must pass in
order to reach him.   Latour-Maubourg, relying on the
immense superiority of numbers which he possessed, was
reckless in his tactics.   After sending off a brigade of light
horse to turn Lumley's position, by a very long detour and
distant fords, he pushed his other three brigades into the
village, with orders to cross the bridge and press the enemy
in front.   Lumley was showing nothing but a line of
Portuguese vedettes, having withdrawn his squadrons
behind the sky line.   He was apprised of the turning
movement, but, knowing the ground better than the
French, was aware that it would take a very much longer
time than the enemy expected, so resolved to hold his
position to the last moment.   He allowed the two leading
regiments of Bron's dragoons to pass the bridge and form
on the nearer side, and then, while the third regiment was
crossing the river, and the second brigade was entering the

long village, charged suddenly in upon the first brigade,
with six English squadrons in front and six Portuguese
squadrons on the right flank. The two deployed French
regiments were thrown back on the third, which was jammed
on the bridge. Hence they could not get away to reform and
rally, the road behind them being entirely blocked, while
the second brigade in the village could not get to the front
to give assistance. All that Latour-Maubourg could do
was to dismount its leading regiment and occupy with it the
houses on each side of the bridge, from which they kept
back the victorious British by their carbine fire. Lumley,
meanwhile, dealt with the three routed regiments at his
leisure, killing or wounding 250 men and capturing 80
prisoners before the disordered wrecks succeeded in re-
crossing the river. Latour-Maubourg, warned by this bloody
check, showed for the future no anxiety to press in upon
Beresford's cavalry screen.

How *not* to deal with an exactly similar situation, it
may be remarked, was shown on the 23rd October of the
following year, 1812, by two British brigadiers, who, charged
with the covering of the retreat of Wellington's army from
Burgos, were holding a position behind the bridge of Venta
del Pozo or Villadrigo, when the part of the French cavalry
immediately opposed to them, the brigade of Faverot, ten
squadrons strong, came down to the defile. Faverot, like
Latour-Maubourg at Usagre, took the hazardous step of
ordering his leading regiment to pass the bridge at a trot,
and form on the other side. This Bock, the senior British
brigadier, allowed it to do, and was right in so doing, for
the proper moment to strike was when the enemy should
have half or three-quarters of his men across the bridge,
and the rest jammed upon it. But Bock allowed the psycho-
logical moment to pass, and did not charge till the French
brigade had almost entirely crossed, and could put very
nearly equal numbers in line against him. Then, moving
too late, with some squadrons of Anson's brigade in support, he came to a desperate standing fight with the enemy,

in which both suffered very heavily. But when all the
British and German Legion regiments were already engaged,
the rearmost squadrons of the French, which had crossed
the bridge under cover of the fighting line, fell upon Bock
from the flank, and turned one of his wings ; the British
cavalry had to give way and retreat, till it was covered by
the infantry of the 7th Division. If Bock had charged
five minutes earlier, he would have nipped the French
column in the middle, and probably have destroyed the
leading regiments. The French brigade, as it was, lost
18 officers and 116 men, Anson and Bock about 200, among
whom were four officers and 70 men prisoners.

On the whole, I am inclined to think that Wellington
was a little hard on his cavalry. There was, of course, considerable justification for his criticisms. There was a want
of decision and intelligence among some of his brigadiers,
and a tendency to headlong and reckless charging straight
ahead among many of his regimental officers. But looking
dispassionately at the cavalry work on both sides, it is impossible to say that the French marshals were any better
served. There is no striking instance in the annals of the
British campaigns of 1809–14 of the army, or even a division,
being surprised for want of vigilance on the part of its
cavalry screen, while several such can be quoted on the
French side—especially Ney's surprise at Foz d'Arouce on
March 15, 1811—caused by his light cavalry under Lamotte
having completely failed to watch the roads, or the better-
known rout of Girard at Arroyo dos Molinos later in the
same year. On that occasion an infantry division, accompanied by no less than two brigades of light cavalry, was
attacked at dawn and dispersed with heavy loss, owing to
the fact that the cavalry brigadiers, Bron and Briche, had
taken no precautions whatever to feel for the enemy. They,
like the infantry, were completely surprised, being caught
with the horses unsaddled, and the men dispersed among
houses ; hence the chasseurs were taken prisoners in large
numbers by Hill's sudden rush, one of the brigadiers and a

cavalry colonel being among the 2000 unwounded prisoners taken.   There is no such large-scale surprise as this among all the records of the British cavalry.   The worst that I know were those of a squadron of the 13th Light Dragoons on April 6, 1811, near Elvas, and a very similar one of the 11th Light Dragoons two months later, not far from the same place.   In the last case the disaster is said to have happened because the regiment had only just landed from England after long home-service, and the captain in command lost his head from sheer inexperience.   With regard to this I may quote the following pregnant sentence, from the *Diary* of Tomkinson, who wrote far the best detailed account of the life of a cavalry regiment during those eventful years.   " To attempt giving men or officers any idea in England of outpost duty was considered absurd, and when they came abroad they had all to learn.   The fact was that there was no one to teach them.   Sir Stapleton Cotton (who afterwards commanded the cavalry in Spain) once tried an experiment with the 14th and 16th Light Dragoons near Woodbridge in Suffolk.   In the end he got the supposed enemy's vedettes and his own all facing the same way.   In England I never saw nor heard of cavalry taught to charge, disperse, and reform, which of all things, before an enemy, is most essential.   Inclining in line right or left is very useful, and that was scarcely ever practised."   He adds in 1819 : " On return to English duty, after the peace, we all continued the old system, each regiment estimating its merit by mere celerity of movement.   Not one idea suggested by our war experience was remembered, and after five years we shall have to commence all over again, if we are sent abroad."

In short, the proper work of cavalry, apart from mere charging, had to be learnt on Spanish soil when any regiment landed.   But it was in the end picked up by the better corps, and on the whole the outpost and reconnaissance work of the Peninsular Army seem to have been well done, though some regiments had a better reputation than others.   Much of the work of this kind speaks for itself. The most admirable achievement during the war was undoubtedly that of the 1st Hussars of the K.G.L., who, assisted afterwards by the 14th and 16th Light Dragoons, kept for four months (March to May, 1810) the line of the Agueda and Azava, 40 miles long, against a fourfold strength of French cavalry, without once letting a hostile reconnaissance through, losing a picket or even a vedette, or sending a piece of false information back to General Craufurd, whose front they were covering.

Allusion has been made in the opening words of this chapter to Wellington's memorandum for the tactical management of cavalry. It was only issued after Waterloo, in the form of "Instructions to Officers commanding Brigades of Cavalry in the Army of Occupation," but, no doubt, represents the tactics which he had evolved from his Peninsular experience.* Too long to give in entirety, it is worth analysing. The heads run as follows :—

(1) A reserve must always be kept, to improve a success, or to cover an unsuccessful charge. This reserve should not be less than half the total number of sabres, and may occasionally be as much as two-thirds of it.

(2) Normally a cavalry force should form in three lines : the first and second lines should be deployed, the reserve may be in column, but so formed as to be easily changed into line.

(3) The second line should be 400 or 500 yards from the first, the reserve a similar distance from the second line, if cavalry is about to act against cavalry. This is found not too great a distance to prevent the rear lines from improving an advantage gained by the front line, nor too little to prevent a defeated front line from passing between the intervals of its supports without disordering them.

(4) When, however, cavalry is charging infantry, the second line should be only 200 yards behind the first, the object being that it should be able to deliver its charge

* *General Orders* (collected volume), pp. 481, 482.

without delay, against a battalion which has spent its
fire against the first line, and will not be prepared for a
second charge pushed in rapid succession to the first.

(5) When the first line delivers its attack at a gallop, the
supports must follow at a walk only, lest they be carried
forward by the rush, and get mingled with the line in
front at the onset. For order in the supports must be
rigidly kept—they are useless if they have got into confusion, when they are wanted to sustain and cover a checked
first line.

A note as to horses may finish our observations on the
cavalry side of Wellington's tactics. In countless places,
in diaries no less than dispatches, we find the complaint
that the trooper of 1810 was, when not well looked after by
his officers, a bad horse-master—careless as to feeding his
mount, and still more so as to saddle-galls and such like.
It is often remarked that the one German light cavalry
regiment in the original Peninsular Army, the 1st Hussars
of the King's German Legion, set an example which some
other regiments might have copied with advantage, being
far more conscientious and considerate to their beasts. It
is interesting to find that the French cavalry reports have
exactly the same complaints, and the number of dismounted
men shown in French regimental states as a consequence of
sick horses was as great as our own. Several times I have
found the report that when a considerable number of French
cavalry had been captured, quite a small proportion of
their horses could be turned over to serve as remounts for
their captors, because of the abominable condition in which
they were found. The fact was that the climate and the
food seem to have been equally deleterious to the English
and French horses : a diet of chopped straw and green
maize—often all that could be got—was deadly to horses
accustomed to stable diet in England or France. Wellington sometimes actually imported hay and oats from
England ; but they could not be got far up country, and
only served for regiments that chanced to be put into winter

quarters near the sea. Practically all the remounts came
from England—the Portuguese and Spanish horses having
been tried and found wanting many times. In 1808 the
20th Light Dragoons were embarked without horses, being
ordered to mount themselves in Portugal; but the experiment failed wholly.

Only a short note is required as to Wellington's use of
artillery. In his early years of command he was almost as
weak in this arm as in cavalry. There was not one British
battery per division available in 1809. But the Portuguese
artillery being numerous, and ere long very efficient, was
largely used to supplement the British after 1810. Yet
even when it had become proportioned to the number of his
whole army, the Duke did not use it in the style of Bonaparte.
He never worked with enormous masses of guns manœuvring in front line, and supporting an attack, such as the
Emperor used. Only at Bussaco, Vittoria, and Waterloo
do we find anything like a concentration of many batteries
to play an important part in the line of battle. Usually the
Duke preferred to work with small units—individual
batteries—placed in well-chosen spots, and often kept
concealed till the critical moment. They were dotted
along the front of the position rather than massed, and in
most cases must be regarded as valuable support for the
infantry that was to win the battle, rather than as an arm
intended to work for its independent aims and to take a
special part in war. Of several of Napoleon's victories we
may say that they were artilleryman's battles; nothing of
the kind can be predicated of any of Wellington's triumphs,
though the guns were always well placed, and most usefully
employed, as witness Bussaco, Fuentes de Oñoro, and
Waterloo.

As to Wellington's use of siege artillery, we must speak
in a later chapter.* It was, through no fault of his own,
the weakest point in his army: indeed till 1811 he never
had a British battering train, and in the early sieges of

* See Chapter XVIII., "A note on Sieges."

Badajoz he worked *in forma pauperis*, with improvised material, mainly Portuguese, and very deficient in quality. The record is not a cheerful one ; but it must be said that the home authorities, and not Wellington, were the responsible parties for any checks that were suffered. A great general who is not an artillery or engineering specialist must trust to his scientific officers, and certainly cannot be made responsible for shortage of men and material due to the parsimony of his masters at home.

So much for the great Duke's tactics. We shall presently be investigating his system of military organization—the inner machinery of his army. But before dealing with it, we shall have to spare some attention for his greater lieutenants, whose individualities had an important share in the management of his army.

CHAPTER VI

WELLINGTON'S LIEUTENANTS—HILL, BERESFORD, GRAHAM

THERE can be no stronger contrast than that between the impression which the Iron Duke left on his old followers, and that produced by his trusted and most responsible lieutenant, Sir Rowland Hill. Hill was blessed and kindly remembered wherever he went. He was a man brimming over with the milk of human kindness, and the mention of him in any diary is generally accompanied by some anecdote of an act of thoughtful consideration, some friendly word, or piece of unpremeditated, often homely charity. A wounded officer from Albuera, who is dragging himself painfully back to Lisbon, reports himself to Hill as he passes his headquarters. Next morning " the general himself attended me out on my road, to give me at parting a basket with tea, sugar, bread, butter, and a large venison pasty." * A grateful sergeant, who bore a letter to Hill in 1813, remembers how he expected nothing but a nod and an answer from such a great man, and was surprised to find that the general ordered his servant to give the messenger a supper, arranged for his billet that night, and next morn had his haversack stuffed with bread and meat, presented him with a dollar, and advised him where to sleep on his return journey.† He would give an exhausted private a drink from the can that had just been brought for his

* See the Diary of Major Brooke, in *Blackwood* for 1908, p. 448, which I edited.

† *Memoirs of Sergeant Donaldson* (94th), ii. p. 217, and *cf.* for a similar story, *Rifleman Harris*, pp. 30, 31.

personal use, or find time to bestow a piece of friendly advice
on an unknown subaltern.   This simple, pious, considerate
old officer, whose later portraits show a decided resemblance
to Mr. Pickwick, was known everywhere among the rank
and file as "Daddy Hill."   An officer of the 2nd Division
sums up his character in a well-written letter as follows * :
"The foundation of all his popularity with the troops was
his sterling worth and heroic spirit, but his popularity was
strengthened and increased as soon as he was personally
known.   He was the very picture of an English country
gentleman : to the soldiers who came from the rural districts
of old England he represented *home ;* his fresh complexion,
placid face, kind eyes, kind voice, the absence of all parade
or noise in his manner delighted them.   The displeasure of
Sir Rowland was worse to them than the loudest anger of
other generals.   His attention to all their wants and com-
forts, his visits to the sick in hospital, his vigilant protection
of the poor peasantry, his just severity to marauders, his
generous treatment of such French prisoners and wounded
as fell into his hands, made for him a warm place in the hearts
of his soldiery ; and where'er the survivors of that army
are now scattered, assuredly Hill's name and image are
dearly cherished still."

The description sounds like that of a benevolent old
squire, rather than that of a distinguished lieutenant-
general.   Nevertheless, Rowland Hill was a very great
man of war.   Wellington liked him as a subordinate
because of his extraordinary punctuality in obedience, and
the entire absence in him of that restless personal ambition
which makes many able men think more of opportunities
for distinguishing themselves than of exact performance
of the orders given them.   Wherever Hill was, it was certain
that nothing would be risked, and nothing would be forgotten.   His beautiful combination of intelligence and
executive power more than once brought relief to his chief's
mind in a critical moment, most of all on the march to

* See Sidney's *Life of Lord Hill*, p. 228.

Bussaco in September, 1810, when it was all-important to Wellington's plans that his own detached force under Hill should join him as soon as Masséna's similar detached force under Reynier should have reached the main French army. Hill executed a long and difficult march over a mountainous country with admirable speed, and was duly up in line on the day before the battle of Bussaco, which could not in common prudence have been fought if he had been late.

This we might have expected from a man of Hill's character; but what is more surprising is that when he was trusted—a thing that did not often occur under Wellington's *régime*—with a command in which he was allowed to take the offensive on his own account, he displayed not only a power of organizing, but a fierce driving energy which none of Wellington's more eager and restless subordinates could have surpassed. Speedy pursuit of an enemy on the move was not one of the great Duke's characteristics; he was often, and not unjustly, accused of not making the best profit out of his victories. But Hill's rapid following up of Girard, in November, 1811, ending with the complete surprise and dispersion or capture of the French force at Arroyo dos Molinos, was a piece of work which for swift, continuous movement, over mountain roads, in vile rainy weather, could not have been surpassed by the best of Napoleon's lieutenants. Another blow of the most creditable swiftness and daring was the storming of the forts of Almaraz five months later, when Hill, with a light force, plunged right into the middle of the French cantonments and broke the all-important bridge by which Soult and Marmont were wont to co-operate. The forts were stormed, the bridge thoroughly destroyed, and Hill was off, and out of reach, before the neighbouring French divisions were half concentrated.

But the crowning glory of Hill's Peninsular service was the one general action in which he was fortunate enough to hold independent command. This was at the end of the war, the battle of St. Pierre, near Bayonne. He was forming the right flank of Wellington's line when his communication with the main army was cut off by a rise in the river Nive, which carried away the bridges by which he communicated with the main host. Soult, transferring the bulk of his field force, then in front of Wellington, by means of the bridges in Bayonne town, fell upon Hill with five divisions. Hill had only two, those which he had commanded for the last three years, the 2nd and Hamilton's (now Le Cor's) Portuguese. With 15,000 men he fought a defensive battle against 30,000 for the greater part of the short December day. His reserves were used up, every regiment had charged many times, the losses were heavy, and it seemed hardly possible to hold on against such odds. But Hill did so, and at last the reinforcements from the other side of the river Nive began to appear in the late afternoon, and Soult desisted from his attack and drew off beaten. This was one of the most desperate pieces of fighting in the Peninsular War, and Hill was the soul of the defence. He was seen at every point of danger, and repeatedly led up rallied regiments in person to save what seemed like a lost battle. Eye-witnesses speak of him as quite transformed from his ordinary placidity—a very picture of warlike energy. He was even heard to swear, a thing so rare that we are assured that this lapse from his accustomed habits only took place twice during the whole war. The first occasion was in the desperate melée in the night attack that began the battle of Talavera.

It is clear that Hill was a man capable of the highest feats in war, who might have gone very far, if he had been given the chance of a completely independent command. But such was not his fortune, and in his last campaign, that of Waterloo, he was almost lost to sight, as a corps-commander whose troops were operating always under the immediate eye of Wellington. He survived to a good old age, was made Commander-in-Chief of the British Army when Wellington gave up the office on accepting the

PLATE II.

LORD HILL, G.C.B.

Premiership in 1827, and held it till within a few months of his death in 1842. Almost the last recorded words of the kindly old man upon his death-bed were, "I have a great deal to be thankful for ; I believe I have not an enemy in the world." And this was literally true : to know " Daddy Hill " was to love him.

The other lieutenant to whom Wellington repeatedly entrusted a semi-independent command was one who was neither so blameless nor so capable as Rowland Hill. Yet William Carr Beresford was by no means to be despised as a soldier. The illegitimate son of a great Irish .peer, he was put into a marching regiment at seventeen, and saw an immense amount of service even for those stirring days of the Revolutionary War, when a British officer was liable to be sent to any of the four continents in rapid succession. This was literally the case with Beresford, who was engaged in India, Egypt, the Cape of Good Hope, Buenos Ayres, and Portugal in the eight years between 1800 and 1808.

When the Portuguese Government asked for a British general to reorganize their dilapidated army in 1809, Beresford was the man selected—partly because he had the reputation of being a good disciplinarian, partly because he knew the Portuguese tongue, from having garrisoned Madeira for many months, but mostly (as we are told) because of political influence. His father's family had never lost sight of him, and he was well " pushed " by the Beresford clan, who were a great power in Ireland, and had to be conciliated by all Governments.

If this appointment to command the Portuguese Army was a job, we may say (with Gilbert's judge) that so far as organization went, it was "a good job too." For he did most eminent service in creating order out of chaos, and produced in the short space of a year a well-disciplined force that was capable of taking a creditable part in line with the British Army, and won well-deserved encomiums from Wellington and every other fair critic for the part that it took at Bussaco, its first engagement. The new

army had not been created without much friction and
discontent : to clear out scores of incapable officers—many
of them *fidalgos* with great court influence—to promote
young and unknown men to their places, to enforce the
rigour of the conscription in a land where it existed in
theory but had always been evaded in practice, gained
Beresford immense unpopularity, which he faced in the
most stolid and unbending fashion. At last the Portuguese
Army was up to strength, and had learnt to obey as well
as to fight. The teaching had been by the most drastic
methods : Beresford cashiered officers, and shot deserters
or marauders in the rank and file, with a rigid disregard
alike for personal and court influence, and for public
opinion, which Wellington himself could not have surpassed.
He was, indeed, an honest, inflexible, and hard-working
administrator ; but with this and with a personal courage
that ran almost to excess his capacities ended. His virtue
in Wellington's eyes was that, after one short tussle of wills,
he completely and very wisely submitted himself to be the
mere instrument of his greater colleague, and did everything that he was told to do, working the Portuguese army
to the best effect as an auxiliary force to the British, and
making no attempt to assert an independent authority.
Instead of being kept under his hand in a body, it was cut
up into brigades, each of which, with few exceptions, was
simply attached to a British division.

It was no doubt because Beresford showed himself so
obedient and loyal, and exhibited such complete self-
abnegation, that Wellington, both in 1809 and 1811, entrusted him with the command of large detached forces
at a distance from the main army. But the marshal was
by no means up to the task entrusted to him, and after
the unhappy experiment of the first siege of Badajoz, and
the ill-fought battle of Albuera, Wellington removed him
from separate command, on the excuse that more organizing
was needed at Lisbon, and kept him either there, or with the
main army (where he had no opportunities of separate

command) till the last year of the war. In 1814 he was for a few weeks entrusted with the conduct of the expedition to Bordeaux, but as it was unopposed by the enemy—and was bound to be so, as Wellington well knew—this was giving him no great responsibility. During the three last years of the war he was really in a rather otiose and equivocal position, as titular Commander-in-Chief of an army which was not treated as a unit, but dispersed abroad among the British divisions. Occasionally he was used as a corps commander under Wellington's own eye, as at Toulouse, where he led the turning column of the 4th and 6th Divisions which broke down Soult's flank defences. For such a task, when hard fighting and obedience to orders was all that was needed, he was a fully competent lieutenant. It was when thrown on his own resources and forced to make decisions of his own that he showed himself so much inferior to his successor Hill.

Beresford was a very tall and stalwart man of herculean strength—every one knows of his personal encounter with a Polish lancer at Albuera : he parried the Pole's thrust, caught him by the collar, and jerked him out of his saddle and under his horse's feet, with one twist of his powerful arm. His features were singularly rough-cast and irregular, and a sinister appearance was given to his face by a discoloured and useless left eye, which had been injured in a shooting accident when he was quite a young man. The glare of this injured optic is said to have been discomposing to culprits whom he had to upbraid and admonish, a task which he always executed with thoroughness. He had been forced to trample on so many misdemeanants, small and great, during his five years in command of the Portuguese army, that he enjoyed a very general unpopularity. But I have never found any case in which he can be accused of injustice or oppression ; the fact was that he had a great many unsatisfactory subordinates to deal with. His own staff and the better officers of the Portuguese service liked him well enough, and the value of his work cannot be too

highly praised. He came little into contact with the British
part of the army, but I note that the 88th, whom he had
commanded before the war in Spain began, much preferred
him to their later chief, Picton, and had a kindly memory
of him. There are singularly few tales or anecdotes connected with his name, from which I deduce that in British
military circles he was neither much loved nor much
hated.

A far more picturesque figure is the third of the three
generals to whom, at one time or another, Wellington
committed the charge of a detached corps, Thomas Graham
of Balgowan, later created Lord Lynedoch. I have already
alluded to him in my preface, as in one way the most typical
figure of the epoch—the personification of all that class of
Britons who took arms against France when the Revolutionary War broke out, as a plain duty incumbent upon
them in days when the country and Crown were in danger.
He had seen the Jacobin mob face to face in its frenzy, in
a sufficiently horrid fashion. In 1792 he had taken his
invalid wife—the beautiful Mrs. Graham of Gainsborough's
well-known picture—to the Riviera, in the vain hope that
her consumption might be stayed. She died, nevertheless,
and he started home towards Scotland with her coffin, to
lay her in the grave of his ancestors. On the way he passed
through a town where the crazy hunt after impossible royalist
conspiracies was in full swing. A crowd of drunken National
Guards were seized with the idea that he was an emissary
in disguise, bearing arms to aristocrats. The coffin, they
declared, was probably full of pistols and daggers, and
while the unhappy husband struggled in vain to hold them
off, they broke it open, and exposed his wife's long-dead
corpse. After this incident Thomas Graham not un-
naturally conceived the idea that his one duty in life was
to shoot Jacobins. When he had buried his wife at Methven
he was ready for that duty, and the war with France
breaking out only five months after, his opportunity was
at hand. Though a civilian, a Whig member of Parliament,

and forty-four years of age, though he had no knowledge of military affairs, and had never heard a shot fired in anger, he went to the front at once, and fought through the siege of Toulon as a sort of volunteer aide-de-camp to Lord Mulgrave. It is odd that both Julius Cæsar and Oliver Cromwell started at this same age as soldiers. This was the first of an endless series of campaigns against the French ; Graham got a quasi-military status by raising at his own expense the 90th Foot, or Perthshire Volunteers, of which he was in reward made honorary colonel. With the curious rank of honorary colonel—he never held any lower—he went as British attaché to the Austrian Army of Italy, getting the post because Englishmen who could speak both German and Italian were rare. He saw the unhappy campaigns of 1796–97 under Beaulieu, Würmser, and the Archduke Charles, being thus one of the few British observers who witnessed Bonaparte's first essays in strategy. Then he held staff appointments during the operations in Minorca and Malta, and again served with the Austrians in Italy in 1799. After much more service, the last of it as British attaché with the army of Castaños in Spain, during the Tudela campaign, he was at last informed that—all precedents notwithstanding—from an honorary colonelcy he was promoted to be a major-general on the regular establishment, on account of his long and distinguished service. Down to 1809 he had seen more fighting than falls to most men, without owning any proper military rank, for his colonelcy of 1794, which he had held for fifteen years, was only titular and temporary, and gave him no regular rank. He had technically never been more than a civilian with an honorary title !

Yet in 1810 he was entrusted with the important post of commander of the British troops in Cadiz, and commenced to take an important part in the Peninsular War. He was now sixty-two years of age, and would have been counted past service according to eighteenth century

notions. But his iron frame gave no signs of approaching
decay, no fatigue or privation could tire him, and he was
one of the boldest riders in the army. His portrait shows
a man with a regular oval face, a rather melancholy expression—there is a sad droop in the eyelids—and abundant
white hair, worn rather long. His mouth is firm and
inflexible, his general expression very resolute, but a little
tired—that of a man who has been for nearly twenty years
crusading against an enemy with whom no peace must be
made, and who does not yet see the end in sight, but
proposes to fight on till he drops. He was a fine scholar,
knew six languages, had travelled all over Europe, and
was such a master of his pen that both his dispatches and
his private letters and diary are among the best-written
and most interesting original material that exists for this
period.

The crowning exploit of Graham's life was the victory
which he won, with every chance against him, at Barrosa
on March 7th, 1811, a wonderful instance of the triumph
of a quick eye, and a sudden resolute blow over long odds.
Caught on the march by a sudden flank attack of Marshal
Victor, owing to the imbecile arrangements of the Spanish
General La Peña, under whose orders he was serving,
Graham, instead of waiting to be attacked, which would
have been fatal, took the offensive himself. His troops
were strung out on the line of march through a wood, and
there was no time to form a regular order of battle, for the
French were absolutely rushing in upon him. Victor
thought that he had before him an easy victory, over a
force surprised in an impossible posture. But Graham,
throwing out a strong line of skirmishers to hold back the
enemy for the few necessary minutes, aligned his men in
the edge of the wood, without regard for brigade or even for
battalion unity, and attacked the French with such sudden
swiftness that it was Victor, and not he, who was really
surprised. The enemy was assailed before he had formed
any line of battle, or deployed a single battalion, and was

driven off the field in an hour after a most bloody fight.
Graham led the centre of his own left brigade like a general
of the Middle Ages, riding ten yards ahead of the line with
his plumed hat waving in his right hand, and his white
hair streaming in the wind. This was not the right place
for a commanding officer; but the moment was a
desperate one, and all depended on the swiftness and sudden-
ness of the stroke; there was no manœuvring possible,
and no further orders save to go straight on. Improvising
his battle-order in five minutes, with only 5000 men against
7000, and attacking rather uphill, he won a magnificent
victory, which would have ended in the complete destruction of the French if the Spaniard La Peña had moved to
his aid. But that wretched officer remained halted with
his whole division only two miles from the field, and did
not stir a man to aid his colleague.

A few months after Barrosa, Graham was moved
from Cadiz to join the main army in Portugal, at the request
of Wellington, who gave him the command of his left
wing during the autumn campaign of 1811, and again
through the whole of that of 1813. For the greater part of
that of 1812 Graham was away on sick leave, for the first time
in his life, his eyes having given out from long exposure to
the southern sun. Unluckily for him, his promotion to
command a wing of the grand army meant that he was
generally under Wellington's own eye, with small opportunity of acting for himself. But his chief chose him to
take charge of the most critical operation of the Vittoria
campaign, the long flank march through the mountains
of the Tras-os-Montes, which turned the right wing of
the French and forced them out of position after position
in a running fight of 200 miles. Still outflanking the enemy,
it was he who cut in across the high-road to France at Vittoria, and forced the beaten army of Jourdan to retire
across by-paths, with the loss of all its artillery, train,
baggage, and stores.

For the dramatic completeness of this splendid old

man's career, we could have wished that it had ended in 1813. But the Home Government, seeking for a trust-worthy officer to command the expedition to Holland in the following winter, chose Graham to conduct it, and his last campaign was marred by a disaster. He drove, it is true, the remnants of the French army out of Holland, though his force was small—only 7000 men, and formed of raw second battalions hastily collected from English garrisons. But his daring attempt to escalade the great fortress of Bergen-op-Zoom, the one stronghold still held by the enemy, was a sad failure. Taking advantage of a hard frost, which had made the marsh-defences of that strong town useless for the moment, Graham planned a midnight attack by four columns, of which two succeeded in crossing all obstacles and entering the place. But when all seemed won, the general's part of the scheme having succeeded to admiration, the officers in immediate charge of the attack ignored many of their orders, dispersed their men in unwise petty enterprises, and finally were attacked and driven out of the town piecemeal by the rallied garrison. The loss was terrible, fully 2000 men, of whom half were prisoners. But the bold conception of the enterprise rather than its failure should be put down to Graham's account. The mismanagement by his subordinates was incredible. Wellington, looking over the fortress a year later, is said to have observed that it must have been extremely difficult to get in. "But," he added, "when once in, I wonder how the devil they ever suffered themselves to be beaten out again."

Graham's last campaign was marred by this check. But, in the general distribution of rewards at the peace of 1814, he was given a peerage, by the title of Lord Lynedoch, and shared in the other honours of the Peninsular Army. Though sixty-six years old when the war ended, he survived. till 1843, when he had reached the patriarchal age of ninety-six. He did a good service to his old comrades by founding

PLATE III.

GENERAL THOMAS GRAHAM, BARON LYNEDOCH, G.C.B., G.C.M.G.
From the picture by Sir George Hayter.

the United Service Club, which he originally designed as a
place of rendezvous for old Peninsular officers, of whom he
had noticed that many were lonely men without family
ties, like himself, while others, stranded in London for a
few days, had no central spot where they could count on
meeting old friends.* His portrait hangs, as is right, in
the most prominent place in the largest room of the institution which he founded.

I have never found one unkindly word about General
Graham, in the numerous diaries and autobiographies of
the officers and men who served under him. All comment
on his stately presence, his thoughtful courtesy, and his
unfailing justice and benevolence. " I may truly say he
lives in their affections ; they not only looked up to him
with confidence as their commander, but they esteemed and
respected him as their firm friend and protector, which,
indeed, he always showed himself to be." † " What could
not Britons do, when led by such a chief ? " asks another.‡
I might make a considerable list of the names of British
officers who relate their personal obligation to his kindness ; § but perhaps the most convincing evidence of all is
that of the French Colonel Vigo-Roussillon, one of the enemies
whom he captured at Barrosa, who has no words strong
enough to express the delicate generosity with which he
was treated while a wounded prisoner at Cadiz. Graham
came to visit him on his sick bed, sent his own physician
to attend him, and made copious provision for his food and
lodging. For a conscientious hatred for French influence,
whether that of the red Jacobin republic, or that of the

---

* He wanted, he wrote, " to have a place of meeting where they
can enjoy social intercourse combined with economy, and cultivate
old acquaintance formed on service." Hitherto " officers coming
to town for a short period were driven into expensive and bad
taverns and coffee-houses, without a chance of meeting their friends
or any good society."

† *Twenty-five Years in the Rifle Brigade*, by Surtees of the
95th.

‡ Caddell of the 28th, p. 99.

§ Especially Bunbury, Dallas, and Blakeney.

Napoleonic despotism, did not prevent him from showing his benevolence to individual Frenchmen thrown upon his mercy.*

* " Le général était de haute stature," says Vigo-Roussillon : " il avait les cheveux tous blancs, et était encore alerte et tres vif, quoiqu'il avait soixante ans.   Sa physionomie noble et ouverte m'avait inspiré le respect, même sur le champ de bataille."—*Revue des deux Mondes,* August, 1891.

CHAPTER VII

WELLINGTON'S LIEUTENANTS—PICTON, CRAUFURD, AND OTHERS

IF Graham had no enemies, and was loved by every one with whom he came in contact, the same cannot be said of the two distinguished officers with whom I have next to deal, General Robert Craufurd and Sir Thomas Picton. They were both men of mark, Craufurd even more so than Picton; they both fell in action at the moment of victory; they were both employed by Wellington for the most responsible services, and he owed much to their admirable executive powers; but both of them were occasionally out of his good graces. Each of them had many admiring friends and many bitter enemies, whose reasons for liking and disliking them it is not hard to discover. Both of them were to a certain extent embittered and disappointed men, who thought that their work had never received adequate recognition, a view for which there was considerable justification. In other respects they were wholly unlike; their characters differed fundamentally, so much so that when they met it was not unfrequently to clash and quarrel.

Picton, a Welsh country gentleman by birth, was a typical eighteenth century soldier, who had (after the old fashion) entered the army at thirteen years of age, and had gone on foreign service at fifteen. His manners, we gather, were those of the barrack-room; he was a hard drinking, hard swearing, rough-and-ready customer. Wellington, who was not squeamish, called him " a rough, foul-mouthed

devil as ever lived,* but he always behaved extremely
well on service." The notorious Duke of Queensberry,
"Old Q," was his friend and admirer, and left him a good
legacy of £5000 in his will. Old Q's model heroes were not
of the Wesleyan Methodist type. One of the strongest
impressions left on one's mind by the diaries of those who
served under him is that of his astounding power of maledic-
tion. Kincaid's account of the sack of Ciudad Rodrigo is
dominated by "the voice of Sir Thomas Picton, with the
power of twenty trumpets proclaiming damnation to all
and sundry." † But if he was destitute of all the graces
and some of the virtues, Picton was a very fine soldier,
with a quick eye, unlimited self-confidence, and the courage
of ten bulldogs. He had, when once the Revolutionary
War commenced, made his way to the front with great
rapidity. A captain in 1794, he had become a brigadier-
general by 1799, and his promotion had been won by un-
deniable good service. For his ultimate misfortune, he
was made in 1797 governor of the newly conquered Spanish
island of Trinidad in the West Indies, while still only a
colonel. This was the beginning of his troubles; the post
was lucrative, dangerous, and difficult. The garrison was
insufficient, and the island was swarming with disbanded
Spanish soldiers, runaway negro slaves, French adventurers,
and privateers and pirates of all nations from the Spanish
Main. Picton had to create order from chaos, and then to
keep it up; his methods were drastic: the lash and the
pillory, the branding-irons, and, where necessary, military
execution. It does not appear on impartial examination
that he ever showed himself self-seeking, partial, or corrupt
in his administration; he merely tried, in his own rough
way, to dragoon into order a very unruly and lawless
community. The majority of the better classes approved
his rule, which, as one of them said, "was of the sort
required by the colony" where a governor "had to make

* Stanhope's *Conversations with Wellington*, p. 69.
† *Kincaid*, p. 116.

himself feared as well as beloved." Naturally he made
many enemies, white, black, and brown, English and
Spanish, adventurers and officials. They kept up a rain
of petitions against him at the Colonial Office, in which he
was represented as a sort of Nero. The most acrid and
ingenious of them, a Colonel Fullarton, succeeded in finding
a method of attack which was certain to have a great
vogue when tried in England. The old Spanish law still
ran in Trinidad, and under it various forms of durance and
torture were permitted against suspected persons under
arrest. A case had happened in which a mulatto girl, who
had been concerned in stealing 2000 dollars from a Spanish
tobacco merchant, was put to the barbarous punishment
of picketing (standing with the heels on a stake) by the local
magistrates, to make her confess who had taken the money,
and where it was hidden. After a few minutes she admitted
that her lover had stolen it, with her aid and consent ;
and this was proved to be the fact. Thus under Picton's
rule, and (as it turned out) with his knowledge, a woman
had been put to the torture, though the torture was slight
and the woman guilty.

Picton, on returning to England, was therefore accused
by Colonel Fullarton of many tyrannical acts, but, above
all, of having put a woman to the torture in order to extract
a confession, a thing abhorrent alike to the laws of England
and to the common sentiments of humanity. There followed a long political trial, (for it became a matter of Whig
and Tory partizanship), in which the Government finally
dropped the prosecution, because it was amply proved that
Spanish, not English, law was running in Trinidad in 1801,
since the island had not been annexed till the peace of
Amiens in the following year, and that the governor had
simply allowed the local magistrates to act according to
their usual practice. The other charges all fell through.

Nevertheless, the mud stuck, as Fullarton had intended,
and Picton was generally remembered as the man who had
permitted a woman to be tortured. The trial had dragged

over several years, and had been most costly to the accused. Since there had been no verdict, owing to the prosecution having simply been dropped, he had not even the satisfaction of being able to say that he had been acquitted by a jury of his countrymen. There was a sort of slur, however unjust, upon his name.

It therefore argued considerable independence and disregard of public opinion on the part of Wellington, when he wrote home to ask that Picton might be sent out to him to command a division,* purely on his military record as a hard fighter. The general came out to Portugal with a name unfavourably known, and to colleagues and subordinates who were prepared to view him with a critical eye. "It is impossible to deny," writes an officer who served under him, " that a very strong dislike towards the general was prevalent. His conduct in the island of Trinidad . . . had impressed all ranks with an unfavourable opinion of the man. His first appearance was looked for with no little anxiety. When he reached the ground, accompanied by his staff, every eye was turned towards him, and his appearance and demeanour were closely observed. He looked to be a man between fifty and sixty, and I never saw a more perfect specimen of a splendid-looking soldier. In vain did those who had set him down as a cruel tyrant seek to find out such a delineation in his countenance. On the contrary, there was a manly open frankness in his appearance that gave a flat contradiction to the slander. And in truth Picton was *not* a tyrant, nor did he ever act as such during the many years that he commanded the 3rd Division. But if his countenance did not depict him as cruel, there was a sarcastic severity about it, and a certain curl of the lip, that marked him as one who despised rather than courted applause. The stern countenance, robust frame, caustic speech, and austere demeanour told in legible characters that he was

* That he made the request is definitely stated in Stanhope's *Conversations*, p. 69.

one not likely to say a thing and then not do as he had said. In a word, his appearance denoted him a man of strong mind and strong frame." *

It was considered characteristic that he ended his first inspection of the division by holding a drum-head court-martial on two soldiers who had stolen a goat, and witnessing their punishment. He then rode up to the regiment to which the culprits belonged, the 88th, and "in language not of that bearing which an officer of his rank should use," said, "You are not known in the army by the name of Connaught Rangers, but by the name of Connaught *foot-pads*," with some unnecessary remarks on their country and their religion.

This untoward incident was the commencement of a long feud between Picton and the 88th, which endured all through the war, and led, at the end of it, to the Rangers refusing to subscribe to the laudatory address and plate which the rest of the 3rd Division offered to their general, after nearly five years of glorious service. Yet the feud was not incompatible with a good deal of reluctant esteem on both sides. On the morning after the storm of Ciudad Rodrigo, in which the Rangers had taken a most gallant part, we are told that some of the men, more than usually elated in spirits, called out to their commander, "Well, general, we gave you a cheer last night : it's your turn now." Picton, smiling, took off his hat and said, "Here, then, you drunken set of brave rascals, hurrah ! And we'll soon be at Badajoz," to which scene of even greater glory for the 3rd Division he did conduct them within a few weeks.

The considerable string of stories, true, half-true, or apocryphal, which cling round the name of Picton relate in about equal proportions, on the one hand, to his extreme intrepidity and coolness in action, and, on the other, to his vehemence alike of language and of action, which struck terror into the objects of his wrath. The best of the former with which I am acquainted comes from the

* Grattan's *Adventures with the Connaught Rangers*, p. 16.

same diarist, Grattan, of the 88th, whom I have already been quoting. It relates to the day of El Bodon (September 25, 1811), when the 3rd Division, caught in a somewhat isolated position owing to one of Wellington's few tactical slips, was retreating in column across a level upland, beset by Montbrun and three brigades of French cavalry. " For six miles across a perfect flat, without the slightest protection from any incident of the ground, without artillery, almost without cavalry, did the 3rd Division continue its march. During the whole time the French cavalry never quitted us, and six light guns, advancing with them and taking the division in flank and rear, poured in a frightful fire of grape and canister. General Picton conducted himself with his accustomed coolness. He rode on the left flank of the column, and repeatedly cautioned the different battalions to mind the quarter distance and the ' tellings off.' At last we got within a mile of our entrenched camp at Fuente Guinaldo, when Montbrun, impatient lest his prey should escape from his grasp, ordered his troopers to bring up their right shoulders and incline towards our column. The movement was not exactly bringing up his squadrons into line, but it was the next thing to it. They were within half pistol-shot of us. Picton took off his hat, and holding it over his eyes as a shade from the sun, looked sternly but anxiously at the French. The clatter of the horses and the clanking of the scabbards were so great, as the right squadron moved up, that many thought it the forerunner of a general charge. Some mounted officer called out, ' Had we not better form square ? ' ' No,' replied Picton ; ' it is but a *ruse* to frighten us, and it *won't do*.' In half an hour more we were safe within our lines." *

This was a fine example of cool resolution, and ended happily what had been a very anxious hour for Wellington. But I imagine that the occasion on which the Commander-in-Chief owed most to the commander of the 3rd Division

* *Grattan*, pp. 116, 117.

was the storm of Badajoz. It will be remembered that on that bloody night the main attack on the breaches failed completely, despite of the desperate exertions of the 4th and Light Divisions. The attempt by escalade upon the towering walls of the castle, which proved successful and caused the fall of the fortress, had not been in Wellington's original plan, but was suggested to him by Picton, who had viewed the breaches, and had not been convinced that they could be carried. Picton pleaded that he might be allowed to try the castle with his own division as a subsidiary operation.* He succeeded triumphantly, and so saved the day. If he had not made his offer, the chance of the city's falling would have been infinitely less, even though a brigade of the 5th Division did succeed in entering Badajoz at another point remote from the fatal breaches. Though Picton got plenty of praise for his courage on this night, it was not generally known that he ought to have been praised even more for his prescience.

Numberless instances of Picton's skill and tenacity might be quoted, all through the six years of his service under Wellington. But the anecdote which best illustrates his Spartan courage is one which belongs to the last three days of his life. At Quatre Bras, where his division so long held back the vehement attacks of Ney, he received a musket ball in his left side, which, though it gave a somewhat glancing blow and did not penetrate, broke two of his ribs. Believing that the battle would be continued next day, he resolved not to return himself as wounded, lest the surgeons should insist on sending him to the rear. He roughly bound up the wound with the assistance of his soldier servant, and was on his horse throughout June 17, conducting the retreat of his division. On the 18th, as every one knows, he was killed—shot through the head—while leading the decisive charge which beat d'Erlon's corps from the heights of Mont St. Jean. Only when

* See McCarthy's *Siege of Badajoz*, p. 35, and Robinson's *Life of Picton*, ii. p. 170.

his body was stripped, to be laid in the coffin, was it discovered that he had gone into action at Waterloo with a dangerous, perhaps mortal, wound two days old upon him. For his side was so swollen and blackened around the broken ribs, that the surgeons thought that the neglected wound might very possibly have caused his death, if he had come unharmed through the battle of June 18.

Such virtues were not incompatible with grave faults. Picton's violent language and reckless disregard of common forms of propriety form the subject of many tales. When he thought that the assistant engineer who guided the 3rd Division at the storm of Badajoz had led them astray, he drew his sword, and with an oath said that he would cut the blind fool down if he had gone wrong. This we have on the first-hand evidence of that officer, who was fortunately able to demonstrate that the right path had been taken.* A better-known tale is that of Picton and the commissary, a story which has also been attributed to Craufurd, and recently by Mr. Fortescue to General Sherbrooke. The commissary had been ordered, during one of Wellington's long marches, to have the rations of the 3rd Division ready at a certain spot at a certain hour. They were not forthcoming, but only a series of excuses, to account for their non-arrival. Picton grimly pointed to a neighbouring tree and said, " Well, sir, if you don't get the rations for my division to the place mentioned by twelve o'clock to-morrow, I will hang you on it at half-past." The commissary rode straight to Lord Wellington and complained, with much injured dignity, of the general's violent and ungentlemanly language. His lordship coolly remarked, " Oh, he said that he'd *hang* you, did he ? " " Yes, my lord." " Well, General Picton is a man of his word. I think you'd better get the rations up in time." Further advice was unnecessary ; the rations were there to the moment.† It is odd to find that many years after Picton's death a question

---

* McCarthy's *Siege of Badajoz*, p. 41.
† Robinson's *Life of Picton*, ii. p. 390.

was asked in Parliament, and a controversy raged in the newspapers, as to which of three named commissaries was the object of Picton's anger.

It would be wrong, however, to paint Picton as a mere vial of wrath, foaming into ungovernable rage in and out of season. When he was angry he generally had good cause; it was only the over-vehemence of his language that caused him to become a centre of legends. Odd as it may seem, the rank and file did not consider him a tyrant; it was acknowledged that he was very just, that he never punished without hearing the defence, that he was capable of pardoning, that when he hit hard he did so not without reason. A sergeant of the 45th wrote on him thus: " He was strict sometimes, especially about plunder, always talking about how wrong it was to plunder the poor people because countries happened to be at war. He used to flog the men when they were found out; but where he flogged, many generals took life. Besides this, the men thought that he had their welfare at heart. Every soldier in the division knew that if he had anything to complain of, ' Old Picton ' would listen to his story, and set him right if he could. On the whole, our fellows always thought him a *kind* general, in spite of his strong language."

This same sense of justice is brought out in the diaries of several officers, who speak in feeling terms of his endeavours to get obscure merit rewarded, and to keep down jobbery in promotion,* or tyranny of senior officers over their juniors. He was very accessible, and even friendly and considerate, to his subordinates. This familiarity, which endeared him to subalterns, was (as we have already noticed) not agreeable to Lord Wellington. Their intercourse was formal and not very frequent. Wellington once went out of his way to say that it was not true that he had ever had a quarrel with Picton, or been on anything but good terms with him. But while acknowledging his

* See especially McCarthy, quoted above, and Macpherson (notes in *Robinson*, ii. pp. 394–397).

services, he never pretended that he had any personal liking for him.

Picton always thought that he suffered grave injustice at the end of the war, by not being included in the list of five Peninsular officers who were made peers for their services. "If the coronet were lying on the crown of a breach, I should have as good a chance as any of them," was his caustic remark. The explanation formally given for his omission was that all the five generals honoured, Beresford, Hill, Graham, Hope, and Stapleton Cotton, had held for some time "distinct commands," and that Picton had not. But though this explanation held good for the first three, it did not really cover the cases of Hope and Cotton, whose independent commands had been little more than nominal; and Picton had on several occasions— notably in the Pyrenees—exercised independent authority in a very similar way. The fact was that he was an un-popular man, and that the Ministry omitted him, while Wellington made no effort to push his claims. He showed his displeasure by announcing his intention to retire from the army in 1814, and would have done so in the next year, if Napoleon's return from Elba had not called him into the field, to die at Waterloo.

To finish our sketch of this curious and contradictory character, we must mention that Picton was a profound despiser of all sorts of pomp and ceremony. His dress, except on gala days, was careless and often unmilitary. He fought Quatre-Bras, as several witnesses remarked, in a tall beaver hat, and in the Vittoria campaign, because he was suffering from his eyes, wore a very broad-brimmed variety of the same type. His aide-de-camps copied him, as was natural, in their disregard for appearance, and it is said that from their manners and dress they were known as "the bear and ragged staff," * a term that has been applied on several more recent occasions to similar parties.

* Cole's *Peninsular Generals*, ii. p. 84.

PLATE IV.

General Sir Thomas Picton, K.C.B.

A very different man from Sir Thomas Picton was the last of the divisional generals whose character we have to deal with, Robert Craufurd. They were both effective weapons in the hands of Wellington, but Picton's efficiency was rather that of the battering ram, while Craufurd's was rather that of the rapier. Robert Craufurd, like Picton, came to the Peninsula as rather a disappointed man, his grievance being that, despite much brilliant service, he had dropped behind in promotion, and found himself a junior brigadier general, when men several years his junior, like Hill, Beresford, and Wellington himself, were holding posts of much greater importance. Craufurd was one of our few scientific soldiers ; he had studied so far back as 1782 the tactics of the army of Frederic the Great at Berlin, and had translated into English the official Prussian treatise on the Art of War. His knowledge of German, which none other of Wellington's officers save Graham possessed, had caused him, in 1794, to be given the important post of military attaché with the Austrian Army in the Netherlands, and afterwards on the Rhine, and he followed Coburg and the Archduke Charles for three years through a series of campaigns, in which failure was much more frequent than success. When the war broke out once more between Austria and the French republic, he was again sent in 1799 to serve with his old friends, and accompanied the head-quarters of General Hotze's army in Switzerland, till he was called off to share in the Duke of York's ill-managed invasion of Holland in the end of the same year. Like Graham, therefore, Craufurd had the sorrow of witnessing a long series of disasters, for which he was not in the least responsible. As his reports and dispatches show, he discharged his duty with zeal and excellent capacity ; but his sarcastic tongue and violent temper seem to have stood in the way of his promotion. A major in 1794, after thirteen years' service, he was still only a lieutenant-colonel in 1801, and during these years had seen numberless comrades climb over his head, though he had all the while been discharging important duties in a fashion which won the admiration of all with whom he came into personal contact. It looks as if the constant reports of disaster, which he had to make, had connected his name in official circles with the notion of ill-luck. In 1801, disappointed of an official post in Ireland for which he had applied, he went on half-pay, and entered Parliament as member for a pocket-borough which chanced to be in his brother's gift.* For the next five years he was a constant speaker in Parliament on military topics, and a very bitter critic of the policy of Pitt, Dundas, and Addington. His views as to the proper organization of the British forces, in first and second line, for the beating off of French invasion were set forth at vast length, and always clashed with those of ministers. It is only fair to say that he was in the main right, and they wrong ; he pleaded for the reduction of the numberless ill-disciplined volunteer corps, and wished to see in the first line a very large regular army raised for short service, and behind it the second line, levied by conscription, as a sort of *levée en masse* trained for irregular fighting, and not expected to manœuvre or to take part in pitched battles. Craufurd's virulent criticism was very telling, but hardly likely to help his promotion as a military man, so long as the Addington and Pitt ministries were in power. When, however, Pitt died, and the Whig administration called "All the Talents" came into power, the new War Secretary, William Windham, was disposed to do everything possible for Craufurd, who was not only his personal friend, but often advised him on matters of organization and technical military subjects.

At last, after five years spent in rather acrid parliamentary criticism, Craufurd was given an opportunity by his friend Windham to see service in a higher post than had ever before fallen to his lot. Though only just

* His brother, Sir Charles Craufurd, had married the Dowager Duchess of Newcastle, and as the duke was a minor, his mother and her husband disposed of the Pelham pocket-boroughs and other patronage.

promoted to a full colonelcy, he was given the command of a brigade of 4000 men, destined for a distant expedition. This adventure was one of the most hare-brained of the many futile schemes of the unlucky cabinet then in power. Craufurd was to take in hand nothing less than a voyage round Cape Horn, for the conquest of Chili ! He never saw the straits of Magellan, however, for his force, after it had sailed, was distracted to form part of the unhappy armament under General Whitelocke, which made the disastrous attack on Buenos Ayres in 1807. Placed in the front, in command of Whitelocke's Light Brigade, and thrust forward into the tangle of streets among which the incapable general dispersed his troops in many small columns, Craufurd fought his way so far on that he was surrounded, cut off from the main body, and compelled to capitulate with the remnants of his men. Thus his first chance of distinction in the field, at the head of a considerable force, ended in absolute disaster. He was acquitted of all blame at Whitelocke's court-martial, but the thought that he was remembered as the officer who had surrendered a British brigade rankled in his mind, and sat heavy on his soul down to the end of his life.

The fact that he was held blameless, however, was marked by his appointment to the command of a brigade in the Peninsular Army in 1808. But his usual ill-luck seemed at first to attend him. He arrived too late for Vimeiro ; when serving under Moore he was detached from the main army, and did not fight at Corunna. In the next year, returning to serve under Wellesley, he was late for Talavera, though to reach the battlefield he made his well-remembered march of forty-three miles in twenty-six hours, which Napier, by a slip of memory, has converted into an impossible achievement—a march of sixty-two miles in that time, which not even Craufurd and the famous 43rd, 52nd, and 95th could have accomplished.

From 1809 onward Craufurd at last got his chance, and

for the greater part of three years * was in command of Wellington's advance, his "Light Brigade" of 1809 becoming the "Light Division" in 1810. At length he got what Fate had denied him in all his earlier career, a post of great distinction and responsibility, and a sight of victory ; for fifteen years he had been witnessing nothing but retreats and disasters. On his happy days, and they were many, Craufurd was undoubtedly the most brilliant lieutenant that Wellington ever owned. Yet he was not trusted by his chief as Hill, for example, was trusted, because of his occasional lapses from caution, and from the blind obedience which his chief exacted. Occasionally he took risks, or ventured to modify the orders given him—the faults of an eager and ambitious spirit in an hour of excitement.

His achievements were great and noble. The most splendid of them was the protection of the north-east frontier of Portugal throughout the whole spring and summer of 1810, when he was set with his own small division and two regiments of cavalry to lie out many miles in front of the main army, and to watch the assembling host of Masséna, till the moment when it should make its forward move for serious invasion. For five months he guarded a long front against an enemy of sixfold force, without allowing his line to be pierced, or suffering the French to gain any information as to what was going on in his rear. This was a great feat, only accomplished by the most complete and minute organization of his very modest resources. There were fifteen fords along the Agueda, the river whose line he had to keep, all of which had to be watched in dry weather, and many even when the stream was high. The French had 3000 cavalry opposite him in March and April, 5000 in May and June, the latter a force exceeding in numbers the total of his whole division.

* He was absent on leave from the winter of 1810 till May 1811, and only just rejoined in time for the battle of Fuentes de Oñoro.

Behind the hostile cavalry screen he knew that there were two full army corps, or over 40,000 men ; and many detachments of this infantry lay only four or five miles from Craufurd's outposts, and might attack him at any moment. Yet he never suffered any surprise ; so well were his observation-posts placed and managed, that the least movement of the enemy was reported to him in an incredibly short time. The whole web of communications quivered at the slightest touch, and the Light Division was concentrated ready to fight or to retreat, as prudence dictated, long before the attack could develop. So wonderfully had he trained his troops that any battalion, as Napier records, was ready under arms within seven minutes from the first alarm signal, and within a quarter of an hour could be in order of battle on its appointed post, with its baggage loaded and assembled ready for departure at a convenient distance to the rear.

As his aide-de-camp, Shaw Kennedy, the historian of this summer, writes, " To understand Craufurd's operations the *calculation* must never be lost sight of, for it was on calculation that he acted all along." Special reports were made of the numerous fords of the Agueda *every* morning, and the rapidity of its rises was periodically marked. Beacons were placed on conspicuous heights, so as to communicate information as to the enemy's offensive movements. To ensure against mistakes in the night, pointers were kept at the stations of communication, directed to the beacons. The cavalry regiment at the outposts was the first Hussars of the King's German Legion, a veteran corps, chosen because its officers were considered superior in scouting power to that of any other light cavalry unit with the army. Craufurd, knowing German well, communicated with each of its squadron leaders directly ; each knew his own duty for the front that he covered, and each worked out his part admirably. The general was untiring, could remain on horseback unwearied for almost any length of time, and knew personally every

ford, defile, and by-path.   Hence nothing was left to
chance.*

It was a pity that Craufurd ended this splendid piece
of service, which lasted over five months of daily danger,
by fighting the unnecessary " Combat of the Coa " on
July 4, 1810.   Staying a day too long beyond that stream
despite of Wellington's clear direction to retire the moment
that he was hard pressed, he was suddenly attacked by the
whole of Ney's corps, 20,000 men or more, and forced over
the Coa, with loss which might have been great but for the
excellence of the battalions he had trained and the cool-
headed tactical skill of his regimental officers.   He held the
bridge of the Coa successfully when he had crossed it, and lost
no more than 300 men ; but he had disobeyed orders and
risked his division.   Wellington was justly displeased, and
let his lieutenant know it.   But he did not rebuke him in
his dispatches, and continued him in his command.   He
wrote home in a confidential letter, " You will say, ' Why
not accuse Craufurd ? '   I answer, ' Because if I am to be
hanged for it, I cannot accuse a man who meant well, and
whose error was one of judgment, not of intention.' "
But for the future he kept Craufurd nearer to himself, and
did not place him so far away that he had much chance of
trying strategical experiments on his own responsibility.
Even so, there were other occasions on which the general's
proneness to think for himself got him into trouble.   One
was on September 25, 1811, on the day of the combat of
El Bodon, when Craufurd, thrown forward into a hazardous
position by his chief's orders, was twelve hours late in
joining the main army.   He had been told to make a night
march, but waited till dawn, because he was moving in
a difficult and broken country full of ravines and torrents,
where he judged that movement in the dark was dangerous.
By his delay the army was concentrated half a day later

* All this comes from Shaw-Kennedy's Diary, which is printed
at length in a most unlikely place,—the Appendix to Lord F. Fitzclarence's *Manual of Outpost Duties*, a book of the 1840's.

than Wellington intended. " I am glad to see you safe," observed the Commander-in-Chief with some asperity, as the Light Division filed into the scantily manned position at Fuente Guinaldo. " Oh, I was in no danger, I assure you." " But *I* was, from your conduct," answered Wellington. Whereupon Craufurd remarked to his staff, "He's d——d crusty to-day." * In this case it must be remarked, in justice to Craufurd, that it was his chief who had placed him in the hazardous position, not himself, and that his judgment that the night march was impracticable was very probably correct. But he had disobeyed an order, and it was remembered against him by the inflexible Wellington.

Against these lapses must be set a long career of careful and scientific soldiering, with movements of brilliant manœuvring, and sudden strokes, in which no other Peninsular general could vie with him. The repulse of Ney's corps at Bussaco was perhaps the most glorious exploit of Craufurd and his Light Division. The way in which the French on this occasion were detained and harassed by light troops, and then, just as they reached the crest of the position, charged and swept downhill by the rush of a much inferior force, launched at the right moment, was a beautiful example of tactics. The most astonishing part of it was that, by his careful choice of a position, and judicious concealment of his line till the critical minute, Craufurd beat his enemy with hardly any loss ; he had only 177 casualties, the French opposed to him over 1200. Yet there was another feat which, though less showy, was probably an even greater example of tactical skill than the stroke at Bussaco. This was the advance and retreat of the Light Division at Fuentes de Oñoro (May 5, 1811), when Craufurd was sent out of the main British position to rescue the 7th Division, which was cut off and nearly surrounded by an overwhelming force of French cavalry. Having disengaged the compromised division, Craufurd

* See *Larpent's Journal*, p. 85, and Alex. Craufurd's *Life of General Robert Craufurd*, pp. 184, 185.

had to retreat back to the main body with five brigades of fine cavalry, aided by horse artillery, surging round him on all sides, and seeking for an opportunity to burst in. To retreat in square across two miles of open plateau, very well adapted for the action of horsemen, was a delicate and dangerous task. Yet Craufurd achieved it with perfect security, and brought in his whole division to Wellington's position with a loss of less than fifty men. As an exhibition of nerve and skill it even exceeded Picton's retreat at El Bodon, for the French horse on this occasion were more numerous, and flushed with previous success, and the Light Division was a smaller body than the 3rd division by 4000 men to 5200. The distance covered, however, during the crisis of retreat at Fuentes was much shorter, only two miles to seven at El Bodon.

Craufurd fell in action before 1812 was many days old, being killed by a chance shot while watching and directing the storm of the lesser breach at Ciudad Rodrigo from the further side of the glacis (January 19). Otherwise his peculiar talents would no doubt have been exhibited in commanding the rear-guard during the retreat from Burgos, and the advance during the campaign of Vittoria. The character of the fighting in the Pyrenees would also have suited admirably his particular style of management. He was bitterly missed by his officers, Charles Alten, his successor in command of the Light Division being a general of much more pedestrian quality,* who might never fail to make an attempt to obey Wellington's orders to the best of his ability, but could never supplement them by any improvisation of his own, of which he was incapable. The operations of the Light Division after Craufurd's death were always admirable so far as the conduct of officers and men went, but there was no longer any genius in the way in which they were led.

* William Napier refused to subscribe to a testimonial to Alten at the end of the war, openly saying that he saw no sufficient merit in him.

Craufurd, unlike Hill or Graham, and like his rival Picton, had many enemies. He was a strict disciplinarian, to his officers even more than to his men, and had a quick temper and a caustic tongue. His anger used to vent itself not in bursts of swearing, such as Picton would indulge in, but by well-framed and lucid speeches of bitter sarcasm, which probably gave more offence than any amount of oaths. Being a highly educated man, and a practised parliamentary speaker, he could put an amount of polished contempt into a rebuke which was not easily forgotten. It was probably this trick that made enemies of the Napiers, both of whom speak very bitterly of him in their diaries and other writings, though William Napier in his history gives him the due credit for his many brilliant achievements.* Several others of his officers speak bitterly of his intellectual arrogance; one calls him a "tyrant"; another says that he never forgot a grudge. But he had no fewer friends than enemies; many of the best of his subordinates, like Shaw Kennedy and Campbell, loved him well, and (what is more surprising) the rank and file, on whom his wrath often fell in the form of the lash, felt not only confidence but enthusiasm for him. The best of all his eulogies comes from a 95th man, Rifleman Harris, and is well worth quoting, for its simple manliness.

"I do not think I ever admired any man who wore the British uniform more than I did General Craufurd. I could fill a book with descriptions of him, for I frequently had my eye upon him in the hurry of action. The Rifles liked him, but they feared him, for he could be terrible when insubordination showed itself in the ranks. 'You think because you are riflemen that you may do whatever you think proper,' said he one day to the miserable and savage crew around him on the retreat to Corunna; ' but

---

* For a bitter story of how his brigadiers, Barclay and Beckwith, spoke of him, see Moore-Smith's *Life of Colborne*, p. 174. *Cf.* too p. 35 of Hay's *Reminiscences* of 1808–15, for an anecdote of Craufurd's occasional snubbing of his officers. *Cf.* also George Simmond's *British Rifleman*, pp. 26, 27.

I'll teach you the difference before I have done with you.' I remember one evening during that retreat he detected two men straying away from the main body ; it was in an early stage of that disastrous flight, and Craufurd knew that he must keep his division together. He halted the brigade with a voice of thunder, ordered a drum-head court-martial on the instant, and they were sentenced to a hundred a-piece. While the hasty trial was taking place, Craufurd, dismounting from his horse, stood in the midst, looking stern and angry as a worried bulldog. He did not like retreating, that man.

" When the trial was over, it was too dark to inflict the punishment. He marched all night on foot, and when morning dawned his hair, beard, and eyebrows were covered with the frost ; we were all in the same condition. Scarcely had dawn appeared when the general called a halt, among the snow on the hills. Ordering a square to be formed, he spoke to the brigade.

" ' Although I shall obtain the good will neither of the officers nor of the men here by so doing, I am resolved to punish those men according to the sentence awarded, even though the French are at our heels. Begin with Daniel Howans.'

" The men were brought out, and their Lieutenant-Colonel, Hamilton Wade, at the same time stepped forward, and lowering his sword, requested he would forgive these men, as they were both of them good soldiers, who had fought in all the battles of Portugal. ' I order *you,* sir,' said the general, ' to do your duty. These men shall be punished.' After seventy-five lashes, Craufurd stopped the flogging. But before he put the brigade in motion again, he gave us another short address, pretty much after this style—

" ' I give you all notice that I shall halt the brigade again the very first moment I perceive any man disobeying my orders, and try him by court-martial on the spot.' He then gave the word, and we resumed our march.

" Many who read this may suppose that it was a cruel and unnecessary severity, under the dreadful and harassing circumstances of that retreat : but I, who was there, a common soldier in the regiment to which these men belonged, say that it was quite necessary. No man but one formed of stuff like General Craufurd could have saved the brigade from perishing altogether. If he flogged two, he saved hundreds from death by his management."

There was a curious anecdote concerning Craufurd's funeral published in the *Saturday Review* lately,* from the unpublished reminiscences of a contemporary, which illustrates well enough the reverence with which the Light Division looked upon its old chief. One of his strongest principles had been that troops on the march must never make a detour to avoid fordable streams or deep mud, nor break their ranks to allow each man to pick shallow water, or hard stones among the wet. The delay so caused was, he held, such a hindrance to rapid movement that it must not be allowed. He had been known to flog men who straggled from the ranks in the water, in order to fill their bottles, or to stoop down to take a long drink.† He had even caused an officer, whom he caught evading a wetting by riding pick-a-back upon his soldier-servant, to be set down with a splash in the middle of a stream.‡ Coming back from Craufurd's funeral, the leading company of the Light Division passed by an excavation at the rear of the siege works, half-filled by mud and water. Instead of turning its end to avoid the wet, the men looked at the inundation, pulled themselves together, and marched straight through it, with great regularity and steadiness, as if they were passing before a general officer at a review. The whole division followed through the slush. It seemed to them that the best testimony to their old commander's memory was to honour his best-known theory, when he was

* Jan. 20, 1912, in a letter from Colonel Willoughby Verner.
† See Hay's *Peninsular Reminiscences*, 1808–15.
‡ See *Rifleman Harris*, p. 206.

no longer there to enforce its acceptance by his usual drastic methods.

I could write much more of this notable character, with all its faults and merits. But so much must suffice. Nor have I space to tell of the other senior generals of the Peninsular War, though some of them, such as Leith and Cole, were great fighting men, just the tools that suited Wellington's hand. They were, however, never trusted with independent commands, so that it is impossible to judge of their full mental stature. I should be inclined to think very highly of Cole from his conduct at Albuera, for it was he who ordered, on his own responsibility, without any permission from Beresford, the famous advance of the Fusilier Brigade and Harvey's Portuguese, which turned into a victory that most perilous battle.* But of most of Wellington's divisional officers we can only say that they were competent for the task set them—the vigorous carrying out of orders which were given them, but in whose framing they had no part. At the most, tactical skill in execution can be attributed to them, and of this there was no lack, as witness details of Salamanca, Vittoria, and the scattered fighting in the Pyrenees. Almost as much can be predicated of some of the great brigadiers, who managed their details well, but never had the chance of showing their full powers. It would be easy to make a long list of them ; at least Kempt, Pack, Barns, Mackinnon, Colborne, Hay, Lumley, Ross, Halkett, Byng, Pakenham, Beckwith, and Barnard should be included in the list. Some of them died or were invalided early, others commanded brigades at Waterloo again, but none, save Byng, of this string of names, was ever given permanent command of a division, though several of them had held the interim charge of one in the Peninsula, when their regular chiefs were sick or absent. Ross and Pakenham alone were

---

* Hardinge advised the advance, but it was Cole who, being in responsible command, ordered and executed it. He it is who should have the credit both for the resolve and for the tactics.

promoted to a separate command, both in America. The former had charge of the expedition which went to the Potomac and Chesapeake in 1813–14 ; he took Washington by a vigorous stroke, but fell in action shortly after, while conducting an attack on Baltimore, which ceased when he fell. Pakenham's expedition to New Orleans was a series of misfortunes, of which some part at least must be attributed to his own fault. It is certain that Wellington never trained a general who proved himself a first-rate exponent of the art of war ; but his system (as we have said above) was not calculated to foster initiative or self-reliance among his lieutenants.

Other subordinates Wellington possessed, of whom we can say that they were not up to their work, even in the carrying out of the orders given them with common self-reliance and clear-headedness. Such were Spencer and Slade, who were only capable of going forward to carry out a definite order ; it was necessary, so to speak, that they should simply be put like trams on a line, and shoved forward, or they would slacken the pace and come to a stop, from want of initiative and moving power. Some few, like Sir William Erskine, who was Wellington's pet aversion—yet irremovable because of the political influence that backed him—were positively dangerous from a combination of short-sightedness, carelessness, and self-will. In one dispatch Wellington says that he thinks that he is a little wrong in his head.* It is astounding that after Erskine's mistakes at Casal Novo and Sabugal, Wellington did not get rid of him at all costs ; but he simply tried to shunt him on to commands where it was unlikely that he could do much harm, and continued solemnly to rehearse his name with approval in his dispatches, along with those of all other officers of his rank, till the unfortunate man committed suicide, in a moment of insanity, in the interval between the campaigns of 1812 and 1813. This was the

* See Wellington to Torrens (the patronage secretary at the Horse Guards), August 4, 1810.

strongest case of difficulty which Wellington, for reasons
of politics and patronage at home, did not care to face by
the decisive step of sending home the general in disgrace.
But there were several brigadier-generals whom he had not
asked for, whom he disliked, and whose departure from the
Peninsula he saluted with a small psalm of thanksgiving in
his private letters.* It is certainly astonishing that, even
after 1811, he was not given a free hand to get rid of subordinates whom he knew to be incompetent or recalcitrant,
any more than he was given the power to promote officers
without a tedious reference to the Horse Guards. It is
true that in the later years of the war his recommendations
were generally (but not always) carried out; yet it took
whole months for a request made in a letter from Salamanca
or Madrid to reach London, to be there acceded to, and
then to take effect by a publication of the *Gazette*. The
power to punish or reward with promptness was never
granted; there was always a long delay. And both
punishment and reward lose much of their salutary effect
when there is an interval of months between the act and its
consequence. Napoleon had a unique advantage in being
at once the commander-in-chief and the dispenser of
favours and chastisement; with him there was no time lost
in lengthy reference to a home government.

* See, *e.g.*, Wellington, *Dispatches*, vi., under Oct. 4, 1810.
Among the generals whose departure he viewed (for various reasons)
with equanimity, were Sir Robert Wilson, Lightburne, Tilson, and
Nightingale.

CHAPTER VIII

HAVING dealt with the greater personalities among Wellington's lieutenants, it remains that we should speak of the organization by which his army was set in motion.

Some great commanders have trusted much to their staff, and have kept their ablest subordinates about their person. This was pre-eminently not the case with Wellington : he was as averse to providing himself with a regular chief-of-the-staff, as he was to allowing a formal second-in-command to accompany his army. The duties which would, according to modern ideas, fall to the chief-of-the-staff, were by him divided between three officers, one of whom was of quite junior standing, and only one of whom held a higher rank than that of colonel. These officers were the Military Secretary, the Quartermaster-General, and the Adjutant-General.

The Military Secretary was merely responsible for the correct drawing out, and the transmission to the proper person or department, of the correspondence of the commander-in-chief. The post was held from April 27, 1809, to September 19, 1810, by Lieutenant-Colonel Bathurst, of the 60th. On the last-named date he went home on leave, and Captain Lord Fitzroy Somerset was given the status of acting-secretary, and confirmed as actual secretary three months later on January 1, 1811. This officer, better remembered by his later title as the Lord Raglan of the Crimean War, held the office till the end of the war—by which time he had reached the rank of colonel. He was one of Wellington's best-trusted subordinates, and his personal friend, but being very young, and junior in rank to all heads of departments, he was in no sense an appreciable factor in Wellington's conduct of the war. In fact, he was nothing more than his title of secretary indicated, and was in no way responsible for organization, or entitled to offer advice.

Much more important were the two great heads of departments, the Quartermaster-General and Adjutant-General. The former was charged with all matters relating to the embarkation or disembarkation, the equipment, quartering, halting, encamping, and route-marching of the various units of the army. He had to convey to all generals in command of them the orders of the general-in-chief, and for this purpose had under his control a number of officers bearing the clumsy titles of assistant-quartermaster-generals, and deputy-assistant-quartermaster-generals. Of the former there were five, of the latter seven, when the army was first organized in April, 1809, but their numbers were continually increasing all through the war, for each unit had an assistant-quartermaster-general and a deputy-assistant-quartermaster-general attached to it, and as the divisions and brigades grew in number, so did the officers of the Quartermaster-General's department told off to them. There was also a parallel growth in the number of those who remained at headquarters, directly attached to their chief.

There is an interesting minute by Wellington, laying down the relations between the divisional generals and the staff-officers of the department : he points out that, though the latter are the organs of headquarters in dealing with divisions, yet they are under the command of the divisional general : and the responsibility both for the orders given through them being carried out, and for their acts in general, lies with the division-commander. " Every staff officer," he says, " must be considered as acting under the direct orders and superintendence of the superior officer for whose assistance he is employed, and who is responsible

for his acts. To consider the relative situation of the
general officer and the staff officer in any other light, would
tend to alter the nature of the Service, and, in fact, might
give the command of the troops to a subaltern staff officer
instead of to their general officer." *

The officers of the Quartermaster-General's department,
besides their duties with regard to the moving of the army,
or the detachments of it, had often to undertake independent
work at a distance from headquarters, and sometimes
remote from the theatre of war. It was they who made
topographical surveys, reports on roads and bridges, and
on the resources of districts through which the army might
have to move in the near or distant future. There was
issued early in 1810 a little manual called *Instructions for
the officers in the department of the Quartermaster-General*
which was given to all its members : it contains a selection
of orders and forms, relating to every possible duty with
which its recipients might be entrusted. The most interesting section is that on topographical surveys, to which there
is annexed a model report of the road from Truxillo to
Merida, containing notes on everything which a staff officer
ought to notice,—positions, defiles, size of villages, character
of sections of the road, amount of corn-land as opposed
to pasture or waste, warnings as to unhealthy spots, notes
as to the depth of rivers and the practicability of fords, etc.

So far as I can ascertain, Wellington had only two
Quartermaster-Generals during the whole of the long period
of his supreme command. Colonel George Murray of the
3rd Guards held the post from April, 1809, to May 28,
1812 : he must be carefully distinguished from two other
Murrays, who sometimes turn up in the dispatches. One
is Major-General John Murray, who commanded a brigade
in the Oporto campaign, went home because he considered
that Beresford had been unjustly promoted over his head,
and came out later to the Peninsula on the Catalan side,
where he was responsible for the mismanaged operations

* *Minute* on p. 572 of the *Collected General Orders.*

about Tarragona. The other is John Murray, the Commissary-General. When Wellington sometimes uses such a phrase in his dispatches as "Murray knows this," or "see that Murray is informed," it is often most difficult to be sure which of the three men is meant. Early in 1811 Colonel George Murray became a major-general, and in the following May he appears to have gone home. He was replaced as Quartermaster-General by Colonel James Gordon—who, again, must not be confused with Colonel Sir Alexander Gordon, who was one of Wellington's senior aides-de-camp, and was killed at Waterloo. This is another of the confusions between homonyms which often give trouble. If a diarist speaks of "Colonel Gordon" we have to find which of the two is meant. James Gordon, having acted as quartermaster-general from May, 1811, to January, 1813, went home, and George Murray, returning early in that year, worked out the remaining fifteen months of the war in his old position.

Parallel with the Quartermaster-General was the other great departmental chief at headquarters, the Adjutant-General, whose sphere of activity was disciplinary and statistical. He was charged with all the detail of duties to be distributed, with the collecting and compiling for the use of the commander-in-chief of all returns of men and horses in "morning states," etc., with the supreme supervision of the discipline of the army, and with much official correspondence that did not pass to the Military Secretary. Roughly speaking, the internal condition of the troops fell to his share, while their movement belonged to the Quartermaster-General. He had to aid him on the first organization of the army in 1809, eight assistant-adjutant-generals and six deputy-assistant-adjutant-generals, but (as in the Quartermaster-General's department) the number of subordinates mounted up, as the war went on, and new units were from time to time created, since an assistant-adjutant-general was attached to each division.

The first holder of the office was Major-General the Hon,

Charles Stewart (afterwards Lord Londonderry, the earliest historian of the Peninsular War), who was discharging its functions from April, 1809, till April, 1813, just four years. He was then sent on a diplomatic mission to Berlin, and Wellington offered the post to his own brother-in-law, Major-General Edward Pakenham, who, while in charge of the 3rd division, had made the decisive charge at Salamanca. Pakenham was adjutant-general for the last year of the war, April, 1813, to April, 1814, and went straight out from Bordeaux to command the unlucky New Orleans expedition, in which he lost his life.

It will be noted that Wellington had actually only two Quartermaster-Generals and two Adjutant-Generals under him during the five years of his Peninsular command—a sufficient proof that when he had found his man he stuck to him. Charles Stewart, who served him so long, was a person of some political importance, as the brother and confidant of Lord Castlereagh. In the early part of his tenure of office he seems sometimes to have made suggestions to his chief, but met little encouragement, for Wellington loved his own way, and was not to be influenced even by his own highest staff officers.* He did not wish to have a Gneisenau or a Moltke at his side : he only wanted zealous and competent chief clerks.

Attached to headquarters in addition to the three great functionaries already named, were the heads of several other departments of great importance. These were—

(1) The general officer commanding the Royal Artillery, who had a general supervisory charge of the batteries attached to the divisions, and a more specific control of the battering train and reserve artillery, when these came into existence in 1811, as well as of the ammunition columns. The first artillery chief was Brigadier-General E. Howarth, who arrived at Lisbon in 1809, about the same time as Wellington himself. He was promoted major-general in

---

* Stewart chafed at his checks, and wrote bitterly to Castlereagh about the insignificance of his position.

1811, and went home that year.   The command then went
through a rapid succession of hands.   Howarth was followed
by Major-General Borthwick, who apparently crossed
Wellington, and went home in March, 1812, after less than
a year's tenure of the post.   Borthwick was succeeded by
Colonel H. Framingham, and he within a few months by
Colonel G. B. Fisher, who (like Borthwick) fell out with
the commander-in-chief, and applied for leave to go home
ere 1813 was six months old.   Wellington then appointed
Colonel Alexander Dickson to the command late in May.
This officer had been for the last two years in charge of the
Portuguese artillery under Beresford.   He had given such
satisfaction at Rodrigo and Badajoz that Wellington re-
transferred him to the British service, and finished the
campaign of 1814 with Dickson in chief charge of this
branch.

(2) After the artillery chief we encounter as a prominent
figure at headquarters the commanding officer of Royal
Engineers.   He had the superintending duty over his own
staff and the engineer officers attached to the divisions, and
control over the " Royal Military Artificers," as the rank
and file of the scientific corps were named till 1812, when they
changed their title to Royal Sappers and Miners.*   The
commanding engineer had also charge over the engineers'
park and the pontoon train.   The officer who held this post
from 1809 till he was killed at St. Sebastian in September,
1813, was Colonel Richard Fletcher, who has left a fame
behind him as the designer of the Lines of Torres Vedras.
On his death the command fell to Lieut.-Colonel Elphinstone,
who was responsible for the celebrated bridge of boats
across the mouth of the Adour which made the siege of
Bayonne possible in 1814.

(3, 4) At headquarters were also to be found the officers
commanding the Staff Corps Cavalry, and the Corps of
Guides.   The former, a small unit of some 200 men, created
in 1812, discharged the police duties of the army, and were

* See Chapter XVIII. on Sieges, p. 286.

worked along with the Provost Marshal. They were occasionally also employed as orderlies, and in other confidential positions.* The Guides were a small body also, some 150 or 200 strong, partly British, partly Portuguese, the latter preponderating. They were detached in twos or threes, to act as interpreters as well as guides to bodies of troops moving in country not known to them. For this reason they had to be bilingual, either English knowing some Portuguese, or Portuguese knowing some English, as they had always to be acting as intermediaries between the army and the peasantry, in making inquiries about roads, supplies, etc. The officer commanding the Guides had also the charge of the post office, and the transmission of letters to and from the front.

(5) The Provost Marshal was also attached to headquarters : he had charge of all prisoners to be tried by general court-martial, of deserters, and prisoners of war. He had powers of jurisdiction on offenders caught red-handed, but as Wellington remarks, " Whatever may be the crime of which a soldier is guilty, the Provost Marshal has not the power of inflicting summary punishment for it, unless he should see him in the act of committing it." † Men arrested on evidence only, had to be tried by court-martials. For the better management of these last, Wellington added a Judge-Advocate-General to his staff in 1812, whose duty was to see that trials were conducted with proper forms and due appreciation of the validity of evidence—in which the commander-in-chief considered that they had often failed. Mr. Francis Larpent, who has left an interesting diary of his duties and his personal adventures, discharged the

---

* For special note as to the functions of the " Staff Corps of Cavalry " raised in March, 1813, see the *General Order* of that date. This body must be carefully distinguished from the Staff Corps, concerning which see Fortescue's *British Army*, iv. p, 881 : it was a kind of subsidiary corps of military artificers, independent of the Ordnance Office to which " Royal Military Artificers " belonged. This was a vicious duplication of parallel organizations.

† *General Order*, Freneda, Nov. 1, 1811.

function of this office from his arrival late in 1812 down to the end of the war.*

As to aides-de-camp, Wellington kept a very limited number of them—he only employed some twenty in the course of the war, and not more than eight or ten at once. They were nearly all young men of the great political families,† nearly half of them were Guards' officers, and the rest mostly belonged to the cavalry. The Prince of Orange served among them in 1811–12. None of them, save Lord Fitzroy Somerset (Lord Raglan) and Colonel Cadogan, came to any very great military position or reputation.

So much for the military side of headquarters. There were also attached to it seven civil departments, small and great, of which it may be well to give a list. On one or two of these we shall have to speak at some length in later chapters—notably the Commissariat and the Medical department. They consisted of—

(1) The Medical Department under an Inspector of Hospitals, who was in general charge of the physicians, surgeons, assistants, etc., attached to the various units of the army. There is an excellent account of the management of this department, and all its difficulties, in the *Autobiography* of Sir James McGrigor, chief of the Medical Staff in 1812–13–14. His predecessor since Wellington's first landing in 1809 was Dr. Frank, who was invalided in the autumn of 1811.

(2) The Purveyor's Department was independent of the medical, though it might well have been attached to it : the establishment consisted of a Purveyor to the Forces, with deputies and assistants, who had charge of the hospitals and all the material and details required for them—from

---

* *Private Journal of Judge-Advocate Larpent*, 1812–14, published London, 1853.

† Names may suffice to show the class from which they were drawn : Marquis of Worcester, Lord March, Bathurst, Bouverie, Burghersh, Canning, Manners, Stanhope, Fremantle, Gordon, de Burgh, Cadogan, Fitzroy Somerset.

the drugs for the sick to the burial expenses of the dead.

(3) The Paymaster-General, with his assistants, was responsible for the transmission of the money received to the regimental paymasters of the various units. He was a much-worried man, generally from three to six months in arrears with his specie, from no fault of his own, but from the immense difficulty of obtaining the hard dollars, doubloons, and "cruzados novos," which alone had currency in the Peninsula till a late period in the war. It was useless to issue English money to the troops, for the natives would not accept crowns and guineas, and refused even to look at the one-pound notes which were almost the sole circulating medium in Great Britain during this period. It was only in a late year of the war that the gold guinea was at last tariffed by the Spanish and Portuguese Governments, and became readily current.*

(4) Most important of all the Civil Departments was the Commissariat, under the Commissary-General, who had under him Deputy-Commissary-Generals, Assistant and Deputy-Assistant-Commissaries, Commissariat Clerks, and many other subordinates. The department was divided into two branches, stores and accounts. The post of Commissary-General was successively held by John Murray (already mentioned above) from 1809 to June, 1810, by Kennedy from June, 1810, to September, 1811, and by Bisset from September, 1811, onward. An assistant commissary was attached to each brigade of infantry and each regiment of cavalry, but a single official had to attend to the needs of the whole of the artillery with the army, and another to the needs of headquarters.†

The whole future of the army in 1809 depended on whether the Commissariat Department would be able to rise to the height of its duties. It was absolutely necessary that Wellington should be able to keep his army

---

* See note on page 270 of chapter xvi on "Impedimenta."
† See *General Order* of May 4, 1809.

concentrated, if this small force of 20,000 or 30,000 men was to be of any weight in the conduct of the war in the Peninsula. The much-cursed and criticized Commissariat succeeded in doing its duty, and the length of time for which the British army could keep concentrated was the envy of the French, who, living on the country, were forced to disperse whenever they had exhausted the resources of the particular region in which they were massed. In a way this fact was the key to the whole war. Wellington's salvation lay in the fact that he could hold his entire army together, while his adversaries could not. On this advantage he relied again and again : his whole strategy depended upon it. How the Commissariat worked we shall show in a later chapter.

(5) The Storekeeper-General had charge of the field equipments, tents, and heavy baggage of the army. Often the heavy baggage was left at Lisbon, and all through 1809–10–11 no tents were taken to the front. It was only in the Vittoria and South-French campaigns that the whole army regularly carried them. In the days when the transport trains were not fully organized, it was necessary to leave even valuable impedimenta behind.

(6) To the Controller of Army Accounts all departments, save the Commissariat, rendered their statistics of money received and spent.

(7) Last, we may name the Press, for a travelling Press and a small staff of military printers accompanied the headquarters when possible, and printed general orders, and other documents and forms, of which many copies were required. I have seen much of its work at the Record Office,* but have never come across an account of its organization, or of any anecdotes of its wandering life, in which it must have passed through many vicissitudes. The press was under the general supervision of the Adjutant-General.

* Its most ambitious efforts were a small volume of maps printed at Cambray, during the occupation of France after Waterloo, with notes by Col. Carmichael Smith, R.E., and the *General Orders* for 1815, printed at Paris, by Sergeant Buchan, 3rd Guards, head printer to the Army of Occupation.

CHAPTER IX

THE ORGANIZATION OF THE ARMY : BRIGADES AND DIVISIONS

IT will probably surprise some readers to learn that Sir Arthur Wellesley fought out the first campaign in which he held supreme command, that of Oporto in May, 1809, with no higher organized unit than the brigade. But this is the fact : the 18,000 infantry of which he could dispose were distributed into eight brigades of two or three battalions each, varying in strength from 1400 up to 2500 bayonets. But Wellesley was not so belated, in failing to form divisions, as might be thought. They were still rather an abnormal than a usual unit for a British army : indeed, in the large majority of the expeditions in which Great Britain had been engaged since 1793, the numbers were so small that no unit above the brigade had been necessary. But it is notable that neither in the Duke of York's first expedition to the Netherlands in 1793–94, nor in his second in 1799, nor in Abercrombie's Egyptian Campaign of 1801 had divisions been formed—though in each of these cases a very large force had been assembled. When several brigades acted together, not under the immediate eye of the commander-in-chief, the senior brigadier present took temporary charge of the assemblage. In the Low Countries York generally speaks of his army as being divided into " columns " of two or three brigades each,* but there was no fixity in the arrangement. Abercrombie, on the other hand, in the last dispatch which he wrote before his victory and death at Alexandria, lays down the theoretical organization

* See, for example, York's Alkmaar dispatch of Oct. 6, 1799.

that the army is to be considered as being divided into
three " lines "—the first composed of three brigades, the
second and third of two each.   If the *word* division is used
in any official documents of these campaigns, the term has
no technical military sense, but is used as a vague synonym
for a section or part of the army.* Indeed, so far as I know,
the first British force during the great French War which
was formed into divisions, in the proper modern sense, was
the army which went on the Copenhagen Expedition of
1807, which was regularly distributed into four of such
units, each under a lieutenant-general, and each composed
of two, three, or four weak brigades, generally of only two
battalions.   This was a force of some 26,000 men.

The original Peninsular Army of 1808, which landed at
the mouth of the Mondego, and won the battle of Vimeiro,
was not far, therefore, from being the first British force
organized in divisions.   It may be noted that they were
rather theoretical than real, for several brigades had not
yet landed when Vimeiro was fought, and Wellesley, while
in temporary command, worked the incomplete army on a
brigade system : no trace whatever of the use of the
divisions as real units will be found in that battle.   Indeed,
even the theoretical composition of some of the brigades
differed from that actually seen in action.   No genuine
divisions were formed in the Peninsula, till Sir John Moore
took command of the army from which its old chiefs, Dal-
rymple, Burrand and Wellesley himself had been removed
and sent home.   We must not, therefore, be surprised
to find that for three months after he landed at Lisbon in
April, 1809, Wellesley worked his 21,000 British troops in
detached brigades, only connected in a formal and temporary
way, under the senior brigadier, when two or more chanced
to form a marching or fighting unit.

But two other points concerning Wellesley's Oporto

* *E.g.* in Walsh's *Expedition to Holland* in 1799, p. 22, the whole
original landing force of the British, 15,000 bayonets, is called the
" first division," but only in contrast to the troops not yet landed,
not technically.

campaign deserve notice. This was the first and only occasion on which he tried the experiment of mixing British and Portuguese regiments in the same brigade.* To five of the eight brigades forming his infantry a Portuguese battalion was attached, picked as being one of the best of the rather disorderly assembly which Beresford had collected at Abrantes and Thomar. Though the Portuguese fought not amiss during this short campaign, and are mentioned with praise in Wellesley's dispatches, yet the experiment was not continued, evidently because it was found not to work happily. The five Portuguese battalions were sent back to Beresford not long after the fall of Oporto.

The other point to be noted in considering Wellesley's organization of his army in the Oporto campaign, is that already he had begun the system of strengthening his skirmishers by the addition to them of a rifle company per brigade, all taken from the 5/60th. The importance of this arrangement in the general scheme of his tactics has been already explained in an earlier chapter.†

So much for Wellesley's first organization of his army. It did not endure for so much as three months, for on June 18, 1809, a General Order, dated from the Adjutant-General's office at Abrantes, gave to the army the organization in divisions, under which it was to win all its subsequent victories. In the midst of some insignificant directions as to forage and ammunition, appears the clause that "as the weather now admits of the troops hutting, and they can move together in large bodies, brigades can be formed into divisions, as follows."

The original disposition was for four divisions only, of which the first consisted of four brigades, the other three of two brigades each. All the battalions in them were in the British service, no Portuguese being included. The

---

* With the exception, of course, that the 1st and 3rd Caçador battalions served all through the war in the two brigades of the Light Division.

† See p. 83.

four line battalions of the King's German Legion were arranged first as one, and then as two brigades of the First Division. Of the ten brigades into which the infantry of the army were now divided, seven had two battalions only, the other three three battalions each. The cavalry, which had recently been increased by the arrival of two regiments from England, was organized as a division of three brigades of two regiments each. The artillery, of which only five field batteries (or " companies " as they were then called) had reached the front, was not yet told off to the individual divisions in a permanent fashion, though certain units are generally found acting with the same division.

As to the command of the divisions, Wellington contemplated that each should ultimately be in the charge of a lieutenant-general ; but as he had only three officers of such rank at his disposition—Hill, Sherbrooke, and the cavalry commander Payne—the General Order directs that " the senior general officers of brigades will respectively take the command of the division in which their brigades are placed, till other lieutenant-generals shall join the army." This placed two brigadiers, McKenzie and A. Campbell, in temporary charge of the 3rd and 4th divisions, Sherbrooke taking the 1st, and Hill the 2nd. Sherbrooke went home before a year was out, but Hill was to remain in command of the 2nd division throughout the war, except during the short periods when he was on leave. But during his last three years in the Peninsula, when he was practically acting as commander of an army corps, the 2nd division was, in fact, under the leadership of William Stewart as his substitute. The only modification caused in internal organization by the creation of the new divisions was that an assistant-adjutant-general, and quartermaster-general, and a provost-marshal were attached to each of them, and that the brigadiers acting as division-commanders were authorized to take on some extra aides-de-camp.

It was with this organization that Wellington's army went through the Talavera campaign, and the retreat to the Guadiana which terminated it. The whole force was British, no single Portuguese battalion accompanying it. The troops of that nation were being employed under Beresford during this summer, to cover the frontier of Beira, between the Douro and the Tagus. Long before the campaign was over, more British reinforcements had begun to arrive at Lisbon, and had been pushed forward some distance into the interior. One brigade, that composed of the three light battalions,* under Robert Craufurd, afterwards to be famous in Peninsular annals as the nucleus of the "Light Division," got to the front after a tremendous march—somewhat exaggerated by Napier and by tradition —only a day after the battle of Talavera. Wellesley incorporated it for a movement in the 3rd division, in which it finished the campaign. There were seven other battalions † which did not get so far forward, and ultimately joined Beresford's Portuguese on the frontier of Spain. In September Wellington drew down these troops to join him in Estremadura, and made from them a third brigade each for his 2nd and 4th Divisions. But there was about this time a shifting about of battalions from division to division, which it would be tedious to give in detail. The net result was that at the end of 1809 Wellington had four much stronger divisions than he had possessed in the summer, the 1st counting nine battalions instead of its old eight, the 2nd ten instead of six, the 3rd still six, but the 4th eight instead of five.

The early months of 1810 were spent by Wellington in an expectant attitude, behind the Portuguese frontier, as he waited for the inevitable French invasion under Masséna, so long announced and so long delayed. In this time of long-deferred anxiety, while the Lines of Torres Vedras were being busily urged towards completion, Wellington carried out some most important changes in the organization of

---

* 1/43rd, 1/52nd, 1/95th.

† 2/5th, 1/11th, 2/28th, 2/34th, 2/39th, 2/42nd 2/58th. The 1/40th and 2/24th joined Wellington in time for Talavera.

his army, which made it (except in the matter of mere numbers) exactly what it was to remain till the end of the war.

The most notable of these changes was that he made up his mind to revert to his old plan of April, 1809, for mixing the Portuguese and British troops. It took a new form, however : instead of placing battalions of each nationality side by side in his brigades, he attached a Portuguese brigade of four or five battalions to most of his British divisions, as a distinct unit. This system was started with the 3rd and 4th Divisions on Feb. 22, 1810. A complete Portuguese brigade consisted of two line regiments (each of two battalions) and one caçador or rifle battalion. The latter was always employed for the brigade's skirmishing work ; when joined by the four light companies of the line battalions, it gave a very heavy proportion of light troops to the unit. This Wellington considered necessary, because of the untried quality of the whole Portuguese Army, which had not yet taken a serious part in any general action. In the autumn they justified Wellington's confidence in them at the battle of Bussaco, where all of them, and especially the two caçador battalions attached to the Light Division, played a most creditable part.

The second great innovation made in the spring of 1810 was the creation of the celebrated Light Division, which came into existence on Feb. 22, 1810 ; it was formed by taking Robert Craufurd's brigade, the 1/43rd, 1/52nd, and 1/95th out of the 3rd division, and adding to them the above-mentioned two Portuguese caçador battalions. Wellington's design was to produce for the whole army, by the institution of this new unit, what he had already done for the individual brigades when he added their rifle companies to them in April, 1809. The Light Division was to be, as it were, the protective screen for the whole army,—its strategical skirmishing line, thrown out far in front of the rest of the host, to keep off the French till the actual moment of battle, and to hide the dispositions of the main body.

At the head of this small corps of picked light troops was placed Robert Craufurd, whom Wellington rightly considered his best officer for outpost and reconnaissance work. How well this trusted subordinate discharged the duty laid upon him has been told in the chapter dealing with his character and exploits. All through the war Wellington used the Light Division as his screen, for his advanced guard when he was moving to the front, for his rearguard when he was on the retreat, and he was never betrayed by it, even after Craufurd's death had left its conduct in the hands of chiefs who were not always men of special ability.

After the creation of the Light Division, Wellington had five instead of four divisions, and another was added to them in the summer of 1810, when in August he created the 5th Division, so long commanded by General Leith. This was formed by adding to a British brigade, newly arrived from England,* two of the hitherto unattached Portuguese brigades. A second British brigade was provided in October for Leith, from troops newly come from Cadiz.† These having come to hand, the 5th Division dropped one of its Portuguese brigades, and became a unit of the normal shape and size, two-thirds British, one-third Portuguese. It did not, however, receive its caçador battalion (drawn from the Lusitanian Legion) till 1811.

During the campaign of Bussaco, therefore, Wellington had six divisions—the old ones numbered 1st to 4th, the Light Division, and the newly-created 5th. In addition to the Portuguese brigades which had now been absorbed into the divisions, there remained six more brigades of that nation which were still unattached. Of these two, under the Brigadiers Archibald Campbell and Fonseca, were formed into a division under General Hamilton, which always marched with Hill's 2nd Division, but was never formally made part of it. But since Hamilton invariably moved

* The original British brigade of the 5th division consisted of the 3/1st, 1/9th, and 2/38th.

† The 2/30th and 2/44th, to which the 1/4th was subsequently added.

along with Hill, this pair of units, with their ten British and eight Portuguese battalions, practically formed a double division, or a small army corps, if a term which Wellington never used in the Peninsula may be applied to it.* There remained four more independent Portuguese brigades, those of Pack, Alex. Campbell, Coleman, and Bradford. By the next year these were reduced to two, as one brigade was withdrawn to serve with the new British 7th division, and another with the 2nd. The surviving units continued as unattached brigades till the end of the war, under a series of commanding officers, whose succession is sometimes hard to follow.† They often accompanied the main army, but were sometimes separated from it for special duties, when some force less than a division was wanted, as a detachment for a subsidiary operation.

The completion of the Peninsular Army in its final shape, which was not again to be varied, took place during its stay by the Lines of Torres Vedras, in the winter of 1810–11. It was then that the two junior divisions were created, the 6th in October, the 7th early in March. Their appearance in the field was, of course, due to the arrival of a considerable number of fresh battalions from England during the autumn and winter. But Wellington did not take all the new-comers and build up fresh divisions from them. The 6th Division was made by taking an old brigade (Archibald Campbell's) from the 4th Division, and uniting it to the extra Portuguese brigade of the 5th Division.‡ The second British brigade of the 6th division was provided some months later from newly-arrived troops from England.§

* The name Army-Corps appears first in the Waterloo Campaign of 1815.

† The succession of brigadiers seems to have been, in the one brigade, Pack followed by Wilson and Alex. Campbell ; in the other Bradford continued almost through the whole war, but McMahon was in command in part of 1811–12. After June, 1811, Ashworth's Brigade was regularly attached to the 2nd division.

‡ Now no longer wanted, as Leith had received his second British brigade.

§ 2nd, 1/36th, and (added long months after) the 1/32nd.

The 4th Division was compensated for the brigade it had given to the 6th by taking over a brigade (Pakenham's) from the 1st Division—while the 1st Division, to replace this last unit, received three battalions * which had just come out from home.

This was a complicated shift and transfer, intended to secure a level quality in the divisions by the mixture of recently arrived and veteran battalions.   But in organizing his last creation, the 7th Division, Wellington was prevented by circumstances from carrying out the same wise plan. Much belated in their arrival at Lisbon by contrary winds, the last batch of reinforcements sent to him for the campaign of 1811, landed when the main army was already in pursuit of Masséna, who had just started on his retreat from Santarem.   Wellington was forced to keep them together, since he had no time to distribute them when the troops were all on the move.   The 7th division was at first very weak, containing only one brigade in British pay, consisting of two English and two foreign corps,† and one Portuguese brigade (Coleman).   Two more foreign corps belonging to the German Legion ‡ formed the second brigade of the 7th Division, but did not join it till the summer, being distracted meanwhile to another field of operations.

The 7th Division was for some time looked on as the " ugly duckling," or backward child of the army.   Having only two British to four foreign battalions, it was sometimes called " the Mongrels ; " its first début in action at Fuentes de Oñoro was not a very happy one, as it was the outlying flank force that was turned and partly cut up by French cavalry.   After this it was never seriously engaged in battle for more than a year.   Moreover, its foreigners earned a bad reputation for their habit of desertion—a

* 1/50th, 1/71st, and 1/92nd.

† 51st, 85th, with the Chasseurs Britanniques and the Brunswick Oels Jägers.   The 68th joined in July, but the 85th went home in October.

‡ 1st and 2nd Light Battalions, K.G.L., which landed very late, joined Beresford's army in Estremadura, and only united with their proper division in June.

habit not altogether unnatural, for they had been largely
recruited from the pontoons and prison-camps in England.*
Hence a cruel joke in the list of divisional nicknames
given by several Peninsular diarists. The sobriquets run :
Light Division, *The* Division ; no doubt the title given
to it by its own proud members.   First Division : " The
Gentlemen's Sons," because it contained one, and afterwards two, brigades of the Foot Guards. The Second
Division is called " the Observing Division," because it was
so often detached as a containing force against Soult, on the
side of Estremadura and Andalusia, while the main body
was more actively engaged on the side of Leon. So much
was this its duty that it was only present at one general
action, Albuera, between the autumn of 1810 and the summer
of 1813.   There were some brilliant episodes between those
dates, such as the surprise of Arroyo dos Molinos, and
the storming of the forts at Almaraz. The 3rd Division was
called " the Fighting Division," its fiery leader, Picton,
having led it into the forefront of the battle both at Bussaco
and Fuentes de Oñoro, not to speak of smaller fights like
Redinha or El Bodon ; it had also done the hardest of
work at the storms of Ciudad Rodrigo and Badajoz. The
4th Division was called the "Supporting Division ;" I suppose
because it was sent off to support the 2nd in Estremadura,
and most effectually discharged that duty at Albuera.† The
5th division was called " the Pioneers," a name whose
source I cannot explain : possibly it refers to some road-
making work done in 1810. The 6th was the " Marching
Division," mainly, I believe, so-called because down to
Salamanca it was accompanying all Wellington's great
movements from north to south and south to north, yet
never had the good fortune to get into the thick of the
battle. At Salamanca, however, it had as much fighting
as any man could crave. The note to the 7th Division,
however, is very malicious, being " We have *heard* that

* See notes on these battalions in the chapter on "The Auxiliaries."
† After Albuera their nickname was changed to "the Enthusiastics."

there is a Seventh Division, but we have never *seen* it."
The fact is, that after its mishap at Fuentes, and some
unsuccessful siege work at the second leaguer of Badajoz,
this unit was very little engaged for two years.   In 1813,
however, it was gloriously prominent in the battles of the
Pyrenees, and the dash at the French line, made by Barns's
brigade, was called by Wellington about the best and most
effective attack that he had ever seen.

After the creation of the 7th Division in March, 1811,
Wellington never again organized a new divisional unit.
He received, of course, a great number of new battalions
during the years 1811–12–13, but contented himself with
adding them in ones or twos to existing brigades, or at
most gave two or three of them as a fresh brigade to one of
the old divisions.   The former practice was the more usual :
the only instances of the latter that I recall being that in
1812 the 1st Division got a second Guards brigade, and in
1813 a new line brigade (Lord Aylmer's) from reinforcements
that had just come out.   The increase of the total number
of battalions at the front was not so great as might have
been expected, because from time to time corps that had
got thinned down almost to the point of extinction, were
sent back to England to be recruited and reorganized.   The
number of British battalions (including the King's German
Legion and two other foreign corps) with Wellington's field
army in March, 1811, was fifty-eight ; in March, 1814, it was
no more than sixty-five, a gain of only seven units.   There
had been a considerable exchange of service between the 1st
and 2nd battalion of regiments—in several cases when the
2nd battalion had been the original unit in the Peninsular
Army, it went home when the first battalion came out,
returning as a mere *cadre* of officers and sergeants, after
turning over its serviceable rank and file to the newly-
arrived sister unit.*

* This happened with the 5th, 28th, 38th, 39th, 42nd.   The 2/4th
and 2/52nd came out for a short time, and then discharged their
serviceable men into their 1st battalion, and went home.

There was only two more considerable rearrangements of the internal organization of a division. One took place in May, 1811, owing to the fearful losses suffered by the 2nd Division at Albuera. Of the seven battalions forming the brigades of Colborne and Hoghton, which had been so dreadfully mauled in holding the all-important heights, two were sent home, and the four others shrank into a single brigade. To fill the place of the vanished unit a whole brigade (Howard's) was transferred from the 1st to the 2nd Division, and became part of it for the rest of the war. There was also a shifting about of two brigades from one unit to another during the winter of 1812–13, after the Burgos retreat.

The normal divisional organization, however, remained unchanged from 1811 onwards, viz. with three exceptions, each division for the remaining three years of the war consisted of two British brigades and one Portuguese, the former having usually three battalions each, and the latter five. This rule worked for the 3rd, 4th, 5th, 6th, 7th divisions. The Light Division, smaller than the rest, had only three (or three and a half) British battalions, and two of Portuguese caçadores. The 1st Division alone had no Portuguese attached, but one of its three (after 1813 *four*) brigades was foreign, consisting of the line battalions of the King's German Legion. The 2nd Division (as explained above) had three British brigades and no Portuguese, but to it was attached Hamilton's (and in 1812–14 Ashworth's) Portuguese, so that it did not vary from the normal arrangement so much as the 1st Division.

It would not be quite accurate to say that a British brigade always had precisely three battalions. Several had four, one five, a few appeared with only two, but Wellington generally made these last up to the three-battalion total as soon as he was able, save in two cases. In the Guards brigades of the 1st Division the two battalions were always so strong that between them they gave 1800 or 2000 bayonets at the beginning of a campaign—which was as

much as most three-battalion brigades produced. Moreover, there was an objection to brigading together units of
the Guards and of the line. In the Light Division the
1/43rd and 1/52nd were also very strong and well recruited:
each formed the nucleus of a small brigade, of which the
rest was composed of a Portuguese caçador battalion and
a certain number (often six) companies of the 95th Rifles.

Roughly speaking, then, an Anglo-Portuguese division
usually amounted to something under 6000 men, save the
Light Division, which numbered under 4000, and the
1st Division, which in 1810, and again in 1813, had four
brigades, and over 7000 men. Of the 5500 or 5800 men in
one of the normal divisions about 3500 were British and
2000 (or a little more) Portuguese. The 2nd Division,
however, was a double-unit, with 5500 British, and attached
to it 6500 of Hamilton's and Ashworth's Portuguese.

The mixture of nationalities in the divisions, normal
with the infantry, was nearly unknown in the cavalry arm.
The very few Portuguese regiments which took the field—
never more than seven, I believe—often four only—were
normally kept separate. Wellington, for the first three years
of the war, had so few cavalry regiments of either nation
that there was no possibility of dividing them into divisions.
In 1809, as has been already stated,* there were only in the
Peninsula six British cavalry regiments, divided into three
weak brigades. Only one more corps joined them in 1810,
and in the spring campaigns of 1811, when he had left three
regiments with Beresford in the south, he had only four to
take with him for the pursuit of Masséna and the battle of
Fuentes de Oñoro—a miserable provision—1500 sabres for
an army of over 30,000 men, about a fourth of the proper
proportion in those days.

It was not till later in 1811 that Wellington got cavalry
reinforcements which more than doubled his mounted
strength, bringing him up to fifteen regiments of British
and German horse. He did then at last divide them into

* See p. 166.

two divisions, one of eleven regiments, which followed his main army, the other of four regiments only, which he left with Hill in Estremadura. But no Portuguese regiments were put into either—though he took one brigade with himself (D'Urban's) for the Salamanca campaign, and left two brigades (or four regiments) with the southern force (those of Otway and Madden).

But the organization in two cavalry divisions was dropped in the spring of 1813—Wellington had had sickening experience of the incapacity of General Erskine, who commanded the small second division, and, Erskine being now dead, for the rest of the war all the seven cavalry brigades were theoretically again made into one division, under Wellington's chosen cavalry leader, Sir Stapleton Cotton. As a matter of fact, Cotton was not allowed any independent command of them, and the brigades were moved in twos and threes under the direct orders of the commander-in-chief. Wellington never used his cavalry in mass for any great separate manœuvre. He employed them for scouting, for covering his front, and for protecting his flanks, sometimes (but rarely and in small units) for a blow in battle, such as that which Le Marchant's heavy dragoons gave at Salamanca, or Bock's Germans at Garcia Hernandez on the following day. But of this we have already spoken when dealing with the general character of Wellington's tactics.

The rule of the combination of British and Portuguese units which prevailed in the infantry, though not in the cavalry, was to be found in the artillery also. In 1810, when Wellington drafted a Portuguese brigade of foot into each of his divisions, he also attached to several of them batteries of Portuguese artillery. So small was his allowance of British gunners, that in 1811, when he had created his two last infantry divisions, he would not have been able to provide one field battery for each of his eight units, unless he had drawn largely for help on his allies. At the time of Fuentes de Oñoro and Albuera there were in the field only three British horse artillery batteries (attached to the cavalry and the Light Division) and five British field batteries attached to infantry divisions. The 3rd and 7th Divisions had only Portuguese guns allotted to them. But by utilizing the very efficient artillery of the allied nation, to the extent of eight units, Wellington was able to put thirteen field batteries in line, which enabled him to provide the 2nd, 3rd, 5th, 6th, and Hamilton's Portuguese divisions with two batteries apiece, the 1st, 4th, and 7th with one each. The two nations were worked as successfully in unison in the artillery as in the infantry organization.

Owing to the arrival of new batteries from home Wellington was able, in 1812, not only to allot one or two field batteries to every division except the Light (which kept its old horse artillery troop, that of Major Ross), but to collect a small reserve which belonged to the whole army and not to any particular division. In 1813–14 he was stronger still, though the mass of guns of which he could dispose was never so powerful in proportion to his whole army as that which Napoleon habitually employed.

CHAPTER X

THE ORGANIZATION OF THE ARMY : THE REGIMENTS

IN the year 1809, when Wellington assumed command in Portugal, the infantry of the British Army consisted of 3 regiments of Foot Guards and 103 regiments of the line, beside 10 battalions of the King's German Legion, the 8 West India regiments, the 8 Veteran Battalions, and some ten more miscellaneous foreign and colonial corps. Of the 103 regiments of the line the majority, 61, had 2 battalions. Of the remainder one (the 60th or Royal Americans) had 7 battalions, one (the 1st Royal Scots) 4, three (the 14th, 27th, and 95th) 3 each, while the remaining 37 were single-battalion regiments.* As the 1st Foot Guards had 3 battalions, and the Coldstream and Scots Fusiliers 2 each, the total number of British battalions embodied was 186.

The reason for the curious discrepancy between the number of battalions in the various regiments was that (putting aside the Guards, the Royal Scots, and the Royal Americans, who had always more battalions than one, even in the eighteenth century) the British Army at the time of the rupture of the Peace of Amiens in 1803 had been composed of single-battalion regiments. On the outbreak of war fifty regiments in the British Isles and other home stations were ordered to raise second battalions,† and a

---

* These thirty-seven were the 2nd, 12th, 13th, 16th, 17th, 19th, 20th, 22nd, 29th, 33rd, 37th, 41st, 46th, 49th, 51st, 54th, 55th, 64th, 65th, 68th, 70th, 74th, 75th, 76th, 77th, 80th, 85th, 86th, 93rd, 94th, and 97th to 103rd.

† Which were intended for hcme service only, and were called the " Army of Reserve." But ere long they were utilized for general service.

little later the same directions were given to a few more. Two corps (the 14th and 27th) succeeded in raising two fresh battalions, as did also the Royal Scots, which was already a double battalion corps. But few of the regiments serving beyond seas were ordered to carry out the same expansion, owing to their remoteness from recruiting centres ; they remained single-battalion regiments, save that the 35th, 47th, and 78th, though they were quartered respectively in Malta, Bermuda, and India, provided themselves with a second battalion. Seven new regiments raised in or after 1804 (these numbered 97 to 103) remained from the first to the last single-battalion corps.

A considerable number of the corps which were on foreign or colonial service in 1803–4 had returned to Great Britain since that time. But they were never, save in a very few cases, able to raise additional battalions, the number of such created after 1805 being only eight * in all. Hence the regiments from which Wellington's Peninsular Army was drawn must be divided with care into one-battalion corps and those which owned more than one battalion.

The Estimates presented to the House of Commons in 1809 show that there were several " establishments " of varying strength for regiments in Great Britain and other European stations. For corps absent in the East Indies there was a wholly different set.†

A regiment of two battalions, with both of them on active service, stands on the higher establishment at either 2250 or 2031, or thereabouts. When the senior battalion was sent on active service it was generally completed to 1000 rank and file, which, with sergeants, officers, and musicians, should have made up a total of over 1100. Its less effective men were drafted into the second battalion,

---

* The regiments which raised belated second battalions were the 12th (in 1813), the 22nd (in 1814), the 37th (in 1811), the 41st (in 1814), the 73rd (in 1809), the 86th (in 1814), the 93rd (in 1814). The 95th (in 1809), and the 56th in 1813, raised a *third* battalion.

† For all the establishments see Table in Appendix I.

which, if the establishment was full (which was by no means always the case), would have left somewhat over 900 for the second battalion. And, indeed, we find such figures as 906, 929, 916, etc., given for the strength of several second battalions whose senior sister-unit had gone overseas.

But these 900 and odd men of all ranks now included not only the weak and ineffective men of the second battalion, but also those of the first. Therefore if a second battalion was sent out to the war, it had to leave behind a disproportionately large number of men unfit for active service, and would be lucky if it sailed for Portugal with 700 bayonets. Many cases are on record where a far smaller number disembarked at Lisbon or elsewhere. More than 200 would often have to be left behind to form the depôt, wherefore second battalions were usually much weaker than first battalions when at the front.

For single-battalion regiments, such as the 2nd, 29th, 51st or 97th, we find very various " establishments " given in the Army Estimates of 1809. They vary down from 1151 to 696 ; one or two exceptional corps are even smaller. As a rule, it may be taken that the ideal would be to recruit such a corps, when it was sent on active service, up to the higher figure : but having to leave 200 men or so at home— the inefficients who were drafted off for the depôt—it would be lucky if it landed 800 in the Peninsula. And to keep up the battalion the depôt could not always suffice ; it was full of unserviceable men, and could only send out recruits newly gathered.

Single-battalion regiments not on active service are those which are found with the smaller establishments—of such figures as 716, 696, etc. Not being expected to take the field, they have not been brought up to the higher establishment, either by drafts from the militia or by specially vigorous recruiting.

The three regiments of Foot Guards had much higher establishments than any line battalion. The three battalions of the 1st Guards mustered no less than 4619 of all ranks, the Coldstream and Scots Fusiliers each 2887. Thus the former could easily send abroad two strong battalions of 1100 or 1200 men apiece, and the two latter one each, while leaving behind a battalion and a big depôt on which to draw for recruits for the active service units. Therefore a Guards battalion in the Peninsula seldom fell under 800 men, and was sometimes up to 1000. The Cadiz detachment of the Guards, which fought at Barrosa, was made up from the home battalions as a sort of extra contribution. It consisted of six companies of the 1st Guards, two of the Coldstream, and three of the Scots Fusiliers. They are sometimes called a brigade—for which they were too small in reality—sometimes a provisional regiment. Their total force was about 1200 or 1300 of all ranks.

With these figures before us, we begin to see why individual battalions came and went in the Peninsular Army. A regiment which had two battalions, one at home and one in Portugal, was always able to keep up the strength of the service unit by regular and copious drafts from the home unit. Or if the original one serving in the Peninsula was a *second* battalion, the first could be sent out to relieve it. Second battalions were never sent out to replace first battalions, it being always the rule that the senior unit had a right to preference for active service. But occasionally both battalions of a regiment were absent from Great Britain, and in a few cases they were both in the Peninsula.* When this happened the second battalion was invariably sent home after a time, discharging its effective rank and file into the sister battalion, and returning to Great Britain as a *cadre* of officers and sergeants, with a few old, unserviceable, or nearly time-expired rank and file.

Having laid down these general rules, we shall see how it came to pass that of Wellington's original army of 1809 some battalions stopped with him for the whole war, while others were successively sent away and replaced by fresh units.

* This was the case with the 7th, 48th, 52nd and 88th in 1811.

The greater part of the British Army which had been in the Peninsula in 1808 went home from Corunna at the end of Sir John Moore's retreat. Of these units some never came back at all to share in Wellington's triumphs ; * others returned only in time to see the end of the war in 1812, 1813, and 1814.† Only Craufurd's three famous light infantry battalions, the 1/43rd, 1/52nd, and 1/95th came back, after an absence of no more than a few months, in the summer of 1809.

The real nucleus of the permanent Peninsular Army was composed, not of the regiments which had operated under Moore, but of that small fragment of the original landing force of 1808 which had not followed Moore to Salamanca, Sahagun, and Corunna, but remained behind in the Peninsula.‡ To this mere remnant of eleven battalions and one cavalry regiment there were added the reinforcements which preceded or accompanied Sir Arthur Wellesley when he came to take up the command in April, 1809, which amounted to twelve battalions more, with four regiments of cavalry.§ The whole, when first divided into brigades and organized as an operating force at Coimbra on May 4, 1809, only amounted to 23,000 men—a modest nucleus for the army which was destined not only to save Portugal, but ultimately to thrust out of Spain a body of invaders which at

* The 3rd Hussars, K.G.L., 2/14th, 2/23rd, 2/43rd, 2/81st, never returned to serve under Wellington in 1809–14.

† In 1810 the following returned to Portugal 3/1st, 1/4th, 1/9th, 1/50th, 1/71st, 1/79th. In 1811 the following: 2nd, 1/26th, 1/28th, 1/32nd, 1/36th, 51st, 2/52nd, 1st and 2nd Light K.G.L. In 1812 the following: 1/5th, 1/6th, 20th, 1/38th, 1/42nd, 2/59th, 1/82nd, 1/91st. In 1813 the 7th, 10th, 15th, 18th Hussars, the first and third battalions of the 1st Foot Guards, and the 76th.

‡ These were the 1/3rd, 2/9th, 29th, 1/40th, 1/45th, 5/60th, 97th, the 1st, 2nd, 5th, 7th Line Battalions of the K.G.L., and the 20th Light Dragoons, the last-named incomplete.

§ The regiments which arrived with Wellesley, or before him, during the spring and the preceding winter of 1808–1809, were 3/27th, 2/31st, and 14th Light Dragoons, during the winter ; in April, 1st Coldstream Guards, 1st Scots Fusilier Guards, 2/7th, 2/30th, 2/48th, 2/53rd, 2/66th, 2/83rd, 2/87th, 1/88th, 16th Light Dragoons, 3rd Dragoon Guards, 4th Dragoons.

this moment amounted to over 200,000 men, and which in 1810–11 was brought up to 300,000, a figure which it maintained till drafts began to be made upon it for the Russian War in 1812.*

Moore's host had been, as he himself wrote to Castlereagh in a noteworthy dispatch, not so much *a* British army as the *only* British army fit for the field. Since no more than an infinitesimal fraction of this picked force was able to return to the Peninsula at once, it followed that Wellesley's army of 1809 was composed, for its greater part, of troops that had been considered of secondary quality, and less fit for service than the battalions which had been put *hors de combat* for a long space by the exhaustion which they had suffered in the terrible retreat to Corunna. Excluding the Guards and the King's German Legion units, Wellesley's Field Army in July contained eighteen British battalions, of which only six were first battalions of regiments of full strength, two (the 29th and 97th) were single-battalion corps, and the remaining ten were junior battalions, *i.e.* were the usually depleted home-service units of regiments which already had one battalion abroad, or of which the first battalion had just returned from Corunna unfit for immediate use.† It was an army whose quality was notably inferior to that of the force which had marched into Spain under Moore six months before. And the second battalions were invariably under strength, because they had, until their unexpected embarkation for the front, been engaged in supplying their sister units abroad

* Since April there had come out the 23rd Light Dragoons, 1st Hussars, K.G.L., 1/61st, 1/48th, 2/24th ; but the 20th Light Dragoons had been deducted (sent to Sicily), while the 2/9th and 2/30th had been sent back to Lisbon, for passage to Gibraltar. The net gain, therefore, between April and July was only one cavalry regiment.

† To recapitulate again. 1st battalions : 1/3rd, 1/40th, 1/45th, 1/48th, 1/61st, 1/88th. 2nd battalions : 2/7th, 2/31st, 2/24th, 2/48th, 2/53rd, 2/66th, 2/83rd, 2/87th. Other junior battalions : 3/27th (left at Lisbon), 5/60th. Single battalion regiments, 29th, 97th. There were also two " Battalions of Detachments."

with the necessary drafts for foreign service. Many of them were woefully weak in numbers, showing, instead of the theoretical 900 bayonets, such figures as 638, 680, 749, 776, which, after deducting sick and men on command, meant under 600 for the field. Indeed, a few months later, at Talavera,* six of the second battalions and both the single-battalion corps showed less than that number present, all ranks included.

Bearing in mind the fact that a British regiment, owing to the difficulties of recruiting, in a time when men were scarce and bounties high, could not as a rule provide drafts to keep up to strength more than one battalion on active service, we can already foresee the fates that were destined to attend the battalions of Wellington's original Peninsular Army. Nearly all the second battalions in time were worn down by the exhaustion of war to a figure so low that they could no longer be worked as regular battalion units. When they had reached this stage one of two things happened to them. If their first battalions were available, being on home service and fit for the field, they came out to the Peninsula and replaced the depleted second battalions. But if the first battalion of any corps was already abroad in India or elsewhere, the Peninsular battalion was, during the earlier years of the war, sent home to recruit, and its regimental number disappeared from Wellington's muster-rolls. In the later years of the war this was not so regularly done : for reasons which will be explained, several of the veteran second battalions, which had survived at the front till 1812, were retained with the army, but cut down to four companies each, and worked together in pairs to make a unit of serviceable size. Of the eight original second battalions of 1809, two were drafted into their first battalion, which had come out to the Peninsula ; † one (2/87th) was sent away for a time to Cadiz, though it returned to the field

* The strongest battalions at Talavera were 1/3rd Foot Guards 1019, 1st Coldstream 970, 1/48th 807 ; the weakest were 2/66th 526, 97th 502, 2/83rd 535.
† Viz. 2/7th, 2/48th.

army in 1812 ; four were cut down in 1811–12 to half battalions.* Only one, the 2/83rd, remained continuously in the Peninsula as a full battalion till the end of the war.

The same fate attended the single-battalion regiments, which had no sister battalion at home to draw upon, but only a depôt. Both the 29th and the 97th went home, reduced to skeletons, in 1811.

But the six first-battalions present with the field army in May, 1809, were still at the front in fair strength at the termination of the war in 1814, and this, though two of them had been among the worst sufferers in the bloody field of Albuera. Indeed, there is throughout the war, I believe, only one case in which the first battalion of a complete regiment went out to the front, and was sent away before the end of the campaigning in 1814.

The reinforcements which were sent out to Wellington from 1810 to 1812 may be divided into two sections, of which the larger was composed of the reorganized and recruited battalions of Moore's Corunna army. Of these, six battalions came out in 1810, nine in 1811, eight in 1812, and three in 1813–14. The greater number of them were first battalions, or putting aside the Guards and German Legion units, fifteen out of twenty-three : of these all save one (the 1/26th) fought out the rest of the war. Of single-battalion regiments there were four (2nd, 51st, 20th, 76th) ; of junior battalions belonging to corps which already had one battalion abroad, there were also only three (3/1st, 2/52nd, 2/59th). Of these two last classes the 2/52nd was soon sent home, after drafting its men into the 1/52nd. The 2nd got so depleted that it was cut down to four companies, and put into a provisional battalion in 1812 till the end of the war. The 76th on its return was only in the field for a few months in 1813–14, so that it had no time to get worked down. The 3/1st, though a junior battalion, belonged to a large regiment of four battalions, and for that

* 2/24th, 2/31st, 2/53rd, 2/66th. The first battalions of three of these were in the East Indies, that of the fourth in Sicily.

reason never shrank below its proper size, there being a sister unit at home to send it drafts. We may therefore say that, of the eight battalions which were not first battalions of full regiments, only three saw long service, yet survived unimpaired to the peace of 1814 (20th, 51st, 2/59th) ; and of these three two only came out in 1812, and were less than two years in the Peninsula. It is clear, then, that the same rule prevailed in the reinforcements as in the original 1809 army ; only first battalions could be relied upon not to melt.

The battalions sent out as reinforcements to Wellington which had not formed part of Moore's Corunna army, were decidedly less numerous than the other class, amounting to only nineteen. Of these six were first battalions,* eight second battalions,† and five single battalion corps.‡ All of the first-named category fought out the whole war : but several of the other two were sent home, either when they had been depleted to reinforce their first battalions, or for other reasons. The proportion would have been larger but for the fact that several of them were among the last arrivals in the Peninsula, who only joined in the later autumn and winter campaigns of 1813–14, and had not time to get worn down.§ One second battalion (2/58th) was worked as a four-company unit during the last two years of the war.

The net result of all the interchange of battalions, and of the sending home of weak units, was that in 1814, when the struggle with Napoleon had come to its end, out of fifty-six British line battalions present at the front, only thirteen were second battalions, and of these last five ‖ were (as has been already mentioned) so depleted in numbers that they were being worked in pairs, being each only four

---

* 1/7th, 1/11th, 1/23rd, 1/37th, 1/39th, 1/57th.
† 2/5th, 2/34th, 2/38th, 2/44th, 2/47th, 2/58th, 2/62nd, 2/84th.
‡ 68th, 74th, 77th, 85th, 94th.
§ This was the case with the 2/62nd, 77th, 1/37th, 2/84th.
‖ The sixth of the units of the provisional battalions being a single battalion corps, the 2nd Foot or Queen's.

companies strong, and not mustering more than 250 or
300 men.

That such weak half-units were detained in the Peninsula was due to a resolve of Wellington's, made after
the campaign of 1811. During the latter part of that year
the chief of his worries was that he had been sent out
among his reinforcements a number of corps which had
served in the Walcheren expedition, where almost every
man had the seeds of ague in him, from a sojourn in the
marshes of Holland. The heat of the Portuguese summer
and the torrential rains of the autumn at once brought
out the latent weakness in the constitution of men who were
little more than convalescents, and regiments which had
landed at Lisbon in July 850 strong showed only 550 in
the ranks in October.* So appalling was the accumulation
of fever and ague cases in the hospitals † that Wellington
wrote home to beg that not another unit which had been
at Walcheren might be sent out to him. He now made up
his mind to keep old regiments, even when they had dwindled
rather low in numbers, rather than to send them home to
recruit, and to receive new battalions in their stead. The
reason was that it took a corps many months before it
learnt to shift for itself, and to grow acclimatized. During
their first few months in the Peninsula, newly arrived units
always showed too many sick and too many stragglers.
For men fresh from barrack life in England were at first
prostrated by the heat of the climate and the length of the
marches. They had still to pick up the old campaigner's
tricks, and were very helpless. Veteran troops were so
superior in endurance to new regiments from England,
most of whom had been on the pestilential Walcheren
expedition, and were still full of rickety convalescents,

* Typical figures are 77th, landed in July 859 of all ranks—
had only 560 present in September. The 68th, landed about the
same time, had 233 sick to 412 effective : the 51st, landed in April,
246 sick to 251 effective ! But the 51st had lost men in the second
siege of Badajoz. The other two regiments had not seen much service.

† Over 14,000 men in October, 1811.

that Wellington determined to keep even remnants of old
corps accustomed to the air of the Peninsula, rather than
to ask for more unacclimatized battalions from home.
Hence came the institution, in the end of 1812, of two
of the "provisional battalions" already mentioned.* At
an earlier period of the war they would undoubtedly have
been sent back to England.† But now these fractions of
depleted veteran corps were taken, with excellent results,
all through the campaign of 1812-13-14.

It is perhaps worth while to make a note how curious
was Wellington's attitude in face of that rather exceptional
occurrence the appearance of two strong battalions of the
same regiment in his army. If the second battalion was
weak, he soon drafted it into the first and sent it home. But
when, from some chance, both had full ranks, it did not by
any means always strike him as necessary to brigade them
together. For example, the 1/7th and 2/7th were both at
the front from October, 1810, to July, 1811 ; but for several
months of the time one was in the 4th Division, the other in
the 1st. A still more striking instance is that of the 48th.
Its two battalions were both from their first arrival placed
in the 2nd Division, but they served from June, 1809, to
May, 1811, in different brigades of it.‡ The occasions when
the two battalions of the same regiment served for any

* Wellington wrote to the Secretary of War (Lord Bathurst),
" I assure you that some of the best battalions with the army are the
provisional battalions. I have lately seen two of these engaged,
that formed of the 2/24th and 2/58th, and that formed from the 2nd
Queen's and 2/53rd : it is impossible for any troops to behave better.
The same arrangement could now be applied with great advantage
to the 51st and 68th, and also to other regiments " (*Dispatches*, x.
p. 629). There was another " provisional battalion " composed of
the 2/30th and 2/44th for a short time in 1812-13.

† Probably a year later Wellington would not have allowed the
29th and 97th, both old single battalion regiments sent home after
Albuera, to depart, but would have worked them together as a
" provisional battalion." He expresses great regret in his private
correspondence at losing two excellent units because they had
fallen to about 250 men each.

‡ After Albuera, where they both suffered heavily, the 2nd was
sent home, discharging its serviceable men into the 1st, which was
the first connection with the sister-battalion that it had.

PLATE V.

PRIVATE, INFANTRY OF THE LINE.
1809.

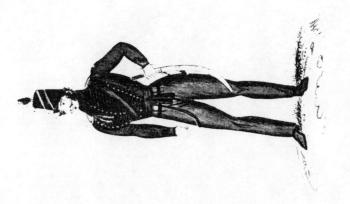

OFFICER OF RIFLES.
1809.

time in one brigade were very rare—I only know of the cases of the 1st and 3rd battalions of the Foot Guards in 1813–14, of the two battalions of the 52nd between March, 1811, and March, 1812, and of those of the 7th Fusiliers, who (after some service apart) had been brigaded together in the 4th Division six months before Albuera. In the last two cases the first battalion presently absorbed the second, which was sent home as a skeleton *cadre* when its strength at last began to run low. All other cases of juxtaposition were so short that it would seem that Wellington only brought the two battalions together for the purpose of drafting the second into the first at the earliest convenient moment. In this way the 2/88th (long in garrison at Lisbon) were brought up to the front to be amalgamated in less than four months with the 1/88th (March–July, 1811). The 1/5th, coming out in the summer of 1812, seems to have served along with the 2/5th for about the same number of months, the latter being sent home in October. The 1/38th similarly arrived at about the same time, and served from June to November beside the 2/38th, which then departed. These are very different cases from those of the two battalions of the 7th, the 48th, and the 52nd, all of which were present for a year or more together in the army.

The working unit of the Peninsular Army was always the ten-company battalion, commanded by a lieutenant-colonel. When, as in the exceptional cases just named, it chanced that two battalions of a regiment got together, the senior of the two commanding officers had no authority over the other. Both were directly responsible to the brigadier. The battalion theoretically had thirty-five officers and 1000 rank and file, besides sergeants and drummers. A pestilent practice prevailed in all British general returns, of giving in statistics of the larger sort only the number of rank and file (*i.e.* corporals and privates), officers, sergeants, and musicians being all omitted. To bring the figures up to the real general total in such a case, an allowance of about one-eighth or one-ninth has to be added to

the number given. Fortunately detailed returns of all
ranks are always available, when absolute correctness is
required, from the fortnightly general states at the Record
Office.

The theoretical establishment of about 1150 of all ranks
for a first battalion was, of course, hardly ever seen in the
field. Regiments which landed at Lisbon with a full
complement soon dwindled, even before they got to the
front, and nothing was rarer than a battalion in line of
battle with a total strength in the four figures.* A good
well-managed corps which had not been in action of late,
and had not been stationed in an unhealthy cantonment,
might keep up to 700 and even 800 men throughout a
campaign. The Guards battalions, which had a decidedly
larger establishment than those of the line, were frequently
up to 900 men or more.

On the other hand, a battalion which had seen much
fighting, which had not received its drafts regularly, and
had long starved on the bleak mountains of Beira, or
sweltered in the pestilential valley of the Guadiana, often
worked down to 450 men or less, even if it were a first
battalion which had landed with its full 1000 rank and file.
A second battalion under similar circumstances might
shrink to 250 or 300. At the end of the very fatiguing
campaign of 1811, which had included the toilsome pursuit
of Masséna, the Fuentes de Oñoro fighting, and the long
tarrying on the Caya during the unhealthy summer heats,
of forty-six battalions present with Wellington's main
army only nine (all save one first-battalions, and two of
them belonging to the Guards) showed more than 700 of all
ranks present. Sixteen more had between 500 and 700,
ten between 400 and 500. No less than eleven were down
to the miserable figure of under 400 men, and it is to be
noted that of these nearly all were either second battalions

---

* Such figures are, however, occasionally found, e.g. the 1/4th
at Bussaco, and the 1/43rd in September, 1811, had over 1000
of all ranks. So had the 1/42nd at Salamanca.

or single-battalion regiments ; there were six of the former three of the latter among them. The average of the whole, it may be seen, was about 550 men per unit ; the extreme variation was between 1005 for the strongest battalion and 263 for the weakest.* At this time, it should be noted, the army was more sickly than it had ever been before, having over 14,000 men in hospital to 29,300 present with the colours. Wellington was never again so encumbered with sick, save for one period of a few weeks—that which followed the end of the retreat from Burgos to Ciudad Rodrigo in October–November, 1813. During the first months of this winter the troops, tired by incessant marching in the rain, and low feeding, sent into hospital a number of cases not less distressing than those which had been seen in September, 1811. But a short period of rest served to re-establish their health, and in 1813–14 the troops were very healthy, even during the trying weeks when many of them were cantoned high among the snows of the Pyrenean passes.

So much for the infantry regiments. A few words as regards the cavalry must be added to this chapter on organization. From first to last Wellington had under him twenty-one regiments of British horse, besides four more of the light and heavy cavalry of the King's German Legion. But at no time had he such a force as would be represented by this total. He started in 1809 with eight regiments. Before he had been many weeks in command one of his units (a fractional one, composed of two squadrons of the 20th Light Dragoons) was taken from him and shipped off to Sicily. Before the end of the year another (23rd Light Dragoons), which had been badly cut up at Talavera, and lost half its strength there, was sent home to recruit. Thus he had only six regiments † on

---

* These chanced to be the 1/43rd and the 2/38th respectively. The two Guards battalions were each just under 900 of all ranks at this time.

† 3rd Dragoon Guards, 1st and 4th Dragoons, 14th and 16th Light Dragoons, 1st Hussars, K.G.L.

January 1, 1810, and as only one joined him that year,* seven was his total force, till he at last received large reinforcements in the late summer and autumn of 1811. But he started the campaign of 1812 with sixteen regiments,† which was almost the highest figure that he was to own. For although during the campaign of 1813 he was sent four new Hussar regiments, yet at the same time four depleted corps were sent home to be recruited and re-organized. This would have left his total at the same figure of sixteen units as in 1812, if he had not also received a large composite regiment (or weak brigade) composed of two squadrons from each of the three units of the House-hold Cavalry. By this addition alone did his cavalry force in 1813–14 exceed that which he had possessed in 1812. If we reckon the Household squadrons as roughly equivalent to two units, the total at the end of the war was eighteen regiments.

Unlike the infantry, the cavalry of the British Army was organized without exception in isolated units, as it is to-day. A corps sent to the Peninsula left a depôt squadron behind it, and there was no source except this depôt from which it could draw recruits. Nothing resembling the sister-unit on which an infantry battalion depended was in existence. Hence if a cavalry regiment sank low in numbers, and exhausted the drafts which the depôt squadron could send out, it had to return to England to recruit. During the whole war only one corps (the 23rd Light Dragoons at Talavera) suffered a complete disaster, corresponding to that which the 2nd Infantry Division incurred at Albuera, and this unlucky regiment was sent home that autumn, when the British Army had retreated to the Portuguese frontier. But four others worked down so low in strength, and especially in horses, during the campaign of 1812, that, although

* 13th Light Dragoons.
† 3rd, 4th, 5th Dragoon Guards; 1st 3rd, and 4th Dragoons; 9th, 11th, 12th, 13th, 14th, 16th Light Dragoons; 1st and 2nd Heavy Dragoons, K.G.L.; 1st and 2nd Hussars, K.G.L.

they had none of them been thinned down in a single
action like the 23rd, they had become ineffective, and had
to quit the Peninsula. It is most noteworthy that all of
these four corps were comparatively recent arrivals ; they
had come out in 1811, and in little over a single year had
fallen into a state of inefficiency far exceeding that of the
regiments whose service dated back to 1809, and who had
seen two years more of hard campaigning.* The moral
to be drawn is the same that we have noted with the
infantry : the regiments which had served Wellington since
his first arrival had become acclimatized, and had learnt
the tricks of the old soldier. They could shift for themselves, and (what was no less important) for their horses,
far better than any newly-arrived corps. We find bitter
complaints of the defective scouting and outpost work of
the new-comers. After a petty disaster to the outlying
pickets of two of the lately-landed regiments Wellington
wrote : " This disagreeable circumstance tends to show
the difference between old and new troops. The old regiments of cavalry throughout all their service, with all
their losses put together, have not lost so many men
the 2nd Hussars of the Legion and the 11th Light Dragoons
in a few days. However, we must try to make the new as
good as the old." † This was evidently not too easy to
accomplish ; at any rate, at the end of the next year it was
four of the new corps ‡ which were sent home as depleted
units, not any of the seven old ones. All these, without
exception, endured to the last campaign of 1814, though
they nearly all § had to be reduced from a four-squadron

---

* Tomkinson in his diary observes (p. 230) that the 11th Light
Dragoons was not in such bad state as the other condemned regiments, but that their colonel was so senior that he stood in the way
of the promotion of several more capable officers to command
brigades—hence Wellington resolved to get him out of the country.

† *Dispatches*, vii. p. 58. To Lord Liverpool.

‡ 9th and 11th Light Dragoons, 4th Dragoon Guards, 2nd
Hussars, K.G.L.

§ Viz. the 1st Royals, 13th, 14th, and 16th Light Dragoons, and
1st Hussars, K.G.L. See *General Orders*, October 2, 1811.

to a three-squadron establishment in the autumn of 1811, owing to their shrunken effective.   But they never fell so low as the four corps condemned to return to England in the next year.   No more regiments went home after the winter of 1812–13 ; the campaign of Vittoria and the Pyrenees did not bear heavily on the cavalry, most of whom, during the mountain fighting in the autumn, were comfortably cantoned in the Ebro Valley.   They only moved forward again in the spring of 1814 for that invasion of France which was brought to such an abrupt end by the fall of Napoleon.

The theoretical establishment of the regiments of cavalry (putting aside the Household Cavalry) was in 1809 fixed at 905 men in nearly every case.   But a large depôt was always left behind in England, and if a regiment landed 600 sabres in Portugal, in four squadrons, it was up to the average strength.   At the front it would seldom show more than 450, as horses began to die off or go sick the moment that they felt the Peninsular air and diet. A regiment which had been reduced from four squadrons to three might show only 300 men on parade in the middle of a campaign.

PLATE VI.

OFFICER OF LIGHT DRAGOONS.
UNIFORM OF 1813.

OFFICER OF LIGHT DRAGOONS.
UNIFORM OF 1809.

CHAPTER XI

HITHERTO we have been dealing with the regiment considered as a whole, and mainly with its place in the brigade and division to which it had been allotted. We must now pass on to consider it not as a whole, but as an assemblage of parts—officers, staff, sergeants, rank and file, and musicians.

To understand the mechanism of a regiment it is first necessary to say something about the establishment of officers. Battalions and cavalry regiments were normally commanded by a lieutenant-colonel: there were very few full colonels with the army, and almost the only ones who commanded a unit were those of the brigades of Guards, where owing to the "double rank" which made all lieutenants "captains in the army," all captains lieutenant-colonels, and all majors and lieutenant-colonels *full* colonels, it resulted that the battalion commander always held a colonelcy.

When the lieutenant-colonel in a battalion was dead, wounded, or sick, the unit was often commanded by the senior major—there were normally two of them—sometimes for many months at a time, till the absent officer returned, or his place was filled by promotion. Cases were known where, owing to great mortality or invaliding in the senior ranks, a captain might be found in command of the battalion for a certain space. I note that about the time of Bussaco the "morning state" of the army shows two units (both of the Guards) commanded by colonels, 30 by lieutenant-colonels, 16 by majors, one by a captain, and this, I think, was a fairly normal proportion.

In addition to the colonel and the two majors, an infantry battalion at full strength would possess ten captains and twenty subalterns, or a trifle more, giving the allowance of three officers per company, with a few over. How many of the subalterns would be lieutenants and how many ensigns (called 2nd lieutenants in the rifle regiments) was a matter of mere chance, but the lieutenants were nearly always in a majority.* A glance down the morning state of the Bussaco army of September, 1811, shows that one battalion (1/45th) had no more than one ensign, another (the 74th) as many as eleven. It was very rare for a regiment to have its full establishment of ten captains present ; there were nearly always one or two companies commanded by their senior lieutenants. In addition to its company officers every battalion had its " staff," composed of the adjutant, paymaster, quartermaster, and the surgeon, with his two assistant surgeons. The adjutant was usually a lieutenant, but occasionally an ensign ; in the Guards (where most ranks counted a step higher than in the line), he was usually a " lieutenant and captain." In addition to the officers regularly commissioned, a battalion had often with it one or two " volunteers "—young men who were practically probationers ; they were allowed to come out to an active-service battalion on the chance of being gazetted to it without purchase, on their own responsibility. They carried muskets and served in the ranks, but were allowed to wear uniforms of a better cloth than that given to the rank and file, and messed with the officers.

The most astonishing case of devolution of acting rank through the death or wounding of many seniors was at the battle of Albuera. On the morning after that action the wrecks of the second brigade of the 2nd Division, temporarily united into one battalion because of the dreadful losses which had fallen on every one of the three units of which

* In the Talavera army, taking the general totals, there were 536 lieutenants to 259 ensigns ; in the Bussaco army 624 to 237 ; in the 1811 army (March) 739 to 323—in each case more than two to one.

it consisted, were commanded by the senior captain of the 1/48th regiment—and he (as it chanced) was a French *emigré*, with the somewhat lugubrious name of Cimitière. The brigade had been reduced (it may be remarked) from a strength of 1651 to 597 in the battle, no less than 1054 officers and men being killed, wounded, or missing, and the brigadier, with five lieutenant-colonels and majors senior to Cimitière having been killed or wounded.* But the Albuera losses were, of course, the record in the way of heavy casualties ; there is nothing that can be compared to them in the annals of Wellington's army for general slaughter extending all through an army, though certain individual regiments in particular engagements suffered almost as heavily—*e.g.* in the storm of Badajoz and at Waterloo.

The chances of temporary command were sometimes curious. The gallant Colborne, whom I have already had occasion to mention, though only a lieutenant-colonel, commanded a brigade at Albuera, owing to the absence of the brigadier—he being the senior of four battalion commanders. He then commanded his own regiment only during 1811-13, but succeeded as senior lieutenant-colonel to the charge of a brigade of the Light Division for the last six months of the war. Though he had thus twice commanded a brigade with distinction in the Peninsula, we find him in the Waterloo campaign once more at the head of his own 52nd Foot, in Adam's brigade. It is true that with his single battalion he there did more than most of the generals, by giving the decisive stroke which wrecked the attack of the French Guard.

Not only did lieutenant-colonels practically become brigadiers, in an interim fashion, pretty frequently, but once at least an officer with no higher rank commanded a whole division for some months. This was Colonel Andrew Barnard, who after Craufurd fell at Ciudad Rodrigo, and

---

* Viz. killed, the Brigadier-Gen. Hoghton and one major, wounded two lieutenant-colonels and two majors.

the only other general with the division (Vandeleur) was wounded, had charge of the most precious unit of Wellington's whole army for nearly five months, and headed it at the storm of Badajoz. There seems to have been a simila, but a shorter phenomenon of this sort with the 3rd Division, after the fall of Badajoz, when, Generals Picton and Kempt being both disabled, Colonel Wallace of the Connaught Rangers commanded the division for a week or two—till Wellington drafted in his brother-in-law, General Pakenham, to lead it, which he did with great distinction at Salamanca.*

Promotion in the British Army at this period was working in the most irregular and spasmodic fashion, there being two separate influences operating in diametrically opposite ways. The one was the purchase system, the other the frequent, but not by any means sufficiently frequent, promotion for merit and good service in the field. The practice at the Horse Guards was that casualties by deaths in action were filled up inside the regiment, without money passing, but that for all other vacancies the purchase system worked. When a lieutenant-colonelcy, majority, or captaincy was vacant, the senior in the next lower rank had a moral right to be offered the vacancy at the regulation price. But there were many cases in which more than the regulation could be got. The officer retiring handed over the affair to a "commission broker," and bidding was invited. A poor officer at the head of those of his own rank could not afford to pay the often very heavy price, and might see three or four of his juniors buy their way over his head, while he vainly waited for a vacancy by death, by which he would obtain his step without having to pay cash. The system of exchanges, which prevailed on the largest scale, also pressed very hardly on the impecunious ; officers from

* Picton, though wounded in the foot at Badajoz, rode with his division for some time after it marched from Estremadura for the North, but the wound getting inflamed he was compelled to go into hospital, and Wallace had his place for some weeks in June, Pakenham appearing as divisional commander in July.

other corps, where there was a block in promotion, managed for themselves a transference into battalions where there seemed to be a likelihood of a more rapid change of rank, by paying large differences for an exchange to those who stood at the head of the list. But there was also a good deal of exchanging for other reasons—officers whose regiments were ordered to unhealthy or unpopular stations, such as the West Indies or New South Wales, offered considerable sums to others who were ready to accept the ineligible destination in return for hard cash. By careful management of this sort, a wealthy officer could procure himself very rapid promotion—*e.g.* a lieutenant might buy a captaincy in a West India regiment for a comparatively modest sum, and then, as a captain in such a corps, exchange on a second payment with a broken or needy captain in some other regiment on a European station, to whom money was all-important, and so get well established in his new rank, without ever really having quitted home, or served in the corps into and out of which he had rapidly come and gone—on paper only. It is said that one young officer, who had the advantages of being wealthy, a peer, and possessed of great family influence in Parliament, was worked up from a lieutenancy to a lieutenant-colonelcy in a single year. This, of course, was a very exceptional case, and happened long ere the Peninsular War began ; but it may be remembered that Wellington himself, was, through similar advantages on a smaller scale, enabled to move up from ensign on March 7, 1787, to lieutenant-colonel in September, 1793—five steps in seven years, during which he had been moved through as many regiments—two of horse and five of foot. He was only nineteen months a captain and six months a major, and he had seen no war service whatever when he sailed for Flanders in command of the 33rd at the age of twenty-three ! The Duke of York later insisted on a certain minimum service in each rank before promotion could be obtained.

Contrast with such promotion that of the poor and

friendless officer who, after twenty-five years of service, six Peninsular campaigns, and two wounds, found himself still a captain at the age of 43! * But there were plenty of unlucky men who at the end of the war were still only lieutenants after six campaigns, and were placed on half-pay as such, at the great disbandment of the second battalions which took place in 1816–17. The juxtaposition of rapid promotion obtainable by influence and the purchase of steps, with absolute stagnation in a low rank, which often fell on the impecunious officer, whose regiment did not chance to have many casualties in action, was appalling and monstrous.

I take it that the most pernicious of all the disturbing causes which told against the right distribution of promotion was political influence. As a contemporary pamphleteer wrote : " Instances are very few indeed of preferment being obtained by other corrupt means † compared to the omnipotence of Parliamentary interest. Thence originates the shameful practice of thrusting boys into a company over the heads of all the lieutenants and ensigns of the regiment. The Duke of York has done something to check it, but he can never remove the Colossus of Parliamentary interest, an interest that disdains solicitation, and imperiously *demands* from the minister of the day that which no minister ever found it convenient to deny. To this species of influence the commander-in-chief must give way—for it is capable, when slighted, of removing both commander-in-chief and minister." ‡

It was to the unscrupulous use by great men of their parliamentary influence upon the ministry of the day that the

---

* See the bitter remarks on pp. 367–369 on Blakeney's Autobiography. For a number of illustrative anecdotes see Leach's curious little book, *Rambles on the Banks of Styx,* which is full of Peninsular grievances.

† The allusion is to the obscure business of influence in distributing commissions said to have been used by the Duke of York's mistress, Mrs. Mary Ann Clarke.

‡ For more of this pamphlet, see Stocqueler's *Personal History of the Horse Guards,* pp. 60–67.

army owed a great proportion of its " King's hard bargains "
in the commissioned ranks. The obscure but necessary
instruments of one of the great borough-mongers—Whig no
less than Tory—were often paid by the nomination of their
sons or other young relatives to a commission, by the influence
of their patron : and the families that did the dirty work of
a great politician were not likely to be distinguished for
high morals or uprightness. Sometimes the nominations
were absolutely shameful—it is said that the son of the
keeper of a fashionable gaming-house in St. James' was
slid into the list of ensigns on one occasion, by a politician
whom his father had obliged. Whether this be true or not,
it is certain that there was a sprinkling of officers who were
not gentlemen in any sense of the term serving throughout
the war.* Others about whose gentle blood there was no
doubt, were undesirable in other ways—prominent among
them a section of young Irish squireens with the bullying
and duelling habits, as well as the hard-drinking, which
were notoriously prevalent among the less civilized strata of
society beyond St. George's Channel. I find in one memoir
a note of a newly-joined ensign after mess addressing the
assembled officers as follows : " By Jasus, gentlemen, I
am conscious you must have the meanest opinion of my
courage. Here have I been no less than six weeks with
the regiment, and the divil of a duel have I fought yet.
Now, Captain C., you are the senior captain, and if you
please I will begin with you first : so name your time and
place." As the diarist very wisely writes, " one could not
be too guarded in one's conduct with such heroes." †

Duels, I may remark in passing, were much less frequent
in the Peninsular Army than might have been expected.
Wellington (though long after he most foolishly " went
out " with Lord Winchelsea in 1829) set his face against
them on active service, because he could not afford to lose

---

* For an astounding story of an ensign who had been a billiard-
marker in Dublin, and who was ultimately cashiered for theft, see
Col. Bunbury's *Reminiscences*, vol. i. pp. 26–28.

† *Memoirs of Captain George Ellers, 12th Foot*, p. 43.

good officers on account of personal quarrels. There
certainly were much fewer duels proportionately in the
Peninsula than in England at the time—not to speak of
Ireland and India, where they were beyond all reason
common. I have only found records of four fatal duels in
the records of court-martials, and though non-fatal ones
could have been (and were) hushed up, they cannot have
been very numerous, for one may read through scores of
memoirs and diaries without running upon the mention of
one. It is curious to note that when they did occur, and a
court-martial followed, that body invariably found that
though there was no doubt that Captain A. or Lieutenant
B. was dead, yet there was no conclusive proof that he had
been killed by C. or D.—the mouths of the seconds being
sealed by the fact that they were also on their trial for
having acted in such a capacity.* The whole matter was
clearly a solemn farce. But the fact remains that duels
were not frequent, and that duellists had a bad mark
against them. Good commanding officers took immense
trouble to prevent a duel from arising over silly mess-table
quarrels, exerting every influence to make one party, or
both, apologize for words spoken in anger, or in liquor.†

The body of officers of a Peninsular regiment was often
a very odd party—there might be a lieutenant-colonel of
twenty-six, who had risen rapidly by purchase or interest,
and captains of fifty or even sixty ; I found a note of one
who had attained that age in the 73rd. At the head of
each rank there might be several impecunious and disappointed men, waiting for the promotion that could only
come by casualties in action, since they could never hope to
purchase their step. Nevertheless, the feuds that might

* See the instances in *General Orders* for April 23, 1910, and
July 16, 1812.
† For a good example, see *Dickson Papers*, pp. 622, 623, where
the good Dickson gets one officer to own that he was " betrayed in
a moment of intoxication " into insulting words, and the other to
say that the counter-charge with which he replied was made " in a
moment of great irritation and passion." The apologies were both
passed as satisfactory.

have been expected to follow such a situation do not seem to have been so many, or so bitter, as might have been expected. The grudge was set against the system rather than the individual, in most cases, and the sight of a mess cut up into cliques and coteries of enemies, though it can be found recorded occasionally, was quite exceptional.* The saving fact was that there was always the chance of promotion for merit, in reward of some specially gallant deed, and it often came—though the Duke was occasionally incomprehensible in the way in which he mentioned or did not mention officers in dispatches. The lieutenant who brought down the French flag from the castle of Badajoz, and who was sent with it by Picton to the commander-in-chief, was thanked and asked to dinner, but was still a lieutenant years after, in spite of his general's vehement remonstrances.† Dozens of such instances could be quoted.

Professional training for officers had perforce been non-existent in the early years of the French war. There was no institution which supplied it, and all military knowledge had to be acquired by rule of thumb at regimental head-quarters. An improvement of the greatest importance was made by the establishment in December, 1801, of the " Royal Military College " at High Wycombe for the use of young officers, followed by the creation of its " Junior Department" in May, 1802, "for the instruction of those who from early life are intended for the military pro-fession." The latter, the origin of the college at Sandhurst, to which the department was removed in 1811, accepted boys as early as thirteen. Its first inspector-general was the French *emigré* Jarry, to whom we owe the " Instructions

* A series of court-martials in one Peninsular battalion shows us such a picture, with the colonel on one side and the two majors on the other. The former prosecuted the senior major for embezzle-ment, while at the same moment a subaltern was " broke " for alleging that the junior major had shown cowardice in the field. The Horse-Guards finally dispersed all the officers into different corps, as the only way of ending the feud.

† See pp. 121–2 of vol. ii. of Robinson's *Life of Picton*.

for Light Infantry in the Field" of 1804, while Colonel John Gaspard Le Marchant was "Lieutenant-governor and Superintendant General." This was the accomplished cavalry officer who fell in 1812, at the head of his brigade, in the crisis of the battle of Salamanca, when he had just delivered a decisive charge. The military college men were already numerous when the Peninsular War began.

The French General, Foy, a witness whose authority can hardly be called in question, for he is making grudging admissions, says that he considered the general mass of the British officers excellent.* The more we study detailed records, the more willingly do we acknowledge that his praise is well deserved. The weaker brethren were very few—so few that an enemy did not even notice them. Misconduct on the field was the rarest of offences; there are hardly half a dozen court-martials for suspected slackness, among the hundreds that were held for other offences. There were an appreciable number of officers "broke" for faults that came from hard drinking, "incapable when on duty," and so forth, or brawling, and a very few for financial irregularities; but considering the unpromising material that was sometimes pitchforked into a regiment by the unscrupulous exercise of patronage at home, they were exceedingly few. The only class of failures who had any appreciable numbers, and earned a special name, were the "Belemites," so called from the general depôt at the convent of Belem in the suburbs of Lisbon. This was the headquarters of all officers absent from the front as convalescents or on leave, and the limited proportion who stayed there over-long, and showed an insufficient eagerness to return to their regiments, were nicknamed from the spot where they lingered beyond the bounds of discretion. Wellington occasionally gave an order to Colonel Peacocke, the military governor of Lisbon, to rout up this coterie—there were always a sprinkling there who were not over-anxious

* Letter printed in *Vie Militaire*, ed. Girod de l'Ain, p. 98.

to resume the hard life of campaigning, and loved too much
the gambling-hells and other sordid delights of Lisbon.*
Occasionally the notices which appear in General Orders
about these gentry are rather surprising—one would not
have thought that such men could even have obtained a
commission. Take, for example, " The commanding officer
at Lisbon (or the commanding officer of any station at
which Captain —— of the 88th may happen to be found),
will be pleased to place that officer under arrest, and send
him to join his regiment, he having been absent for several
months without leave, and having been in Portugal since
October 20th last, without reporting himself to or com-
municating with his commanding officer." †

Wellington in his moments of irritation sometimes
wrote as if the majority of his officers were slack and dis-
obedient. Such men existed; but, as one who knew the
Duke well observed, " by long exercise of absolute power
he had become intolerant of the slightest provocation, and
every breach of discipline, no matter how limited its range,
made him furious with the whole army. Hence frequent
General Orders, as violent as they were essentially unjust,
wherein, because of the misdeeds of a few, all who served
under him were denounced—the officers as ignorant of their
duty, the rank and file as little better than a rabble." ‡

But the duty-shirking officer, and still more the disreputable officer was, after all, a very rare exception. The
atmosphere of contempt which surrounded him in his
regiment as a rule sufficed to make him send in his papers,
after a longer or a shorter period of endurance, in proportion as his skin was tough or thin. Opinion was not
so hard upon the man who was merely quarrelsome and

* See the heading " Lisbon " in the collected volume of *General
Orders*, pp. 206, 207.
† *General Orders*, Freneda, December 4, 1811. For anecdotes
about this officer's shirking propensities, see pp. 27–36 of the second
series of Grattan's *Adventures with the Connaught Rangers*. He was
ultimately cashiered.
‡ Gleig's *Reminiscences of Wellington*, p. 303.

ungentlemanly in his cups. But there were limits even
to the boisterousness permitted to the tippler, and drunkenness when in face of the enemy, or in a position of
military responsibility, was always fatal.

There was, throughout the war, a perceptible proportion
of officers who had risen from the ranks. Meritorious
service, showing good capacity as well as courage, not
unfrequently led to the promotion of a sergeant to an
ensigncy. A well-remembered case is that of the Sergeant
Newman of the 43rd who rallied the stragglers during the
march from Lugo to Betanzos, in the Corunna retreat, and
beat off the pursuing French dragoons. Another is that of
Sergeant Masterson of the 2/87th, who captured the eagle
of the 8th Ligne at Barrosa. Many more might be quoted,
though none of them is so striking as that of a man who
did not serve in the Peninsula, but in contemporary campaigns in India, the celebrated John Shipp. He was *twice*
given a commission for deeds of exceptional daring. After
winning his first ensigncy in the storming party at the
Siege of Bhurtpoor in 1805, he was forced to " sell out "
a little later by improvident living. He enlisted as a private
in another regiment, and was again promoted from the
ranks for a single combat with a Nepaulese chief during
the first Goorkha War of 1815. Conducting himself with
more wisdom on his second chance, he served long as an
officer, and when he went on half-pay became chief-con-
stable of Liverpool. His autobiography is an artless and
interesting piece of work well worth perusal.

When a regiment had greatly distinguished itself in
the field, Wellington not unfrequently directed its colonel
to recommend a sergeant for a commission. This, for
example, was done for all three battalions of the Light
Division after their splendid exploit at Bussaco. Yet he
did not approve of this system of promotion as anything
but a very exceptional measure, and in his table-talk with
Lord Stanhope we find some very harshly worded verdicts
on old rankers, " their origin would come out, and you

could never perfectly trust them," * especially in the matter of drink. This seems to be a typical instance of the Duke's aristocratic prejudices—but there was something in what he said. The position of the promoted sergeants was certainly difficult, and it required a man of exceptional character to make it good. As a rule, they drifted into the position of paymasters, recruiting officers, barrack masters, and such-like posts. But many of them made useful and efficient adjutants. In command they were not as a rule successful,† and I have only come on a single case of one who reached the rank of full colonel, and of two who were fortunate enough to obtain a majority. It is clear that the purchase system pressed very hardly upon them : with no private resources it was impossible for them ever to buy a step, and, after reaching the rank of captain, they almost invariably went upon half-pay or looked for employment in some civil or semi-civil capacity.

Concerning the equipment of the officer, his baggage, his horses and mules, and his servants, information will be found in another chapter. Here we are dealing with him as an item in the machinery of the regiment.

---

* *Conversations with Duke of Wellington*, pp. 13 and 18.
† See, for an instance, pp. 249–50.

CHAPTER XII

HE who would make himself acquainted in detail with the
many experiments by which British Governments, from the
rupture of the Peace of Amiens onward, strove to keep on
foot in full numbers the very large army that it had raised,
must satisfy his curiosity by studying the admirable volumes
of Mr. Fortescue. Here we are concerned only with the
methods which prevailed from 1809 till 1814, and gave
Wellington the invincible, though often attenuated, battalions which conquered at Talavera and Bussaco, at
Salamanca and Toulouse.

In the Peninsular Army the system of territorial names
prevailed for nearly all the regiments of the line, but in
most cases the local designation had no very close relation
with the actual *provenance* of the men. There were a
certain number of regiments that were practically national,
e.g. most of the Highland battalions, and nearly all of the
Irish ones, were very predominantly Highland and Irish
as to their rank and file : but even in the 79th or the 88th
there was a certain sprinkling of English recruits. And
in some nominally Scottish regiments like the 71st Highland
Light Infantry, or the 90th Perthshire Volunteers,* the
proportion of English and Irish was very large. Similarly
in almost all the nominally English regiments there was a

---

* When the 90th was raised in 1794, out of the 746 men 165
were English and 56 Irish—not much less than a third of the whole.
Cf. Delavoye's *History of the 90th,* p. 3. In the Waterloo campaign
the 71st had 83 English and 56 Irish in its ranks.

large sprinkling of Irish, and a few Scots. This came partly from the fact that, though the corps recruited in their own districts, yet they were often allowed to send recruiting parties to great centres like London, Bristol, Liverpool, Glasgow, or Dublin. But still more was it due to the fact that the larger half of the recruits were raised not in the old normal fashion, but by volunteering from the embodied militia, and that in this system practically no attempt was made to confine the choice of militiamen wishing to join the regular army to their territorial regiment. Nothing, for example, was more usual than to find such things as 100 of the King's County Militia joining the 31st or Huntingdonshire Regiment. When the 77th or East Middlesex Regiment returned from India in 1808, it was completed, before going out to the Peninsula, from the 1st West York, North and South Mayo, Northampton, and South Lincoln Militia, but did not get a single man from the Middlesex Militia.* The Shropshire Regiment (53rd) when allowed in a similar case to call for volunteers, did get 99 from its own county militia, but 144 more from the Dorset, East York, and Montgomery local corps.† The 81st or Loyal Lincoln was filled up in 1808, before sailing for Portugal, from the Dublin, King's County, South Devon, and Montgomery Militia. Instances might be multiplied *ad nauseam*. It was quite exceptional for any English corps to contain a preponderance of men from its own nominal district, and nearly all of them had from a fifth to a fourth of Irish.

It is impossible to exaggerate the advantage to the Peninsular Army of the system, the invention of Castlereagh when War Minister, which enabled it to draw in such a heavy proportion on the militia for recruits. ‡ The men thus obtained had all had at least twelve months' drill and discipline, in a corps which had been under arms for many

---

* Woolwright's *History of the 77th*, p. 29.
† Rogerson's *History of the 53rd*, p. 35.
‡ See Fortescue's *History of the British Army*, **vi.** pp. 180–183.

years : they were trained soldiers of some little experience, much superior in fact to the recruits who had been procured in other ways. The permanent militia represented the force raised by the counties by ballot, though substitutes rather than principals were procured by that device. Being forced to serve at home for a period of years, the militiamen freely volunteered into the line, from love of adventure, dislike of dull country quarters in England or Ireland,* and, it must be added, the temptation of the enormous bounty, running at various times from £16 up to £40, which was given to those changing their service.†

It is a mistake to make a point, as some writers have done, of the fact that many regiments appeared in Spain with their ranks " full of raw militiamen, who sometimes still bore their old militia badges on their knapsacks." So far from their being ineligible recruits, they were the very best, for the militia of 1808–14 was not a body called out for short service during one month of the year, but a permanent institution which practically formed a second line to the field army. And no man was allowed to volunteer into the regulars till he had served a full year in the local corps in which he had enlisted. A regiment must get drafts on active service, and these were the very best sort that could be obtained. Of course a corps filled up hastily

---

* To quote an interesting explanatory note from the autobiography of Morris of the 73rd. " The militia would be drawn up in line, and the officers for the regiments requiring volunteers would give a glowing description of their several corps, describing the victories they had gained, and the honours they had acquired, and conclude by offering the bounty. If these inducements were not effectual in getting men, coercive measures were adopted : the militia colonel would put on heavy and long drills and field exercises, which were so tedious and oppressive that many men would embrace the alternative, and volunteer for the regulars " (p. 13).

† A canny Scot makes his explanation for volunteering in a fashion which combines patriotism, love of adventure, and calculation. " In the militia I serve secure of life and limb, but with no prospect of future benefit for old age (pension) to which I may attain. It is better to hazard both abroad in the regular service, than to have poverty and hard-labour accompanying me to a peaceful grave at home." Anton's *Retrospect of a Military Life*, p. 39.

with a great number of them, would want a little time to shake down, but it would take far longer to assimilate a corresponding number of ordinary recruits, hurried out from its regimental depôt—for these men would neither have had a whole year's drill, nor would they have been accustomed to the daily economy of a full regiment—depôts seem to have been slackly administered, in many cases by officers and sergeants invalided and past service, or who had of their own desire shirked the service at the front.

The other moiety of the recruits who came out to the Peninsula, to fill up the never-ending gaps in the ranks of a battalion at the front, were on the whole worse material than the militiamen. They were the usual raw stuff swept in by the recruiting sergeant—all those restless spirits who were caught by the attraction of the red coat, country lads tired of the plough, or town lads who lived on the edge of unemployment, and to whom a full stomach had been for some time a rarity. We have autobiographies of runaway apprentices who had bolted from a hard master,* and of village Lotharios who had evaded an entanglement by a timely evasion.† Sons of hard fathers, and stepsons of intolerable stepmothers drifted in, and still more frequently the rowdy spirits who were "wanted" by the constable for assault and battery, or for some rural practical joke which had set the parish in an uproar. The oddest cause of enlisting that I have come upon is that of a son of a respectable Edinburgh tradesman's family, whose account of the fortunes of the 71st in 1808–15 is one of the best written of all the soldier-biographies. A stage-struck youth with a little money in his pocket, he had often gone on (no doubt as a super) at the Theatre Royal, carrying a banner or a five-word message. At last the summit of his ambition came—a friendly manager gave him a short part, where he had actually some share in the action. He

* See the amusing narrative of Lawrence of the 20th and his two evasions from his stone-mason employer.
† See Stanhope's *Conversations with Wellington*, p. 13.

invited all his friends to the performance to see his glory, came on the boards, and was suddenly struck with stage fright, so that he stood gaping and silent before the audience, and heard the laughter and hooting begin. The poor wretch bolted straight away from the stage in his costume and paint, ran down to Leith, and enlisted with a sergeant of the 71st, whose party was sailing that night for the South. Anything was preferable to him rather than to face next morning the jeers of the friends to whom he had boasted of his histrionic powers, and who had come to see his début.*

But these were the better spirits. There was a much lower stratum among the recruits, drawn from the criminal or semi-criminal classes, whom the enormous bounty offered for volunteers had tempted into the service—generally with the purpose of getting out of it again as soon as possible. Not only were there poachers, smugglers, and street-corner roughs, who had been offered by the local authorities the choice between enlistment and the jail, but pickpockets, coiners, and footpads, who had made London or some other great town too hot for them, often enlisted as a *pis aller*, intending to desert and "jump another bounty" when they could. But sergeants were lynx-eyed when they found that they had enlisted a slippery customer, and the evasive recruit often found himself kept under lock and key in a fort, and shipped off to Spain before he got his opportunity to abscond. The number of these "King's hard bargains" varied much between different regiments, but Colborne, a good authority, says that the battalion was lucky which had not its fifty irreclaimable bad characters, drunkards, plunderers, stragglers, would-be deserters, actual criminals "whom neither punishment nor any kind of discipline could restrain; for the system of recruiting was defective and radically bad." † It was this scum,

* Journal of T. S. of the 71st in Constable's *Memorials of the Late War*, i. p. 25.

† Note by Colborne on p. 396 of his *Life* by Moore-Smith.

a small proportion of the whole, but always swimming to the top when there was mischief to be done—peasants to be plundered or churches to be pillaged—that provided the subject-matter for court-martials, and engrossed the majority of the attention of the Provost Marshal. Officers of undoubted humanity, and men in the ranks who knew what they were talking about, unite in stating that there was a residuum in the Peninsular Army which could only be governed by the lash.

This small percentage of irreclaimables provided the nucleus around which misconduct sometimes grew to a great scale, in moments of special privation or temptation. In abominable orgies like the sack of Badajoz, or the lesser but still disgraceful riots at Ciudad Rodrigo and San Sebastian, it was the criminals who started the game, but the drunkards—a far more numerous class—who took it up. When the drink was in them, the mob was capable of any freak of wanton mischief or cruelty. Wellington more than once complained that the most reckless and ungovernable of his rowdies were the newly-joined Irish recruits. It seems that when in liquor they became irresponsible madmen, and had not undergone enough of discipline to get them into a habit of obedience, which might serve as a substitute for moral sense. And I can well believe this from casual evidence picked up in the diaries of his obscure subordinates. The account of the difficulties of officers and sergeants in getting a large draft of Irish recruits from Cashel to Deal, which I met in one soldier-diary reads like a nightmare *— or a glimpse of some primitive pagan heaven, in which all was objectless fighting in the intervals between frequent and limitless potations. As a side-light on the national failing, I may quote the fact that going through the complete record of general court-martials for the whole period 1809–14, I found that after putting aside all trials of officers, non-combatants, and foreign auxiliaries (the last almost always for desertion) there was an unmistakable over-percentage

* *Rifleman Harris*, pp. 10–16.

of men with Irish names, just as there was an under-percentage of Scots. The offences for which the former were tried were generally desertion and crimes of violence, plundering or maltreating the peasantry.*

The way in which the habitually criminal element makes itself visible in this list of court-martials is in the not infrequent cases of scientific and habitual burglary, robbery of the convoys going to the military chest, or of the private property of officers, and the stealing of church plate—all offences often punished with death, for Wellington rarely pardoned the professional thief, though he sometimes let off a deserter with a sound flogging. But the queerest glimpse into the lowest stratum of the army is the curious anecdote recorded in Napier's fifth volume. Nonplussed in the winter of 1813–14 by the refusal of the French peasantry to accept the dollars or the guineas which were all that he could offer, Wellington determined to set up a mint of his own, which should melt down Spanish and Portuguese silver and recoin it in the form of five franc pieces. He sent private appeals to the colonels to find him all the professional coiners that they could discover in the ranks, collected as many as forty at St. Jean de Luz, and with their aid struck a large quantity of money, of which he was careful to see that the weight and the purity were both correct.†

Occasionally the gentleman-ranker was to be found in a Peninsular regiment. He was generally an "undesirable," who had enlisted in consequence of some disgraceful quarrel with a family who had refused to do anything more for him. Persistent drink, gambling, or dishonesty were the usual causes that had broken him—not undeserved misfortune or dire poverty. Occasionally he pulled himself

* In the Court Martials on privates printed in *General Orders*, out of 280 trials I make out 80 certainly Irish names, and a good many more probably Irish—while there are only 23 Scots. There were certainly not four times as many Irish as Scots in the Peninsular Army, though there were more than twice as many.

† See also Stanhope's *Conversations with Wellington*, p. 6.

together, became a good soldier, and was ultimately promoted to a commission. More often he sank into a persistent drunkard or a criminal. Surtees of the 95th, in an interesting chapter, gives the biographies of the four privates of this class that he had known.* One conducted himself well for some years, became a paymaster-sergeant, and then broke out into a wild fit of dissipation, embezzled the company's money, and committed suicide on detection. The second was always in scrapes: finally he was caught deserting to the French, and was lucky to get off with penal servitude for life instead of death. The third, " always excessively wild," was once made a corporal, but was not fit for that or any other rank. The fourth was one of the exceptional cases—being a retired lieutenant without friends or means, who had enlisted as a private in sheer poverty. He was an exemplary and deserving man, who was soon made secretary, or private clerk, to his colonel, behaved excellently, and was in the end restored to his former rank in the army by interest made in his behalf.

A regiment on Peninsular service depended for its strength on the regularity with which it was fed from its home-battalion or its depôt. Whenever a convoy sailed from Spithead, it contained an immense number of small detachments, varying from a few scores to over a hundred men, under charge of officers newly gazetted to the service battalion, or returning from sick leave. There was often much wrangling on shipboard (unless the weather reduced every one to the same level of nausea and helplessness), not only between the men but between the young officers in charge of them. After an angry comparison of the exact date of commissions, which settled seniority in the choice of berths, and in dealing with the transport-captain, two ensigns in charge of detachments would often settle down to a feud destined to last for the whole voyage to Lisbon. Their men gleefully joined in the wrangle. There are some absurd sidelights, in court-martials, on these frequent

* *Twenty-five Years in the Rifle Brigade*, pp. 47, 48.

shipboard quarrels, which sometimes ended in affrays and " conduct unbecoming an officer and a gentleman."

When a detachment landed at Lisbon, the officer in charge, often a lad of sixteen, had to shepherd his flock to the front, perhaps over 200 miles of mountain roads. Neither officers nor men knew a word of Portuguese, or had the slightest notion of the manners, government, prejudices, or food of the peasantry. They went forward in a perpetual haze of mistakes and misunderstandings. Every draft had its percentage of undesirables, or even of criminals. Hence the young officer, responsible for their safe delivery at the front, found himself embroiled in constant disputes with the natives, often ending in his arrest on his final arrival at headquarters. We must feel nothing but sympathy for the unfortunate young man who delivered only twenty-nine out of a detachment of forty-one entrusted to him ; or the other who found that fourteen men out of twenty had privately disposed of their new blankets.* The only way of managing the draft was by reliance on the sergeant or two who formed a part of it : and if the sergeant was himself a sluggard or a tippler, ill fared his superior. Imagine the feelings of the second-lieutenant who having left his one non-commissioned officer behind, to hunt up footsore stragglers, found no one arrive at the nightly billet, and returning for miles to seek the lost ones, discovered his sergeant dead drunk and snoring in the middle of the high-road.† Ability to conduct a draft to the battalion was one of the greatest tests of the character and capacity of a junior officer.

The responsibility of the non-commissioned officer cannot be exaggerated. It was easy to make sergeants, but not easy to secure them of the proper quality. Too often the man promoted for an act of courage or of quick cleverness had to be reduced to the ranks again, for some

* Both court-martialled, of course : see *General Orders*, vol. vii.
† This incident occurs in the unprinted letters of F. Monro, R.A., lent to me by his kinsfolk of to-day.

hopeless failing—he was prone to drink,* or he was an over-harsh or an over-slack administrator of discipline. One of the commoner types of court-martial was that of the non-commissioned officer who connived at and profited by the misdeeds of the men under his charge—whose silence was bought by a percentage, when peasants were plundered, or convoys lightened of food, shoes, or clothing. It was often difficult to get at him—to prove that he had known of what was going on, and had contrived to see nothing. But the numbers of reductions to the ranks were notable, and lashes were often added when part of the *corpus delicti* was found in the sergeant's pack.

However, the ideal sergeant was not unfrequently found, and when found he was invaluable ; he had to be a steady man with a modicum of education and a sense of duty, who could be relied upon neither to connive at his men's graver faults, nor, on the other hand, to be perpetually spying on them and reporting them to their captains for every minute breach of discipline. Tact was as necessary as the power to get orders carried out. The bullying sergeant would, in the end, get left in some quandary or dilemma by the men that he was always harrying, while the considerate sergeant would get the benefit of his popularity by receiving loyal and intelligent service instead of mere obedience.

Most important of all non-commissioned officers was the sergeant-major, concerning whose position I cannot do better than quote the homily of a Highland soldier more given to philosophical disquisitions than most of the diarists from the ranks.†

" The sergeant-major has an arduous duty to perform ; in all the arrangements of regimental duty he takes, or ought

---

* One of the Duke's acrid generalizations on this point was " the non-commissioned officers of the Guards regularly got drunk once a day, by eight in the evening, and got to bed soon after—but they always took care to do first what they were bid."—Stanhope's *Conversations with the Duke of Wellington*, p. 18.

† See Anton's (42nd, Black Watch) *Retrospect of a Military Life*, pp. 239, 240.

to take, the most active concern. He has, of course, been
considered by his colonel a meritorious man, before he ap-
points him to this highest step to which a non-commissioned
officer can attain : and, as it is frequently found necessary
to consult him on the interior economy of the regiment, if
he is possessed of any talents they are sure to be seen and
called forth. Fortunate is the regiment which possess a
good sergeant-major. His rank is not such as to make him
above associating with and advising the other non-commissioned officers : his own personal example is the means
of swaying their actions : he cautions them against unjust
oppression, yet shrinks not from pointing out the cases
which require coercive measures. He recommends for
promotion those who meritoriously aspire to rise from the
ranks. His commanding officer is seldom troubled with
complaints, for he settles them to the satisfaction of the
accuser and accused. No mercenary motive actuates his
conduct in reconciling differences, and his hands are never
soiled with the gift of an inferior. To those who are un-
acquainted with the influence which sergeant-majors
generally possess this may seem a hyperbole ; but to me
it appears a fact ; I speak not of one regiment but of many.
A sergeant-major, on the other hand, can be a little tyrant
in the corps, without the knowledge of his colonel : his
unnecessary acts of oppression may be made to appear to
his superiors as laudable zeal, and his severity as merit
deserving reward. . . . If the commanding officer be of
an easy, complying turn, or again of a repulsive, haughty,
don't-trouble-me disposition, and the adjutant (which is
often the case) not over well informed, the sergeant-major
is consulted on all occasions. His opinion is asked as to
character, he can establish or injure at pleasure, for who
will be called in to contradict him ?   In short he has much
more to say between the non-commissioned officers and
the colonel, concerning the poor soldiers' conduct, than all
the captains and subalterns of the regiment." *

   * *Retrospect of a Military Life,* pp. 57, 58.

The gap between the sergeant and the men in the ranks was necessarily a well-marked one. The non-commissioned officers kept together and formed messes of their own. " Pride and propriety " kept them from joining in the carouses of the rank and file. " He who has once joined the company of sergeants is disincluded for any other," * writes one veteran proud of well-deserved promotions. The non-commissioned officer who was too familiar with his inferiors was generally one of those who profited by their misdeeds, and would some day be convicted of sharing their plunder, or conniving at their excesses.

* *Memoirs of Sergeant Morley, 5th Foot,* p. 101.

CHAPTER XIII

THE AUXILIARIES : THE GERMANS AND THE PORTUGUESE

OF the two classes of foreign troops which assisted to
make up the invincible divisions of the Peninsular Army,
the one formed at the time an integral part of the British
military establishment ; the other was the contingent of
an allied Power, placed at the disposition of Wellington,
and incorporated with the units of his host, but preserving
its own national individuality.

We must deal with the first class before we proceed to
explain the position of the second. Copying old British
precedent, the governments of George III. had taken into
pay a number of foreign corps from the very commencement of the Revolutionary War. They were the successors
of the Hanoverians against whom the elder Pitt had railed
so fiercely in his hot youth, and of the Hessians who had
taken such a prominent part in the War of American
Independence.

The regiments raised in the early years of the great
struggle with France had mainly been composed of Swiss,
or of French royalist *emigrés*. Most of these corps had
disappeared by 1809, and of those of them which survived
the majority were doing garrison duty in the Mediterranean
and elsewhere.* Wellington never had them under his
hand. The foreign troops which came under his command
were nearly all German, and consisted of regiments raised
after the rupture of the Peace of Am iens.

* The survivors in 1809 were the regiments of de Meuron, Rolle,
Dillon, and de Watteville.

By far the largest number of them belonged to that
admirable corps the King's German Legion, whose history
was written with great care and enthusiasm by Ludlow
Beamish, while the generation which fought in the Peninsula
was still alive. They were the legitimate representatives
of the old Electoral army of Hanover, the comrades of the
British troops in many a fight of the War of the Austrian
Succession and of the Seven Years' War. When in June,
1803, Napoleon invaded Hanover, and overran it with the
troops of Mortier, the 15,000 men who formed the standing
army of the electorate could make no effective resistance.
They laid down their arms in accordance with the Convention of Lauenburg (July 5, 1803), which disbanded them,
and permitted officers and men to go where they pleased,
with the proviso that none of them would bear arms
against France till they should have been exchanged
for French officers or men in the hands of the English
Government.*

The best and most loyal of the Hanoverian officers
began at once to betake themselves to England, and by
the end of the year were streaming thither by dozens and
scores. Men soon began to follow in considerable numbers, and after two provisional infantry regiments had been
formed in August, a larger organization, to be called the
King's German Legion, was authorized in December. It
included light and line infantry, heavy and light cavalry,
artillery and engineers. All through 1804 new units were
being rapidly created, mainly from Hanoverians, but not
entirely, for other recruits of German nationality were
accepted. But all the officers, nearly all the sergeants,
and the large majority of the rank and file came from the
old Electoral army. By January, 1805, there were in

---

* This proviso was neither submitted to nor approved by the
British Government, who refused to take notice of it. Napoleon,
during many disputes as to the exchange of prisoners in later
years, always found a good excuse for breaking off negociations in
the fact that he held that 4000 or 5000 Hanoverians of the K.G.L.
should be reckoned as men requiring exchange.

existence a dragoon and a hussar regiment, four Line and two Light battalions, and five batteries of artillery.

In November, 1805, when Lord Cathcart's expedition sailed for the Weser, to make a diversion in favour of Austria, the whole German Legion went with him. For a few short weeks the invaders were in possession of Bremen and Verden, Stade, and Hanover city, before the news of the disastrous peace that followed Austerlitz came to hand. During this space immense numbers of Hanoverians flocked to the colours, some old soldiers, others volunteers who had not served before. When the army evacuated Hanover in February, 1806, it brought back so many recruits that the Legion was raised to ten battalions of infantry and five regiments of horse.

These were almost the last genuine Hanoverians that were raised for service in the corps, for when the electorate was annexed to Jerome Bonaparte's " Kingdom of West-phalia," it became part of the French Imperial system, and was subjected to the conscription for Jerome's service. Only a few individuals henceforth succeeded in getting to England and joining the Legion by circuitous ways. But there were some good recruits obtained at Stralsund and in Denmark during the Copenhagen Expedition at the end of 1807, when the Legion was for some weeks in the Baltic.

The battalions and squadrons were still mainly Hano-verian, when, in 1808, the larger half of them was sent to the Peninsula. In that year one Hussar regiment (the 3rd), two Light and four Line battalions (Nos. 1, 2, 5, 7), landed in Portugal. Of these only the two Light battalions and the Hussars marched with Moore, and re-embarked for England after his disastrous retreat. The four Line battalions remained in Portugal, as did two German batteries, and made part of Wellesley's original army of 1809. They were joined in the spring of that year by the 1st Hussars, who (as has been already mentioned) were considered the most efficient light cavalry regiment in Portugal, and

were long the chosen comrades of Craufurd's Light
Division.

In the spring of 1811 the K.G.L. contingent in Portugal
was increased by the 2nd Hussars and the two Light Battalions, who returned about two years after their departure
in the company of Moore. In the winter of 1811–12 the
two heavy dragoon regiments joined Wellington's army.
Thus in the beginning of 1812 four of the five cavalry
regiments, and five (the 7th Line battalion had gone home)
of the ten infantry battalions were serving in Spain. But
at the end of the year the 2nd Hussars were drafted back
to England, owing to depleted numbers.

It had now become impossible to keep the ranks of the
Legion filled with the genuine Hanoverians who had been
its original nucleus. Communication with the electorate
was completely cut off, and German recruits of any kind
had to be accepted. Many of them were volunteers from
the English prison camps, where thousands of Napoleon's
German troops were lying. Of these only a fraction were
Hanoverians born. The large majority could not, of
course, share in the loyalty and enthusiasm of the original
legionaries, being subjects of all manner of sovereigns in
the Rheinbund, who had marched at Napoleon's orders.
The quality of men was much worse, and many enlisted only
to escape from prison life, and readily deserted when they
reached the front, having no interest in the cause for which
they were fighting. From 1811 onward desertion, not at
all usual in the early years of the Legion, became very
common, and plunder and misconduct (previously very
rare) were also rife. Matters became still worse when,
later in the war, German recruits of any sort became so
hard to obtain that Poles, Illyrians, and miscellaneous
foreigners of any sort * were drafted out to fill the shrinking

* I note among the deserters from the German Legion in 1812–14
the strange and non-Teutonic names of Gormowsky, Melofsky,
Schilinsky, Wutgok, Prochinsky, Borofsky, Ferdinando, Panderan,
Kowalzuch, Matteivich, etc.

ranks. But the splendid Hanoverian officers still continued to get good service out of a rank and file that was
no longer so homogeneous or loyal as it had been when the
war began, and the regiments of the German Legion, the
cavalry in especial, continued to be among Wellington's
most trusted troops. The charge of Bock's Heavy Dragoons
at Garcia Hernandez, on the day after Salamanca, was, as
has been already stated, considered by Foy to have been
the most brilliant and successful cavalry attack made in
the whole Peninsular War. After the peace of 1814 all
the "mongrels" were discharged, and the officers and
native-born Hanoverian rank and file became the nucleus
on which the new Royal Army of Hanover was built up.
The fact that the aliens had been discharged in 1814 was
the cause of all the K.G.L. battalions appearing at
Waterloo in the following year with very small effectives,
in no case reaching 500 of all ranks.

Another foreign corps which served under Wellington
from the end of 1810 till 1814 had an origin and a history
much resembling that of the German Legion. This was
the Brunswick Oels Jägers, whose history starts from
1809. The hard-fighting Frederick William, Duke of
Brunswick, the nephew of George III., had made a gallant
diversion in Northern Germany during the Wagram Campaign. At the head of a small body of adventurers, he had
thrown himself into the middle of Jerome Bonaparte's
Kingdom of Westphalia, and had stirred up an insurrection
there, particularly in his own old hereditary states. He
was joined by several thousands of patriotic volunteers,
and inflicted a series of small defeats on the Westphalians.
But surrounded in the end by overwhelming numbers of
enemies, he cut his way to the sea, and embarked the
remnants of his followers aboard English ships at Brake
on the Frisian coast. The British Government at once
offered to take the refugees into its service, and from them
organized the Brunswick Oels Jäger and Hussar regiments,
whose black uniform reproduced that of the duke's old troops.

The kernel of this corps was originally excellent—the
officers were North-Germans, largely Prussians, who had
risked their lives by joining an insurrection contrary to
the orders of their sovereign, and could never return to
their homes: while the rank and file had been patriotic
volunteers. But, like the German Legion, the Brunswick
regiment could find no more recruits of this sort when it
had left Germany, and soon had to depend for the continuance of its existence on the men in the English prison
camps, who could be induced to buy a release from confine-
ment by enlisting in the British service. It is clear that
the German Legion got the best of these turncoats, and
that the worst fell to the lot of the Brunswick corps. Not
only Germans but Poles, Swiss, Danes, Dutch, and Croats
were drafted into it. They were a motley crew, much
given to desertion—on several occasions large parties went
off together. One great court-martial in 1811 sat on ten
Brunswick Oels deserters in a body, and ordered four to be
shot and the rest to be flogged. Such men had all the
vices of the mercenary, though in time of battle they
displayed many of the virtues. Their officers had a hard
task to keep them together, and they could never be trusted
at the outposts. But the regiment was full of good shots
and bold adventurers, and furnished several of the detached
rifle companies with which Wellington strengthened the
light infantry of his brigades.

There was, however, one foreign regiment which was
even more tiresome to manage than the Black Brunswickers.
This was the *Chasseurs Britanniques*, a corps formed early
in the Revolutionary War from French royalists, and taken
into the British Service in 1801. It was recruited entirely
from deserters of all sorts when it came out to Portugal in
the spring of 1811. At absconding it was far worse than the
Brunswickers—the latter were raised from many races, but
at least they were not born Frenchmen as were the most
important section of the Chasseurs. A glance down the
names of the rank and file of the corps seems to show that

after Frenchmen the next most important section were Italians, and that there were a few Poles and some Swiss, the latter supplying the men with Teutonic names. It seems to have been the working rule with the officers who accepted volunteers from the prison-camps to draft French and Italians into the Chasseurs, while Germans of all sorts went into the Legion or the Brunswick Corps, and Swiss partly into the Chasseurs, partly into Watteville's old Swiss regiment: Poles and Croats went anywhere. Now a German prisoner who volunteered into the British service might do so from patriotic motives, and make an excellent soldier. A Swiss or an Italian or an Illyrian could not be very heavily blamed for desertion—he had been conscribed, and sent to fight for Napoleon, in a quarrrel that was not his own. But the French deserter was no longer an old royalist, like the *emigré* soldiers of 1794, but one of two things. Either he was a man who enlisted in the Chasseurs simply to get a chance of deserting back to his own friends, or else he was a *mauvais sujet*, a man without patriotic feeling or morality, who was ready to fight against his own country-men for pay or plunder. Both classes were amply repre-sented : the former fled back to the French ranks when they could, often taking valuable information with them. The latter were the worst class of mercenaries, since they had no inspiring cause to keep them true to their colours, while individually they were for the most part bad characters who had been the curse of their regiments while in the French service.

The unenviable task of keeping together this body of deserters and adventurers fell to a body of officers who were almost without exception furious French royalists, the second generation of the *emigrés*. They looked upon the war with Bonaparte as a family feud, in which they fought under any colours (many of their kin were in the Russian or the Austrian, or the Spanish service) in order to avenge the death of Louis XVI., the atrocities of the Terror, or the Massacres of Quiberon. With old loyalty to the Bourbons, and personal hatred for the new French *régime* as their inspiration, they were fierce and desperate fighters. They kept the miscellaneous horde committed to their charge under an iron discipline, and used the lash freely. All that their personal courage could accomplish was done, to make the Chasseurs an efficient fighting force. But they could not stop desertion, nor frequent misconduct. The most astonishing court-martial in the war was that held on October 5, 1812, upon no less than 18 Chasseurs who had deserted in a body, two corporals and 16 men, of whom all but two bore Italian names.* This was only the largest case of a constant series of defections. The regiment melted away whenever it came near the French lines, and Wellington had a standing order that it must never be trusted with the outposts. Yet as a fighting body it had no bad record—as witness Fuentes de Oñoro and many other fields. This was the work of the zealous service of its officers—and was indeed a wonderful *tour de force*. The material with which they had to work was detestable.

These were the only foreign corps, strictly speaking, in Wellington's army, but there were two more units which had a large, indeed a preponderating, German element in them, though they were numbered in the British line. These were the 5/60th, the rifle battalion of the " Royal Americans," and the 97th, a single-battalion corps which started its existence as Stuart's " Minorca Regiment," but got a place in the British line in 1804 as the " Queen's Germans." Neither of these battalions were purely German either in officers or men : of the 5/60th the disembarkation roll on its original landing in Portugal shows eighteen officers with German and ten with British names.† The colonel, De Rottenbourg, was a foreigner, but the second in command,

---

* The other two names are one Swiss the other Croatian.
† Names such as Davy, Woodgate, Galiffe, Andrews, McKenzie, Holmes, Linstow, Wynne, Joyce, Gilbert are unmistakably British. See Colonel Rigaud's *History of the* 5/60th, Appendix i.

Davy, an Englishman. The British element was not proportionally so strong in the rank and file at the commencement of the war, but was apparently increasing as it went on. English and Irish recruits were drafted in, in order that such a fine corps might not be spoilt with the bad class of German recruit such as was alone procurable in 1812 or 1813. When the corps returned from the Peninsula in 1814 it had only nine officers with German names and twelve with British, and I fancy the balance in the rank and file between the nationalities had changed in the same way. When amalgamated with the 1/60th, after the end of the war it had certainly 400 British to something under 300 Germans in its ranks.

This was a most distinguished corps : the green-coated rifle companies which it supplied to many brigades of the Peninsular Army were universally praised for their cool courage and admirable marksmanship. The battalion had very few deserters save for one period in 1808–9, when it had received a batch of recruits from Junot's Army of Portugal, who proved unsatisfactory. It would be an absolute insult to the 5/60th to class them with the Brunswickers or the Chasseurs Britanniques.

The 97th being a single-battalion corps, with nothing to maintain it but a depôt which could only collect German recruits in the same fashion as the K.G.L., wasted down to a very small remnant after two years of war, and was sent back to England in 1811, with a handsome epitaph of praise by Wellington. It never got to the front again, remained at home on a very weak establishment, and was disbanded at the end of the war. Like the 5/60th it was not wholly German ; among the officers we find individuals with British names like Carter, Biscoe, Wilson, Lyon. Its colonel and one of its two majors were English, and there was a proportion of non-Germans among its rank and file. Its Peninsular record if short was distinguished.

It remains to speak about the Portuguese, who formed

about two-fifths of Wellington's fighting force. We have already had occasion to speak of the way in which they were distributed among the British troops, when dealing with the character of Beresford,* and the composition of the Peninsular divisions.† But the inner mechanism of the Portuguese army remains to be detailed. It consisted in 1809 of twenty-four regiments of infantry of the line, each of two battalions, save the 21st which had been cut up at Soult's storm of Oporto in March, and only mustered one.‡ There were also six light infantry battalions of caçadores, all raised in 1808–9, and twelve weak regiments of horse. The artillery, divided into four local regiments of unequal strength (those of Lisbon, Oporto, Elvas, and Algarve), supplied nine or ten field batteries, and a number of garrison companies which manned the guns of Elvas, Almeida, Abrantes, Peniche, and many other minor fortresses. There was in addition an abnormal corps, the Loyal Lusitanian Legion, raised by Sir Robert Wilson at Oporto in 1808, which furnished three battalions of light infantry, a squadron of horse and an incomplete battery. This legion, which had done very good service in 1809–10, was absorbed into the regular army in 1811, its three battalions becoming the 7th, 8th, and 9th caçadores. At the same time Wellington ordered the raising of three new light battalions bearing the numbers 10, 11, and 12.

The establishment of a Portuguese two-battalion line regiment was nominally 1540 men, that of a caçador battalion 770 men : they were each divided into six strong companies. The cavalry regiments, with a nominal effective of 590 men, seldom showed 300 apiece in the field. The infantry corps, with the conscription to keep their ranks full, could from 1809 onward generally take the field with over 1200 of all ranks, not including men in hospital or detached, and very seldom shrank as low as 1000. The caçador battalions were generally somewhat weaker in proportion

* See p. 120.   † See pp. 168–9.
‡ This corps only raised its second battalion in 1811.

to their nominal effective, rarely showing more than 500
men in line.

The organization of the Portuguese Army was made on
a strictly local basis, each of the twenty-four line regiments
having its proper recruiting district. Two corps were
furnished by the province of Algarve, five by the Alemtejo,
four by Lisbon city and its surrounding district, three by
the rest of Portuguese Estremadura, four by the Beira,
four by Oporto and the Entre-Douro-e-Minho, and two by
Tras-os-Montes.* Some of the recruiting-districts being
less populous than others, had a greater difficulty in keeping
up their territorial regiments. This was especially the case
with the five corps of the Alemtejo, where the waste bears
a greater proportion to the inhabited land than in other
provinces of Portugal.

The caçador battalions were mainly raised in the better
peopled north, which supplied not only the three (Nos. 7,
8, 9), formed from the Lusitanian Legion (all raised in and
about Oporto), but also numbers 3, 4, 6, and after 1811 the
additional numbers 10, 11, 12. The southern provinces
only provided numbers 1, 2, 5. These brown and dark
green battalions, whose sombre colours contrasted strongly
with the bright blue and white of the Portuguese line,†
supplied, along with the green British riflemen, the main
skirmishing line of Wellington's army. Eight of the
twelve were raised and commanded by British officers, only
the remaining four by Portuguese colonels.

Portugal is not a country abounding in horses, and
of the twelve dragoon regiments of which its cavalry

* Algarve, Nos. 2 (Lagos) and 14 (Tavira). Alemtejo, Nos.
5 and 17 (1st and 2nd of Elvas), 8 (Evora), 20 (Campomayor), 22
(Serpa). Lisbon, Nos. 1, 4, 10, 16. Estremadura, No. 7 (Setubal),
19 (Cascaes), 11 (Peniche). Beira, Nos. 3 and 15 (raised in the
Lamego district), 11 and 23 (1st and 2nd of Almeida). Oporto
region, Nos. 6 and 18 (1st and 2nd of Oporto), 9 (Viana), 21
(Valença). Tras-os-Montes, Nos. 12 (Chaves), and 24 (Braganza).

† The three Lusitanian battalions wore a uniform of ivy-green,
the nine others a dark brown dress. The cut of both was fashioned
in imitation of that of the British Rifle Brigade.

consisted, three (Nos. 2, 3, 12) were never put into the field
at all, but utilized as dismounted troops in garrison duty.
Of the other nine corps several were mere fragments, and
none ever took anything like its establishment of 500 sabres
to the front. Three hundred was as much as was usually
shown : in the 1811 campaign the two regiments which
Wellington used in the Fuentes de Oñoro campaign had
not 450 mounted men between them.

Beresford's conversion of the disorganized and depleted
army of which he took the command in 1809 into a serviceable and well-disciplined force was a remarkable achievement
He found it in a chaotic state—Junot had disbanded the
whole, save a few battalions which he sent to France to
serve Napoleon. The regiments had collected again as
best they could, but the cadres were incomplete, and the
corps of officers left much to be desired. The Portuguese
army before 1808 had all the typical faults of an army of
the *ancien régime* which had rusted in a long period of peace.
It was full of old or incapable officers put into place by court
intrigues or family influence. Promotion was irregular and
perfectly arbitrary ; the lower commissioned ranks of the
regiments were choked with officers whose want of education
and military knowledge made them unfit for higher posts.
They had often grown grey as lieutenants, and were perfectly useless in a crisis. The pay was very low, and the
temptation to make up for the want of it by petty jobbing
and embezzlement too strong.

When Beresford took command, in the early spring of
1809, he had found about 30,000 regular troops in arms
on an establishment which ought to have shown nearly
60,000. The deficiency in mere numbers could be remedied
by a stringent use of the conscription : but the deficiencies
of organization could not. Beresford complained that
" Long habits of disregard of duty, and consequent laziness,
made it not only difficult but almost impossible to induce
many senior officers to enter into any regular and continued
attention to the duties of their situations, and neither

reward nor punishment would induce them to bear up
against the fatigue." * In the lower ranks there was a
good deal of zeal, there being great numbers of young
officers from the higher classes, who had just accepted
commissions from patriotic motives; but there was also a
heavy dead-weight of old and slack officers, and an appalling
want of professional knowledge.

Beresford made it a condition of accepting his post that
he should be allowed a free hand to retain, dismiss, or
promote, and should be permitted to introduce a certain
amount of British officers into the army. The Regency
granted his request, of necessity and not with enthusiasm.
He then proceeded to use his permission with great energy.
A vast number of old officers, both in the higher and lower
ranks, were put on half pay : only a minority of the colonels
and generals were retained on active service. All the
regiments which had been cursed with notoriously inefficient
commanders were placed in charge of British officers, of
whom four or five were drafted into every unit. Beresford's
system was that " since national feeling required management," and "he must humour and satisfy the pride of the
nation," a sufficient number of the higher places must be
left to natives, but each must have British officers either
immediately over or immediately under him. Where a
Portuguese general commanded a brigade, it was managed
that the colonels of his two regiments should both be
English. Where there was a Portuguese colonel, his senior
major was English; where an English colonel, his senior
major was Portuguese. In addition there were two, three,
or four British captains in each regiment, but hardly any
subalterns. For, to encourage good officers to volunteer
into the Portuguese service, it was provided that every
one doing so should receive a step in promotion, lieutenants
becoming captains, and captains majors. This system
seems to have worked well, though friction was bound to
occur, since the blow to Portuguese national pride, when

* Beresford to Wellington, *Supplementary Dispatches*, vi. p. 774.

so many high posts were given to foreigners, was a heavy one.

Yet according to those who had the working of the newly organized army in their hands, the effect was very satisfactory. "The Portuguese captains are piqued into activity and attention, when they see their companies excelled in efficiency by those under English, and do from emulation what a sense of duty would never, perhaps, bring them to. There are a variety of oblique means and by-paths by which the parts of a Portuguese corps are constantly, and almost insensibly, tending to return to their old habits, to which they are so much attached. To nip this tendency, from time to time, in the bud, it is necessary to be aware of it : without the constant surveillance of English subordinate officers (who ever mingling with the mass of the men cannot but be aware of what is going on) the commanding officer can rarely be warned in time." * D'Urban, the author of this memorandum, adds that one of his great difficulties was to secure that the junior officers of the old noble families were kept up to their work. " Even supposing a sufficient energy of character in a native officer, he does not, and will not, unless he be a *fidalgo* himself, exercise coercive or strong measures to oblige one of that class to do his duty. He is aware that by doing so he will make a powerful enemy, and all the habits of thought in which he has been educated inspire him with such a dread of this, that no sense of duty will urge him to encounter it. Whenever a regiment is commanded by a non-*fidalgo* it never fails to suffer extremely : the noblemen are permitted to do as they please, and set a very bad example." The only remedy was to see that any regiment where the *fidalgos* were numerous had an English colonel.

Such were the difficulties under which Beresford and the body of picked British officers whom he selected as

---

* From a memorandum by Benjamin D'Urban, Beresford's Quartermaster-General, or rather Chief of the Staff, in the unpublished D'Urban papers.

his subordinates built up the army, which by 1811 was fit to take its place in battle line along with its allies, and in 1812–14 did some of the most brilliant service of the Peninsular War. Some of the exploits of the Portuguese brigades hardly obtain in Napier's history the prominence that is their due. While he acknowledges the good service of the Light Division caçadores at Bussaco and elsewhere, there is scarcely praise enough given to Harvey's brigade at Albuera, who received and repulsed *in line* the charge of Latour-Maubourg's dragoons, a feat of which any British troops would have been proud. And the desperate resistance for many hours of Ashworth's Portuguese at St. Pierre near Bayonne is hardly noticed with sufficient gratitude— forming the centre of Hill's thin line, pressed upon by overwhelming numbers, and with both flanks turned from time to time, they fought out a whole long morning of battle, and never gave way an inch, though their line was reduced to a thin chain of skirmishers scattered along a hedge and a coppice. The advance of the 13th and 24th Portuguese at the storm of St. Sebastian, across a ford 200 yards wide and waist-deep, swept by artillery fire from end to end, does however receive from Napier its due meed of admiration. This was a great achievement—every wounded man was doomed to drowning: on the other side was the blazing breach, where the British assault had come to a dead stop after dreadful slaughter, but the Portuguese regiments won their way over the deadly water, and took their share in the final assault with unflinching courage.

On the whole, the caçador battalions had the finest record in the Portuguese Army, the cavalry the least satisfactory. Some good work is recorded of them, *e.g.* the charge of Madden's squadrons saved the whole of La Romana's army at the combat of Fuente del Maestre in 1810, and that of D'Urban's brigade gave efficient help to Pakenham's great flank attack at Salamanca in 1812. But there were some "untoward incidents," such as the general bolt at the battle of the Gebora, and the panic at the combat of Majadahonda, just before Wellington's entry into Madrid. Of the last D'Urban writes,* " My poor fellows are still a most daily and uncertain sort of fighting people. At Salamanca they followed me into the enemy's ranks like British dragoons ; yesterday they were so far from doing their duty that in the first charge they just went far enough to land me in the enemy's ranks. In the second, which (having got them rallied) I rashly attempted, I could not get them within 20 yards of the enemy—they left me alone, and vanished before the French helmets like leaves before the autumn wind. They require a little incentive of shouts, and the inspiring cheers of a British line advancing near them. I am afraid they will never be quite *safe* by themselves, or in silence." These are bitter words, but the record of Majadahonda is not a creditable one.

Of the Portuguese militia and the irregular levies of the Ordenança it is not necessary to speak here at length. They formed part of Wellington's tools for carrying on the war, but not of his army. For, excepting in the Lines of Torres Vedras, he never put the militia side by side with the regulars, but always left them out in the open country, to watch frontiers or harass French lines of communication. They were under strict orders not to fight—orders which enterprising officers like Silveira and Trant sometimes disobeyed, to their own sorrow. Their duty was to screen the country-side against small French detachments, to make the movement of the enemy save in large bodies impossible, to capture convoys, or to cut off stragglers. Their most brilliant exploit was the capture of Masséna's hospitals at Coimbra in 1810. More could not be expected from levies only intermittently under arms, not furnished with proper uniforms, and officered by civilians, or by the inefficients weeded out of the regular army. They were a valuable asset in Wellington's hands, but not a real fighting

* From a letter to his friend, J. Wilson, in the unpublished D'Urban Correspondence.

force. Even far on in the war, so late as 1812, whole brigades of them broke up in panic in face of a very small force of cavalry—as at the unhappy combat of Guarda, where Trant and Wilson tried to do too much with these amateurs.

As to the ordenança or *levée en masse*, it had not even the organization of the militia, and was largely armed with pikes for want of muskets. Its only duty was to infest the countryside and prevent the enemy from foraging. The French shot them as " brigands " whenever caught; it was their natural practice to retaliate by making away with all stragglers and marauders who fell into their hands. Wellington offered a bounty for prisoners, but it was not very often asked for, or paid.

CHAPTER XIV

DISCIPLINE AND COURT-MARTIALS

In the chapters that dealt with the officers and the men of the Peninsular Army, we have had occasion to speak of the percentage of undesirables that were to be found in every rank, and of their special weaknesses and crimes. It is necessary to explain the way in which the British military code of the day dealt with them.

For the officers there was a long gradation of punishments, ranging down from a simple reprimand to discharge from the service with ignominy. For the non-commissioned officers reduction to the ranks was the most usual chastisement inflicted ; but in cases of a particularly disgraceful sort, the lash was not infrequently allotted as an additional penalty. For the rank and file flogging was the universal panacea ; the amount of strokes might range up from a minimum twenty-five strokes—which was a mere nothing to the habitual offender, but a serious thing for the good soldier who lost much of his *morale* when once he had " gone to the halberds," even for such a light punishment. The maximum, a very unusual one, was 1200 strokes, an amount calculated to kill many men, and to permanently disable many more. But this awful tale of lashes was not very frequently awarded, being reserved for bad cases of desertion to the enemy, robbery with violence, or striking an officer, all of them offences which might have had death as their punishment. As far as I can count, 1200 lashes were only awarded nine or ten times by general court-martial during the whole six years of the war.

The hardly less severe sentence of 1000 lashes was given more frequently—over 50 cases may be reckoned up—the offences were the same as those which earned the still heavier maximum amount. During the latter years of the war, from 1811 onward, two additional forms of punishment for very serious crimes were invented. The first, mainly reserved for deserters who had not gone over to the enemy, but had simply left the colours and hidden themselves in the Peninsula, was long service in a colonial corps, such as the African or the New South Wales Regiment. The other, a much more severe sentence, was that of penal servitude, either for a term of years (seven was the usual period), or for life. The penal settlement to which the convict was sent is generally stated, and is almost invariably New South Wales. This sentence was generally awarded for cases of repeated desertion (not to the enemy) and habitual theft without violence. The moment that violence was added to robbery, the offender came within a near distance of the gallows or of the much-dreaded 1000 lashes—which often had the same meaning in the end.

It may be interesting to give some account of the various causes for which an officer might incur the heaviest penalty that could be laid on him—to be cashiered. This sentence was awarded some thirty times during the war. Twice only was it the reward of shirking or cowardice. In three or four cases it was inflicted for swindling merchants ; in as many more for embezzling public money or stores. Five or six were instances of insulting or openly disobeying a commanding officer. Three or four cashierings were the direct result of drink—the offender having been found intoxicated and incapable while on duty in a responsible position. The most repulsive case of the whole list was one where drunkenness was the indirect, but not the actual, cause of disgrace. Three young officers, at the break up of a debauch, found the corpse of a priest lying in state in a room in the quarters where two of them were lodged. They mishandled it, and cast it forth, stripping off the vestments, and breaking the candles, etc., with which it was laid out.* This disgusting freak, apparently caused by drunken resentment at finding a corpse in close proximity to their bedroom, drew down a commentary from Wellington as to the noxious effects of drink—which not only makes men incapable of performing their duty, but renders them " unaware of the nature or effect of their actions."

The remaining cases of cashiering were for such offences as public and disgraceful brawling, violently resisting arrest, and flagrant immorality.† There is just one case of dismissal from the service for tyranny—that of a colonel who habitually bullied his officers and inflicted arbitrary and illegal punishments on his men.‡ Of this I shall have to say more in its place.

All the thirty cashierings cited above are those of combatant officers. There are about an equal number of cases in which persons employed under the civil departments of the army were dismissed the service—commissaries, purveyors, surgeons, hospital mates, etc. In the commissariat department (as might have been foreseen) embezzlement was the snare to unscrupulous men, often far from the eye of their superior—it was too easy to issue false vouchers as to the number of men or horses rationed, or to make corrupt agreements with contractors or local authorities, certifying that a larger amount of food or forage had been supplied than had really been given in. Selling public mules or horses, and returning them as dead, was another profitable fraud. Two non-combatant employés of the army (a paymaster and a conductor of stores) were " broken " for absconding from the army during the battle of Talavera, and spreading false reports of disaster in the rear.

The medical staff, not nearly such frequent offenders

* General Orders, Santa Marinha, March 25, 1811.
† The case of an officer who openly cohabited with the wife of a private, and fought with and thrashed her not-unreasonably jealous husband.
‡ See General Orders, July 2, 1813.

as the commissariat staff, are occasionally dismissed the service for brawling and drunkenness, which last inevitably resulted in the neglect of the wounded on the march or in hospital.

After cashiering, the next most serious punishment inflicted on an officer was suspension from pay and rank for a term of months, six and three were the usual periods named. This might be inflicted for any one of a great variety of offences. By far the most frequent fault was neglect of details of duty, such as quitting the regiment or detachment for many hours without leave, allowing a convoy or a draft to straggle, permitting the rank and file to pull down cottages for firewood, or to waste crops, or to fell fruit trees. Sleeping away from the company, in a rather distant house or village, was another frequent misdemeanour. We may place second in the category of offences the one that may be called quarrelling with native authorities. Owing to high-handed action on the one side, and provocative sulkiness on the other, these wrangles were very common. Officers in charge of detachments fell out with a *juiz de fora* or a *corregidor*, or the governor of some petty garrison, about billets or payments due, and ended by insulting, occasionally by assaulting, him. This generally cost the offender six months' suspension, for Wellington was resolved that the officers of his army must not override lawful local authority, and sometimes, in his comments on a court-martial sentence, asks what would be thought of a lieutenant who should treat in such a fashion the mayor of an English borough, or the commandant of an English fort.

The third list of offences which were usually visited with shorter or longer " suspension " may be put together under the general head of relations of officers to each other. This includes equally oppressive or insulting acts of superiors to inferiors, and insubordinate conduct of inferiors to superiors. The latter was far the more common failing, if the statistics of court-martials may be trusted. But no

doubt allowance must be made for many cases in which a
bullied subaltern preferred to hold his tongue, rather than
to appeal against the acts or language of his captain or
colonel—the failure of his case would leave him in a very
dangerous and unpleasant position for the future. Intemperate language, or " improper " letters from inferiors
to superiors, are a not uncommon cause of court-martials.
Even colonels occasionally wrote or spoke in insubordinate
terms to generals.* But " answering back " on the part
of subalterns to captains or majors was of course far more
frequent. Wellington grew, on occasion, exceedingly
wrath at reading the reports of court-martials on petty
cases of this kind. We may give a typical comment.

" I cannot but consider the transaction which has been
the subject of this court-martial as simply a private quarrel,
it has as little connection with the public service or the
discipline and subordination of the army, as any that has
ever come under my notice. It is certainly true that the
private quarrels of officers may be proper subjects for the
investigation of a court-martial. But the complainant, in
order to obtain a decision in his favour, must come with a
fair case. He must not himself have been guilty of any
breach of the general order of the army, or of discipline.
His authority as a superior must not have been exerted
over his inferior (of whom he complains) in order to enjoy
the advantage of his own improper conduct. Above all,
he must have refrained from the use of abusive or improper
language and gestures." †

Another comment is—

" The Commander of the Forces cannot but feel that both
his time, and that of the officers composing court-martials,

* There is a long quarrel of this sort between Colonel Cochrane
of the 36th and General A. Campbell, whose original cause was in
details of mismanagement at the escape of Brennier from Almeida.
† General Orders, Lesaca, September 20, 1813. In this case a
lieutenant of the 5/60th had been condemned for violently resisting
the turning out of his horses from a stable by his senior, " using
opprobrious and disgraceful language " and threatening to strike him.

is occupied very little to the advantage of the public service, in considering the unbecoming and ungentlemanlike behaviour of officers to each other." *

The mildest form of punishment for officers was the reprimand, which varied much in shape. It might amount to no more than the publication of the fact that an officer *was* reprimanded in the General Orders, without any further publicity. Or, on the other hand, the sentence of the court-martial might be directed to be read out to his regiment, or even to his division, in the most public fashion. And to the sentence there might be added a caustic and scathing postscript by the Commander-in-Chief. Take, for example, " This person may think himself very fortunate that the sentence of the court has been so lenient. A different view of the evidence on the charge would have rendered his dismissal from the service necessary under the Articles of War. The Commander of the Forces hopes that he will take warning by what has occurred, and will in future conduct himself on all occasions as a gentleman should. This reprimand is to be read to him by the commanding officer at the station where he may happen to be, in presence of the officers and troops, paraded for that purpose." †

Reprimands were generally the punishment for the smaller derelictions of duty, such as failing to report arrival at a station, striking a soldier who was insolent instead of arresting him, brawling with a civilian or a Portuguese militia officer, or boisterous and unseemly conduct in the streets when off duty.

There was no court-martial on an officer for desertion during the whole war, and only one case of the sort in the commissioned ranks. This was that of an Irish lieutenant who passed over to the French outposts while Masséna's army was lying behind the lines of Santarem in February, 1811. He was discovered to be insane or suffering from delusions, being captured during Masséna's retreat, while

---

* General Orders, Garris, February 24, 1814.
† *Ibid.*, Freneda, February 3, 1813.

wandering in an objectless way in the rear of the enemy's march : he was sent to a mad-house.*

As to the punishments of the soldier, the heaviest was death, either by the bullets of a firing party, or by the Provost Marshal's gallows. Shooting was almost exclusively reserved for the military offence of desertion to the enemy ; but it was two or three times awarded for mutiny and striking an officer or sergeant, and once only (as far as I can make out) to a non-commissioned officer for robbing valuable stores which he had been set to guard.† It would have been more usual to hang for the latter offence, and I do not know why this particular case was punished with shooting. There seem to have been 78 men shot in all during the war, of whom 52 were British, and 26 foreigners. The disproportion, of course, is enormous, as there were some fifty or sixty British battalions in the army, and only ten foreign battalions.‡ Among the last the main body of deserters were supplied by two battalions only, the *Chasseurs Britanniques* and Brunswick Oels Jägers, both of which corps were largely recruited, as has been already explained, from Germans, Italians, Poles, and other aliens from prison camps at home. They had volunteered into the British service in order to get the chance of escape, and took it at the first opportunity. The deserters from the King's German Legion were in proportion very few. During the last two years of the war many of these foreign deserters were not shot, but given life service in a colonial corps, in places such as New South Wales, from which they could not desert again. Some others got off with a heavy sentence of flogging.

Hanging was the penalty for practically all capital offences except desertion to the enemy. It was not so frequent as shooting. The records of the General Court-Martials

* See *Wellington Dispatches*, vol. ii., pp. 330 and 369, and for his recapture Stepney's *Diary*, p. 55.

† Case of Corporal Hammond of the 87th, January 24, 1810.

‡ Viz. 5/60th, 97th, 1, 2, 5, 7 Line of the K.G.L., 1 and 2 Light K.G.L., Brunswick Oels and *Chasseurs Britanniques*.

show a total of about forty executions, and a few more were apparently carried out by the Provost Marshal on criminals caught *flagrante delicto* murdering or wounding peasants.

The punishment of hanging covered many offences. It is rather surprising to find that two men who killed their officers (one in the Buffs, one in the 42nd) were hanged rather than shot—but apparently each case was ruled to be one of private spite, and not of mutiny, and was treated as simple murder. There were six or eight instances of men who slew a comrade in the ranks, by deliberate assassination, not in a quarrel, and were hanged for it. It may be noted, however, that one private who stabbed an unfaithful wife, at the moment of detection, was found guilty of manslaughter and given one year's imprisonment only. Far the most frequent cause for the use of the gallows, however, was the killing or wounding of peasants who attempted to defend their houses or cattle from plunder. This was a crime for which Wellington seldom if ever gave pardon; he was as inflexible on the point in the hostile land of France as in the friendly Spain and Portugal. It did not matter whether the peasants were killed or not—the use of musket or bayonet against them in pursuit of plunder was the thing that mattered. There are certainly some most atrocious cases in the list, where a whole family had been murdered or left for dead. But in others, where the violence had been no more than a blow with a butt-end, or a bayonet prod in the shoulder, the offenders seem to have been unlucky in not getting off with a sound flogging. But in Wellington's code petty stealing without violence was punished with the lash, but armed robbery with death.

In an age when in England theft to the value of over forty shillings was still punishable in theory with death, (though the penalty was more often evaded than not), it is not surprising to find that some of the cases of hanging in Wellington's army were for mere stealing. But it was always for stealing on a large scale, or under aggravated

circumstances. Mere petty larceny led to the lash only.
The most notable achievement in this line was that of
two foreigners who succeeded in breaking open the commissary-general's chest and stole no less than £2000 from
it ; others were those of a soldier-servant who absconded
with his master's mule, baggage, and purse ; of a sentry
over the tent of a brigadier, who took the opportunity of
making off with the general's silver camp-equipage and
plate ; and of a man who being on treasure-escort, succeeded in opening a barrel and stealing some hundreds of
dollars from it. In two or three instances large sums of
£40 or £60, burglariously stolen from the house or tent of
an officer, a commissary, or a sutler, brought men to the
gallows. Finally, there was one case of hanging for the
crime of sodomy—which was still a capital offence in
English law for more than thirty years after the Peninsular
War ended.

There are one or two instances on record of rather surprising leniency in the sentences inflicted by court-martial
for crimes which in most other cases entailed the death-
penalty—*e.g.* plundering and wounding a peasant was on
two occasions in 1814 punished with 900 and 1000 lashes
only, and three artillerymen, who stole the watch, purse,
and papers of the Spanish General Giron, got off with
transportation to New South Wales, instead of suffering
the hanging that was usual for such a serious offence. A
dragoon convicted of rape in 1814 was lucky also in
receiving no more than a heavy flogging. No doubt there
was in such light sentences some consideration of previous
good conduct and steady service on the part of the
offenders.

We have already spoken of the penalties which came
next after death in the list—the terrible 1200 and 1000
lash awards, and of the crimes which usually earned them.
Much more frequent were the 700, 500, and 300 lash sentences, which are to be numbered by the hundred, and
were awarded, as a rule, for casual theft without violence,

making away with necessaries (*e.g.* selling blankets or
ball-cartridge to peasants), or "embargoing" carts and
oxen, *i.e.* pressing transport from the countryside without
leave, to carry baggage or knapsacks when a small party,
without an officer in charge, was on the move. Purloining
shoes or food from a convoy was another frequent offence,
worth about 500 lashes to the detected culprit. The bee-
hive stealers of the retreat from Talavera got 700 lashes
each—a heavy sentence for such a crime. The tale concerning them is too good to be omitted.

After the general order against plundering from the
peasantry was issued at Jaraicejo to the half-starved army,
Sir Arthur Wellesley, in a cross-country ride, saw a man
of the Connaught Rangers posting along as fast as his legs
could carry him, with his great coat wrapped around his
head, and a bee-hive balanced upon it, with a swarm of
furious bees buzzing around. Furious at such a flagrant
breach of orders issued only on the previous day, the
Commander-in-Chief called out to him, "Hullo, sir, where
did you get that bee-hive ? " Pat could not see his inter-
locutor, having completely shrouded his face to keep off
stings : he did not pay sufficient heed to the *tone* of the
question, which should have warned him, and answered
in a fine Milesian brogue, "Just over the hill there, and,
by Jasus, if ye don't make haste they'll be all gone." * The
blind good-nature of the reply stayed the General's anger ;
he let Pat pass, and told the story at dinner with a laugh.
But the order was no joke to the men of the 53rd caught
at the same game a few days after.† They got the nickname of the "honeysuckers" along with their flogging.

There is another tale of "embargoing" belonging to
the regimental history of the Connaught Rangers, which
may serve as a pendant to that about the bee-hives.

Early in 1812 a commissary had pressed country carts

---

* The tale comes from p. xxxi. of the Introduction to the *Collected
General Orders.*
† General Orders, September 22, 1809.

to go to the Douro, to bring back pipes of wine for the troops. On such occasions, with a hilly country and very tedious work, the men would often contrive, in spite of the vigilance of the subaltern in charge of the convoy, to let the driver escape with his bullocks for a pecuniary consideration. Other carts were then illegally pressed as substitutes. On one of these occasions a detachment of the 88th regiment was sent to St. João da Pesqueira for some wine. On their return, the commissary observed that the two fine white bullocks, which he had sent with one cart, had been exchanged for two very inferior blacks. He made his regular complaint, and the two men in charge, a corporal and private, were brought to a court-martial. On the trial everything was proved, save the act of receiving money from the driver to allow the white bullocks to escape ; and the president, on summing up the evidence of the commissary, said to the prisoners, " It is quite useless denying the fact ; it is conclusive. You started from hence with a pair of fine white bullocks, and you brought back a pair of lean blacks. What can you have to say to that ? " Private Charles Reilly, noways abashed at this, which every one thought a poser, and ready with any excuse to save himself from punishment, immediately exclaimed, " Och ! plaise your honour, and wasn't the white beasts lazy, and didn't we bate them until they were black ? " The court was not quite satisfied of the truth of this wonderful metamorphosis, and they were condemned to be punished (*see* General Order, Freneda, January 22, 1812)—the corporal to be broke and get 700 lashes, Reilly to get 500. But in consideration of the great gallantry displayed by the 88th at the storm of Ciudad Rodrigo a few days before, the culprits were in the end pardoned.

All these cases quoted are from records of general courtmartials. But of course the huge majority of floggings were inflicted by regimental courts, which had jurisdiction over all minor offences, such as drunkenness, disobedience, and petty breaches of discipline inside the regiment, but could not give the heavier sentences such as death or transportation, or the 1000 lashes.

A glance through the records of court-martials shows that some battalions gave much more than their proper percentage of criminals, some much less. Two main causes governed the divergence: the first was that some corps got more than their share of bad recruits—wild Irish or town scum; but I fancy that the character of the commanding officer was even more important than the precise proportion of undesirables drafted into the ranks. A colonel who could make himself loved as well as feared could reclaim even very unpromising recruits : a tyrant or an incapable could turn even well-disposed men into bad soldiers. It is clear that an excessively easy-going and slack commanding officer, who winked at irregularities, and discouraged zeal among his officers, ruined a battalion as surely as the most inhuman martinet. Among the court-martials of the Peninsular Army there are very few on colonels—not half a dozen. But one chances to be on a tyrant, and the other on a *fainéant*, and the evidence seems to show that the latter got his corps into quite as wretched condition as the former. Though he received over the regiment, as every one allowed, in excellent order, in a few months of slack administration and relaxed discipline, it became not only drunken and slovenly, but so slow on the march, and at the rendezvous, that the other units in the brigade had always to be waiting for it, and the brigadier complained that he could not trust it at the outposts. The officers, gradually coming to despise their colonel, treated him with contempt, and finally sent in a round-robin to the Horse Guards, accusing him not only of incapacity but of cowardice, which last, in the court-martial which followed, was held to be an unfounded charge.* The colonel, as a result of the investigation, was reprimanded, and put on half-pay; his subordinates, for grave breach of

* See the printed report of the Long *Court-Martial on Colonel Quentin*, London, 1814, p. 272.

discipline, were all drafted into other regiments, and a new body of picked officers was brought together, to reorganize a corps which was evidently in a thoroughly demoralized condition; the new-comers got the nickname of the " Elegant Extracts."

The reverse-picture, of a regiment ruined by arbitrary strictness and inhuman exaggeration of punishments, may be studied in the records of a court-martial held in the spring of 1813.* In this case a commanding officer was found guilty not only of " violent conduct " and " using intemperate and improper language to his officers, being in breach of good discipline, and unbecoming the character of an officer and a gentleman," but of inflicting corporal punishment at large without any form of trial, when there were sufficient officers present to form a proper regimental court-martial ; of disobeying the direction of the Commander-in-Chief by piling up sentences of flogging passed on men on different occasions, so as to inflict several separate punishments at the same time, and of releasing men sentenced to punishment in order to send them into action, and then returning them to arrest after the battle in order to receive their lashes. This last was specially in conflict with Wellington's orders, for he held that good conduct in action ought to work out a sentence, pronounced but not inflicted, and that no man convicted of a disgraceful offence ought to be put into line till he had expiated it by undergoing his punishment. This officer was dismissed the service, but, in consideration of a good fighting record in the past, was allowed the value of his commission as major.

One diary from the ranks, that of Donaldson of the 94th, gives a very interesting and complete picture of the fate of a battalion which, by the invaliding of its colonel, had fallen into the hands of a major who had the soul of a tyrant. This was a case of an old ranker who knew too

---

* Printed in *General Orders*, vol. v. 1813, the accused being Col. Archdall of the 1/40th.

much of soldiers' tricks, and had a sort of system of espionage through men who were prepared to act as his toadies and secret informers. " By this eaves-dropping he knew all the little circumstances which another commanding officer would have disdained to listen to, and always made a bad use of his knowledge. When he got command of the regiment he introduced flogging for every trivial offence, and in addition invented disgraceful and torturing modes of inflicting the lash. But this was not enough—he ordered that all defaulters should have a patch of black and yellow cloth sewed on to the sleeve of their jacket, and a hole cut in it for every time they were punished. The effect was soon visible : as good men were liable to be punished for the slightest fault, the barrier between them and hardened ill-doers was broken down, and those who had lost respect in their own eyes became broken-hearted and inefficient soldiers, or else grew reckless and launched out into real crime. Those who were hardened and unprincipled before, being brought by the prevalence of punishments nearer to a level with the better men, seemed to glory in misconduct. In short, all idea of honour and character was lost, and listless apathy and bad conduct became the prevailing features of the corps. Reckless punishment changed the individual's conduct in two ways—he either became broken-hearted and useless, or else shameless and hardened. . . . The real method of accomplishing the desired end of keeping good discipline, is for the officers to make themselves acquainted with the personal character and disposition of each man under their command. A commanding officer has as good a right to make himself acquainted with the disposition of his men, as the medical officer with their constitutions." * When the colonel came back from sick leave he was shocked to find the men he had been so proud of treated in this manner. His first act was to cut off the yellow badge ; his second to do away with the frequent punishments. But though the regiment was again on a

* Sergeant Donaldson's *Eventful Life of a Soldier*, pp. 145, 146.

fair footing, it was long before the effect of a few months'
ill-usage disappeared.

What certain misguided officers tried to maintain by a
reign of terror, was sought in other ways by wiser men.
It is to the Peninsular War period that we owe the first
of our " Long Service and Good Conduct " medals—all at
first regimental, and not given by the State.   Honorary
distinctions for the well-conducted man are both a more
humane and a more rational form of differentiation between
good and bad than the black and yellow badge for every
man punished for any cause, which the detestable major
quoted above tried to introduce.*   In addition some
regiments instituted a division of the men into classes, of
which the best behaved had graduated privileges and
benefits.   Any man after a certain period of certified good
conduct could be moved up into a higher class, and the
emulation not to be left among the recognized black-sheep
had a very good effect.†   But even without " classes " or
good-conduct medals, the best could be got out of any
regiment by wise and considerate conduct on the part of
the officers.   There were corps where the lash was practically
unknown,‡ and others where it had only been felt by a very
small minority of hopeless irreclaimables.

On the other hand, there is a record or two of punishments in a unit, inflicted by officers who do not seem to
have been regarded by public opinion as specially tyrannical
or heartless, which fills the reader with astonishment.   I
have analysed the list of men noted for chastisement in
one battery of artillery, where on an effective of 4 sergeants
and 136 rank and file, three of the former had been " broken,"
and 57 of the latter had received punishments varying

* There are Peninsular-period Good-Conduct medals for the
10th and 11th Hussars (starting 1812), 5th Foot (Northumberland
Fusiliers), 7th Fusiliers, 22nd, 38th, 52nd, 71st, 74th, 88th, 95th,
97th, and some other corps, not to speak of others which were medals
for special deeds of courage or for marksmanship.

† See Hope's *Memoirs of an Infantry Officer*, 1808–15, pp. 459–60.

‡ This is said to have been the case in the 1/48th when it was
under Colonel Donnellan, who fell at Talavera.

downwards from 500 lashes, in the space of twelve months (July, 1812, to July, 1813), over which the record extends. Though some of the offences were serious enough, there were others for which the use of the cat appears altogether misplaced and irrational. As an observer in another corps wrote " the frequency of flogging at one time had the effect of blinding the judgment of officers who possessed both feeling and discrimination. I have known one who shed tears when his favourite horse was injured, and next day exulted in seeing a poor wretch flogged whose offence was being late in delivering an order."

Floggings were inflicted by the drummers of the regiment, under the superintendence of the drum-major and the adjutant. The culprit was bound by his extended arms to two of three sergeants' halberds, planted in the ground in a triangle, and lashed together at the top. The strokes were inflicted at the tap of a drum beaten in slow time. Each of the wielders of the cat retired after having given twenty-five lashes. The surgeon was always present, to certify that the man's life was not in danger by the further continuance of the punishment, and the prisoner was taken down the moment that the medical man declared that he could stand no more. Often this interference saved a culprit from the end of his punishment, as if the tale was fairly complete he might never be called upon to undergo the balance. But in grave cases the prisoner was merely sent into hospital till he was sufficiently convalescent to endure the payment of the remainder of his account. Inhuman commanding officers sometimes refused to allow of any abatement, even when the crime had not been a very serious one, and insisted that the whole sentence should be executed, even if the culprit had to go twice into hospital before it was completed.

The autobiographical record of a flogging is rather rare—the diarist in the ranks was generally a steady sort of fellow, who did not get into the worst trouble. The following may serve as an example, however. It is that of

William Lawrence of the 1/40th, who in 1809 was a private, though he won his sergeant's stripes in 1813.

"I absented myself without leave from guard for twenty-four hours, and when I returned I found I was in a fine scrape, for I was immediately put in the guard-room. It was my first offence, but that did not screen me much, and I was sentenced to 400 lashes. I found the regiment assembled all ready to witness my punishment : the place chosen for it was the square of a convent. As soon as I had been brought up by the guard, the sentence of the court-martial was read over to me by the colonel, and I was told to strip, which I did firmly, and without using the help that was offered me, as I had by that time got hardened to my lot. I was then lashed to the halberds, and the colonel gave the order for the drummers to commence, each one having to give me twenty-five lashes in turn. I bore it very well until I had received 175, when I got so enraged with the pain that I began pushing the halberds, which did not stand at all firm (being planted on stones), right across the square, amid the laughter of the regiment. The colonel, I suppose thinking then that I had had sufficient, 'ordered the sulky rascal down' in those very words. Perhaps a more true word could not have been spoken, for indeed I was sulky. I did not give vent to a sound the whole time, though the blood ran down my trousers from top to bottom. I was unbound, and a corporal hove my shirt and jacket over my shoulder, and convoyed me to hospital, presenting as miserable a picture as I possibly could.

"Perhaps it was as good a thing for me as could then have happened, as it prevented me from committing greater crimes, which might at last have brought me to my ruin. But I think a good deal of that punishment might have been abandoned, with more credit to those who then ruled the army." * Yet to be absent twenty-four hours when on guard was certainly a serious crime.

* *Autobiography of Sergeant William Lawrence*, pp. 48, 49.

Lawrence got off with 175 lashes out of 400 ordered, but was in hospital nearly three weeks. But 300 or 400 lashes were often inflicted at a time, and there were men who could take them without a groan.

"Corporal punishment was going on all the year round," writes a veteran officer of the 34th,* "men were flogged for the small offences, and for the graver ones often flogged to death—the thousand lashes were often awarded by court-martial. I have seen men suffer 500 and even 700 before being 'taken down,' the blood running down into their shoes, and their backs flayed like raw red-chopped sausages. Some of them bore this awful punishment without flinching for 200 or 300 lashes, chewing a musket ball or a bit of leather to prevent or stifle the cry of agony : after that they did not seem to feel the same torture. Sometimes the head drooped over to one side, but the lashing still went on, the surgeon in attendance examining the patient from time to time to see what more he could bear. I *did* see, with horror, one prisoner receive the 700 before he was taken down. This was the sentence of a court-martial, carried into effect in the presence of the whole brigade, for an example.† We certainly had very bad characters sent out to fill the gaps in our ranks, sweepings of prisons in England and Ireland : but such punishments were inhuman, and I made up my mind that, if ever I had the chance of commanding a regiment, I would act on another principle. That time *did* come. I *did* command a gallant corps for eleven years, and I abolished the lash."

But enough of such horrors. The memory of them is a nightmare.

---

* *Rough Notes*, by Sir George Bell, i. p. 120.
† Probably the case of a private of the 34th who had struck his captain, in a rage. This flogging (1813) was the only one of such severity which occurred in the regiment while Bell was serving with it in 1812–1814.

CHAPTER XV

THE ARMY ON THE MARCH

IT is rare in Peninsular literature to find any general descriptions of the normal working of the military machine. In personal diaries or reminiscences the author takes for granted a knowledge of the daily life of the army, which was so familiar to himself, and only makes remarks or notes when something abnormal happened. Official documents, on the other hand, are nearly always concerned with changes or modifications in routine. They explain and comment upon the reasons why some particular detail of practice must be abandoned, or be more strictly enforced, but they do not give descriptive accounts of the whole system of which that detail is a part. A notion as to the methods on which Wellington's army was moved could be got together by the comparison of a great many of his " General Orders." But, fortunately, we are spared much trouble in the compilation of such a sketch by the fact that, for once, it is possible to lay one's hand on a careful detailed narrative of how the army marched. It is to be found in the anonymous introduction to the second edition of *Selected General Orders*, which Gurwood published in 1837. It was apparently not by the editor himself, as he states in his introductory note that it "was written, as a critique, at the suggestion of the author of a distinguished periodical review ; but being found too long and too professional for columns usually destined to literature or politics, it was not inserted." * Since authors do not review their own

* See footnote to p. xxv. of *Selected General Orders*.

books, it is clear that this critique was written by some
friend, not by Gurwood himself. It extends to about
thirty-seven pages, of which nine are devoted to the long
and interesting sketch of Wellington's army on the march,
which is reproduced in the following paragraphs. The author,
writing for the general public, not for the professional
public, tells us precisely what we want to know.

" The orders for movement from the Commander of the
Forces were communicated by the Quarter Master General
to the General Officers commanding divisions, who detailed
them, through their Assistant Quarter Master Generals, to
the Generals of brigades, who gave them out immediately
to the battalions of their brigades, through the Brigade
Majors. The drum, the bugle and the trumpet sounded the
preparation for the march at a certain hour, generally one
hour and a half before daylight, in order that the several
battalions might be assembled on the brigade alarm-posts,
so as to be ready to march off from the ground precisely at
daylight. It must be observed that the alarm-post is the
place of assembly in the event of alarm ; it was generally,
and should always be, the place of parade.

" It is singular to refer to these orders to see how a
division of 6000 men, and so on in any proportion, rolled
up in their blankets ' in the arms of Murphy,' were all
dressed, with blankets rolled, packed, equipped, squadded,
paraded in companies, told off in subdivisions, sections,
and sections of threes, marched by companies to the
regimental alarm-posts, and finally to that of the brigade,
formed in close columns, all by sounds as familiar to the
soldier as the clock at the Horse-Guards to a corporal of the
Blues. Guns were paraded, baggage packed and loaded,
Commissariat mules with the reserve biscuit, the Store-
keeper with the spare ammunition-bullocks placed under
charge, all assembled with the same precision and order,
ready to march off under the direction of the Assistant
Quarter Master General attached to the division or corps,
who had previously assembled the guides, whom he attached

to the column or columns directed to be marched to the
points or towns named in the Quarter Master General's
instructions.   In the mean time the formidable Provost
Marshal attached to the division made his patrols.

"The report of ' All Present ' being made in succession
by the Brigade Majors to the Assistant Adjutant General,
and by him to the General commanding the column, the
word ' By sections of threes, march,' was given, from the
right or left, as directed in the Quarter Master General's
instructions, the whole being formed either right or left in
front, according to the views of the General in command of
the army.   The advanced guard of the column was then
formed under the superintendence of the Brigade Major
of the Brigade, right or left in front.   This advanced guard
consisted of one company of varying strength.   The whole
was marched off at sloped arms, with the greatest precision
and regularity, and remained in that order until the word
' March at ease ' was given to the leading battalion, which
was successively taken up by the others in the rear.   The
women, in detached parties, either preceded the column or
followed it—none were permitted to accompany it ; they
generally remained with the baggage, excepting when their
finances enabled them to make little speculations in bread
and *comfort* in the villages or towns in the neighbourhood
of the line of march.   The Assistant Provost Marshal with
his guard and delinquents brought up the rear of the column,
followed by the rear guard, under an officer who took up
all the stragglers, whom he lodged in the main guard on his
arrival, where those who had received tickets of permission
to fall out were directed to join their corps, non-commissioned officers being in waiting to receive them.

"The first halt was generally made at the expiration of
half an hour from the departure, and afterwards once an
hour ; each halt lasted at least five minutes after the men
had piled their arms ; this might vary a little, as the
weather, distance, or other circumstances of the march
might point out.   The object of halting was for the purpose

of allowing those who had fallen out to rejoin their companies,
which, excepting in cases of sickness, usually occurred;
as a man wanting to fall out was obliged to obtain a ticket
from the officer commanding his company so to do, and to
leave his pack and his firelock to be carried by his comrades
of his section of threes; he therefore lost no time to return
to his rank, and give back his ticket. This first halt was
generally passed in eating a piece of bread or meat set aside
for the march—arranging the accoutrements, pack, haversack, and canteen, so as to sit well—in jokes about the last
night's quarters or bivouac, or in the anticipations of the
next. At the expiration of the halt the drum or bugle
sounded the 'Fall-in,' and, by word of command, the
leading battalion proceeded in the same order as in the
beginning of the march; the other battalions following in
succession, always with music; then 'March at ease' as
before; but when the word 'Attention' was given, the
whole sloped arms and marched in the same order as at a
field-day; this was always done in formations previous to
the halt.

" When the army was not near the enemy, two officers
preceded each battalion on its march, one of them twenty-
four hours before the battalion, and, on his arrival at the
station pointed out, received the necessary information
from the Assistant Quarter Master General. The other
officer marched the same day in charge of the camp-
colour men of each company, so as to arrive early, and take
over the quarters from the officer who went on the day
before.

" The Deputy Assistant Quarter Master General always
preceded these officers, to make arrangements with the
magistrates as to quarters: and the town was parcelled
out by him, in proportion to the strength of the several
battalions or corps, to their respective officers; they
divided it according to their judgment to the ten orderlies,
who chalked on the doors the letter of the company and
number of men to occupy, as also the officers' quarters,

which invariably were in the quarters of the company. The officer first marked off the quarters of the Commanding Officer, staff, orderly-room, guard-room, Quarter Master's stores, all in the most central position in the quarters of the regiment. The first officer then proceeded to the next station ; the second officer and the ten orderlies proceeded to the road by which the troops were to arrive, and accompanied them to the alarm-post fixed for them : which spot the Assistant Quarter Master General, under the direction of the General in command, had pointed out, either in front or in rear of the town. Here they halted in column, as also assembled the following morning, or at any other time that the alarm or assembly might be sounded. The brigades, the battalions, and the companies each had their respective alarm-posts or places of formation in the most central parts of their quarters. The officers commanding companies then put their men up, and made reports to the Officer Commanding as to the accommodation, or the want of it, the officers commanding battalions to those commanding brigades, and the Generals of Brigades to the General of the Division. The Assistant Quarter Master General was always ready to be appealed to, in case of a battalion being crowded, to afford further accommodation, as there was generally some building or street reserved in a central position for this purpose, or in the event of detachments of other corps arriving.

" When the column was to bivouac in huts, or, as afterwards, encamp in tents, there occurred less difficulty. On arrival on the position pointed out in the Quarter Master General's instructions, the General commanding chose what he considered the most favourable ground in accordance with needs as to front, communications with his flanks and rear, reference to wood and water, and the health of the ground, avoiding proximity to marshes, where the night damps might affect the troops. The Assistant Quarter Master General disposed of this ground to the several officers sent on in advance by the battalions for that purpose, as before described in quarters. The General then proceeded to the front, and indicated where he wished his advanced piquets to be posted, to be in communication with the outposts of the cavalry in front, or, if there were none, to cover all the approaches with detached posts and sentries, so that nothing should be able to arrive by any of them without being seen and stopped ; or if patrols or other movements of the enemy should take place, either by night or day, that the same might be made known by the chain of sentries to the detached posts and outlying piquets, and communicated to the main body, if thought necessary, by the Field Officer of the outlying piquets. Preconcerted signals of setting fire to beacons, or a certain number of musket shots fired, communicated the alarm more quickly, and allowed the troops more time to get under arms, until the precise cause of the alarm was ascertained.

" The division having arrived on its ground, the out-lying piquets were immediately marched off to take the covering of the front just described. The temporary division-hospital, and the Commissariat magazines, being pointed out to the Commanding Officers, Surgeons, and Quarter Masters, the brigades and battalions proceeded to their respective alarm-posts and ground for the encampment or bivouac, accompanied by the officers and the camp-colour men as before stated. The quarter and rear guards were then mounted, to be relieved always in two hours afterwards by fresh troops. The sentries from the quarter guards watched the communications to the front, and to the detached posts between the camp and the out-lying piquets, to communicate alarm if announced in any manner from the front.

" If the troops were to encamp, the tent mules, which always immediately followed the column, under charge of an officer, preceding all other baggage, were unloaded, and the company's tents pitched in column on the alignment given to the battalion, brigade, and division.

" If there were no tents, then the bill-hooks came

speedily into play : regular squads were formed for cutting branches, others for drawing them to the lines, and others as the architects for constructing the huts : this was an amusement more than a duty, and it was quite wonderful to see how speedily every one was under cover. It was the pride of each company that their officers' huts should be the first and the best built. The soldier became quite re-invigorated by the mere act of piling arms, getting off his accoutrements, pack, haversack, and other incumbrances, which weigh generally about sixty pounds, and set to work in right earnest at the hut-building. Although the huts were not quite so speedily erected, or pitched with the same regularity, as the tents, yet still the order and alignment were preserved when the ground permitted. This might not have been essential, yet still no opportunity should be allowed to escape in inculcating the habit of order and regularity in whatever is done by the soldier ; and, however simple the act, it should be impressed on his mind, that what is ordered is the easiest, and that what is his duty is his interest.

" The regular fatigue parties for bread, meat, and spirits were regularly told off and warned, before the companies were dismissed to pitch tents or build huts. These parties consisted generally of two or three men per company, under a corporal, for each particular article of provisions, to be ready to turn out when that article was called at the quarter guard. A company's guard or watch, of a corporal and four privates, furnishing one sentry with side arms only, always remained in the lines of the company to repeat communications and preserve order.

" The Commanding Officers made their reports through the Majors of brigade, that their respective battalions had received bread, meat, spirits, and forage, specifying the number of days for each ; that they had marched off one or more companies, of such and such strength, for the outlying piquets, to the posts directed under the orders of the Field Officer of the outlying piquets ; and that the orderlies

who had accompanied them had returned, knowing where
to find them. The outlying piquets were under the Field
Officer of the day, who again received his instructions from
the Assistant Adjutant General of the division. The
Commanding Officers at the same time reported the force
of the company or inlying piquet, which were ready to turn
out to support the outlying piquet in the event of being
required, and were under the Field Officer of the day of the
inlying piquets, and kept on their accoutrements, although
in other respects, like the remaining companies, not on duty,
and in their tents or huts. The company on inlying
piquet, as also the Field Officer of the day in charge of the
whole of the companies of the brigade, were always first
for the outlying piquet.

" All particular duties were taken by companies, under
their own officers, and not by the old way of individual
roster of so many men per company ; such were the company
for outlying piquet ; the company for inlying piquet, which
gave the quarter and rear guards within the lines ; the first
company for general fatigue, from which the Quarter
Master's fatigues were taken for ammunition, equipment,
working parties, and all other fatigues, excepting rations ;
all these duties were taken by the roster of companies.

" The issue of rations was regulated by the Quarter
Master and Commissariat, agreeably to the instructions of
the General commanding the division or brigade, communicated in orders to the battalions, and was done regi-
mentally by individuals from all the companies, and not
by the company on general fatigue. On the issue of any
article, such as bread, meat, wine, or forage, the fatigue
parties from each company, as before described, were
summoned from the quarter guard by the Quarter Master,
who called out the watch in the lines of each company ;
those previously warned for each article turned out under
their respective non-commissioned officers, and assembled
under the officer of the inlying piquet named in the orders
at the quarter guard. He then proceeded with the Quarter

Master or Quarter Master Sergeant to the place of issue ; after the delivery he returned to the quarter guard, reported to the Captain of the Day, who was the captain of the in-lying piquet, the regularity or irregularity of the particular issue under his superintendence, and then dismissed the parties under their several non-commissioned officers to their respective companies, where the delivery was imme-diately made under the orderly Officer of each company. The same routine took place when in quarters ; and, although the recapitulation may appear tedious, still the whole was performed with a celerity which leaves more time to the soldier when in camp than in any other situation.

"At an appointed hour the sick reports were gathered from the companies, and the men paraded for the inspection of the Surgeon ; he reported to the Staff Surgeon, who, in his turn, reported to the General commanding the division, sending his own report to the Inspector General of Hospitals.

"The General commanding the division made his reports to the Adjutant and Quarter Master Generals for the information of the Commander of the Forces, according to the importance of the report and the circumstances of the moment.

"When before the enemy, the issue of the provisions and the cooking were attended to with every consideration to the position of things, so that what was to be done should be done with speed as well as precaution ; for it would be bad management to throw away the soup before it was well made, or swallow it boiling hot, in case of interruption, and still worse to leave it to the enemy. All this is sufficiently dwelt upon in the Duke's 'Circular Letter,' and in the admirable orders of General Robert Craufurd, from whence the greater part of the foregoing details were learned and proved in the field.*

"The new tin camp-kettle, carried alternately by the

* These can be found in *Fitzclarence on Outpost Duty*, mentioned above, in which they were printed at full length. It is still easy to procure.

men of each squad, was a great improvement upon the old
Flanders iron cauldron, which required a whole tree, or the
half of a church door, to make it boil ; and which, being
carried on the camp-kettle mule (afterwards appropriated
to carry the tents), only arrived with the baggage. This
improvement, as the Duke truly observed in his 'October
Minute,' left much valuable time disposable for other
purposes. It is to be hoped that in any future wars some
improvement will also take place in the weight and temper
of the old bill-hook, which, in the early part of the
Peninsular War, was immoderately heavy, and had edges
which, on attempting to cut any wood not absolutely green,
bent like lead : many of the men threw these away, but the
more prudent *exchanged* them for the lighter and better
tempered bill-hook used by the Portuguese in their vine-
yards, exchange being no robbery with our fellows.

"In the camp or bivouac, in fine weather, all went on
merrily, but there came moments of which the mere
remembrance even now recalls ancient twitches of rheumatism, which the iron frame of the most hardy could not
always resist. On the night previous to General Craufurd's
affair on the Coa, on those previous to the battle of Salamanca and the battle of Waterloo, and on many other less
anxious nights, not hallowed by such recollections, deluges
of rain not only drenched the earth, but unfortunately all
that rested or tried to rest upon it ; the draining through
the hut from above by some ill-placed sticks in the roof,
like lightning conductors, conveyed the subtle fluid where
it was the least wanted ; while the floods coursing under,
drove away all possibility of sleep : repose was, of course,
out of the question, when even the worms would come out
of the earth, it being far too wet for them. 'In such a night
as this' it was weary work to await the lagging dawn with
a craving stomach ; and, worse still, to find nothing but a
bellyful of bullets for breakfast. But, on the Pyrenees, in
the more fortunate and healthy days of tents, it was not
unusual, when the mountain blast and torrents of rain

drew up the pegs of the tents, for them to fall, as nothing in nature falls, squash on the soldier, who lay enveloped and floundering in the horrible wet folds of canvas. Then nothing but the passing joke ' Boat a-hoy ! ' or the roars of laughter caused by some wag, who made this acme of misery into mirth, could re-animate to the exertion of scrambling out of these clammy winding-sheets. These are recollections, however, which, notwithstanding the sufferings in the experience of them, and their legacies of rheumatism, still afford pleasurable feelings to the old soldier, now laid up by his Christmas fireside."

To this long and lively description by an anonymous Peninsular veteran (probably from the Light Division) of the way in which Wellington's army moved, we need only add a few words by way of caution and supplement. The smoothly-working regularity which it described could not always be secured in actual practice. There were marches where the system could not be carried out, by reason of hurry, unexpected changes of direction, and the vagaries of the weather. When some sudden movement of the French forced the Duke to throw his army on a route that he had not intended to take, the elaborate provision of officers going before to act as harbingers could not be carried out. When a division halted, late at night, at some unforeseen destination, there could be neither the selection of billets, nor (in the open field) the erection of huts described above. All had to be done more or less haphazard in the dark. In hot or stormy weather stragglers were numerous, and the " ticket " routine broke down altogether. The description above will do for long orderly movements like the advance on Madrid in 1812, or the march to Vittoria, in 1813, but it fails to reproduce the impression of confusion and misery caused by the perusal of any good narrative of the Burgos retreat, or of the disorder in the hasty marches to intercept Soult on the eve of the battles of the Pyrenees. A quotation from a diarist in the ranks,* giving a picture

* Donaldson of the 94th, pp. 179–181.

of the first-named march may suffice to give the reverse of the shield.

" Retreating before the enemy at any time is a grievous business, but in such weather as that of November, 1812, it was doubly so. The rain pouring down in torrents drenched us to the skin, the road, composed of clay soil, stuck to our shoes so fast that they were torn off our feet. The nights were dismally dark, the cold winds blew in heavy gusts, and the roads became gradually worse. After marching in this state for hours, we halted in a field by the roadside, piled our arms, and were allowed to dispose of ourselves as we best could. The moon, wading through dense masses of clouds, sometimes threw a momentary gleam on the miserable beings huddled together in every variety of posture, and trying to rest or to screen themselves from the cold. Some were lying on the wet ground rolled in wetter blankets, some placed their knapsack on a stone, and sat on it, with their blankets wrapped about them, their heads resting on their knees, their teeth chattering with cold. Long before daylight we were again ordered to fall in, and proceeded on our retreat. The rain still continued to fall, the roads were now knee-deep in mud. Many men got fatigued and could not follow : the spring waggons could not hold them all; they dropped behind to fall into the hands of the French cavalry. By some mismanagement the commissary stores had been sent on ahead with the baggage, toward Rodrigo, and we were without food. The feeling of hunger was very severe : some oxen that had remained with the division were killed and served out to us, but our attempts to kindle cooking fires with wet wood were abortive. Sometimes we just managed to raise a smoke, and numbers would gather round a fire, which then would go out, in spite of their efforts.

" A savage sort of desperation took possession of our minds : those who lived on most friendly terms with each other in better times now quarrelled with each other, using the most frightful imprecations on the slightest offence.

A misanthropic spirit took possession of every breast. The streams from the hills were swollen into rivers, which we had to wade, and vast numbers fell out, among them even officers. It was piteous to see the men, who had long dragged their limbs after them with a determined spirit, finally fall down in the mud unable to proceed further. The despairing looks that they gave us, when they saw us pass on, would have pierced the heart at any other time ; but our feelings were steeled, and we had no power to assist, even had we felt the inclination.

" At last the rain somewhat abated, but the cold was excessive: at the nightly halt many men threw themselves down in the mud, praying for death to relieve them from their misery. And some prayed not in vain, for next morning, starting in the dark, we stumbled over several who had died in the night. Setting my foot inadvertently on one, I stooped down to feel, and I shall never forget the sickening thrill that went to my heart, as my hand touched his cold, clammy face. This day we halted earlier than usual, and the weather being clearer, got fires lighted ; but there was nothing to eat save acorns from a wood in which we encamped—we greedily devoured them, though they were nauseous in the extreme. Next day's sufferings were of the same nature—only more aggravated, till at last we neared Rodrigo in the dark, halted, and heard at last the well-known summons of ' Turn out for biscuit,' ring in our ears. We had got to food at last. Instead of the usual orderly division each man seized what he could get, and began to allay the dreadful gnawing pain which had tormented us for four days of unexampled cold and fatigue.

CHAPTER XVI

IMPEDIMENTA : THE BAGGAGE—LADIES AT THE FRONT

THE train of Wellington's army was very heavy. In addition to the long droves of mules and ox-waggons which carried public stores, there was a very large accumulation of private baggage. The field equipment of officers—especially of officers of the higher ranks—strikes the modern student as very heavy, and was much commented on by French observers at the time. "To look at the mass of impedimenta and camp-followers trailing behind the British," says Foy, "you would think you were beholding the army of Darius. Only when you have met them in the field do you realize that you have to do with the soldiers of Alexander." The cause of this accumulation was partly a survival of the lax customs of the eighteenth century, but it resulted still more from the character of the country over which Wellington's host moved. In the interior of Spain or Portugal absolutely nothing was to be procured. The simplest small luxuries, tea, sugar, coffee, were ungettable, save in the largest towns ; to renew clothing was equally impossible. He who required anything must carry it with him. It was not like campaigning in France, Belgium, Germany, or Italy. At the commencement of his term of command Wellington laid down the rule * that no private baggage was to be carried upon carts : "those who have baggage to carry, must be provided with mules and horses." This order is repeated again and again during later years.† A regular scale of the amount of horses and

* General Order, May 23, 1809.
† See reproofs in 1811 and 1812 in *Collected General Orders*, p. 20.

mules allowed to officers of different rank was shortly
produced. Two subalterns must share one sumpter-beast
between them, a captain was allowed a whole mule or horse,
and so on, in a mounting scale.* But as early as September
1, 1809, it would seem that a more liberal allowance was
made legal. In a " general order " of that day we get an
elaborate table of rations of forage for all ranks, from the
commander-in-chief downwards. While subalterns are
allowed one ration each, the number rises enormously for
the seniors, a captain commanding a company is set down
for five rations, a major for seven, a lieutenant-colonel in
charge of a battalion for ten, the Adjutant-General for
twenty, etc., etc. This was a far too liberal allowance for
the senior ranks, and led to an accumulation of beasts,
both riding horses and pack-mules, far surpassing what was
reasonable. To enable them to equip themselves for field
service, all officers (whether staff or regimental) when
ordered for the first time to join the army, were allowed
to draw 200 days " bât, baggage, and forage money." This
presumably would go towards the purchase of their animals.
The forage allowed was 14 lbs. of hay or straw of the
country, and 12 lbs. of oats, or 10 lbs. of barley or Indian
corn. When English hay was procurable (as at Lisbon)
only 10 lbs. of it might be issued instead of the 14 lbs. of
native stuff. On this system the captain would provide
himself with a riding horse, generally a small Portuguese
nag, and have a mule for his baggage. The subaltern
must walk if he kept a mule : but it seems that very soon
the juniors also took to riding. At any rate, lieutenants
and other juniors often appear with a riding horse. Nothing
is more common in a diary than to find, on his first arrival
in Portugal the young officer procuring himself not one but

* " Under the orders of Sir John Moore a horse or mule was
allowed to each captain of a company of infantry, and a horse or
mule in common among the subalterns. And under the orders of Sir
John Cradock, which have been the rule for this army, the
subalterns were allowed a horse or mule between them " (*General
Orders*, p. 122).

two beasts, generally a nag and a mule. Sometimes he brought out a horse of his own from England.* More usually he bought—

> "A mule for baggage, and a 'bit of blood'" †

in the horse-market at Lisbon, of which one who had been through the business writes:—

"The only convenient opportunity to make the purchase was at a sort of fair held every Tuesday in the lower part of the town. There horses, mules, and asses were bought and sold, and (as in all markets) the price chiefly depended on the demand. The Portuguese horse-dealer has all the avidity of the English jockey to pick your pocket, but is not so *au fait* at the business. At this Fair you buy or sell your animal, the bargain is struck, the money paid, and the contract is indissoluble. English guineas had no attraction: the dollar or the moidore was the medium; but since the guinea has been introduced in the payment of the army (1813) the Portuguese begin to appreciate its value. It was customary for officers who wanted cash to give their draft on some house in London; but it was purchasing money very dearly, giving at the rate of six and sixpence for a dollar that would only bring five shillings, so losing eighteen pence on every crown." ‡

Good and large Spanish mules cost as much, or almost as much, as the small horses of the country. Fifty to ninety dollars was an ordinary price. Thirty to forty-five

---

* I find, *e.g.*, in diaries, that 2nd Lieut. Hough, R.A., got "two domestics, a country horse, and a mule" immediately on landing. Geo. Simmons and Harry Smith of the 95th were certainly habitually riding when only lieutenants. So was Grattan of the 88th. Bell of the 34th being impecunious had "only half a *burro* along with another lad." Bunbury of the Buffs had half a horse and half a mule in conjunction with another subaltern. Hay of the 52nd was just in the regulation with one mule to himself, on his first campaign, but bought a Portuguese mare before he had been a year in the field.

† From that amusing piece of doggerel (strictly contemporary *The Military Adventures of Johnny Newcome.*

‡ Notes to *Johnny Newcome*, p. 30.

pounds was considered cheap for an English riding horse.*
A Portuguese nag might be bought for fifteen or twenty.

"In consequence of the difficulty of transporting
baggage," writes one of the liveliest commentators on daily
life at the front, "a regiment on active service could not
keep up a regular mess, as in England. Each officer was
obliged to manage for himself: they generally divided
themselves into mess-parties by twos and threes. This
greatly incommoded the subaltern: allowed only the
carriage of half an animal [or at the most of one] it was not
possible to admit, for the purpose of having extra eatables,
any addition to his share of baggage. The mere ration
was all that he got, with a camp-kettle for culinary purposes. Besides we must recollect the difficulty of getting
extra food, and also the want of money. So the bit of beef
and the ration of biscuit was frequent fare for perhaps
two-thirds of the officers—with the allowance of ration-rum
or wine (generally execrable stuff). The prime luxuries
were a drop of brandy and a segar. With respect to articles
of dress, the contents of a small portmanteau being all that
could be taken about, if a subaltern wore out or lost his
regimental jacket, he had to improvise a substitute, e.g. his
great coat. Waistcoats were as fancy directed, black, blue,
or green, silk or velvet."

Nevertheless, though the officer, or at least the junior
officer, thought himself much stinted in baggage, the private
mules of the regiment, and in particular those of the senior
officers, made up quite a drove—at least some thirty or
forty. In addition there were the public mules of the corps,
some thirteen in number—one for each company's camp
kettles, one for entrenching tools, one for the paymaster's
books, one for the surgeon's medical paniers. If we add
to these the private riding horses of the senior officers and

* Grattan of the 88th, selling his horse on leaving the Peninsula
at the Lisbon Horse-Fair, says that he got 125 dollars for it,
equalling at the then rate of exchange £31 5s. Boothby, R.E.,
buying a red English stallion, considers himself very lucky to get it
for 30 guineas. A donkey fetched about 15 dollars only.

such of the juniors as could afford them, there was quite a cavalcade—enough to block a road or to encumber a ford. And unfortunately the mules and horses presupposed drivers and attendants. Wellington set his face against the withdrawal from the ranks of soldier-servants to act as muleteers.* Each officer, of course, had one; but they were supposed to be available for service, and could only look to their master's business in the halts and encampments. Hence native servants had to be hired—even the poorest pair of ensigns wanted a Portuguese boy to look after their single mule. The colonel had probably three or four followers. Thus to take charge of its baggage, private and public, each battalion had a following of twenty or thirty such attendants, a few English, the large majority Spanish or Portuguese.

It cannot be denied that these fellows had a villainous reputation, and largely deserved it. Though many decent peasant lads were picked up in the countryside by the earlier comers, and made trustworthy and loyal servants, the majority were not satisfactory. The sort of followers whom the officers of a newly-landed regiment engaged at short notice upon the quays of Lisbon, when only two or three days were given them for selection, were mostly "undesirables." If there were a few among them who were merely "broken men,"—ruined peasants seeking bread at any hand that would give it,—the majority were the scum of a great harbour city, ruffians of the lowest sort. The best of the Portuguese were with the army: the net of the conscription was making wide sweeps, and few young men of the decent class escaped the line or the militia. Personal service under an English officer, who was certainly an incomprehensible foreigner, and might well be a hard and unreasonable master, was not so attractive as to draw the pick of the Portuguese working classes. It did, on the other hand, appeal to needy rascals who wanted the chance

* There are several court-martials on officers who (disregarding this order) kept a soldier-servant or bâtman out of the ranks.

of cheating an employer who knew nothing of the country, its customs, and its prices. There was splendid opportunity for embezzlement. Moreover, many looked for more lucrative, if more dangerous gains. The diaries show that a very considerable proportion of the hastily-hired muleteers and servants absconded, after a few days, with their master's mule and portmanteau, and were never seen again. Those who did not, were looking after the plunder of the battle-field, the camp, and the wayside. It was they who robbed drunken soldiers, ill-guarded commissary stores, or lonely villages. They slunk out at night to make privy plunder in the lines of the regiments in which they were not employed. On the battlefield they were ruthless strippers of the wounded—English and Portuguese no less than French —as well as of the dead. Unless report much mistreats them, they habitually knocked a wounded Frenchman on the head, if they were out of sight of the red-coats.* Considering the atrocities of which the French had been guilty in Portugal, this might pass for not unnatural retaliation; but it is certain that the British wounded were also frequently plundered, and there is more than a suspicion that they were sometimes murdered. The Spanish camp-followers passed as being even more blood-thirsty than the Portuguese. Of course it was not the officers' private employés alone who were guilty of these misdemeanours; the public muleteers of the commissariat staff, and other hangers-on of the army, had an equally bad reputation. The most daring theft of the whole war, as has been already mentioned, was done by two "authorized followers," who

---

* One officer relates that he came upon his own mule-boy, aged ten or twelve, deliberately beating out the brains of a wounded Frenchman, at Salamanca, with a large stone. Another diarist speaks of making a wounded Frenchman comfortable while he went for a surgeon, and returning to find him stabbed and stripped. A third (F. Monro, R.A.) says, "I found myself among the dead and dying, to the shame of human nature be it said, *both* stripped, some half-naked, some wholly so, and this done principally by those infernal devils in mortal shape, the cruel, cowardly Portuguese followers, unfeeling ruffians. The Portuguese pillaged and plundered *our own wounded officers* before they were dead!"

burglariously entered the house of the Commissary General in 1814, and got off with no less than £2000 in gold. They were detected, and naturally suffered the extreme punishment of the law. By their names one would seem to have been French, the other a Spaniard. There is an awful story, told in two diaries, of a camp follower who in a time of starvation sold to British soldiers as pork slices cut off a French corpse.* He got away before he could be caught and shot. But enough of these ghouls !

The followers of a British army were by no means exclusively foreign. One of the worst impediments to the free movement of the host came from the unhappy practice that then prevailed of allowing corps on foreign service to take with them a proportion of soldiers' wives—four or six per company. Forty or sixty of these women, mostly mounted on donkeys, formed the most unmanageable portion of every regimental train. They were always straggling or being left behind, because they could not keep up with the long marches that the army had often to take. Wayside tragedies of this sort are to be found recorded in almost every Peninsular memoir—often of the most harrowing sort. In especial we may mention the number of these poor women who dropped in the Corunna retreat, and died in the snow, or fell into the hands of the French. The interesting little book of a married sergeant of the 42nd, who took his wife about with him during the last three years of the war, is full of curious little shifts and anxieties that they went through.† The best description of this curious stratum of the Peninsular Army that I know is in the autobiography of Bell of the 34th.‡

" The multitude of soldiers' wives stuck to the army like bricks : averse to all military discipline, they impeded our progress at times very much, particularly in retreats. They

---

* See Ross Lewin's *With the 32nd in the Peninsular War*, p. 205.
† Sergeant Anton's *Retrospect of a Military Life*, pp. 60, 61.
‡ *Rough Notes of an Old Soldier*, vol. i. pp. 74, 75.

became the subject of a General Order, for their own special
guidance. They were under no control, and were always
first mounted up and away, blocking up narrow passes
and checking the advance of the army with their donkeys,
after repeated orders to follow in rear of their respective
corps, or their donkeys would be shot. On the retreat
from Burgos I remember Mrs. Biddy Flyn remarking, ' I
would like to see the man that wud shoot *my* donkey :
faith, I'll be too early away for any of 'em to catch me.
Will you come wid me, girls ? ' ' Aye, indeed, every one
of us.' And away they started at early dawn, cracking
their jokes about divisional orders, Wellington, commanding
officers, and their next bivouac. Alas ! the Provost Marshal
was in advance—a man in authority, and a terror to evil
doers : he was waiting a mile or two on, in a narrow turn
of the road, for the ladies, with a party all loaded. He gave
orders to shoot the first two donkeys *pour exemple*. There
was a wild, fierce and furious yell struck up, with more
weeping and lamentation than one usually hears at an
Irish funeral, with sundry prayers for the *vagabone* that had
murdered the lives of the poor darling innocent *crathers*.
' Bad luck to the ugly face of the Provost, the spy of the
camp, may he niver see home till the vultures have picked
his eyes out, the born varmint,' and so on. The victims
picked up what they could carry, and marched along with
the regiment, crying and lamenting their bitter fate. It
was wonderful what they endured—but in spite of this
warning they were foremost on the line of march next
morning again. As Mrs. Skiddy, their leader, said, ' We
must risk something to be in before the men, to have the
fire and a *dhrop* of tay ready for them after their load and
their labour : and sure if we went in the *rare* the French,
bad luck to them, would pick me up, me and my
donkey, and then Dan Skiddy would be lost entirely
without me.' "

The soldiers' wives were indeed an extraordinary community—as hard as nails, expert plunderers, furious

partisans of the supreme excellence of their own battalion, much given to fighting. Many of them were widows twice and even thrice over—for when a married man was shot, and his wife was a capable and desirable person, she would receive half a dozen proposals before her husband was forty-eight hours in his grave. And since the alternative was a hazardous voyage back to relatives in England or Ireland, who had probably broken off with the "girl who ran away with a soldier," most of the widows concluded to stop with the battalion, with a new spouse and a new name. As the war dragged on many of the men picked up Portuguese and Spanish helpmates, who joined the regimental drove, and made it strangely polyglot. At the end of the struggle in 1814 there was a most harrowing scene at Bordeaux, when the general order was issued that all these foreigners who could not prove that they had been legitimately married to soldiers, with the colonel's leave, were to be refused transport to the British Isles.* There were hundreds of them, and only in a few cases could the men find money to get them taken home in private merchantmen. The bulk marched back to the Peninsula in charge of a brigade of homeward bound Portuguese—a most melancholy and distressful assembly.†

It is extraordinary to find that a sprinkling of the officers of the Peninsular Army were unwise enough to take their wives with them to the front—thereby securing a life of wearing anxiety for both, and of dire hardship for the poor ladies. One of the best known cases was that of Hill's senior aide-de-camp, Captain Currie, whose wife I have found mentioned half a dozen times as making tea for the second division staff, and holding a little reception whenever the division was settled down for a few days. Another

* Wellington (General Order of April 26, 1814) makes the concession that colonels may permit "a few who have proved themselves useful and regular," to accompany the soldiers to whom they are attached "with a view to being ultimately married."

† For details see Donaldson's *Eventful Life of a Soldier*, pp. 231, 232.

was Mrs. Dalbiac, wife of the colonel of the 4th Dragoons, whose adventures on the field of Salamanca are mentioned by Napier.* But the best chronicle of the ups and downs of a young married couple may be found in the breezy autobiography of Sir Harry Smith, then a subaltern in the 95th Rifles. His tale is well known—he rescued a young Spanish lady among the horrors of the sack of Badajoz, married her two days later, and had her with him for the remaining three years of the war. The story of their Odyssey, as related by him, is one of the most touching narratives of loyal love, and hardship cheerfully borne, that any man can read. They lived together for forty years in storm and sunshine, and she survived to christen the town of Ladysmith by her name, while her husband was commanding the forces in South Africa. He gave his name to the sister town of Harrismith, less well remembered now than the long-besieged place with which the memory of Juana Smith is linked.

There is a sketch in Paris by the well-known artist, Colonel Lejeune, who, when a prisoner at Elvas, made a drawing of an English military family which passed him. As he describes it in his diary, "The captain rode first on a very fine horse, warding off the sun with a parasol : then came his wife very prettily dressed, with a small straw hat, riding on a mule and carrying not only a parasol, but a little black and tan dog on her knee, while she led by a cord a she-goat, to supply her with milk. Beside madame walked her Irish nurse, carrying in a green silk wrapper a baby, the hope of the family. A grenadier, the captain's servant, came behind and occasionally poked up the long-eared steed of his mistress with a staff. Last in the procession came a donkey loaded with much miscellaneous baggage, which included a tea-kettle and a cage of canaries ; it was guarded by an English servant in livery, mounted on a sturdy cob and carrying a long posting-whip, with which

* *History of the Peninsular War*, vol. iv. p. 276. Also mentioned in Tomkinson's *Diary*, p. 185.

he occasionally made the donkey mend its pace." *   If this
picture is not exaggerated, it certainly helps us to understand the strong objection which Wellington had for ladies
at the front, and all forms of impedimenta.

* *Memoirs of Lejeune*, vol. ii. p. 108. I am a little inclined to
think that this may have been the household establishment of
Hill's senior aide-de-camp, Currie, as the sight was seen by Lejeune
in the Elvas-Olivenza direction, where the 2nd division was then
quartered.

CHAPTER XVII

A NOTE ON SIEGES

EVERY one knows that the record of the Peninsular Army in the matter of sieges is not the most brilliant page in its annals. It is not to the orgies that followed the storm of Badajoz or San Sebastian that allusion is here made, but to the operations that preceded them, and to the unhappy incidents that accompanied the luckless siege of Burgos. Courage enough and to spare was lavished on those bloody leaguers ; perseverance was shown in no small measure ; and to a certain extent professional skill was not lacking. But the tale compares miserably with the great story of the triumphs of Wellington's army in the open field. Reckless bravery had to supply the place of the machinery and organization that was lacking, and too much blood was spilt, and sometimes spilt to no effect.

The responsibility for these facts is hard to distribute. As is generally the case when failures are made, it is clear that a system was to blame rather than any individual, or body of individuals. Great Britain had been at war with France for some sixteen years ; but in all her countless expeditions she had never, since 1794, been compelled to undertake regular sieges on a large scale. The battering of old-fashioned native forts in India, the blockades of Malta or Alexandria, the bombardments of Flushing or Copenhagen, need hardly be mentioned. They were not operations such as those which Wellington had to carry out in 1811 or 1812. For a long time the Peninsular War had been considered as a purely defensive affair ; it was concerned with the protection of Portugal, almost (we might say) of Lisbon, from the French invader. The home Government kept sending reinforcements to Wellington, but they were under the impression that an over-powerful combination of the enemy's forces might some day force him to re-embark. He himself regarded such a contingency as by no means impossible.

But in the spring of the year 1811 it became clear that a defensive war may have offensive episodes. After Masséna's retreat from before the Lines of Torres Vedras, Wellington had to protect the frontiers of Portugal; and to guard them efficiently he needed possession of Almeida, Ciudad Rodrigo, and Badajoz, which had all been in the hands of the allies in the summer of 1810, but were now French fortresses. To subdue these three places he required a large battering-train, properly equipped for movement, and such a thing was not at his disposition. There were a number of heavy guns mounted on the Lines of Torres Vedras, and on the ramparts of Elvas, Abrantes, and Peniche. There were also many companies of Portuguese gunners attached to those guns, and a lesser number of British companies which had been immobilized in the Lisbon lines. But heavy guns and gunners combined do not complete a battering train. An immense amount of transport was required, and in the spring of 1811 it was not at Wellington's disposition. Well-nigh every available ox-cart and mule in Portugal was already employed in carrying the provisions and baggage of the field army. And water transport, which would have been very valuable, could only be used for a few miles of the lower courses of the Tagus and Douro. To begin a regular siege of Almeida in April, 1811, was absolutely impossible, not because there were not guns or gunners in Portugal, but because there were no means of moving them at the time. Wellington did not even attempt it, contenting himself with a mere blockade. On the other flank an endeavour was made to besiege Badajoz, but this was only possible because within a few miles of that city lay the Portuguese fortress of Elvas, from whose walls was borrowed the hastily improvised and imperfect battering-train with which the Spanish stronghold was attacked.

The first two sieges of Badajoz in 1811 were lamentable failures, precisely because this haphazard battering-train was wholly inadequate for the end to which it was applied. Alexander Dickson, the zealous and capable officer placed in charge of the artillery, was set an impossible task. He had about 400 Portuguese and 120 English gunners, all equally untrained in siege duty, to work a strange collection of antiquated and unserviceable cannon. The pieces borrowed from Elvas were of irregular calibre and ancient pattern. Almost incredible as it may appear, some of these long brass 24-pounders were nearly two hundred years old—observers noted on them the arms and cyphers not only of John IV. the first king of the Braganza dynasty, but of Philip III. and Philip IV. of Spain, the contemporaries of our James I. and Charles I.*   Even the better guns were of obsolete eighteenth-century types.   No two had the same bore, nor were the shot supplied for them uniform in size ; it was necessary to cull and select a special heap of balls for each particular gun.   The whole formed, indeed, a sort of artillery museum rather than an effective battering-train.   The guns shot wildly and weakly, and their gunners were inexperienced.   No wonder that their effect was poor.

But this was not all : indeed, the inefficiency of the guns was perhaps the secondary rather than the primary cause of the failure of the two early sieges of Badajoz. More important still was it that Wellington was as weak in the engineer as in the artillery arm.   The number of trained officers of engineers with the Peninsular Army was very small—not much over thirty ; but of rank and file to serve under them there were practically none.   Of the corps called the " Royal Military Artificers," the ancestors of the " Royal Sappers and Miners," there were actually

* See Dickson Papers I., p. 448.

only thirty-four attached to the army in 1810, and it was far on in 1811 before their numbers reached a hundred. Many of them were with Wellington's field army on the distant frontier of Beira, and before Badajoz, in May, there were little more than a score. For the trench-work of the siege untrained volunteers had to be borrowed from the line battalions, and to be instructed by the engineer officers actually under the fire of the French guns. Their teachers were almost all as ignorant of practical siege operations as themselves ; the British Army, as has already been remarked, had done little work of the sort for many years.

The officers, it is true, were zealous and often clever ; the men were recklessly brave, if unpractised in the simplest elements of siegecraft. But good-will could not atone for want of experience, and it seems clear that in these early sieges the plans were often unwise, and the execution unskilful. The points of attack selected at Badajoz were the strongest and least accessible points of the fortress, not those against which the French had operated in their earlier siege in February with success. This choice had been made because the British were working " against time " ; there were French armies collecting for the relief of Badajoz, and if the leaguer took many weeks, it was certain that an overwhelming force would be brought against the besiegers and compel them to depart. Hence the engineer officers, in both the unsuccessful sieges, tried to break in at points where victory would be decisive ; they thought it would be useless to begin by capturing outworks, or by making a lodgment in the lower parts of the city, which would leave its stronger points intact and capable of further defence. They battered the high-lying fort of San Cristobal, and the citadel on its precipitous height, arguing that if they could capture either of them the whole fortress was at their mercy. Both the points assailed turned out to be too strong : the stony hill of San Cristobal proved impossible for trench work ; desperate attempts to storm the fort that crowned it, by columns advancing across the open, were beaten off with heavy loss. The castle walls, after long battering, refused to crumble into practicable breaches. Before anything decisive had been accomplished, the French armies of succour came up. Beresford beat the first at Albuera in May and renewed the siege ; the second (Soult and Marmont combined) was so strong that Wellington dared not face it, and withdrew from his abandoned trenches to within the Portuguese frontier in July.

A great change for the better in Wellington's position as regards sieges had been made by the autumn of 1811. He had at last received a number of good modern British iron guns, much superior to the old Portuguese brass 24-pounders. And with infinite trouble and delay he had at last created a battering-train that could move. This was the work of Alexander Dickson, already mentioned, who was occupied from July to November in accumulating at the obscure town of Villa da Ponte, behind Almeida, masses of waggon-transport and trains of mules and oxen, for the moving of the heavy cannon and the immense store of ammunition belonging to them. The guns were brought up the Douro to Lamego, where the river ceased to be navigable, and then dragged over the hills by oxen. Several companies of Portuguese and British gunners were attached to the park, and instructed, so far as was possible, in siege work. At the same time the military artificers—still far too few in numbers—were instructing volunteers from the line in the making of a great store of gabions, platforms, fascines, and other necessaries.

This long preparation, which was almost unsuspected by the French, because it was unostentatious and made at a great distance from the front, enabled Wellington to execute the siege of Ciudad Rodrigo in January, 1812, with unexampled rapidity and success. The fortress was not one of the first class, the garrison was rather weak, the battering-train was now ample for the task required of it, and, to the surprise and dismay of Marmont, Rodrigo fell after a siege of only twelve days at midwinter (January 7–19) long before he could collect his scattered divisions for its relief.

The third attack on Badajoz, in March–April, 1812, turned out a much less satisfactory business, though it ended in a triumphant success. Like the two sieges of the preceding year, it was conducted "against time"; Wellington being fully aware that if it went on too long the relieving armies would be upon him. The means employed were more adequate than those of 1811, though only a part of the battering-train that had subdued Ciudad Rodrigo could be brought across the hills from the distant frontier of Beira. The remainder was composed of ship-guns borrowed from Lisbon. But though the artillery was not inadequate, and the walls were thoroughly well breached, both the trench-work and the storm cost over-many lives. Indeed, the main assault on the breaches failed, and the town fell because two subsidiary attacks by escalade, one carried out by Picton, the other by General Walker with a brigade of the 5th Division, were both triumphantly successful. Wellington laid the blame of the fearful loss of life upon the fact that his engineers had no trained sappers to help them, and were unskilled in siegecraft. They had attacked a point of the defences far more promising than those battered in 1811, and had opened up immense gaps in the defences, but nevertheless he was not satisfied with their direction. In a private letter to Lord Liverpool, which is not printed in either of the two series of his dispatches, he wrote :—

"The capture of Badajoz affords as strong an instance of the gallantry of our troops as has ever been displayed. But I anxiously hope that I shall never again be the instrument of putting them to such a test as that to which they were put last night. I assure your lordship that it is quite impossible to carry fortified places by ' *vive force* ' without incurring great loss, and being exposed to the chance of failure, unless the army should be provided with a sufficient

PLATE VII.

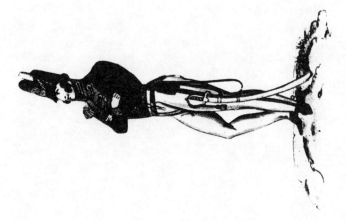

OFFICER OF FIELD ARTILLERY.
1809.

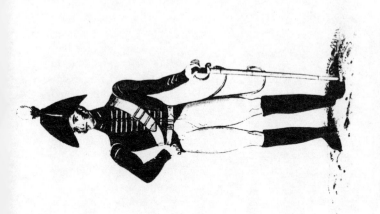

PRIVATE OF HEAVY DRAGOONS.
1809.

trained corps of sappers and miners. . . . The consequence
of being so unprovided with the people necessary to approach
a regularly fortified place are, first, that our engineers,
though well-educated and brave, have never turned their
minds to the mode of conducting a regular siege, as it is
useless to think of that which it is impossible, in our service,
to perform. They think they have done their duty when
they have constructed a battery with a secure communication to it, which can breach the place. Secondly, these
breaches have to be carried by *vive force*, at an infinite
sacrifice of officers and soldiers. . . . These great losses
could be avoided, and, in my opinion, time gained in every
siege, if we had properly trained people to carry it on.
I declare that I have never seen breaches more practicable
in themselves than the three in the walls of Badajoz, and
the fortress must have surrendered with these breaches
open, if I had been able to ' approach ' the place. But
when I had made the third breach on the evening of the 6th,
I could do no more. I was then obliged either to storm or
to give the business up, and when I ordered the assault, I
was certain that I should lose our best officers and men.
It is a cruel situation for any person to be placed in, and I
earnestly recommend to your lordship to have a corps of
sappers and miners formed without loss of time." *

The slaughter of Badajoz, then, in Wellington's estima-
tion, was due partly to the fact that the British Army,
unlike all other armies, lacked regular companies of sappers
and miners, and partly to the inexperience of the engineer
officers in carrying out the last stages of a siege—the
advance towards the glacis and the ditch by scientific
trench-work. They did not, he says, " turn their mind "
towards such operations, because they had never been
furnished with skilled workmen to carry them out. That
sappers and miners did not exist as yet was not the fault
of Wellington, nor of the ministers, but of the professional

---

* This letter, found among Lord Liverpool's papers in 1869, was
communicated to me by Mr. F. Turner of Frome.

advisers of the administration, who should long ago have pointed out that such a corps was wanted. That the Liverpool ministry was not slow to take advice was shown by the fact that they at once converted the already existing "Military Artificers" into sappers. On April 23, less than three weeks after Badajos fell, a warrant was issued for instructing the corps in military field works, and shortly after six companies were ordered to be sent to the Peninsula the moment that they should have received such training. On August 4 the name of the whole corps was changed from Royal Military Artificers to Royal Sappers and Miners.* It was not, of course, till very late in the year that the first of the new sapper companies joined Wellington, but by the next spring he had 300 trained men with him.

Meanwhile they had of course arrived too late for the siege of Burgos, the most unhappy of all Wellington's leaguers, where the whole trench-work was conducted by volunteers from the line directed by precisely eight of the old artificers—of whom one was killed and the remaining seven wounded. The story of the Burgos operations reads like an exaggerated repetition of the first siege of Badajoz. The battering-train that took Badajoz had been left behind, and to attack Burgos (whose strength was undervalued) Wellington had with him no proper means. Only eight guns were brought up—because the transport with the army could only provide a few spare teams, and the whole of Castile had been swept clear of draught-beasts. This ridiculously weak train proved wholly insufficient for the work set it. "Had there been a siege establishment with the army even moderately efficient, so as to have admitted of the performance of the rudiments of the art, the attack (even with the inadequate artillery) might have been carried through," writes the historian of the Peninsular sieges.† But there were only five engineer officers present, just eight artificers, no tools save regimental picks and shovels

---

* See Connolly's *Royal Sappers and Miners*, pp. 187–8 and 194.
† Jones, *Sieges of the Peninsula*, i. p. 169.

borrowed from line regiments, no *material* save wood requisitioned from the town of Burgos, and so little transport that the fire had sometimes to cease, to allow fresh ammunition to be brought up from the distant Madrid. Wellington ordered repeated assaults on the inadequately battered walls ; they all failed, and he finally retired after thirty-two days of open trenches, and with the loss of nearly 2000 men, from before a " bicocque," as the French called it, which could not have withstood a proper battering-train for a third of that time.

The fact is that Wellington had undervalued the strength of Burgos ; he thought it would fall easily. If he had known that it would hold out for more than a month, he could have procured more guns from the captured French arsenal at Madrid, and might have requisitioned all the beasts of the army to draw them. But by the time that it began to be seen that Burgos was not about to yield to a mere demonstration, it was too late to get up the necessary means of reducing it. Finally, the French armies mustered for its relief, and the British had to retire. It may be added that the besieging troops, thoroughly disgusted with the inadequate means used to prepare the way for them, did not act with the same energy that had been shown at Rodrigo or Badajoz. Several of the assaults were not pushed well home, and the trench-work was slack. Wellington wrote, in his General Orders for October 3, a stiff rebuke, to the effect that " the officers and soldiers of this army should know that to work during a siege is as much a part of their duty as to engage the enemy in the field ; and they may depend upon it that unless they perform the work allotted to them with due diligence, they cannot acquire the honour which their comrades have won in former sieges. . . . The Commander-in-Chief hopes he shall have no reason to complain in future." *

The leaguer of San Sebastian, the last of Wellington's sieges, bore a great likeness to the last siege

* *General Orders*, p. 275.

of Badajoz. It was conducted in a time of considerable anxiety, while the army of Soult was making vigorous and repeated efforts to frustrate it. The place was strong by nature—a towering castle with the town at its foot joined to the mainland only by a narrow sandy spit ; the defences of this isthmus were short, and reached from sea to sea : they were fully commanded by the castle behind. The first great assault (July 25, 1813) was made while the trenches were still far from the walls, and while the fire of the besieged had not been silenced. It failed with heavy loss. The second assault (August 31) was successful, but very bloody—2000 men were killed or wounded. The most authoritative commentator writes : "The operations against San Sebastian afford a most impressive lesson on the advantages of proceeding step by step, and with due attention to science and rule. The attempt there made to overcome or trample on such restrictions caused a certain operation of twenty days to extend to sixty. It bears strong testimony to the truth of the maxim laid down by Marshal Vauban : ' La précipitation dans les siéges ne hâte point la prise des places, la retarde souvent, et ensanglante toujours la scène.' " *

There can be no doubt that siege-work was loathed by the rank and file, not so much for its danger—there was never any lack of volunteers for a forlorn hope—but for its discomfort. There was a sort of underlying feeling that entrenching was not soldier's but navvy's work ; the long hiding under cover in cramped positions, which was absolutely necessary, was looked upon as a sort of skulking. With an unwise disregard for their personal safety, which had a touch of bravado and more than a touch of sulkiness in it, the men exposed themselves far more than was necessary. I fancy that on some occasions, notably at the early sieges of Badajoz and at Burgos, there was a general feeling that matters were not being scientifically or adequately conducted, and that too much was being asked of

* Jones' *Sieges of the Peninsula*, ii. p. 97.

the rank and file, when they were made to attempt a hard task without the proper means. It must have been clear to them that there were too few engineer officers, not enough artillery, and no proper provision of tools. Hence came a spirit of anger and discontent.

At Ciudad Rodrigo, and at the third and last leaguer of Badajoz, the weather was so abominable that the siege-work was long looked back on as a perfect nightmare. At Rodrigo, in the high upland of Leon, the month of January was a combination of frost and rain ; the water accumulated in the trenches and there often froze, so that the men were standing ankle-deep in a mixture of ice and mud, and since they could not move about, because of the enemy's incessant fire, suffered horribly from cold. At Badajoz there was no frost : but incessant chilling rain was almost as bad during the early weeks of the siege ; the trenches were often two feet deep in water, and the work of the spade was almost useless, since the liquid mud that was shovelled up ran away in streams out of the gabions into which it was cast, and refused to pile up into parapets for the trenches, spreading out instead into mere broad accumulations of slime, which gave no cover, and had no resisting power against the round shot of the garrison. I imagine that the desperate and dirty toil in those operations, protracted over many days of abominable discomfort as well as danger, accounts in great measure for the ferocious spirit shown by the victors both at Rodrigo and Badajoz. The men were in a blind rage at the misery which they had been enduring, and it found vent, after the storm was over, in misconduct far surpassing that which would have followed a pitched battle where the losses had been equally great. One observer writes : " The spirit of the soldiers rose to a frightful height—I say frightful because it was not of that sort which denoted exultation at the prospect of achieving an exploit which was about to hold them up to the admiration of the world ; there was a certain *something* in their bearing which told plainly that they had

suffered fatigues of which they had not complained, and
seen their comrades and officers slain around them without
repining, but that they had smarted under the one and
felt acutely for the other. They smothered both, so long
as body and mind were employed, but now, before the
storm, they had a momentary licence to think, and every
fine feeling vanished—plunder and revenge took their
place. . . . A quiet but desperate calm replaced their
usual buoyant spirits, and nothing was observable in their
manner but a tiger-like expression of anxiety to seize upon
their prey." *

Preparation for the storm affected different men in
different ways : some tried to make up old quarrels and
exchanged words of forgiveness ; a good many wrote
letters home, which were to be delivered only in the case
of their falling. " Each arranged himself for the combat in
such manner as his fancy would admit of : some by lowering
their cartridge-boxes, others by turning them to the front
for more convenient use ; others unclasped their stocks
or opened their shirt collars ; others oiled their bayonets.
Those who had them took leave of their wives and children
—an affecting sight, but not so much so as might have
been expected, because the women, from long habit, were
accustomed to such scenes of danger." †

One intelligent sergeant speaks of the moment of waiting
for the order to storm as full of a stress that nothing else
could produce : " We felt a dead weight hanging on our
minds ; had we been brought hurriedly into action, it would
have been quite different, but it is inconsistent with the
nature of man not to feel as I have described. The long
warning, the dark and silent night, the known strength
of the fortress, the imminent danger of the attack, all
conspired to produce this feeling. It was not the result of
want of courage, as was shown by the calm intrepidity of
the advance when we came in range of the French

* Grattan's *With the Connaught Rangers*, pp. 193, 194.
† Grattan, dealing with the Storm of Rodrigo, p. 145.

cannon." * That the revulsion from the long waiting took the shape of frenzied violence, when the men were at last let loose, was not unnatural. A certain amount of the horrors which took place at Badajoz and San Sebastian may be ascribed to mere frenzy, if the rest was due to more deliberate wickedness on the part of the baser spirits of the army.

* Sergeant Donaldson, p. 155 : he is speaking of the last assault on Badajoz.

CHAPTER XVIII

UNIFORMS AND WEAPONS

WITHOUT going into the niceties of regimental detail, which were fully developed by 1809, it is necessary to give a certain attention to the dress of the army—we might almost add, to its occasional want of dress.

The Peninsular Army was fortunate in having started just late enough to be rid of the worst of the unpractical clothing—the legacy of the eighteenth century—which had afflicted the troops of the earlier years of the war. The odd hat, shaped something like a civilian beaver, with a shaving-brush at the side, which had been worn in Holland and Egypt, had just been superseded for the rank and file by a light felt shako, with brass plate in front,* and a woollen tuft with the regimental colours (worn sometimes in front, sometimes at the side), and ornamented with white loops and tassels.† This was a light headdress, compared with what had gone before, and no less with the heavy, bell-topped leather shakos that were to come after. Wellington protested against an early attempt to introduce these, saying that he always knew his own troops at a distance, even when great-coated, by the fact that their shakos were narrower at the crown than the base, while the French headgear was always bell-topped, swelling out from the bottom to the crown, and the distinction was useful. The

---

* Instead of the brass plate with regimental badge or number, the Light infantry and rifles had only a bugle-horn.

† Light infantry had a small green tuft on the front of the shako; regiments of the rest of the line a larger upright plume fixed on the side.

felt shako had a peak to protect the eyes from the sun, and a chin-strap. It was a serviceable head-dress, whose only fault was that, after long wear, and exposure to much rain, the felt became soft and might crease or bulge, and then dry into unsightly and lop-sided shapes.*

Down to 1811, officers of the line, except in rifle and light infantry corps, were wearing cocked hats, as had been the custom since the eighteenth century. The new clothing which came out in 1812 had shakos (of a more ornamental sort) for officers as well as men. The very sensible reason for the change was that obvious difference in dress between commissioned and non-commissioned ranks enabled the enemy's marksmen to single out the officers, and to give them more than their fair share of bullets. The discarded cocked hat had been a stupid survival—a "burlesque of a *chapeau* usually topped by some extraordinary-looking feather," says one wearer of it, while others wore it without any feather at all. The "cut-down" hat, exactly a span in height, was all the rage in the Lines of Torres Vedras during the winter of 1810–11.† The felt shako was an enormous improvement in every way. After 1811, only generals and staff officers, engineers, doctors, commissaries, and drum-majors retained the cocked hat. The last case that I remember of its being used in the line was that of Lieutenant Maguire, of the 4th, who, leading the "forlorn hope" at the storm of San Sebastian (Aug., 1813) put on a cocked hat with a white feather "to make himself conspicuous and recognizable." Clearly this headdress was by that date wholly abnormal.‡

Another evil which the Peninsular Army escaped also belonged to the head. Pigtails and hair-powder went out in 1808—an immense boon. As one who had endured them

* Cooke of the 43rd says (in his *Narrative of Events in the South of France*, p. 67) that "distorted by alternate rain and sunshine, as well as by having served as pillows and nightcaps, our caps had assumed the most monstrous and grotesque shapes."

† Grattan's *Connaught Rangers*, p. 51.

‡ See Leslie's edition of the *Dickson Papers*, ii. p. 994.

says, "The hair required to be soaped, floured, and frizzed, in order to be tortured into an uncouth shape, which gave the man acute pain, and robbed him of the power of turning his head easily, unless he brought his body round with it." The grease and flour matted the hair, and inclined towards all sorts of scalp diseases. Wellington, who had discarded hair-powder and dressing long before most officers,* must have been rejoiced when it became legally permissible to do without it in all ranks. It was not every one who agreed with him—a few old-fashioned men still wore pigtails and powder for some time in the Peninsula ; but they soon died out.

In the same year, 1808, that these monstrosities vanished another affliction was relieved. Trousers of a blue-grey colour were substituted for breeches and gaiters, as service dress, just before the first brigades sailed, in 1808. The many-buttoned gaiters to the knee had been an intolerable nuisance ; there was every temptation not to strip them off at all, when it took twelve minutes to button them up efficiently, more if they were wet through. Hence troops liable to be alarmed at any moment were tempted not to take them off at all for many days, which led to uncleanliness and diseases in the legs. Trousers were a great improvement—they were less tight, and could be easily slipped into and out of. Under the trousers short boots (often called shoes) were worn.

The coat for all ranks in the infantry was cut short in front, and had fairly small tails ; it still preserved, more or less, the late eighteenth century cut in this respect, but differed from the earlier type in having the stiff upstanding collar supported by a leather stock, an evil device which constricted the neck and tended to apoplexy. On hard service, such as storming parties, the men unbuttoned their

---

* *Memoirs of Captain Ellers*, p. 124 (dealing with the year 1800). "He never wore powder though it was the regulation to do so. His hair was cropped close. I have heard him say that hair powder was very prejudicial to the health, as impeding perspiration, and he was no doubt right."

collars and threw their stocks aside.* The most characteristic point that strikes the eye in pictures of the rank and
file of the Peninsular period is the series of white stripes
across the front of the coat, caused by the ornamental
prolongation of the button guards. Bayonet and cartouche
box were supported by the broad white leather cross-belts,
ornamented with a brass plate with the regimental badge.
The very heavy knapsack, normally of oilskin or glazed
canvas, was supported by a separate attachment of straps
passing under the arm-pits. The whole kit weighed some
sixty pounds, when the canteen and haversack are taken
into consideration. Officers had only a single leather belt
coming from the right shoulder to the left hip, to sustain the
sword, and wore their red silk sashes girt tight, in several
turns around their waists.

One of Wellington's most sensible traits was an intense
dislike of worrying officers or men about details of uniform
on active service. "Provided we brought our men into the
field well appointed," says Grattan of the 88th, "with their
sixty rounds of ammunition each, he never looked to see
whether trousers were black, blue, or grey: and as to
ourselves, we might be rigged out in any colour of the rain-
bow if we fancied it. The consequence was that scarcely
any two officers were dressed alike! Some wore grey
braided coats, others brown: some again liked blue; many
(from choice, or perhaps necessity) stuck to the "old red
rag." Some wore long-skirted frock-coats, as better
protection to the loins than the orthodox regimental cut.
There are some curious records of the odd clothing in which
officers finished a campaign. One records that he did the
Burgos retreat in a garment improvised from the cassock
of a priest, slit up and cut short and furnished with buttons.
Another, a captain in the 29th, landing in Great Britain in
a braided pelisse and a fancy waistcoat with silver buttons
of Spanish filigree work, was taken for some sort of French

* See for example the description of the 43rd preparing to storm
Rodrigo, in Grattan, p. 145.

prisoner by a worthy general, who congratulated him on being allowed such freedom in the place of his captivity.* As to the men, they wore anything that could be got: a quantity of French trousers found at the capture of Madrid, in the Retiro fort, were issued to some corps. A more rough expedient was that of a colonel with a very ragged regiment in the winter of 1813–14, who allowed blankets to be cut up by the regimental tailors, to make up into trousers for such of the men as were absolutely disreputable in appearance. The battalion made some sensation when it marched into Mont-de-Marsan a few days later.†

All this did not vex Wellington's soul in the least—from Picton's tall beaver hat to the blanket-trousers, he saw and disregarded every detail. He himself was the most simply dressed man in the army, with his small cocked hat unornamented save by the English and Portuguese cockades, his blue, tight-buttoned frock-coat, and the short cloak with cape which has been immortalized by a score of statues and pictures.

I ought, perhaps, to mention that the winter-clothing for the infantry was a grey pepper-and-salt coloured great coat, of very thick cloth, with a cape reaching down to nearly the elbow, so as to give a double thickness of protection to the shoulders. There was also an oilskin cover to the felt shako, which could not always be easily adjusted to the latter, when it had got distorted in shape from much wear. Plate No. 8 gives an illustration of this costume.

When the Peninsular Army first started on its campaigns, the heavy dragoons were the most archaic-looking corps in it, for they still wore the broad and heavy cocked hats, which had prevailed in all armies during the middle years of George III., and jack boots up to the knee. This headgear, which after a single campaign in the tropical rains of the Peninsula always became sodden and shapeless, and hung down limply towards the shoulders, was fortunately

* *Military Journal of Col. Leslie of Balquhain*, p. 229.
† *Memoirs of Captain Cooke*, ii. p. 76.

PLATE VIII.

Sᴇʀɢᴇᴀɴᴛ ᴀɴᴅ Pʀɪᴠᴀᴛᴇ ᴏғ Iɴғᴀɴᴛʀʏ ɪɴ Wɪɴᴛᴇʀ Mᴀʀᴄʜɪɴɢ Oʀᴅᴇʀ.
1813.

abolished by a royal warrant of August, 1812, and during the following winter many of the heavy dragoon regiments received brass helmets of a classical shape, with a crest and plume, which, though rather heavy, were an immense improvement on their former shapeless hats. At the same time they were given instead of jack-boots (which had made skirmishing on foot almost impossible) grey cloth overalls, with a broad red stripe, and short boots. This was the dress of the heavies in 1813–14 and during the Waterloo campaign.

The light dragoons had gone to the Peninsula in 1808 with the black japanned helmet with a bearskin crest along its crown, which had been in use since the time of the American War. With it they wore blue coats with white froggings, and buckskin breeches with Hessian boots. The general effect was handsome, and in use the dress was not unpractical. General Foy mentions it with approval in his history. The French outposts were much puzzled when, at the commencement of the Vittoria campaign, the English vedettes and outposts appeared in a new uniform, which was introduced for light cavalry at the same time as the changes made for heavy cavalry just mentioned above. It was at first suspected that new regiments had been joining from England. The 1813 uniform substituted, for the black helmet with fur, a shako with a small upright plume, slightly bell-topped in shape, and with ornamental cord and tassels. It looks as if it had been suggested by the head-dress of the French *chasseurs à cheval*, and was much too like it to please Wellington. At the same time the blue jacket barred with white lace was changed for a blue coat, with a very broad plastron of the colour of the regimental facings in front, extending from collar to waist, and the buckskin breeches were replaced by tight-fitting breeches of webbing. This was the Waterloo uniform of all light dragoon regiments.

The large majority of the British cavalry regiments in the Peninsula were light dragoons : for the first three years of

Wellington's command there were only three heavy dragoon regiments in the field, and no British hussars. Of the latter, a new introduction in the national Army, there was one brigade present in 1808 during Sir John Moore's operations,* and the same regiments came out in 1813, to see the last year of the war.† During the greater part of Wellington's campaigns the only hussars present with the army were Hanoverians, the very efficient corps belonging to the King's German Legion. The fantastic hussar uniform of the period, a development from a much simpler Hungarian original, is well known. Over a jacket fitting tight to the body, was worn the furred and braided pelisse, which was usually not completely put on, but flung back, so as to hang over the left shoulder. It flapped behind, and was a hindrance rather than a covering. On the legs long overalls were worn. The head-dress was a very large fur cap, or, as it would have been called later, a busby. I find very severe criticisms on this head-gear. One officer says, "These flimsy, muff-like appendages encumber the heads of our soldiers. The awkward cap, being constructed partly of pasteboard, soaks up a great quantity of wet during the violent rains of this country, and so becomes unbearably heavy and disagreeable, while it affords no protection to the wearer. At all times it can be cut down to his skull with the greatest ease." ‡ The cause of its adoption seems to have been rather the Prince Regent's eye for splendour in military costume than anything else. For strength and protection, no less than comfort, the light helmet of the early dragoons was universally preferred by critics. Later improvements made the busby more solid and less heavy, but in 1808 it was evidently a most unsatisfactory head-dress.

Artillery uniform may be described in a few words.

* 7th, 10th, 15th Hussars. The 18th were still called Light Dragoons in 1808.

† In April, 1813, 10th, 15th, 18th Hussars, the 7th Hussars followed in September of the same year.

‡ Ker-Porter's *Letters from Portugal and Spain*, 1808–9, p. 219.

That of the horse artillery was a close copy of that of the
original light dragoon—black japanned helmet with fur
crest, blue jacket laced with gold (instead of the dragoon's
silver) and buckskin breeches. Field artillery, on the other
hand, were clothed almost exactly like infantry of the line,
save that their coats were blue instead of red. Their tall
felt shako and tuft, trousers, and coat with white stripes,
were exactly similar to those of the linesmen. Engineer
officers wore a dress like that of line officers before the
shako came in, having a cocked hat down to the end of the
war, and trousers. The rank and file of that department—
Royal Military Artificers down to 1812,* Royal Sappers and
Miners after—had shako and blue coat down to 1813, but
changed the latter for a red coat, like that of the line, in the
last-named year. It was braided with yellow across the
front instead of white, the only practical difference in
appearance.

Doctors and commissaries down to the end of the war
were wearing a cocked hat, like that of a general or a staff
officer. Hence some queer mistakes, when these peaceful
gentlemen were mistaken for combatant officers, the colour
of their plume, the one differentiating point, failing to be
observed in the dusk or in dirty weather. It is said that
some young commissaries were prone to pass themselves
off as staff officers on the Spanish and Portuguese peasantry,
and even on local authorities. A ridiculous anecdote is
told of Doctor Maurice Quill, the surgeon of the Connaught
Rangers, who was the best-known humorist in the army.†
A general, who caught a glimpse of his cocked hat behind a

---

* The Royal Military Artificers were wearing in the early years
of the century a most extraordinary and ugly head-dress, a tall
top-hat with brim, looking more fit for civilian's wear, and having
nothing military about it except the " shaving-brush " stuck at one
side. It was not unlike, however, the hat of the Marines. For
illustration of it see the plates in Connolly's *History of the Royal
Sappers and Miners*, vol. i.

† There are plenty of stories about him in Grattan's *With the
Connaught Rangers*. This one, however, is from Bell's *Rough Notes*,
i. 95.

hedge, took him for a staff-officer shirking, and hunted him for some time from cover to cover, the doctor meanwhile shouting back to him, " I'm off ; seen plenty of fighting for one day." It was only when he took refuge with his mules and medical panniers, that his irate pursuer discovered that he was not a combatant officer. Other wearers of the cocked hat were the drum-majors of the line, who are said to have had much adulation paid to them by the country-folk, because of their enormous gold-laced head-dress and lavish display of braiding, which caused them to be taken for brigadiers at the least.

The most distinctive infantry uniform in the whole army was that of the rifle battalions, whose sombre colours contrasted in the most marked way with the red of the British and the bright blue of the Portuguese line. The dress of the 5/60th and the two light battalions of the K.G.L. differed from that of the three battalions of the 95th, in that while both wore the dark rifle-green jacket, the three German units had grey-blue trousers not unlike those of the line, while the latter were in green from head to foot. All wore black shakos of a high shape, like those of other regiments, and with a green tuft or ball at the front. The accoutrements were all black, in order to avoid the showing of light or shining points on the body, when the men were dispersed in skirmishing. In the head-dress of the officers there was a certain variety, the 5/60th and 1st Light battalion K.G.L. having a tall shako similar to that of their rank and file, while those of the 95th and the 2nd Light battalion K.G.L. had a peculiar head-dress, something like that of an eighteenth-century hussar ; it was a tall, narrow cap, much adorned with diagonal twists of braid, and destitute of the peak to shade the eyes which formed part of the normal shako ; it had a green tuft at the front. The 95th officers for some time wore over their tight jackets a black furred and braided pelisse, in the hussar style—surely a most absurd and inconvenient encumbrance for men who were continually scrambling through hedges, and working among thick brushwood. When thrown back, as it seems generally to have been, it must have caught in every possible twig. The officers' jackets were distinguished from the plain-breasted coat of the rank and file by having a great quantity of narrow braiding across the front : they all wore falling " wings," instead of epaulettes. The Portuguese caçador uniform, save that it was brown and not bottle-green, reproduced very closely the cut and form of that of the 5/60th.

A word as to armament naturally follows on notes concerning uniform. The weapon that mainly won the Peninsular victories was the " Tower musket " of the line battalions, the famous " Brown Bess." It was a heavy flint-lock, fitted with a pan, and weighing about nine pounds. Its effective range was about 300 yards, but no accurate shooting could be relied upon at any range over 100. Indeed, the man who could hit an individual at that distance must not only have been a good shot, but have possessed a firelock of over average quality. Compared with the rifle, already a weapon of precision, it was but a haphazard sort of arm. At any distance over the 100 yards the firing-line relied upon the general effect of the volley that it gave, rather than on the shooting of each man. Nevertheless, the British musket was decidedly a stronger, better made and more accurate weapon than that used by Continental armies, and was much preferred by our Spanish and Portuguese allies to those of their own manufacture. Its calibre was sixteen, its missile was a round leaden bullet (a little heavier than the French ball, whose weight was twenty to the pound), and made up with a stout paper cartridge, of which each man normally carried sixty. In order to secure certain ignition by the snapping of the flint, the butt-end of the cartridge had to be torn open by the teeth, before it was placed in the musket barrel, and a splash of powder had to be thrown into the pan to catch the spark and communicate it to the cartridge. The latter was driven down the barrel by an iron ramrod. Raw recruits in a moment of excitement, firing too fast, are said not infrequently to have forgotten to withdraw the ramrod after loading, and to have shot it away—which left them helpless.

The greatest hindrance to good musketry was wet. Long-continued rain might penetrate the cartouch box, and damp all the powder, so that every cartridge missed fire. But even a sudden heavy squall might drench the particular cartridge that was being handled, and make its torn-open end incapable of ignition. Or it might wash the priming-powder out of the pan, or damp it into a paste, so that it could not catch fire. In either case, infantry fighting in a rainstorm could not count on any certain fire-effect ; not one shot in four might go off, and troops surprised in open order by cavalry would be very helpless. Their only chance of salvation would be to form square and trust to the defensive power of the bayonet. The latter weapon was long, triangular, and rather heavy ; its weight did not make accurate shooting easier, when it was fixed.

There was a somewhat lighter and more carefully made weapon for light infantry battalions, called the light infantry musket ; except that its sights were more accurately seen to, and that its length was slightly less, I cannot find that it greatly differed from the normal Tower musket. The same may be said of the *fusil*, which was an older type of light musket, which had originally given its name to all fusiliers. The last time that it occurs in use, was when it was given during the latter years of the war to the experimental home battalions, into which boys under seventeen were drafted. To suit their short stature and younger muscles, fusils instead of full-sized muskets were served out to them.

Quite different from all muskets were the rifles served out to the 5/60th, the 95th, and the Light Battalions of the K.G.L. The pattern was called the Baker rifle, from its inventor. It was a short weapon with a barrel two and a half feet long, furnished with seven grooves within, which made a quarter-turn in the length of the barrel. Its calibre was a twenty bore, and it was stiff to load. An interesting letter from one of the majors of the 5/60th to the assistant adjutant-general at Cork, written just before the battalion sailed for Portugal, makes a demand for 450 small mallets, for the purpose of forcing the bullet down the barrel. " They should be made of hard wood, with a handle about six inches long, pierced with a hole at the extremity for fastening a string to it." Major Davy adds that " the instrument is absolutely necessary," and a mallet for every two men should be furnished.* These tools, however, were in use only for a few months, were found not indispensable, and were finally withdrawn. But to ram the ball home was always a hard job, owing to the grooves. The rifleman carried no bayonet, his second weapon being a very short and curved sword, more useful for wood-chopping than anything else.

Sergeants were not yet armed like the rank and file, except in the rifle battalions, where they carried the normal weapon of the " Baker " type. In the Guards and line alike they had a seven-foot spear with a cross-piece below the head, to prevent over-penetration after a thrust.† The names of pike and halberd were used for it indifferently, though the former was the more correct, the original halberd having been a cut-and-thrust weapon with an edge as well as a point. In addition, the sergeant carried a brass-hilted sword at his left side. I have never found any mention of its being used, the halberd being always the preferred weapon—though in action a sergeant often picked up a dead man's musket, and joined in the firing.‡ But,

---

* See the letter in General Rigaud's *History of the 5/60th*.
† See illustration in Plate 8 of a sergeant and private in winter marching order.
‡ There is a curious anecdote in the diary (p. 28) of Cooper of the 1/7th, of a sergeant, who, running with the point of his pike low, caught it in the ground, and fell forward on its butt-end, which went right through his body.

en revanche, I have found a confession by a newly made sergeant of his having caught it between his legs, and had a nasty fall, on his first appearance with the three stripes. The weapon was slightly curved, and meant for cutting rather than thrusting.

On the other hand, the infantry officer's sword was quite straight and rather light, a thrusting weapon essentially. There are many complaints that it was too slight for its work—*e.g.* it had no chance against a French cavalry sword, which would always batter it down, when the two clashed in stroke and parry. I have found it called a " toasting-fork," and other insulting names. Many officers provided themselves with foreign weapons of a heavier make, and better adapted for cutting ; no objection was made to this departure from the regulations. Mounted and staff officers carried a different sword—a curved broad-bladed sabre, of the type of that used by light cavalry. Rifle officers also used a curved sabre, of a rather short make, and not the straight infantry sword.

Heavy cavalry used the broad-sword with steel hilt and guard, straight and very heavy. It could be used for the thrust as well as for the cut, but it would seem that the British dragoons (unlike the French cuirassiers) always preferred the edge to the point. The sabre of the light dragoon and the hussar was a markedly curved weapon, very broad in the blade, and only suitable for the stroke, though very occasionally we hear of a thrust being made.* From the enormous proportion of wounded to killed in engagements where the French and English light cavalry met, it is clear that the sabres of both sides were better suited to maim than to slay. The thrusting sword of the cuirassiers had a much more terrible reputation.

The rank and file of the Royal Sappers and Miners carried muskets and bayonets like infantry of the line, and

---

* *E.g.* there is a Waterloo story of a sergeant of the 18th Hussars, who long engaged with a cuirassier, and unable to get at him because of his armour and helm, ultimately killed him with a thrust in the mouth. I should not like to take it as certain.

their sergeants the regulation halberd. Horse artillery gunners had sabres of the light dragoon type; but field artillery only very short curved swords, like those of the rifle regiments. The drivers, who were organized as a separate corps, had no weapons at all, in order that their attention might not be distracted from their horses. This seems to have been a very doubtful expedient, leaving them absolutely helpless if attacked by hostile cavalry. It may have originated from the fact that the driver, far into the eighteenth century, had not been a soldier at all, but a " waggoner," a civilian without uniform or arms. It was only in 1794 that the corps of Artillery Drivers was formed upon this rather unpromising basis.

This is probably the place in which mention should be made of the standards under which the army fought.* Cavalry banners or *guidons* had just gone out—if used at all in the Peninsular War, it was only in its first year. Reports from the later years show that all regiments had left them either at their depôt in England, or in some cases at Lisbon. But infantry regiments, with few exceptions, took their flags into the field, as was the custom with their successors down to the last generation. It was only in the 1880's that they finally ceased to be displayed on active service. The Rifles, always destined to fight in extended order, never had colours, and the regimental annals of some Light Infantry corps (the 68th and 71st) show that for similar reasons they had left their standards behind in England. But this was not the case with all Light Infantry : the famous 43rd and 52nd carried them all through the war.

Of the two battalion colours the one or " King's Colour " was a large Union Jack, with the regiment's number on a shield or medallion, often encompassed with a wreath, and sometimes also with the badge of the corps, when such existed. The second or Regimental colour was of the same hue as the facings of the corps, and only had a small Union

---

* For ample details about them see Mr. Milne's *Standards and Colours of the Army*, Leeds, 1893.

Jack in its upper left corner, next the pole. On the plain silk of the main surface of the flag were disposed the number of the regiment, often in a wreath, and its badges and battle-honours, where such existed. Since facings had many hues, the main effect of the two flags was very different, the large Union Jack of the King's Colour being contrasted with the yellow, green, crimson, or white, etc., of the Regimental Colour.

The colours were borne in battle by the two junior ensigns of the battalion, who had assigned to them for protection several colour-sergeants. It was the duty of these non-commissioned officers to take charge of the flag if the proper bearer were slain or hurt, and in many battles both colours came out of action in sergeants' hands. The post of colour-sergeant was honourable but dangerous, for the enemy's fire always beat hardest about the standards in the centre of the battalion line. Sergeant Lawrence of the 40th notes, in his simple diary, that at Waterloo he was ordered to the colours late in the day, because both the ensigns and all the colour-sergeants had been hit. "Though used to warfare as any one, this was a job I did not like. There had been before me that day *fourteen* sergeants already killed or wounded around them, and both staff and colours were almost cut to pieces." * This was, of course, very exceptional carnage; but the posts of junior ensign and colour-sergeant were always exceptionally dangerous.

* *Autobiography of Sergt. Lawrence, p. 239.*

CHAPTER XIX

THE COMMISSARIAT

As I have already had occasion to remark, when dealing with the central organization of the Peninsular Army, of all the departments which had their representatives at Head Quarters that which was under the charge of the Commissary-General was the most important.* It is not too much to say that, when the long struggle began, the whole future of the war depended on whether the hastily organized and inexperienced Commissariat Department could enable Wellington to keep his army concentrated, and to move it freely in any direction.

Spain and Portugal are countries where large armies cannot be supplied from local resources, except in a few favoured districts. Any attempt to live on requisitions was bound to fail in the end, as the French realized to their sorrow, after a long series of endeavours to subsist on the countryside in the Peninsula, as they were wont to do in Italy or Germany. Wellington from the first forbade it, and resolved that the main dependence of the troops must be on regular stores brought up from the base of operations. Requisitions were only a subsidiary resource ; they could only be made by an authorized commissary, and must be paid for at once. It was his misfortune that specie was often not forthcoming, and the payments had to be made by Treasury orders or other paper, which the peasants who received them found hard to negotiate. But payment in some form was always made.

* See above, p. 161.

At the best, requisitions were only a secondary aid, and the army relied for the staple of its provisions on the stores which the Commissary-General had to bring up from Lisbon or other bases. This was a hard task for him, when it is remembered that the cross roads of the Peninsula were mule-tracks, on which heavy wheeled traffic could not pass ; and that the army was often operating at a distance of 150 or 200 miles from its depôts. Moreover, in 1809, the staff of the Commissariat had all their work to learn— no British army for many years had been operating in heavy force, and for many months on end, in a thinly-peopled continental theatre of war. The difficulty of bringing up the daily food of the troops seemed at first almost insuperable. At the end of the Talavera campaign the men were well-nigh famished, simply because the attempt had been made to depend more than was possible on local resources, to the neglect of convoys from the base. After this experience Wellington resolved that he must live on his own stores, and this principle was remembered throughout the war. Hence the work which fell on the commissariat, in collecting and forwarding food from the base, was appalling. Most of it had to be conveyed by brigades of pack-mules with native drivers, who were hard to manage and prone to desert. The rest came up on country carts—ox-waggons for the most part. That mistakes and delays occurred, that a brigade or a division was occasionally foodless for several days, and forced to halt in the middle of a critical operation, is not wonderful. But on the whole after much toil and trouble the Commissariat succeeded in doing its duty, and the length of time for which the British army could keep concentrated was the envy of the French, who, living on the country, were forced to disperse whenever they had exhausted the resources of the particular region in which they were massed.

All through the years 1811–12 the central fact in the Peninsula was that if the French armies of Portugal and the North concentrated at Salamanca and Rodrigo, or if (on the other hand) those of Portugal and Andalusia joined on the Guadiana, in the region of Badajoz and Merida, the Anglo-Portuguese were too weak to face the combination. Wellington had to abandon the offensive, and to seek refuge behind the Portuguese frontier. But when he did so, as in June, 1811, and again in September of the same year, he knew that the overwhelming force in front of him could not hold itself together for more than a very short period of days. Troops brought from enormous distances, and destitute of any adequate magazines or transport, could not live on the countryside for more than a limited period. They were forced to disperse, in order to feed, and so the threatening conjunction passed, and, when the enemy had drawn apart, the allied army could once more abandon the defensive, and take some positive project in hand. The same was the case in the late autumn of 1812, during the retreat from Burgos. Wellington on this occasion had on his hands the largest combination of French troops that he ever faced—the four armies of Portugal, the North, the Centre, and Andalusia were all pressing in upon him. It would have been hopeless to fight, and so retreat was persevered in, so long as the enemy continued to advance. But Wellington knew that the progress of the 100,000 men now pursuing him must inevitably come to an end, for in their rapid course they could bring no stores with them, and in the war-worn country between Salamanca and Rodrigo they could obtain nothing. Where his own troops, though returning toward their base and their depôts, were hard put to it for food, the French must be suffering even more. Wherefore he retreated, waiting for the inevitable moment when the pursuit could be no longer urged. It mattered little whether it stopped at Salamanca, or a march or so beyond (as actually happened), or whether it might get a little further, as far as the Portuguese frontier. It was certain, within a period of days, that it must break down. Meanwhile he himself was retreating on to his stores, and could depend upon them;

after Rodrigo the men were getting their full rations once more.

The duties of the Commissariat may be divided into three sections—the first was the accumulation of great masses of sea-borne stores at the regular bases, the second was the distribution of those stores to the troops at the front by an immense system of convoys ; the third and subsidiary task was the supplementing of these base-stores, by getting in what could be procured in the country-side, where the army was operating ; for, of course, every *fanega* or *arroba* of food-stuff that could be obtained at the front was helpful. It had not to be carried far, it saved convoy work, and it kept the magazines at the base from depletion. Yet, as has been already remarked, what was got in the countryside was always considered as the secondary source of supply ; the main reliance was on the food-ships, which poured into the base-depôt of Lisbon corn sought in the ends of the earth, not only in such limited parts of Europe as could be drawn upon in the days of the Continental System, but in Morocco, Turkey in Asia, and America.

The maintenance of the Peninsular War entirely depended on the naval predominance of Great Britain in all seas ; if the army of Wellington had not been able to draw freely on distant resources, his position would have been little better than that of his French enemies. Hence it was that, in one sense, the greatest danger that he ever incurred was the American War of 1812–14, which turned loose upon his line of communications, in the North Atlantic, many scores of active and enterprising privateers, who did considerable damage among British shipping, and for the first time since the war began made the high seas insecure. But fortunately the commencement of the American War exactly synchronized with the beginnings of Napoleon's downfall, and the struggle in Europe took a favourable turn just as the peril on the ocean came into being. If the American War had broken out in 1809 or

1810, its significance would have been of much higher importance.

The normal condition of commissariat affairs, during the first four years of the war, was that there were daily arriving in Lisbon supplies of all sorts, not only food but clothing, munitions, and weapons of war, which had to be got forward to the army as quickly as possible. In the winter of 1810-11, when the whole of Wellington's host lay concentrated behind (or later in advance of) the Lines of Torres Vedras, the problem was comparatively simple, as the troops were close to the magazines. But during the remainder of the years 1811-12 the British divisions were lying out at a long distance from their base— by Guarda, Celorico, or Almeida, or at other times near Merida, Campo Mayor, and Portalegre. In 1812, when Wellington moved forward as far as Madrid and Burgos, the *étapes* between the base-depôt and the field army were even greater.

The Commissary-General's duty was to see that convoys went regularly to the front, so that the army should never be in want. This was a hard business, since most of the transfer had to be made on mule-back, and the rest on ox-carts of primitive construction and small capacity. Water-carriage, which would have been comparatively easy, could only be utilized on a limited scale ; the Tagus was generally navigable to Abrantes, and when the main army lay in Estremadura this was a great help, since stores could be sent up in barges and country boats with much greater ease than by road. When unloaded at Abrantes, they had a comparatively short way to travel by mule or ox-cart to Elvas or Portalegre. But usually only Hill's two divisions were on the Estremadura frontier, and Wellington with the main force was somewhere on the Beira frontier, in the direction of Guarda, Sabugal, and the Coa. These regions are 150 miles or more from Lisbon, and the roads beyond Coimbra on the one side and Abrantes on the other were rugged and badly kept. It was a trying business to secure the constant and regular forwarding of the necessary convoys, and the return of beasts and men to the base, when they had discharged their loads at the front. A very slight assistance was got by using the river Douro as a secondary line of water carriage—but it was only navigable to Peso da Regoa near Lamego, which was so far from the Spanish frontier and the normal haunts of the army, that little was gained by sending stores to Oporto as a secondary base-depôt. In 1811 the only large consignments forwarded on that line were the heavy guns and ammunition, which were to form the siege-train that Dickson was organizing at Villa da Ponte,* which is comparatively close to Lamego, though the roads between them were very bad. In 1812 Wellington's engineers, by patient blasting and dredging in the bed of the Douro, made it navigable as far as Castro de Alva, which is forty miles up-stream from Peso da Regoa, and lies not very remote from Almeida. After this the Douro became much more useful as a line of supply, and it was largely used for the forwarding of stores before the opening of the campaign of 1813. But, just as it had become available on a better scale, Wellington started the great march to Vittoria, whose success took him away for ever from Portugal. During the last year of the war he suddenly shifted his base, and made Santander and Passages his base-ports, so that the improvements in the navigation of the Douro were of no further utility.

A great part of the Commissary-General's staff was kept at Lisbon, with a smaller sub-department at Oporto, receiving from the ships, unloading, and repacking the immense stores that came to hand. Every few days a convoy started for the front, under the charge of a deputy-assistant-commissary, a commissariat-clerk, or some such subordinate. It would usually consist of a large drove of hired mules, worked by their owners, who generally acted together in gangs or parties, of which a *capataz* or head-driver,

* See p. 283.

chosen by his comrades, was the chief, and did the bargaining with the commissariat authorities. The convoy would probably consist of the gangs of five or six *capatazes*, and would number many scores of beasts. The commissariat official in charge had no easy task to make the muleteers get over a reasonable daily stretch of road, and to see that they did not steal from the stores, or (what was not unknown when there was a quarrel) desert with their beasts. When the convoy got near the front, it would have to be provided with an escort—generally convalescents returning to their battalions, or drafts newly arrived from England. But the escorts were not an unmixed blessing—they were terribly prone to picking and stealing from the stores, with or without the connivance of the muleteers. There was nearly always trouble when a small escort, without an officer to keep his men in hand, got associated with a mule train. Brawls were frequent between soldiers and muleteers, and the assistant-commissary in charge could not get the escort to obey him : sergeants looked upon him as a mere civilian in a cocked hat, who might be contemned. Nor was the task of such an unfortunate official rendered more easy by the fact that, owing to sheer want of hard cash, his muleteers were usually in long arrears of their stipulated hire. They naturally grumbled, but on the whole stuck to their service far more faithfully than might have been expected ; there were times when the whole body of them were many months unpaid, yet only a small proportion disappeared. Probably the fact that they escaped the conscription by being registered as authorized followers of the British Army had something to do with their long-suffering : probably also real patriotism had some share, for they all loyally hated the French, and were prone to cut the throats of their wounded, if left unshepherded near a recent battlefield.

Wheeled transport was much less satisfactory than the mule trains for continuous movement. The British waggons sent out to the Peninsula turned out to be quite useless for Portuguese by-roads. Wellington finally gave up all idea of relying on them for load-carrying, and mainly employed them for his sick and wounded. A few of the "spring waggons" (as they were called to distinguish them from the springless Portuguese vehicles) * were attached to each brigade for the carriage of invalids, and the "Royal Waggon Train" in the later years of the war seem to have been almost treated as an ambulance corps. Certainly the army would have been in evil case, if it had been forced to rely on them for the moving of its food.

Such stores as did move upon wheels, and not upon mule-back, were carried on Portuguese ox-waggons, to which Wellington was compelled to have recourse for want of better vehicles. These were very primitive structures —the sides of wicker work, the wheels made of solid circles of wood bounded with iron, turning axle and all, which made their grinding noise almost intolerable. The excruciating thrills caused to the ear by a train of such carts are mentioned with disgust by nearly every Peninsular diarist, on his first introduction to life at the front. The only advantages of ox-waggons were that they were light, easy to repair, and specially built for the bad roads of the country : moreover, every peasant knew how to drive them, or to mend them at a pinch. Their weak points were that they were intolerably slow—two miles an hour was a full allowance— and that they were too small to carry much. However, they had to serve for want of better vehicles—and the army could not have lived without their service. An immense amount of them were employed, some on regular and long terms of hire, as part of the permanent transport of the army, others in a more temporary way, by requisition from the district. These last were always difficult to manage ; professional muleteers would not object to travel, but impressed peasants loathed quitting their own district, fearing that they might be taken far afield—perhaps into Spain—before they were released. They were always

* Cf. p. 266 above.

trying to abscond with their precious bullocks, abandoning the comparatively worthless cart and its stores. A picture of the sort may be taken from Hennegan's lively narrative of a march in 1809, when he had to take an unwilling train of " embargoed " waggoners across the mountains of Northern Beira.

" Leaning on their oxen at nightfall, they contemplated in mute dismay on one side the gigantic hill which they had just descended, on the other the roaring torrent of the Douro, which in its impetuous course seemed to threaten with destruction the temerity that would brave its power. The *Santa Marias* of some were answered by the more emphatic *carajos!* of others, but even these died away before the necessities of the moment, and unyoking the oxen, to afford them the shelter of trees, the drivers spread their large cloaks in the empty sheds, and soon in sleep seemed to forget their disappointment. The poor men, taken from their homes for our service, risked in the loss of their oxen the only means of support for themselves and families.

" The following morning, however, presented a curious scene. There stood the wains, securely packed, but looking as if the earth had brought them forth, for no vestige remained of the means by which they had been brought to this lonely spot. The rumour of the proximity of the French had determined these Portuguese on sacrificing the wains, if only they could ensure the preservation of themselves and oxen. What was now to be done ? " *

As a matter of fact, the non-plussed guardian of the deserted convoy had to remain motionless for many days, risking the possible arrival of the French, till at last he procured boats on the Douro, and shipped his charge down to Oporto. Hennegan's peasants got away with their bullocks—he and his escort were evidently sleepy and unsuspecting : but often a good watch was kept on the teams, and sentries placed over them. In such cases, if the weather

* Hennegan's *Seven Years' Campaigning*, i. p. 52.

was bad, or the French too near, the drivers would often sacrifice even their loved beasts, and simply abscond themselves, abandoning their means of livelihood.

It says much for the general zeal of the Commissariat Department that, even with such difficulties about them, they usually succeeded in keeping the army supplied with food. Occasionally there were desperate pinches of starvation, when the army had out-marched its convoys—this, for example, happened on the Alva in March, 1811, when half of the army, in pursuit of Masséna, had to stop dead for several days, because their rapid advance had left the slow-moving mule-trains several marches behind. To press the French would have been most profitable—but if the troops had gone on, through the depopulated land before them, they must have perished of sheer want of food, and Wellington reluctantly halted till the convoys began to creep up to the front. Another period of empty stomachs was seen during the retreat from Burgos, from the opposite cause; forced to give back, Wellington started his train betimes for Ciudad Rodrigo, to get it out of the proximity of the oncoming enemy. Hence the rear divisions, who had to contain the pursuers and to move slowly, found, when they had eaten what was in their haversacks, that the convoys were all several marches ahead of them. They suffered terribly, and existed for two days mainly on acorns gleaned from the oak forests through which they were marching. But mischances of this kind were hardly to be considered the fault of the Commissariat.

As I have already had to remark, the duty of the officers of this department did not merely consist in bringing up and distributing food forwarded from the base depôts. They had also, as a subsidiary resource, to get what they could out of the countryside. A good assistant-commissary was always casting about, through the villages on either side of the route of the brigade to which he was attached, to find cattle and corn that could be bought. He was forced to pay for them, since Wellington strictly forbade requisition without value given. When the commissary had dollars the matter was not so difficult, for the peasants were generally ready to sell. But when, as often happened, the military chest was empty, and payment could only be made in *vales*—paper promises to pay—the inhabitants soon got wind of the fact, hid their corn, and drove their oxen up into the hills. The good commissary was the man, who, under such circumstances could discover and get possession of the concealed resources of the land. But even if there was money in hand, a good deal of tact was required in dealing with the natives, and it was not every one who would make the most of his store of cash or paper for the benefit of his brigade. How the ingenious man worked may be gathered from a note of Commissary Dallas, dealing with a march through Northern Andalusia in 1812.*

" Having made careful inquiries as to the properties and farms which lay at some distance to right or left of the road, our plan was to seek them, not saying a word of our object, but simply asking hospitality. I do not remember that this was ever refused, though sometimes we failed to gain anything. We usually began with talking of the horrors of the French, of which Andres had many terrible chapters to relate. This led to expressions of grief as to the ravages that the enemy had made : by degrees we introduced a word of rejoicing that some people had so well known how to hide their property from such rapacious robbers. It often happened that at the word *esconder*, to hide, there were indications on the countenances of some of the party which led to further inquiries. On many occasions we drew out hints from various members of the community which enabled us to jump to conclusions, which surprised other members, as to the concealment of stores of wheat, barley, Indian corn, etc. The difficulty was to obtain access to the supplies, when we had become aware of their

* Dallas was taking care of the brigade of Skerrett, then march-ing (Oct., 1812) from Seville to Aranjuez, right across Central Spain.

existence ; but I had power to give a good price, and was armed with plenary authority of Spanish officials to say that my drafts would be honoured in due course.

" An incident or two will illustrate the manner in which we got supplies. At one distant solitary house of poor appearance Andres discovered that, while everything looked poverty-stricken about the place, there was somewhere in a thick wood a barn which contained concealed stores. I told the mistress of the house of the very high price that I would give for wheat, Indian corn, or forage. In the grey October dawn I was awoke by her husband, who told me he could supply what I wanted, if I would give a certain price, which he named. I said that I must see the supplies before I gave money. He bade me rise, and he would show me. He led me two miles to a thick wood, in which was a deep ravine ; here he brought me safely to a receptacle of much hidden store, which I took at his own price, and gave him the proper document. In one part of the Sierra Morena we heard of a considerable flock of sheep secreted in the depth of a forest. I obtained the permission of the owner to possess them for a certain price *if I could get them*, for he himself could not point out the spot where they were to be found. After gathering what information I could, I set forth in the hope of finding them, and did so by following a track of sheep till I arrived in the middle of the flock. I told the two shepherds that I had purchased them—they were doubtful and one very refractory. But at last one of them drove the sheep to the open plain outside the forest, and then disappeared among the trees with his dog, leaving me to drive the flock as I could. It was no easy task—but I got them into an enclosure a considerable way off." *

If these were the experiences of a Commissariat official who had been three years in Spain, and knew the language well, it is easy to guess how inefficient a newly landed clerk

* Autobiography of the Rev. Alexander Dallas, London, 1871, pp. 59, 60

or assistant must have been, when he was sent to sweep the countryside for what he could discover. It was a thankless task—often the seeker came back empty, to be frowned upon by his departmental chief and the brigadier. When he did discover food, it was taken for granted, and he was little thanked. The fighting men seem to have had a general prejudice against their providers—they were accused of being timid, arrogant, and selfish, and the embezzlements of certain black sheep were made to cover a general charge of dishonesty against the whole tribe, which was far from being justified. Misfeasance there certainly was, when an unscrupulous commissary credited a peasant with more *fanegas* than he had received, and divided the balance of cash with the seller. But on the whole the work was well done, despite of the many complaints of the military—from Wellington himself downwards. That the Peninsular War was successfully maintained in 1810–11–12 was surely, at bottom, the work of the much-maligned commissaries, and the motley band of ill-paid and sometimes ruffianly muleteers and waggoners, who, through a thousand difficulties,* generally got the biscuit and the rum-barrels, the droves of bullocks, and the packs of clothing and shoes, to their appointed destination.

* For the maddening delays, caused by the impossibility of finding a mule-train ready to go back to the front, a good example may be found in the autobiography of Quartermaster Surtees of the 95th, stranded at Abrantes for unending weeks in the late autumn of 1812 with the new clothing of his battalion, which (as he knew) was suffering bitterly for want of it.

CHAPTER XX

A NOTE ON THINGS SPIRITUAL

In the first chapter of this volume I had occasion to remark that Wellington's army had in its ranks a considerable sprinkling of men of religion, and that three or four of the better Peninsular memoirs were written by them. Some were Methodists, some Churchmen, so that both sides of the great spiritual movement which had started about the middle of the eighteenth century were represented in their diaries. The spiritual side of the soldier's life during the great war has had so little written about it, that a few illustrative pages on this topic must not be omitted.

We may trace the existence of the admirable class of men who have left us these memoirs to two separate causes. The one, of course, was the way in which the movement started by the Wesleys had influenced all ranks of life, from the lowest upward. Its effects had not been confined to avowed Methodists, but had led to the rise of the Evangelical party within the Church of England, which was developing very rapidly all through the days of the Great War. But I think that even if the Wesleys had never lived, there would yet have been a strong reaction in favour of godly living and the open profession of Christianity, in consequence of the blasphemous antics of the French Revolution. Nothing in that movement so disgusted Englishmen (even those of them who were not much given to practical religion) as the story of the " Goddess of Reason," enthroned on the high-altar of Notre Dame, at the time when an orgy of bloodshed was making odious the flatulent talk about humanitarianism and liberty which was the staple of Revolutionary oratory. The peculiar combination of insult to Christianity, open evil living, and wholesale judicial murder, which distinguished the time of the Terror, had an effect on observers comparable to nothing else that has been seen in modern times. Even men who had not hitherto taken their religion very seriously, began to think that a hell was logically necessary in the scheme of creation for beings like Chaumette or Hébert, Fouquier Tinville or Carrier of the *Noyades*. And, we may add, a personal devil was surely required, to account for the promptings of insane wickedness which led to the actions of such people. A tightening up of religious observances, such as the use of family prayer and regular attendance at Church, was a marked feature of the time. It required some time for the movement to spread, but its effect was soon observable. It naturally took shape in adhesion to Evangelical societies within the Church of England, or Methodist societies without it ; since these were the already existing nuclei round which those whose souls had been stirred by the horrors in France and the imminent peril of Great Britain would group themselves.

Very soon the day was over in which " enthusiasm " was the dread of all normal easy-going men. Something more than the eighteenth century religious sentimentalism, and vague spiritual philosophy, was needed for a nation which had to fight for life and empire against the French Republic and all its works. Those methods of thought were sufficiently discredited by the fact that there was a touch of Rousseau in them : it was easy to look over the Channel, and see to what a belief in some nebulous Supreme Being, and in the perfectibility and essential righteousness of mankind at large, might lead. The God of the Old Testament was a much more satisfactory object of worship to the men who had to face the Jacobin, and Calvinism has always proved a good fighting creed. If ever there was a justification for a belief that the enemy were in a condition of complete reprobation, and that to smite them was the duty of every Christian man, it was surely at this time. The conviction of the universality of sin and the natural wickedness of the human heart was the exact opposite and antidote to the optimistic philosophy of the eighteenth century, and to its belief that man is essentially a benevolent being, and that if he sometimes breaks out into deplorable violence " *tout comprendre est tout pardonner*." As a working hypothesis for an enemy of the French Revolution the Calvinistic . theory had everything in its favour.

The army, like English society in general, contained an appreciable proportion of those whom the stress and terror of the times had made anxious about their souls. Some took their religious experience quietly, and found sufficient edification in accepted forms. Many, however, filled with a fervent belief in original sin and in the blackness of their own hearts, only got comfort by " conversion " in the prevalent form of the day, and in subsequent reliance on complete Justification by Faith.

" Conversion " was frequently a matter of dire spiritual agony and wrestling, often accompanied by fits of horrible depression, which were generally fought down, but sometimes ended in religious mania. Sergeant Donaldson of the 94th, whom I have often had to quote in other chapters, tells a terrible tale from his own regiment of a man whose weak point had been a violent temper, and a tendency to use his fists. Being under strong religious emotion, and having determined never again to offend in this way, he had the misfortune to break out once more in unjustifiable blows, administered to his peasant landlord in the village of Ustaritz. Ashamed of his backsliding he fell into a fit of despair, and brooding over the text " if thy right hand offend thee, cut it off," he resolved that this was the only cure for his irascibility. Whereupon he went, and without any display of emotion or eccentricity, very quietly borrowed a felling-axe from one of the regimental pioneers, placed his right hand upon a window-sill, and cut it off with a single blow delivered very dexterously with his left. He then went and reported his act and its reason to the regimental surgeon, with great calmness and lucidity.*

Such incidents as this were rare among those who were undergoing the process of Conversion, but it was generally accompanied by long spasms of conviction of sin, when, as one memoir-writer records, " all the crimes of his life passed before him in black array, when he felt that if he could but bury himself in a cave or den of the earth, and forego all intercourse with mankind, it would be to purchase pardon and peace easily and cheaply. . . . Life was but the dreadful expectation of that fatal hour when the fiend would be commissioned to seize and carry off the guilty soul to its abode of everlasting misery." † Another diarist records that, as he went down toward the great breach of Badajoz, he was repeating to himself very forcibly, " You will be in hell before daylight " all the time, till he received a disabling wound. This rifleman, when he experienced conversion, received therewith an unexpected gift of metrical exposition. His autobiography is curiously sprinkled with his impromptu verses such as—

> " Then why let our minds be encumbered
> 'Bout what such poor worms may befall,
> When the hairs of our head are all numbered
> By Him who reigns King over all ? "

And again—

> " I shall go where duty calls me,
> Patient bearing what befalls me,
> Jesus Christ will bring me through !
> Bullets, cannon balls or death
> Cannot hurt ' the better part,'
> So I'll list to what He saith
> Till He bids me home depart." ‡

---

* See Donaldson's *Eventful Life of a Soldier*, pp. 219, 220.
† Surtees's *Twenty-five Years in the Rifle Brigade*, pp. 173, 175.
‡ From *Travels and Adventures of Bugler William Green, late of the Rifle Brigade*, Coventry, 1857—a most interesting little book.

This ecstatic confidence of the converted man is very clearly expressed in many a little book. A Guards' sergeant, whose memoirs I have had occasion to quote in earlier chapters, mentions that, all through the hard experience of his brigade at Talavera, he was comforted by the thought that, however disastrous the day was looking, "the Lord can save us now."

"Standing between the enemy and my own men, with the shot ploughing up the ground all about me, the Lord kept me from all fear, and I got back to my place in the line without injury and without agitation. Indeed, who should be so firm as the Christian soldier, who has the assurance in his breast that to depart and to be with Christ is far better than to continue toiling here below ? " * On another occasion this diarist, in a long waiting spell before a dangerous disembarkation, found Wesley's two hundred and twenty-seventh hymn running in his mind all the morning, to the inexpressible comfort of his soul during an anxious time.

This kind of comfortable ecstasy did not by any means preclude a ready and competent employment of musket and bayonet. One or two of the notable personal exploits of the Peninsular War were done by "saints." There is a special mention in several diaries, regimental and general, of John Rae, of the 71st, a well-known Methodist, who at the combat of Sobral (October 14, 1810), being the last man of the skirmishers of his battalion to retire, was beset by three French *tirailleurs*, on whom he turned, and shot one and bayoneted the other two in the twinkling of an eye. He received a medal for his conduct from his brigadier, who had been an eye-witness of the affair.†

The attitude of Wellington toward religion at large, and religious soldiers in particular, was very much what

---

* *Memoirs of John Stevenson*, 3rd Foot Guards, p. 191.

† Recorded in Tancred's *Historical Medals:* for details see Stevenson, as also the *Life of a Scottish Soldier*, which is a 71st book (p. 118).

one might have expected from his peculiar blend of personal characteristics. He was a sincere believer in Christianity as presented by the Church of England, but he had not been in the least affected by recent evangelical developments, and his belief was of a rather dry and official sort ; an officer who took to public preaching and the forming of religious societies was only two or three degrees less distasteful to him than an officer who was foul-mouthed in his language and openly contemned holy things. I fancy that the Duke would have been inclined to regard both as " ungentlemanly." Religion with him was the due recognition of the fact that man has a Creator, who has imposed upon him a code of laws and a system of morality which it is man's duty to remember, and so far as he may, to observe. He was quite ready to acknowledge that he had his own failings, but trusted that they were not unpardonable ones. The two or three Evangelical enthusiasts who had the courage to tackle him in his later days on the subject of his soul, got small profit thereby.*

It is highly to his credit that he made from 1810 onward a serious attempt to organize a system of brigade chaplaincies for his army, and to see that the men should not lack the possibility of public worship. Down to that year the chaplains' department had been much neglected: large expeditions had gone out without a single clergyman attached, and in the first Peninsular Army of 1808 there had been very few—though two of them, Ormsby and Bradford, happen to have left interesting books behind them, the latter's beautifully illustrated by sketches. Wellington complained that the provision that he found in 1809 was wholly inadequate, asked for and obtained an additional establishment, and made arrangements for regular Sunday services in each brigade.

The letter of February 6, 1811, in which he explains

* The absurd semi-religious correspondence of the Duke and 'Miss J.' in the 1840's, published some ten years back may be remembered.

his views to the Adjutant General at the Horse Guards is a very characteristic document. " The army should have the advantage of religious instruction, from a knowledge that it is the greatest support and aid to military discipline and order." But there are not enough chaplains, and those that exist are not always " respectable." The prospects of a military chaplain are not attractive enough ; on retirement he is much worse off than he would have been " if he had followed any other line of the clerical profession besides the army." Hence few good men are obtained. For want of sufficiently numerous and influential official teachers, spontaneous religious life has broken out in the army. There are three Methodist meetings in the 1st Division alone. In the 9th regiment two officers are preaching, in despite of their colonels' dissuasions.

" The meeting of soldiers in their cantonments to sing psalms, or to hear a sermon read by one of their comrades is, in the abstract, perfectly innocent ; it is a better way of spending their time than many others to which they are addicted. But it may become otherwise, and yet, till the abuse has made some progress, their commanding officer would have no knowledge of it, nor could he interfere."

Official religious instruction is the proper remedy. A " respectable clergyman " is wanted, who " by his personal influence and advice, and by that of true religion, would moderate the zeal and enthusiasm of those people, and prevent meetings from becoming mischievous, even if he could not prevail upon them to discontinue them entirely." Wherefore the Adjutant General must provide for a larger establishment of " respectable and efficient clergymen."

The Horse Guards complied at once : chaplains, it was replied, should be sent out " selected with the utmost care and circumspection by the first prelates of the country." Their pay was raised, and they were directed to conclude every service with a short practical sermon, suited to the habits and understanding of soldiers. " Good preaching," adds the Adjutant General, " is more than ever required

at a time peculiarly marked by the exertions and interference of sectaries of various denominations." *

The chaplains duly appeared. There were good men
among them, but they were not, taken as a whole, a complete success. Perhaps the idea, equally nourished by
Wellington and by the Horse Guards, that "respectable"
clergymen rather than enthusiasts should be drafted out,
was the cardinal mistake ; the sort of men that were really
wanted at the front were precisely the enthusiasts, like that
Rev. T. Owen (afterwards secretary of the British and
Foreign Bible Society), of whom we are told that he was in
days of action so far forward in the field that officers
warned him that he would infallibly be killed. His reply
was that his primary duty was " to be of service to those
now departing this life." † This sort of laudable energy,
I am bound to say, does not seem to have been the most
common characteristic of the chaplains, if we may trust
the diaries of the time.

A good many of them were sent straight out from a
country curacy to the front, had no special knowledge of
soldiers and their ways, and were appalled at having to
face the great facts of life and death in their crudest form
day after day. There is one distressing picture of a young
clergyman suddenly confronted in the guard-tent with
five deserters who were to be shot that afternoon. They
were all criminals who had been actually taken in the
French ranks, fighting against their old comrades, at the
storm of Ciudad Rodrigo. The chaplain helplessly read
prayers at them, felt that he could do no more with callous
ruffians who had met the death-sentence with an oath,
and followed them to the execution-place looking very
uncomfortable, quite useless, and much ashamed of
himself.

It was almost as trying, if not so horrible, to be tackled

* Sir H. Calvert, Adjutant General, to Wellington, 8th November,
1811.
† See Stevenson, p. 172.

by a Calvinist in the throes of conversion, who gave glowing
pictures of hell-fire, and asked for the means of avoiding
it, refusing to take as an answer any dole of chapters from
the New Testament or petitions from the Prayer Book.
Here is a picture of the situation from the point of view of
the penitent, Quartermaster Surtees, whom I have already
had occasion to quote.

"From the clergyman, though a kind and sympathizing
man, I, alas! derived but little benefit. He did not direct
me to the only source of a sin-sick being's hopes—the Lamb
of God which taketh away the sins of the world. He tried
to make my hopes centre more on good resolutions, and
after-doings. How thankfully would I have accepted the
true method of salvation pointed out in the gospel; but
already I was but too much (as the natural man always is)
inclined to expect pardon from the acts of penitence which,
if God spared me, I intended to perform. The kind
gentleman wrote me out prayers, and seemed much interested in my welfare. But reading and praying seemed
more like an irksome task than an exercise which brought
spiritual profit. . . . Indeed the Scriptures were still at
this time a 'sealed book' to me; until the grace of God
has dispelled our darkness there is no light in anything." *

Clearly the Quartermaster had come upon one of those
sensible and commonplace clergy whom Wellington had
requisitioned from the Chaplain-general's department,
when he wanted an Evangelist who would have preached
to him Justification by Faith in its simplest form.

There are a good many humorous anecdotes concerning
the race of Chaplains preserved in the Peninsular diaries,
not for the most part imputing to them any serious moral
failing—though several are accused of having become
"Belemites," † and of shirking the front—but tending to
prove that they often failed to rise to the occasion in their
difficult calling. This was indeed to be expected when

---

* Surtees, pp. 177–9.
† For the "Belemites" see above, pp. 204–5.

most of them had not the least knowledge of military life
and customs, and were wandering about for many months
in a world quite new to them. Clearly only men of experience should have been sent—but (as Wellington remarks
in one of his letters) the pay offered was so small that only
enthusiasts or very poor men could be expected to take
it—and enthusiasts, for other reasons, the commander-in-
chief did not like. The soldier seems often to have been
struck by the helplessness of the chaplain—he let himself
be robbed by his servants, wandered outside the picquets
and got captured by the French, or was deceived by obvious
hypocrites. There is one ridiculous story of a young
clergyman who, when first brought forward to take a
brigade Sunday service, and placed behind the big-drum,
which was to serve him as a sort of central mark, mistook
its function for that of a pulpit, and endeavoured to mount
upon it, with disastrous results, and to the infinite laughter
of the congregation.

Not unfrequently the chaplains fell out with the
Methodists among their flocks. They had been specially
imported by Wellington in order that they might discourage
the prayer meetings—" getting up little conventicles " as
one of them called these assemblies. " The Church service
is sufficient for the instruction of mankind," said another,
and " the zeal for preaching " tended to self-sufficiency
and incipient pharisaism. On the whole, however, there
was no regular or normal opposition between Church of
England and Methodist soldiers ; they were in such a
minority among the godless that it would have been absurd
for them to have quarrelled. The Methodists regularly
received the sacrament from the chaplains along with the
churchmen, and the latter were frequently to be found
at the prayer meetings of the former.

Sergeant Stevenson's memoir, a mine of useful information in this respect, informs us that the regular organized
prayer meeting of the Wesleyans in the 1st Division was
begun in a gravel-pit just outside the walls of Badajoz, in

September, 1809, and never ceased from that time forward. During the long sojourn behind the Lines of Torres Védras it was held for many weeks in a large wine-press, holding more than a hundred men, behind the village of Cartaxo, quite close to Wellington's headquarters, where indeed the hymns sung could be clearly heard. There were similar associations in other divisions, some mainly Church of England, some (as in the 79th regiment) Presbyterian. Stevenson says that he never heard of any opposition on the part of commanding officers, save in the case of one captain, whose preaching was finally ended by a course of persecution on the part of his colonel. But of course the " saints " had to endure a good deal of ridicule from their comrades, more especially those of them who took occasion to testify against drunkenness or blasphemy. Stevenson gives a verse of his own, which he says that he pasted up in the sergeants' room of the 3rd Guards, to discourage profane swearing at large.

> " It chills the blood to hear the Blest Supreme
> Rashly appealed to on each trifling theme,
> Maintain your rank : vulgarity despise ;
> To swear is neither *brave, polite,* nor *wise.*"

We may observe a certain canny appeal to the self-respect of the non-commissioned officer, in the insinuation that by blasphemy he lowers himself to the ranks, and is guilty of vulgarity and want of politeness. It is to be feared that these couplets might have been not inappropriately hung up in the mess rooms of certain regiments whose colonels were by no means choice in their language.

Among the senior officers of the Peninsular Army there were a good number who were not merely like Wellington, conformists of an official sort, but zealous Christians, such were Hill, Le Marchant,* Colborne, and

---

* Who "never went into action without subjecting himself to a strict self-examination, when after having (as he humbly hoped) made his peace with God, he left the result in His hands with perfect confidence that He will determine what is best for him."—See Cole's *Peninsular Generals,* ii. 292.

John Beckwith—the Light Division colonel, who devoted his later years to taking care of the Waldenses of Piedmont, among whom he settled down in the evening of his life. Quite a sprinkling of the younger officers took orders when the war was over, after the great disbandment of 1816–17, when all the second battalions were disembodied. Such were three men who have left us excellent Peninsular diaries, Gleig of the 85th, the author of " The Subaltern," and other works, afterwards Chaplain-General to the forces ; Dallas, who made a great name as an evangelist at Burford, was another soldier-parson ; Boothby, who wrote a good journal concerning Maida, Corunna, and Talavera, was a third. The type generally ran to strong Evangelicalism, as was natural, considering that this was the really live and vigorous element in the Church of that day.

It is clear that the religious condition of regiments varied extremely—that in some the influence of serious and devout officers and men was large, in others practically invisible. The character of the colonel made some difference for good or bad, but I imagine that more depended on the existence or non-existence of some small knot of officers or sergeants who did not fear to let their views be known, and formed a nucleus around which steady men gathered. Their names are mostly forgotten, the record of their witnessing has perished, or emerges only in some obscure corner of a little-read biography or an old religious magazine. I could wish that some sympathetic hand could devote a whole book to collecting and recording that which I have only been able to touch upon in this short chapter. It is a side of the life of the Peninsular Army which well deserves recording, since without some notice of it the picture of military society during the great war is wholly incomplete.

APPENDIX I.

(A.) ESTABLISHMENT OF THE BRITISH INFANTRY OF THE LINE. July, 1809.

N.B.—The star * affixed to a battalion's station means that it had just returned from Sir John Moore's Corunna Campaign.

No. of Regiment.	Territorial or other Designation.	Establishment. Officers and men.	Station of 1st Battalion.	Station of 2nd and other Battalions [if any].
1st	Royal Scots	4926	West Indies	2nd East Indies; 3rd Home* [went to Walcheren]; 4th Home
2nd	Queen's Royal	906	Home* [went to Walcheren]	No 2nd battalion raised
3rd	The Buffs	1610	Peninsular Field Army	Home
4th	King's Own	2031	Home* [went to Walcheren]	Home [went to Walcheren]
5th	Northumberland Regiment	2031	Home* [went to Walcheren]	Home
6th	1st Warwickshire	1820	Home* [went to Walcheren]	Home
7th	Royal Fusiliers	2031	Nova Scotia	Home
8th	The King's Regiment	1610	West Indies	Lisbon [later Gibraltar]
9th	East Norfolk	2289	Home* [went to Walcheren]	Home [went to Walcheren]
10th	North Lincoln	1610	Sicily	Peninsular Field Army
11th	North Devon	2031	Madeira [later Peninsula]	Home [went to Walcheren]
12th	East Suffolk	941	East Indies	Home [went to Walcheren]
13th	1st Somerset	1126	West Indies	[Raised a 2nd battalion in 1813]
14th	Bucks Regiment (See Note)	2290	East Indies	No 2nd battalion raised; 2nd Home* [Walcheren]; 3rd Sicily
15th	East Riding Regiment	1400	West Indies	Home
16th	Bedfordshire (See Note)	406	West Indies	No 2nd battalion raised

NOTE.—In 1809 the 14th, formerly Bedfordshire, took the Territorial Designation of Bucks; and the 16th, formerly Bucks, became Beds.

No. of Regiment.	Territorial or other Designation.	Establishment. Officers and men.	Station of 1st Battalion.	Station of 2nd and other Battalions [if any].
17th	Leicestershire	1151	East Indies	No 2nd battalion raised
18th	Royal Irish	1669	West Indies	West Indies
19th	1st York, North Riding	930	East Indies	No 2nd battalion raised
20th	East Devon	930	Home* [went to Walcheren]	No 2nd battalion raised
21st	Royal North British Fusiliers	1820	Sicily	Home
22nd	Cheshire	941	East Indies	[Raised a 2nd battalion in 1814
23rd	Royal Welsh Fusiliers	2079	Nova Scotia	Home* [went to Walcheren]
24th	2nd Warwickshire	2031	Cape of Good Hope	Peninsular Field Army
25th	King's Own Borderers	1400	West Indies	Home
26th	Cameronians	1610	Home* [went to Walcheren]	Home
27th	Inniskillings	3448	Sicily	2nd Battalion Sicily; 3rd battalion Garrison of Lisbon
28th	North Gloucestershire	2031	Home* [went to Walcheren]	Peninsular Field Army
29th	Worcestershire	1126	Peninsular Field Army	No. 2nd battalion raised
30th	Cambridgeshire	2242	East Indies	Gibraltar [late Lisbon]
31st	Huntingdonshire	2079	Malta	Peninsular Field Army
32nd	Cornwall	941	Home* [went to Walcheren]	Home
33rd	1st West Riding	1845	East Indies	No 2nd battalion raised
34th	Cumberland	1820	East Indies	Home [later to Peninsula]
35th	Sussex	1820	Sicily	Home [went to Walcheren]
36th	Herefordshire	1610	Home* [went to Walcheren]	Home
37th	North Hants	706	West Indies	[Raised a 2nd battalion in 1811]
38th	1st Stafford	1820	Home* [went to Walcheren]	Home
39th	Dorsetshire	1820	Malta	Peninsular Field Army
40th	2nd Somerset	1820	Peninsular Field Army	Home
41st	None	696	Canada	[Raised a 2nd battalion 1814]
42nd	Black Watch	2031	Home* [went to Walcheren]	Peninsular Field Army

No. of Regiment.	Territorial or other Designation.	Establishment. Officers and men.	Station of 1st Battalion.	Station of 2nd and other Battalions [if any].
43rd	Monmouth	2031	Peninsular Field Army*	Home* [went to Walcheren]
44th	1st Essex	2030	Sicily	Gibraltar
45th	Nottinghamshire	1610	Peninsular Field Army	Home
46th	South Devon	496	West Indies	No 2nd battalion raised
47th	Lancashire	2242	East Indies	Home [later Cadiz]
48th	Northamptonshire	2251	Peninsular Field Army	Peninsular Field Army
49th	Hertfordshire	906	Canada	No 2nd battalion raised
50th	West Kent	1820	Home* [went to Walcheren]	Home
51st	2nd West Riding	906	Home* [went to Walcheren]	No 2nd battalion raised
52nd	Oxfordshire	2079	Peninsular Field Army*	Home* [went to Walcheren]
53rd	Shropshire	2242	East Indies	Peninsular Field Army
54th	West Norfolk	706	West Indies	No 2nd battalion raised
55th	Westmoreland	706	West Indies	No 2nd battalion raised
56th	West Essex	2301	East Indies	2nd battalion East Indies [raised a 3rd battalion 1813]
57th	West Middlesex	1610	Gibraltar [later Portugal]	Home
58th	Rutland	1820	Sicily	Garrison of Lisbon
59th	2nd Nottinghamshire	1290	East Indies	Home* [went to Walcheren]
60th	Royal Americans	4847	West Indies	2nd battalion West Indies; 3rd battalion ditto; 4th battalion ditto; 5th battalion Peninsular Field Army; 6th and 7th West Indies
61st	South Gloucestershire	1820	Peninsular Field Army	Home
62nd	Wiltshire	1610	Sicily	Sicily
63rd	West Suffolk	1610	West Indies	Home [went to Walcheren]
64th	2nd Staffordshire	916	West Indies	No 2nd battalion raised

No. of Regiment.	Territorial or other Designation.	Establishment. Officers and men.	Station of 1st Battalion.	Station of 2nd and other Battalions [if any].
65th	2nd Yorks, North Riding]	731	East Indies	No 2nd battalion raised
66th	Berkshire	2031	East Indies	Peninsular Field Army
67th	South Hants	2031	East Indies	Home
68th	Durham	716	West Indies	No 2nd battalion raised
69th	South Lincolnshire	1337	East Indies	Home
70th	Surrey Regiment	706	West Indies	No 2nd battalion raised
71st	Glasgow Highlanders	1820	Home* [went to Walcheren]	Home
72nd	Highlanders	1600	East Indies	Home
73rd	2nd Royal Highlanders	1180	Sailing to N.S. Wales	Home [only formed in 1809]
74th	Highlanders	696	Home [went to Walcheren]	No 2nd battalion raised
75th	Highlanders	696	Home	No 2nd battalion raised
76th	Hindostan Regiment	1126	Home* [went to Walcheren]	No 2nd battalion raised
77th	East Middlesex	696	Home [went to Walcheren]	No 2nd battalion raised
78th	Rosshire Buffs	1885	East Indies	Sicily [later Home]
79th	Cameron Highlanders	1820	Home* [went to Walcheren]	Home
80th	Staffordshire Volunteers	1151	East Indies	No 2nd battalion raised
81st	2nd Loyal Lincoln	2079	Sicily	Home* [went to Walcheren]
82nd	Prince of Wales' Volunteers	1820	Home* [went to Walcheren]	Home
83rd	None	2461	Cape of Good Hope	Peninsular Field Army
84th	York and Lancaster	2276	East Indies	Home [went to Walcheren]
85th	Bucks Volunteers	716	Home [went to Walcheren]	No 2nd battalion raised
86th	Leinster Regiment	731	East Indies	[Raised a 2nd battalion 1814]
87th	Prince of Wales', Irish Fusiliers	2299	Cape of Good Hope	Peninsular Field Army
88th	Connaught Rangers	2031	Peninsular Field Army	Lisbon [later Gibraltar]
89th	None	2031	Cape of Good Hope	Gibraltar
90th	Perthshire Volunteers	1610	West Indies	Home
91st	Highlanders	1390	Home* [went to Walcheren]	Home

No. of Regiment.	Territorial or other Designation.	Establishment. Officers and men.	Station of 1st Battalion.	Station of 2nd and other Battalions [if any].
92nd	Gordon Highlanders	1820	Home* [went to Walcheren]	Home
93rd	Sutherland Highlanders	1126	Cape of Good Hope	[Raised a second battalion 1814]
94th	Scotch Brigade	696	Home	No 2nd battalion raised
95th	Rifles	2283	Peninsular Field Army*	2nd Home* [went to Walcheren] 3rd Home [only just raised]
96th	None	1400	West Indies	Home
97th	Queen's Germans	907	Peninsular Field Army	No 2nd battalion raised
98th	None	906	Bermuda	No 2nd battalion raised
99th	Prince of Wales' Tipperary	696	Bermuda	No 2nd battalion raised
100th	County of Dublin	696	Canada	No 2nd battalion raised
101st	Duke of York's Irish	906	West Indies	No 2nd battalion raised
102nd	New South Wales	906	New South Wales	No 2nd battalion raised
103rd	None	486	Canada	No 2nd battalion raised

Total.	1st Battalions.	2nd Battalions.	3rd and Junior Battalions.	Total.
At Home	25*	42†	3§	= 70
Peninsula	11‡	15	2	= 28
Sicily and Malta	10	3	1	= 14
East Indies	21	2	0	= 23
West Indies	21	2	4	= 27
Cape of Good Hope	5	0	0	= 5
Canada and Nova Scotia	6	0	0	= 6
New South Wales	2	0	0	= 2
Gibraltar and Madeira	2	2	0	= 4
			Total	= 179

* Of these 25, twenty had been with Moore's army in the Corunna Retreat, and 23 went to Walcheren.
† Of these 42, seven had been with Moore's army in the Corunna Retreat, and 14 went to Walcheren.
‡ Of these 11, three (1/43rd, 1/52nd, 1/95th) had been with Moore's army.
§ Of these 3, one (3/1st) had been with Moore's army in the Corunna Retreat and went to Walcheren.

z

A consideration of the prefixed table of "establishments" shows the following results. Putting aside the regiments with many battalions (the 1st, 14th, 27th, 60th, 95th), the remainder fall into two-battalion and single-battalion corps.

Of the 61 double-battalion regiments—

> 9 were at a strength of 2250 or thereabouts.*
> 17 were at a strength of 2031 or thereabouts.†
> 16 were at a strength of 1820 or thereabouts.‡
> 12 were at a strength of 1610 or thereabouts.§
> 7 were at a strength of under 1600.||

All the regiments on the two higher establishments (with one exception) had both battalions on active service in 1809, either one in the Indies and one in Europe, or both in Europe. Hence it was necessary to keep them at a very high figure.

Those with 1820 or 1610 men were nearly all regiments which had one battalion on active service and one on home service, though a very few had both overseas (such as the 18th, 34th, 39th, 62nd); in such cases the 2nd battalion, though on service, was very weak.

The two-battalion corps with under 1600 men were almost invariably regiments which had one battalion in the Indies, worked down to very low numbers by disease, and had failed to keep up its strength (the 15th, 25th, 96th in the West, the 59th, 69th in the East Indies).

The 37 single-battalion regiments stood on the following establishments—

> 6 were at a strength of 1126 or thereabouts.**
> 13 were at a strength of 940 or thereabouts.††
> 15 were at a strength of 700–730 or thereabouts.‡‡
> 3 were at a strength of under 600.§§

Those corps on the two higher establishments are either actually

---

* 9th, 30th, 47th, 48th, 53rd, 56th, 83rd, 84th, 87th. The 83rd was far over this figure, 2461, a wholly exceptional strength.
† 4th, 5th, 7th, 11th, 23rd, 24th, 28th, 31st, 42nd, 43rd, 44th, 52nd, 66th, 67th, 81st, 88th, 89th.
‡ 6th, 21st, 32nd, 34th, 35th, 38th, 39th, 40th, 50th, 58th, 61st, 71st, 78th, 79th, 82nd, 92nd.
§ 3rd, 8th, 10th, 18th, 26th, 36th, 45th, 57th, 62nd, 63rd, 72nd, 90th.
|| 15th, 25th, 59th, 69th, 73rd, 91st, 96th.
** 13th, 17th, 29th, 76th, 80th, 93rd.
†† 2nd, 12th, 19th, 20th, 22nd, 33rd, 49th, 51st, 64th, 97th, 90th, 101st, 102nd.
‡‡ 37th, 41st, 54th, 55th, 65th, 68th, 70th 74th, 75th, 77th, 85th, 86th, 94th, 99th, 100th.
§§ 16th, 46th, 103rd.

serving, or are designated for immediate service abroad, and have therefore their establishments fixed high. Those on the lower establishments (730 or under) fall into two classes: either they are regiments in the East or West Indies which have died down to a low figure [*e.g.* 16th, 37th, 46th, 54th, 55th, 65th, 68th, 70th, 86th] or they are battalions quartered in peaceful stations and not expected to be sent on active service, [*e.g.* 41st, 99th, 100th, 103rd, in Canada and Bermuda] or at home [74th, 75th, 77th, 85th, 94th]. All the last-named five, on home service, were raised to a higher establishment and sent to the front in 1810–12.

It will be noted that of the one hundred and three 1st battalions, or single-battalion regiments, a great many were not available, viz. twenty-one in the East Indies, twenty-one in the West Indies (including Bermuda), eleven in the Mediterranean Garrisons, five at the Cape of Good Hope, six in Canada, two in (or bound for) New South Wales. There were only twenty-five 1st battalions at home, and of these twenty had served under Moore in the Corunna retreat and then went on the Walcheren expedition, so that in 1809 they were unavailable. Three more battalions which had not served under Moore had shared in the same descent on the Scheldt (74th, 77th, 85th). There were actually only two single-battalion corps which had neither gone to Corunna nor to Walcheren and were available at home (75th and 94th).* In the way of the strongly organized first battalions, therefore, there was absolutely nil to send to Wellington in 1809 save Craufurd's three Light Infantry battalions, which though they had been with Moore in January were back in the Peninsula by July (1/43rd, 1/52nd, 1/95th).

It is easy to see, therefore, that there was the greatest possible difficulty in finding battalions with which Wellesley's Peninsular Army could be reinforced. Of troops which had not gone to Walcheren there were left in Great Britain only the 75th and 94th, with twenty-eight 2nd (or junior) battalions which had not joined in the expedition to the Scheldt. These were almost without exception very weak units, the first battalions of ten of these were in the Indies, then of five more already in the Peninsula, all their strength was used up in keeping their senior battalions full, of the remaining thirteen only two (2/5th 2/34th, 2/38th), were strong enough to be sent to Portugal. The reinforcements which Wellington was

* The 94th went out to Cadiz in 1810; the 75th, not long back from India, was very weak and did not go on foreign service (Sicily) till 1812.

given in the autumn of 1809 and the summer of 1810 were largely scraped up from foreign garrisons—the 1/7th from Nova Scotia, the 1/11th from Madeira, the 1/57th from Gibraltar. But in 1810 Walcheren battalions began to come out, such as the 3/1st, 1/9th, 1/50th, 1/71st, 1/79th, and to load Wellington's hospitals with ague-stricken convalescents. For later reinforcements see Chapter VII.

ESTABLISHMENT OF CAVALRY IN 1809.

1st Dragoon Guards	905	Home
2nd Dragoon Guards	905	Home
3rd Dragoon Guards	905	Peninsular Field Army
4th Dragoon Guards	905	Home
5th Dragoon Guards	905	Home
6th Dragoon Guards	905	Home
7th Dragoon Guards	905	Home
1st Dragoons	1083	Peninsular Field Army
2nd Dragoons	905	Home
3rd Dragoons	905	Home [went to Walcheren]
4th Dragoons	905	Peninsular Field Army
6th Dragoons	905	Home
7th Hussars	905	*Home
8th Light Dragoons	720	East Indies
9th Light Dragoons	905	Home [went to Walcheren]
10th Hussars	905	*Home
11th Light Dragoons	905	Home
12th Light Dragoons	905	Home [went to Walcheren]
13th Light Dragoons	905	Home
14th Light Dragoons	905	Peninsular Field Army
15th Hussars	905	*Home
16th Light Dragoons	905	Peninsular Field Army
17th Light Dragoons	940	East Indies
18th Hussars	905	*Home
19th Light Dragoons	905	Home
20th Light Dragoons	905	½ Sicily and ½ Peninsula
21st Light Dragoons	905	Cape of Good Hope
22nd Light Dragoons	928	East Indies
23rd Light Dragoons	903	Peninsular Field Army
24th Light Dragoons	928	East Indies
25th Light Dragoons	940	East Indies

N.B.—Note that there was no 5th regiment of Dragoons in 1809. The corps last bearing that number had been disbanded in 1799, and its successor was not raised till 1858.

ESTABLISHMENT OF THE HOUSEHOLD TROOPS IN 1809.

1st Life Guards	416	Home
2nd Life Guards	416	Home
Royal Horse Guards	654	Home
1st Foot Guards (3 batts.)	4619	1st Batt.* Home [went to Walcheren] ; 2nd Batt. Home ; 3rd Batt.* Home [went to Walcheren]
2nd (Coldstream) Foot Guards (2 batts.)	2887	1st Batt. Peninsular Field Army ; 2nd Batt. Home
3rd Foot Guards (2 batts.)	2887	1st Batt. Peninsular Field Army ; 2nd Batt. Home

N.B.—The Second Batts. Coldstream and 3rd Foot Guards both sent their flank companies to Walcheren. The troops sent to Cadiz early in 1810 were detachments, viz. 4 companies of the 2/1st Guards, 3 of the 2/2nd, 3 of the 2/3rd.

MISCELLANEOUS CORPS.

In addition to the regular units shown in these lists, there are on the estimates of 1809 twelve veteran battalions, with effectives ranging from 693 to 1129, and eight garrison battalions, mostly with an establishment of 906. Most of these were at home, but a few in the Mediterranean garrisons.

There were also the foreign corps of Meuron, de Roll, Watteville, Dillon, *Chasseurs Britanniques*, Royal Malta, Royal Corsicans and the Sicilian regiment, all in the Mediterranean, with the York Light Infantry, York Rangers, and Royal West India Rangers in the West Indies. These were all single battalion corps ranging from 1361 men (de Roll) to 694 (York L. I.). The black regiments, eight West India battalions with 1125 men each, could only be used in their own regions.

Of the King's German Legion there were at home the two Heavy Dragoon Regiments with an establishment of 694 each, and the 2nd and 3rd Hussars, with the same numbers. The 3rd Hussars were just back from the Corunna Retreat: the 2nd went to Walcheren. Of the ten infantry battalions, four (1st, 2nd, 5th, 7th Line) were with the Peninsular Field Army, as was the 1st Hussars; four (3rd, 4th, 6th, 8th Line) were in Sicily ; 1st and 2nd Light battalions (just back from Corunna) were at home, and went to Walcheren. Four battalions had establishments of 1062, six of 902, of all ranks.

APPENDIX II

DIVISIONAL AND BRIGADE ORGANIZATION AND CHANGES.

1809—1814.

BY C. T. ATKINSON, M.A., FELLOW AND TUTOR OF EXETER COLLEGE, OXFORD.

1809.

On April 22, when Wellesley arrived the troops were brigaded as follows :—

Cavalry. G.O.C., Cotton. 14th Light Dragoons, 16th Light Dragoons, 2 squadrons 20th Light Dragoons, detachment 3rd Hussars K.G.L.: Fane's brigade (not at the Douro), 3rd Dragoon Guards, 4th Dragoons.

Guards' Brigade (H. Campbell). 1st Coldstream, 1st 3rd Guards (*i.e.* Scots), 1 co. 5/60th.

1st Brigade (Hill). 1/3rd, 2/48th, 2/66th, 1 co. 5/60th.

2nd Brigade (Mackenzie). 2/24th (attached), 3/27th, 2/31st, 1/45th.

3rd Brigade (Tilson). Headquarters and 5 cos. 5/60th, 2/87th, 1/88th.

4th Brigade (Sontag). 97th, 2nd Detachments, 1 co. 5/60th.

5th Brigade (A. Campbell). 2/7th, 2/53rd, 1 co. 5/60th.

6th Brigade (R. Stewart). 29th, 1st Detachments.

7th Brigade (Cameron). 2/9th, 2/83rd, 1 co. 5/60th.

K.G.L. (Murray, Langwerth and Drieberg). 1st, 2nd, 5th, and 7th Line K.G.L., detachment Light Battalions K.G.L.

The 3rd, 4th, 5th, 6th and 7th Brigades each included a Portuguese battalion.

[N.B.—The " Battalions of Detachments " were composed of convalescents and stragglers, left behind from the regiments which had marched from Portugal under Sir John Moore in the preceding autumn.]

The organization in divisions dates from June 18. It was originally as follows :—

Cavalry. G.O.C., Payne. A [Fane], 3rd Dragoon Guards, 4th Dragoons ; B [Cotton], 14th and 16th Light Dragoons ; Unattached, 2 squadrons 20th Light Dragoons, 23rd Light Dragoons, 1st Hussars K.G.L., detachment 3rd Hussars K.G.L.

1st Division. G.O.C., Sherbrooke. A [H. Campbell], 1st Coldstream, 1st Scots ; B [Cameron], 2/9th, 2/83rd ; C [Langwerth], 1st and 2nd Line K.G.L., detachment Light Battalions K.G.L. ; D [Low], 5th and 7th Line K.G.L.

2nd Division. G.O.C., Hill. A [Hill], 1/3rd, 2/48th, 3/66th ; B [R. Stewart], 29th, 1st Detachments.

3rd Division. G.O.C., Mackenzie. A [Mackenzie] 3/27th, 2/31st, 1/45th ; B [Tilson], 5 companies 5/60th, 2/87th, 1/88th.

4th Division. G.O.C., A. Campbell. A [A. Campbell], 2/7th, 2/53rd ; B [Sontag], 97th, 2nd Detachments.

The detached companies of 5/60th at Talavera were with I A, I B, II A, IV A, IV B.

Subsequent changes were as follows :—

Cavalry. 20th Light Dragoons and detachment 3rd Hussars K.G.L., left the Peninsula before the end of July.

By June 21 a new brigade, C, was added, under G. Anson, composed of 23rd Light Dragoons and 1st Hussars K.G.L.

On November 1 Granby Calcroft was commanding A for Fane, absent.

By November 24 1st Dragoons (who arrived at Lisbon in October) replaced the 16th Light Dragoons in B, now under Slade, as Cotton was assisting Payne in command of the division ; 16th Light Dragoons were transferred to C *vice* 23rd Light Dragoons, ordered home after their losses at Talavera.

1st Division. 1/40th, from Seville, replaced 2/9th before June 21, 2/9th going to Gibraltar and relieving 1/61st, who joined before Talavera, on which 1/40th were transferred to IV B.

After Talavera 2/24th and 2/42nd were added to I B, 2/83rd being sent down to Lisbon.

At Talavera, H. Campbell was wounded, Stopford replacing him in command of the division and brigade, but from November 8 to December 15, Hulse had the brigade. Langwerth having been killed at Talavera, Beck of 1st Line K.G.L. succeeded to his brigade, but the two K.G.L. brigades were amalgamated under Löw from November 1.

2nd Division. By June 21 Tilson (from III B) had taken over Hill's own brigade. Before Talavera 1/48th (arrived at Lisbon June 22, on being relieved at Gibraltar by 2/30th) had been added to II B.

In September, a new brigade, C, under Catlin Craufurd, was added, composed of 2/28th, 2/34th, 2/39th, and about the same time 2/31st (from III A) was added to II A.   By November 1, 1/57th (from Gibraltar) replaced 1st Detachments in II B, the Battalions of Detachments having been broken up.

From December 15 on II A was under command of Duckworth of 2/48th.

3rd Division. Tilson, moving to II A, was replaced by Donkin (June 21).

Before Talavera 2/24th replaced 3/27th (sent down to Lisbon) in III A.

Mackenzie was killed at Talavera, and the division passed under the command of R. Craufurd, whose brigade, 1/43rd, 1/52nd and 1/95th, arrived just too late for the battle, and was apparently added to the division in place of Mackenzie's brigade which was amalgamated with Donkin's.   On September 15, 2/87th was ordered down to Lisbon for garrison duty, 2/24th being transferred to II B and 2/31st to II A about the same time.

In October, Donkin gave up his brigade, Mackinnon obtaining command.

4th Division. Myers of 2/7th seems to have commanded IV A for A. Campbell.

By Talavera 1/40th had been added to IV B, of which Kemmis had taken command *vice* Sontag.

At Talavera A. Campbell was wounded, and had to go

home, the division being without a definite G.O.C. till the arrival of Lowry Cole in October.

In September 1/11th (arrived at Lisbon from Madeira in August) was added to IV A. On the Battalions of Detachments being sent home (October), 3/27th, in garrison at Lisbon since after the Douro, replaced the 2nd Battalion in IV B.

1810.

On January 1, the composition of the Army was as follows :—

Cavalry. G.O.C., Payne ; Cotton, second in command.

A [Fane], 3rd Dragoon Guards, 4th Dragoons ; B [Slade], 1st Dragoons, 14th Light Dragoons ; C [G. Anson], 16th Light Dragoons, 1st Hussars K.G.L.

1st Division. G.O.C., Sherbrooke. A [Stopford], 1st Coldstreams, 1st Scots ; B [A. Cameron], 2/24th, 2/42nd, 1/61st ; C [Löw], 1st, 2nd, 5th, and 7th Line, K.G.L., detachment Light Battalions, K.G.L.

2nd Division. G.O.C., Hill. A [Duckworth, temporarily], 1/3rd, 2/31st, 2/48th, 2/66th ; B [R. Stewart], 29th, 1/48th, 1/57th ; C [C. Craufurd], 2/28th, 2/34th, 2/39th.

3rd Division. G.O.C., R. Craufurd. A [R. Craufurd], 1/43rd, 1/52nd, 1/95th ; B [Mackinnon], 1/45th, 5/60th, 1/88th.

4th Division. G.O.C., Cole. A [Myers acting for Cole], 2/7th, 1/11th, 2/53rd ; B [Kemmis] 3/27th, 1/40th, 97th ; C [Lightburne], 2/5th, 2/58th.*

Subsequent changes were :—

Cavalry. Payne went home before June 1, Cotton obtaining sole command from June 3.

On April 1 the 13th Light Dragoons arrived at Lisbon, joining the army in May, and being attached to Hill's division, along with four regiments of Portuguese cavalry, the whole under Fane, who gave over his brigade to de Grey from May 13. Two troops of the regiment went to Cadiz, but rejoined the regiment in September.

* This brigade was added to IV on January 2.

Before the end of the year Fane seems to have gone home ill.

1st Division. On April 26 Cotton was posted to the command of the division, *vice* Sherbrooke, gone home ill, but gave place to Spencer, June 3, on getting the Cavalry Division.

In the " States " of March 8 to August 1, no brigadier is given for I B. On August 4 Lord Blantyre (of 2/42nd) was appointed to command I B " during the absence of Brigadier-General Cameron." Cameron was back in command from October 1, but on November 26 he was invalided home, Blantyre probably commanding again.

By the Orders of September 12, 1/79th (just arrived from Cadiz), was posted to I B *vice* 1/61st, to be transferred to a new brigade to form part of the 1st Division. These orders were suspended from September 14, and at Bussaco 1/7th (arrived from Halifax before end of July), and 1/79th formed a brigade (I D) under Pakenham.

On October 6, orders were given for the transfer of Pakenham's brigade to the 4th Division, the exchange between the 1/61st and 1/79th having been carried out previously, and a new brigade was added under Erskine, comprising 1/50th (arrived September 24), 1/71st (arrived September 26), 1/92nd (arrived in October, before the 6th), and 1 company 3/95th.

2nd Division. On June 20 Leith was appointed to command " Tilson's brigade," and to command the division " under Hill," but in the " State " of July 8 his name appears as commanding the brigade composed of 3/1st, 1/9th, and 2/38th. On August 8 orders were issued to W. Stewart to take command of Tilson's brigade and of the division under Hill. In November Hill went on sick leave.

Leith's name ceases to appear in the returns as commanding II A from July 8, and W. Stewart's name appears in his place from July 27. When Stewart commanded the division, Colborne of 2/66th had the brigade. C. Craufurd died in September, and at Bussaco Wilson of 2/39th commanded II C. On September 30 Lumley was posted to command it.

Before September 1 R. Stewart had gone home ill, and

at Bussaco Inglis (of 1/57th) commanded II B. On October 8 Hoghton was posted to it.

3rd Division. From January 8 on 5/60th no longer appear in the Returns as belonging to the division, and their place in the brigade was taken by 74th, who arrived at Lisbon February 8, and are mentioned in Orders on February 22 as in III B.

On February 22 the division was reorganized, R. Craufurd's brigade becoming, with two battalions of Caçadores, the Light Division. Mackinnon's brigade now became III A, and Lightburne's brigade was transferred from the 4th Division and became III B. The headquarters and three companies 5/60th were posted to Lightburne's brigade, the remaining companies having been posted to I A, I B, II A, II B, II C, IV A, IV B. At the same time a Portuguese brigade composed of the 9th and 21st Regiments (under Harvey) was added to the division.

At Bussaco Champlemond was in command of the Portuguese brigade, by October 29 Sutton had it, Champlemond being wounded at Bussaco.

On September 12 2/83rd was posted to III B, 2/88th having arrived from Cadiz to relieve them September 4. Hurrying to the front they joined their brigade before Bussaco. When they did join, 2/58th was detached from III B for garrison duty at Lisbon. 94th (arrived from Cadiz September 20), were added to III B on October 6, and on October 10 Colville was posted to command the brigade *vice* Lightburne, who went home.

4th Division. On the transfer of Lightburne's brigade to the 3rd Division the other two brigades exchanged places, Kemmis' becoming IV A, and being Cole's brigade, but under the immediate command of Kemmis. A Campbell, who had rejoined, took command of his old brigade.

The 3rd and 15th Portuguese were added to the division in February, as a brigade under Collins.

At Bussaco the Portuguese brigade consisted of the 11th and 23rd, the 3rd and 15th having been removed to the 5th Division.

On October 6 A. Campbell's brigade was removed from the division to become the nucleus of the newly-formed 6th Division, its place being taken by Pakenham's from the

1st Division, *i.e.* 1/7th, 1/61st, to which the Brunswick Oels Light Infantry (arrived Lisbon September 17) were added.

On November 12 the Brunswick Oels were removed to the Light Division, but one company was posted to IV B, two more being detached to provide the newly-formed 5th Division, with extra light troops. Their place in IV B was taken by the newly arrived 1/23rd from Halifax, Nova Scotia.

On November 17 2/7th and 1/61st were ordered to exchange, IV B thus becoming the Fusilier Brigade.

Light Division. Formed on February 22 by the removal of R. Craufurd's brigade from the 3rd Division, the 1st and 3rd Portuguese Caçadores being added to it. On August 4 it was broken up into two brigades, as follows : A [Beckwith of 1/95th] 1/43rd, 4 companies 1/95th, 1st Caçadores ; B [Barclay of 1/52nd] 1/52nd, 4 companies 1/95th, 3rd Caçadores. Barclay having been wounded at Bussaco, Wynch of 1/4th got the brigade (in Orders of November 14th).

A company of 2/95th (from Cadiz) was added to A before October 1. On November 12 nine companies Brunswick Oels joined B.

5th Division. Officially this division first appears in the " State " of August 8, when the 3/1st, 1/9th, and 2/38th,* are first called the " Fifth Division," a Portuguese brigade, Spry's (*i.e.* 3rd and 15th Line), being added, and Leith being G.O.C.

On August 4 J. S. Barns of 3/1st was appointed to command the British brigade, being superseded by Hay September 30.

On October 6 orders were issued that Leith should command the 5th Division, and that it should be composed of Brigadier-General Hay's brigade, a brigade made up of 1/4th (from England, they first appear in the " State " of November 15), 2/30th (from Cadiz), and 2/44th (from Cadiz), and Spry's Portuguese.

---

* These regiments had arrived at Lisbon in April, but having been at Walcheren were not at first sent into the field till July, since the 8th of which month they had been shown as a brigade under Leith.

On November 5 Dunlop was posted to V B, hitherto under its senior battalion commander.

On November 12 a company of the Brunswick Oels was posted to each of the British brigades.

6th Division. Ordered to be formed October 6, by taking A. Campbell's brigade out of the 4th Division and adding Eben's Portuguese (*i.e.* 8th Line and Lusitanian Legion) to it : A. Campbell being G.O.C.

On November 14, Hulse was posted to A. Campbell's brigade.

On November 17 1/61st from IV B exchanged with 2/7th.

In addition to the Portuguese brigades attached to the 3rd, 4th, 5th, and 6th Divisions there were at least five others, two of which, the 4th under Archibald Campbell (= 4th and 10th Line), and 2nd under Fonseca (= 2nd and 14th Line) formed a division under Hamilton, which acted throughout under Hill. Wellington says that he intended to organize this division like the rest, but the heavy losses at Albuera and the consequent necessity of reforming the 2nd Division made it impossible for him to carry out his resolve. [Cf. *Wellington Dispatches*, viii. 111.]

The remaining brigades were the 1st (Pack's), consisting of the 1st and 16th Line and 4th Caçadores, the 5th (A. Campbell's), 6th and 18th Line, and 6th Caçadores; the 6th (Coleman's), 7th and 19th Line and 2nd Caçadores. On the formation of the 7th Division in March, 1811, Coleman's brigade was posted to it, the other two remaining unattached.

The 12th and 13th Line and 5th Caçadores seem to have formed yet another brigade under Bradford, but in October the 13th Line was in garrison at Abrantes.

Spry's brigade ranked at the 3rd, Eben's as the 7th, Sutton's as the 8th, and Collins' as the 9th.

1811.

On January 1 the Army was organized as follows :—

Cavalry. G.O.C., Cotton. A [de Grey], 3rd Dragoon Guards, 4th Dragoons ; B. [Slade], 1st Dragoons, 14th Light Dragoons ; C [G. Anson], 16th Light Dragoons, 1st Hussars, K.G.L. ; unbrigaded, 13th Light Dragoons.

1st Division. G.O.C., Spencer. A [Stopford], 1st Coldstream, 1st Scots, 1 company 5/60th ; B [? Blantyre, acting], 2/24th, 2/42nd, 1/79th, 1 company 5/60th ; C [Löw], 1st, 2nd, 5th, and 7th Line, K.G.L., detachment Light Battalions, K.G.L. ; D [Erskine], 1/50th, 1/71st, 1/92nd, 1 company 3/95th.

2nd Division. G.O.C., W. Stewart. A [Colborne], 1/3rd, 2/31st, 2/48th, 2/66th, 1 company 5/60th ; B [Hoghton], 29th, 1/48th, 1/57th, 1 company 5/60th ; C [Lumley], 2/28th, 2/34th, 2/39th, 1 company 5/60th.

3rd Division. G.O.C., Picton. A [Mackinnon], 1/45th, 1/74th, 1/88th ; B [Colville], 2/5th, 3 companies 5/60th, 2/83rd, 94th ; also Sutton's Portuguese.

4th Division. G.O.C., Cole. A. [Kemmis], 3/27th, 1/40th, 97th, 1 company 5/60th ; B [Pakenham], 1/7th, 2/7th, 1/23rd, 1 company Brunswick Oels ; also Collins' Portuguese.

5th Division. G.O.C., Leith. A [Hay], 3/1st, 1/9th, 2/38th, 1 company Brunswick Oels ; B [Dunlop], 1/4th, 2/30th, 2/44th, 1 company Brunswick Oels; also Spry's Portuguese.

6th Division. G.O.C., A. Campbell. A [Hulse], 1/11th, 2/53rd, 1/61st, 1 company 5/60th; also Eben's Portuguese.

Light Division. G.O.C., R. Craufurd. A [Beckwith], 1/43rd, 4 companies 1/95th, 1 company 2/95th, 1st Caçadores ; B [Wynch], 1/52nd, 4 companies 1/95th, Brunswick Oels, 3rd Caçadores.

Portuguese. Hamilton's Division, brigades under Fonseca (2nd) and Archibald Campbell (4th). Unattached brigades under Pack (1st), Ashworth, late A. Campbell (5th), Coleman (6th), and Bradford (10th).

Subsequent changes were :—

Cavalry. Cotton went home January 15, returning April 22 ; in his absence Slade commanded the division until March 7, when Erskine seems to have been placed in command of both the Cavalry and the Light Division. While Slade had the division, his brigade was apparently under Hawker of 14th Light Dragoons, and from March 1 to May 15, G. Anson being absent, Arentschildt of 1st K.G.L. Hussars, commanded C.

On March 19 Long was posted to command the cavalry of the force usually under Hill, but commanded by Beresford during Hill's absence. At Albuera Lumley (of II C) was in command of Beresford's cavalry, Long's conduct not having given satisfaction to the Marshal. On May 11 Erskine was appointed to command "the cavalry south of the Tagus."

On June 13 a new brigade, D, was formed under Long, composed of 13th Light Dragoons and 2nd Hussars K.G.L., two squadrons of which had landed April 8. On June 18 the 11th Light Dragoons (arrived June 1) replaced the 13th, transferred to Slade's brigade.

On June 19 a reorganization of the cavalry in two divisions was ordered, as follows :—

1st Cavalry Division. G.O.C., Cotton. B [Slade], 1st Dragoons, 13th and 14th Light Dragoons; C [G. Anson], 16th Light Dragoons, 1st Hussars, K.G.L.; also Madden's Portuguese.

2nd Cavalry Division. G.O.C., Erskine. A [de Grey], 3rd Dragoon Guards, 4th Dragoons; D [Long], 11th Light Dragoons, 2nd Hussars, K.G.L.

On July 19 another reorganization took place, the final result being as follows :—

1st Cavalry Division. G.O.C., Cotton. B [Slade], 1st Dragoons, 12th Light Dragoons (arrived July 1), vice 13th (to C) and 14th (to D); C [G. Anson], 13th and 16th Light Dragoons; E [V. Alten, a new brigade], 11th Light Dragoons (from D) and 1st Hussars, K.G.L. (from C); Madden's Portuguese.

2nd Cavalry Division. A [de Grey], 3rd Dragoon Guards, 4th Dragoons; D [Long], 14th Light Dragoons, 2nd Hussars, K.G.L.

On August 1, 9th Light Dragoons (newly arrived) were posted to Long's brigade, together with 13th Light Dragoons, which exchanged from C with 14th.

On August 30, a new brigade, F, was added, comprising 4th Dragoon Guards, arrived August 15, and 3rd Dragoons, arrived before August 20, its commander being Le Marchant. By October 1, 5th Dragoon Guards had been added to this brigade.

On October 5 de Grey's brigade was transferred to the 1st Cavalry Division, to which Le Marchant's was attached by Orders of November 8, the Portuguese brigade being struck off that division.

From December 8 on the States do not give any G.O.C. for the 2nd Cavalry Division.

1st Division. On January 23 Nightingale was posted to I B: on February 6 Howard obtained I D, when Erskine was transferred to the command of the 5th Division.   On June 8 H. Campbell's name is given in the "State" as in command of I A, Stopford being transferred to IV B (in Orders for this June 18).   Nightingale departing to Bengal before June 25 his brigade had no permanent commander till July 28, when Stopford got it.

Owing to the heavy losses of the 2nd Division at Albuera and its consequent reconstruction, Howard's brigade was transferred to it on June 6, and at the same time the detachment of the Light Battalions of the K.G.L., hitherto in I C, rejoined those battalions, which had been posted to VII A.

On June 26 orders were issued for the 7th Line K.G.L., to go home, its rank and file being drafted into the other three battalions.   On July 21 1/26th were added to I B, having recently arrived from England.

On August 9, Graham was appointed to command the division, Spencer having gone home in July, he received leave July 25.   From December 1 onward I B appears in the "States" as having no G.O.C.

2nd Division. The heavy losses at Albuera led to the reorganization of the division, detailed in Orders June 6. Howard's brigade of the 1st Division was transferred to the 2nd Division, becoming II. A. The remainder of the brigades of Colborne and Hoghton (who was killed) were formed into a Provisional Battalion, less 1/48th and 2/48th; 1/48th, to which the rank and file of 2/48th were drafted (the cadre of 2/48th going home), was transferred to IV B.

This Provisional Battalion was placed in Lumley's brigade, of which Abercromby (of 2/28th) had had temporary command at Albuera, while Lumley was in charge of the cavalry.   At the same time, Ashworth's Portuguese brigade

was definitely attached to it: this was the 5th Brigade,
which had been under A. Campbell in October, 1810, but
had come under Ashworth by March 11; it comprised the
6th and 18th Line and 6th Caçadores. Cf. also *Wellington
Dispatches*, viii, 566, and *S. D.* vii. 135.

Before the end of May Hill returned and took over
command of the division, as well as of the whole force commanded by Beresford at Albuera.

On July 22 1/28th (newly arrived from Gibraltar) was
posted to Lumley's brigade.

On August 7 orders were issued for 1/3rd and 1/57th to
resume their separate formations, large drafts having arrived
from their second battalions in England. The division was
again formed in three brigades, Howard's being II A, and
1/3rd, 1/57th, and the Provisional Battalion, [*i.e.* 29th
(3 companies), 2/31st (4 companies) and 2/66th (3 companies)]
forming II B, apparently under Inglis of 1/57th, while 1/28th,
2 28th, 2/34th, and 2/39th under Lumley formed II C.

On August 21 2/28th was drafted into 1/28th, and sent
home, and the company 3/95th, hitherto in Howard's brigade,
were transferred to Beckwith's brigade of the Light Division,
being replaced in II A by a company of 5/60th, there being
three with the division.

On September 21 Byng was posted to command II B,
and on October 9 Wilson was appointed to command II C,
Lumley having gone home sick early in August.

On October 3 orders were issued for 29th to go home to
recruit ; on October 20 1/39th, just arrived from Sicily,
was added to II C, 2/39th being drafted into it and sent home
by Orders issued December 17.

3rd Division.   Orders of March 5 direct the transfer of the
headquarter companies 5/60th to III A, 2/88th, on garrison
duty at Lisbon since September 4, 1810, being added to III B.
On July 10, 2/88th was ordered to be drafted into 1/88th, and
the cadre sent home.

On July 22 the 77th were added to III B.

From July 1 to October 31 Mackinnon was absent from
his brigade, ill, Wallace of 1/88th commanding it in his
place.

On December 22 Colville was transferred to the command
of the 4th Division, in Cole's absence on leave, J. Campbell
of the 94th getting III B.

Champlemond had the Portuguese brigade on March 19 ;
but by Fuentes Power had it.

4th Division. By February 1 the headquarters and 9 companies
Brunswick Oels had been added to IV A, having been
removed from the Light Division, but on the formation of the 7th Division (March 5), they were removed
to it.

On January 23 Houston was appointed to IV B *vice*
Pakenham, but left the brigade again March 5, on being
appointed to command the 7th Division : Myers would
seem to have commanded IV B till Albuera, where he was
killed. On June 18 Stopford was appointed to command
IV B, but was transferred to I B on July 28, Pakenham
again getting IV B. From November 15 onwards the
" States " do not give any brigadier for IV B, but it continued
to be described as " Pakenham's."

After Albuera 2/7th was drafted into 1/7th, the remnants
being sent home June 26 ; 1/48th from the 2nd Division
was added to IV B June 6. On October 3, the 97th, a single
battalion regiment, was ordered home in consequence of its
severe losses.

On December 22 Colville was appointed to command
the division, Cole having gone home ill.

At Albuera Harvey was in command of the Portuguese
brigade of the division, to which 1st battalion Loyal Lusitanian Legion had been added on March 14 : by September
this unit was renamed 7th Caçadores, the brigade was then
again under Collins, who at Albuera had led a provisional
brigade from the Elvas garrison [5th Line, 5th Caçadores].

5th Division. From February 1 to February 6 the division was
without a G.O.C., Leith being absent : on February 6,
Erskine was appointed to command it, but was transferred
to the command of the advanced guard (the Light Division

and cavalry), from March 7 to April 22. During this period Dunlop seems to have commanded the division, Egerton of 2/44th commanding V B.

On May 11 Erskine was appointed to the 2nd Cavalry Division, and Dunlop again had temporary command of the division until October 2, when G. T. Walker was appointed to command his brigade. By December 1 Leith was again in command of the division.

On March 14 the 2nd Battalion Loyal Lusitanian Legion had been added to Spry's Portuguese brigade. By September it had been renamed 8th Caçadores.

6th Division. Orders of March 5 directed the addition to the division of a new brigade under Burne (of 1/36th), comprising 2nd and 1/36th.

It seems to have been intended to put the Brunswick Oels into the 6th Division, but on the formation of the 7th Division (March 5), they were put in C. Alten's brigade.

On July 21 1/32nd, arrived at Lisbon before July 8, was posted to VI B.

A. Campbell leaving for India in November, the division was without a definite G.O.C. till the end of the year, Burne commanding it temporarily.

On March 14 the Loyal Lusitanian Legion was removed from the Portuguese brigade of the division, and distributed as Caçador battalions to the 4th and 5th Divisions, being replaced by the 12th Line, formerly in Bradford's brigade. At Fuentes Madden commanded the brigade.

Light Division. Wynch dying January 6, the 2nd Brigade was without a commander till February 7, when Drummond (of 1/52nd) was appointed to it. Craufurd having gone home on leave before February 8, the division had no G.O.C., but was under Erskine from March 7 on, together with the Cavalry who also were in the advanced guard.

On March 5 2/52nd, newly arrived at Lisbon, was added to Drummond's brigade.

R. Craufurd returned April 22 and took over the division from Erskine.

By August 1 Beckwith had been invalided home, Andrew Barnard of the 95th commanding the brigade in his place.

On August 21 the headquarters and four companies of the 3/95th, which had gone out to Cadiz in 1810, arrived at Lisbon, and were added to the 1st Brigade, the company 3/95th hitherto with II A being also added to the same brigade.

Drummond dying before September 8, Vandeleur was appointed to the vacant brigade on September 30. By October 1 another company 2/95th had been added to the 1st Brigade.

7th Division. Orders were issued on March 5 for the formation of this division, to be composed of two British brigades under C. Alten and Long, and Coleman's Portuguese, *i.e.* 7th and 19th Line and 2nd Caçadores. The composition of the British brigades is not given, but General Orders say that the Brunswick Oels should be in Alten's brigade, and the Chasseurs Britanniques (arrived at Lisbon from Cadiz, January 28) in Long's. The other regiments in the division were 51st (arrived during February), 85th (arrived March 4), which were in Long's brigade, and the 1st and 2nd Light Battalions, K.G.L., in Alten's. These last only landed on March 21, and did not join the division till it came down with Wellington from Almeida to the Guadiana Valley for the second siege of Badajoz. Till then they had been attached to the force under Beresford: Schwertfeger (*Geschichte der K.G.L.,* i. 317) says the battalions formed part of the 2nd Division, but this does not seem accurate. As they had no casualties at the siege of Badajoz, in which the 7th Division suffered severely, one may presume that they finally joined the division after the siege was raised.

Thus the British brigade (at first there was only one) was 51st, 85th, Chasseurs Britanniques, Brunswick Oels. On March 31 Sontag was posted to it *vice* Long, removed to command Beresford's cavalry, March 19.

On July 19 68th (just arrived) was posted to VII B.

Houston was invalided home before August 1, Sontag commanding the division. By October he too was invalided (his A.D.C. received orders to rejoin his regiment on October

29). Alten was in temporary command, C. Halkett commanding his brigade. VII B was without a G.O.C. from October 15 till de Bernewitz got it on December 23.

On October 3 85th (a single-battalion regiment) was ordered to go home to recruit.

Le Cor was posted to Coleman's brigade on March 14; at Fuentes Doyle had it.

Portuguese. No changes seem to have taken place in Hamilton's division, or in Pack's brigade, but the other unattached brigade was under McMahon in September, and included the 13th and 22nd Line and 5th Caçadores, the 12th Line having been transferred to the 6th Division.

1812.

On January 1 the organization of the Army was as follows :—

Cavalry. 1st Division. G.O.C., Cotton. B [Slade], 1st Dragoons, 12th Light Dragoons; C [no G.O.C., G. Anson absent], 14th and 16th Light Dragoons; E [Cuming of 11th Light Dragoons in absence of V. Alten], 11th Light Dragoons, 1st Hussars, K.G.L.; A [no G.O.C., de Grey absent], 3rd Dragoon Guards, 4th Dragoons; F [Le Marchant], 4th and 5th Dragoon Guards, 3rd Dragoons.

Cavalry. 2nd Division. No G.O.C.; D [Long], 9th and 13th Light Dragoons, 2nd Hussars, K.G.L.

1st Division. G.O.C., Graham. A [H. Campbell], 1st Coldstreams, 1st Scots, 1 company 5/60th; B [? Blantyre for Stopford], 2/24th, 1/26th, 2/42nd, 1/79th, 1 company 5/60th; C [Low], 1st, 2nd, and 5th Line, K.G.L.

2nd Division. G.O.C., Hill. A [Howard], 1/50th, 1/71st, 1/92nd 1 company 5/60th; B [Byng], 1/3rd, 1/57th, 1st Provisional Battalion (*i.e.* 2/31st and 2/66th), 1 company 5/60th; C [Wilson], 1/28th, 2/34th, 1/39th, 1 company 5/60th; also Ashworth's Portuguese.

3rd Division. G.O.C., Picton. A [Mackinnon], 1/45th, Headquarters 5/60th, 74th, 1/88th; B [J. Campbell for Colville], 2/5th, 77th, 2/83rd, 94th; also Palmeirim's Portuguese.

4th Division.   G.O.C., Colville (for Cole).   A [Kemmis], 3/27th, 1/40th, 1 company 5/60th ; B [? Pakenham], 1/7th, 1/23rd, 1/48th, 1 company Brunswick Oels; also Collins' Portuguese.

5th Division.   G.O.C., Leith.   A [Hay], 3/1st, 1/9th, 2/38th, 1 company Brunswick Oels ; B [Walker], 1/4th, 2/30th, 2/44th, 1 company Brunswick Oels ; also Spry's Portuguese.

6th Division.   No G.O.C., Burne in temporary charge.   A [Hulse], 1/11th, 2/53rd, 1/61st, 1 company 5/60th ; B [Burne], 2nd, 1/32nd, 1/36th ; also Madden's [?] Portuguese.

7th Division.   No G.O.C., Alten in temporary charge.   A [C. Halkett for Alten], 1st and 2nd Light Battalions, K.G.L., Brunswick Oels ; B [de Bernewitz], 51st, 68th, Chasseurs Britanniques : also Coleman's Portuguese.

Light Division.   G.O.C., R. Craufurd.   A [? Barnard], 1/43rd, 4 companies 1/95th, 2 companies 2/95th, 5 companies 3/95th, 1st Caçadores ; B [Vandeleur], 1/52nd, 2/52nd, 4 companies 1/95th, 3rd Caçadores.

Portuguese.   Hamilton's division, with brigades under Fonseca and Arch. Campbell.   Unattached brigades under Pack and McMahon.

Subsequent changes were :—

Cavalry.   On January 1 the 1st and 2nd Dragoons, K.G.L., under Bock arrived at Lisbon: they remained near there till March 12, joining the army at Estremoz March 23, and being reckoned as the 2nd Brigade (= G) of the 2nd Cavalry Division.

By January 8 V. Alten was again in command of his brigade.

Several changes took place under orders issued January 29 ; the 3rd and 4th Dragoon Guards were posted to Slade's brigade, from which the 12th Light Dragoons were removed to G. Anson's, the 4th Dragoons replaced the 4th Dragoon Guards in Le Marchant's, and de Grey's brigade disappeared. F. Ponsonby of the 12th Light Dragoons took command of C in Anson's absence.

By April 8 Erskine had resumed command of the 2nd

Cavalry Division, to which Slade's brigade was transferred
April 14, Bock's joining the 1st Division.

On July 1, an exchange was ordered between the 11th
and 14th Light Dragoons: G. Anson, who had resumed
command of his brigade, having 11th, 12th and 16th Light
Dragoons, V. Alten 14th Light Dragoons and 1st Hussars,
K.G.L.

At Salamanca Cotton was wounded, and Le Marchant
killed. While Cotton was disabled, Bock commanded the
Cavalry, de Jonquières having his brigade. W. Ponsonby,
of 5th Dragoon Guards, succeeded to Le Marchant's brigade
(by orders of July 23). Cotton rejoined before October 15,
but had to go home again in December invalided. From
August 1 V. Alten was absent, but rejoined by the middle
of September.

By Orders of October 17, 2nd Hussars, K.G.L., were
transferred to V. Alten's brigade.

1st *Division.* Stopford resumed command of I B before
February 1, but was gone again by April 8. On May 7
Wheatley was appointed to command the brigade until
Stopford's return.

1/26th, being too sickly for field service, was out of I B
before March 8, being sent down to Lisbon, and thence to
Gibraltar to relieve 1/82nd. Their place in I B was taken
by 1/42nd, just arrived from England and posted to I B
April 23. On May 19 2/42nd was ordered home, drafting
its rank and file into 1/42nd. 2/58th was posted to I B
by Orders of April 2; on June 1 its transfer to V B
was ordered, but "orders will hereafter be given as to the
regiment joining the brigade." It seems to have remained
with I B till after the retreat from Burgos.

Graham going home ill July 6, H. Campbell was appointed
to command the division, Fermor getting I A.

Wheatley died September 1, Stirling (of 1/42nd) being
appointed to I B September 11.

On October 11 E. Paget was posted to command the
division, but he was taken prisoner November 17, his place
being taken by W. Stewart, who had just returned to the
Peninsula.

After the retreat from Burgos the division was reorganized.

A new brigade of Guards was added, composed of 1/1st
(Grenadier) Guards, who arrived at Corunna from England
October 1 and joined the army on the Carrion October 24, and
3/1st Guards, who had been at Cadiz, and came up to Madrid
with Skerrett's column. This was ordered October 17,
but cannot have been carried out till later. On November
10 Howard was transferred from II A to command this
brigade. On November 11 Stirling's brigade was ordered
to be removed to the 6th Division, the company of 5/60th
attached to it remaining in the 1st Division. On December
6 the 1st and 2nd Light Battalions, K.G.L., were removed
from VII A to the K.G.L. brigade of the 1st Division.

2nd Division. In Orders of April 14, Tilson-Chowne (formerly
Tilson) was appointed to command the division, " under
Hill," but though present at Almaraz in May does not seem
to have been present to the end of the year. Howard being
transferred to the 1st Division, November 10, Cadogan
(of 1/71st) took command of II A.

3rd Division. At Ciudad Rodrigo Mackinnon was killed (January
19), his brigade going to Kempt—in Orders February 8.

At Badajoz Picton and Kempt were wounded (April 6),
Wallace taking over Kempt's brigade, and also having
temporary command of the division when Picton was disabled : Forbes (of 1/45th) then commanded III A.

After the fall of Badajoz 77th (a single battalion regiment)
was sent down to Lisbon, being much reduced.

On June 28 Pakenham was appointed to command
" Colville's brigade in the 3rd Division," *i.e.* III B. At
Salamanca he commanded the division, Picton having gone
sick again, Wallace and J. Campbell having the brigades.

1/5th, which arrived in May, was posted to III B June 1,
both battalions were at Salamanca, but on July 27 2/5th
was drafted into 1/5th, the skeleton going home in October.

By Orders of October 17 2/87th, which had come up
from Cadiz with Skerrett, was posted to III B, then still
called " Colville's."

Wallace was invalided home after the retreat from Burgos.

Pakenham was to retain command of the division till
the return of " Colville or some other " (*W. D.*, v. 399), his

name does not appear in the States as commanding III B after November 1: Colville apparently came back before the end of the year : *D. N. B.* says in October.

On April 8 Power took over the Portuguese brigade, Champlemond, who had it *vice* Palmeirim by March 17, having been wounded at Badajoz : 12th Caçadores were added to it on April 8.

4th Division. On February 9, Bowes was appointed to command "the brigade late under Pakenham," *i.e.* IV B. In April Colville was wounded at Badajoz, and the division was without a G.O.C. till Cole returned—before July 8.

At Salamanca (July 22), Cole was wounded, and was absent in consequence till October 15. In Cole's absence W. Anson, who was appointed to IV A April 9, would have commanded the division. The vacancy in IV A was caused by the departure of Kemmis—before April 1: at Badajoz Harcourt (of 1/40th) commanded IV A.

Bowes was transferred to the 6th Division May 2, and it would appear that Ellis (of 1/23rd) commanded IV B temporarily. He certainly was in charge of it at Salamanca, and apparently kept it till Skerrett took charge of it. It was then still described as "Pakenham's," as was also the case as late as November 28. Skerrett was appointed to it on October 17, but his force from Cadiz only joined Hill on October 26, and the arrangements ordered on October 17 can hardly have been carried out at once.

Skerrett's brigade (3/1st Guards, 2/47th, 2/87th and 2 companies 2/95th) seems to have acted with IV after joining Hill's force, but was broken up when operations ceased.

Orders of October 17 directed 1/82nd, which had come up from Gibraltar in June and was with the 4th Division at Madrid, to join IV B, but the battalion was transferred to VII A by Orders of November 28, the 20th which arrived in December being posted to IV B instead. On 1/82nd joining, 1/48th was transferred to IV A.

On December 6 the 2nd Provisional Battalion (*i.e.* 2nd and 1/53rd) was posted to IV A.

By Salamanca Stubbs had taken over command of the Portuguese Brigade, which had been under Harvey by March 17 and at the siege of Badajoz.

5th Division. At Badajoz Walker was wounded (April 6):
his brigade had no regular G.O.C. till Pringle was appointed
to it June 28.

On May 10 2/4th, arrived at Lisbon during April, was
posted to V B. In June 1/38th came out and was present
at Salamanca, apparently with V A, but it only appears as
part of] that brigade in the "States" of August 8 and
afterwards.

Orders of June 1 directed 2/58th to join V B, but the
battalion seems to have been with I B till reorganized as
part of the 3rd Provisional Battalion in December.

Hay was absent from June 8, Greville of 1/38th commanding the brigade till July 31, when Hulse was transferred to it. Hulse must have also commanded the division,
as Leith was wounded at Salamanca and invalided home.
Hulse dying (September 6), Pringle commanded the division,
until Oswald was appointed to it (October 25), when Pringle
reverted to his brigade, of which Brooke (of 4th) had been
in command.

Orders of June 18 directed 1/9th to exchange with 2/30th
and 2/44th, but these were cancelled June 28. E. Barnes
was in Orders to command V A October 28, but seems to
have been with the brigade at Villa Muriel three days earlier.
On December 6 he was transferred to VII A. Hay
appears to have returned before December 31.

On December 6 Orders directed the drafting 2/4th into
1/4th and 2/38th into 1/38th, the skeletons being sent home,
also for forming 2/30th and 2/44th into a Provisional Battalion, the 4th. By Orders of October 17 2/47th of Skerrett's
column had been posted to V B, which was then described
as Walker's brigade.

6th Division. On February 9 H. Clinton was appointed to
command the division.

By April 1 VI B was without a brigadier: Bowes was
appointed to it May 2, but he was killed in the attack on
the Salamanca forts (June 24). On this Hinde, of 32nd,
commanded the brigade, being appointed definitely to it
September 30, but ante-dated to June.

On Hulse being transferred to V A, July 31, VI A was

without a brigadier, Bingham, of 2/53rd, being actually in command, until the amalgamation of the two brigades by Orders of November 11. At the same time Stirling's brigade was transferred from the 1st Division to the 6th, 1/91st, which arrived at Corunna October 8, being added to it by Orders of November 28—it actually joined December 14.

On December 6 orders were issued for the formation of 2nd and 2/53rd as the 2nd Provisional Battalion, and of 2/24th, and 2/58th as the 3rd Provisional Battalion, and for their transfer to IV A and VII A respectively.

The Portuguese Brigade was under Eben till April 30, when the Conde de Rezende took command. It was joined by 9th Cacadores on April 10. Rezende was invalided in November, and succeeded by Madden.

7th Division.   On May 2 Alten was transferred to command the Light Division : John Hope being given command of the 7th. Halkett of 2nd Light Battalion, K.G.L. seems to have commanded VII A, though in the "States" no brigadier is named from May 2 till December 6, when E. Barnes was appointed to it.

Hope having to quit the army on account of his health September 23, the division had no G.O.C. till October 25, when Lord Dalhousie was appointed to it, having been put on the Staff of the Army September 12.

On November 28, 1/6th, newly arrived from England, was added to VII A, then called " Colonel Halkett's," and 1/82nd, from IV B, was added to VII B.

Orders of December 6 directed the transfer of the Light Battalions, K.G.L., to the 1st Division, the 3rd Provisional Battalion (*i.e.* 2/24th and 2/58th) being added to VII A.

The Portuguese Brigade was under Palmeirim in March : later it seems to have been under Doyle of the 19th Line.

Light Division.   At Ciudad Rodrigo (January 19), Craufurd was killed, and Vandeleur wounded ; Barnard then took command of the division, and Gibbs of 1/52nd of the 2nd Brigade. By April 15 Vandeleur had resumed command, 2/52nd was drafted to 1/52nd by Orders of February 23, the skeleton being sent home.

On May 2 C. Alten received command of the division.

By May 8 1/95th had been united in the 2nd Brigade, but Orders of August 24 again divided it, 3 companies in each brigade: before the end of the year it was again united and placed in the 1st Brigade.

Two more companies 2/95th came out from England in May, and joined those already out, the four being in the 2nd Brigade. Two more came up from Cadiz with Skerrett, and joined the brigade.

3/95th seems to have been transferred temporarily to the 2nd Brigade, but was back in the 1st by the end of the year.

The 20th Portuguese, which had come up with Skerrett, were posted to " Beckwith's brigade," October 17.

Portuguese. In April, 1812, Power had replaced Arch. Campbell in command of the 4th Brigade, while Bradford had the 11th *vice* McMahon : this now included the 5th Caçadores, 13th and 24th Line.

By July Power had exchanged the 4th Brigade for the 8th, which was in the 3rd Division. A. Campbell would seem to have again commanded the 4th, to which on April 8 the 10th Caçadores were added.

1813.

On January 1 the Army was organized as follows :—

Cavalry. 1st Division. No G.O.C., Cotton absent. F [W. Ponsonby], 5th Dragoon Guards, 3rd and 4th Dragoons ; C [G. Anson], 11th, 12th, and 16th Light Dragoons ; E [V. Alten], 14th Light Dragoons, 1st and 2nd K.G.L. Hussars ; G [Bock], 1st and 2nd K.G.L. Dragoons.

Cavalry. 2nd Division. No G.O.C. B [Slade], 3rd and 4th Dragoon Guards, 1st Dragoons ; D [Long], 9th and 13th Light Dragoons.

1st Division. G.O.C., W. Stewart. A [Howard], 1/1st Guards, 3/1st Guards, 1 company 5/60th ; B [Fermor], 1st Coldstreams, 1st Scots, 1 company 5/60th ; C. [Löw], 1st, 2nd, and 5th Line, K.G.L., 1st and 2nd Light Battalions, K.G.L.*

* Some accounts represent the Light Battalions as forming a separate brigade under Halkett.

2nd Division.   G.O.C., Hill.   A [Cadogan], 1/50th, 1/71st, 1/92nd,
1 company 5/60th ; B [Byng], 1/3rd, 1/57th, 1st Provisional
Battalion (= 2/31st and 2/66th), 1 company 5/60th ; C
[Wilson], 1/28th, 2/34th, 1/39th, 1 company 5/60th; also
Ashworth's Portuguese.

3rd Division.   G.O.C., ? Pakenham.   A [no brigadier], 1/45th,
headquarters 5/60th, 74th, 1/88th ; B [J. Campbell for
Colville], 1/5th, 2/83rd, 2/87th, 94th ; also Power's
Portuguese.

4th Division.   G.O.C., Cole.   A [W. Anson], 3/27th, 1/40th, 1/48th,
2nd Provisional Battalion (= 2nd and 2/53rd), 1 company
5/60th ; B [Skerrett], 1/7th, 20th, 1/23rd, 1 company
Brunswick Oels; also Stubbs' Portuguese.

5th Division.   G.O.C., ? Hay, acting.   A [Hay], 3/1st, 1/9th,
1/38th, 1 company Brunswick Oels ; B [Pringle], 1/4th,
2/47th, 4th Provisional Battalion (= 2/30th and 2/44th),
1 company Brunswick Oels; also Spry's Portuguese.

6th Division.   G.O.C., H. Clinton.   A [Stirling], 1/42nd, 1/79th,
1/91st, 1 company 5/60th ; B [Hinde], 1/11th, 1/32nd,
1/36th, 1/61st ; also Madden's Portuguese.

7th Division.   G.O.C., Dalhousie.   A [Barnes], 1/6th, 3rd
Provisional Battalion (= 2/24th and 2/58th), Headquarters
and 9 companies Brunswick Oels ; B [de Bernewitz], 51st,
68th, 1/82nd ; Chasseurs Britanniques ; also Doyle's
Portuguese.

Light Division.   G.O.C., C. Alten.   A [no brigadier present :
still called Beckwith's], 1/43rd, 1/95th, 3/95th, 1st Caçadores ;
B [Vandeleur], 1/52nd, 2/95th, 3rd Caçadores, ? 20th
Portuguese.

Portuguese.   Hamilton's division, brigades under (?) Fonseca
and Campbell.   Unattached brigades, Pack's and Bradford's.
Subsequent changes were :—
  Cavalry.   By January 25 a new brigade (H) was added,
    composed of two squadrons each of 1st and 2nd Life Guards
    and Royal Horse Guards, O'Loghlin had apparently been
    appointed to command it, but by Orders of November 28,

1812, F. S. Rebow was appointed to command it in his place. It ranked as 3rd Brigade, 2nd Division, but was transferred to the 1st on February 5. In March it was under Sir Robert Hill, Rebow having gone home.

Orders of March 13 directed the distribution among the regiments remaining in the Peninsula of the horses of 4th Dragoon Guards, 9th and 11th Light Dragoons, and 2nd K.G.L. Hussars, these regiments going home. Their place was taken by a new brigade (I), under Colquhoun Grant, of 15th Hussars, composed of the 10th, 15th and 18th Hussars: this first appears in the "States" on April 15.

Orders were issued April 21 for the amalgamation of the two divisions, "under the command of Sir S. Cotton": Cotton did not, however, rejoin till June 25, and in his absence Bock seems to have commanded the cavalry, his brigade being under Bülow.

On May 20 Fane, appointed a Major-General on the Staff April 24, was given B vice Slade, who had been ordered home April 23.

On July 2 orders were issued to transfer the 18th Hussars to V. Alten's brigade, vice the 14th Light Dragoons moved to Long's, which had been reduced to one regiment by the departure of the 9th Light Dragoons (out of the "States" by April 4). Lord E. Somerset at the same time was given command of the Hussar brigade vice Grant and Vandeleur, that of C vice G. Anson, removed to the Home Staff.

On September 6 Grant was appointed to take over Long's brigade, Long having apparently gone home before the battles of the Pyrenees, as his name was not among the commanders of Cavalry brigades thanked by Parliament on November 8 for those operations. On November 24 Hussey Vivian was appointed to take Grant's place.

7th Hussars arrived in Spain in September, and were added to the Hussar brigade. They would seem to have been with the brigade by October 21, but were not in Orders till November 24.

In October O'Loghlin seems to have taken over the Household Brigade, he had been placed on the Staff June 17.

1st Division. In March Howard replaced W. Stewart in command, but on May 19 Graham was appointed to command the division Howard acting as his assistant while Graham commanded the left wing of the army. On October 8 Graham resigned command and went home ill. Sir John Hope * took his place : he was placed on the Staff October 10, as from September 25.

While Howard commanded the division his brigade was under Lambert ; it missed Vittoria, being too sickly to take the field with the army and only joined in August.

On July 2 Lambert was transferred to VI B, and Maitland got the brigade.

Löw went home May 6, the K.G.L. being certainly one brigade only at Vittoria, where Halkett commanded them.

Lord Aylmer's brigade (76th, 2/84th and 85th) which is first mentioned in Orders on July 23, and joined the army during August, may be reckoned as part of the 1st Division with which it always acted. By Orders of October 17 2/62nd was added to it *vice* 2/84th transferred to V B. On November 24 the 77th (from Lisbon) was added to it.

On October 20 Hinüber was appointed to command the K.G.L. infantry.

2nd Division. On March 25 W. Stewart was appointed to command the division " under Hill's direction." At the same time G. T. Walker got Howard's brigade, on the latter taking over the 1st Division from Stewart.

Wilson died in January and O'Callaghan of 39th commanded the brigade till July 23, when Pringle was appointed to it. On May 1 Wellington had written that he was keeping it vacant for Oswald, should Leith come out and take over the 5th Division.

At Vittoria Cadogan was killed and J. Cameron of 92nd took over II A ; he was wounded at Maya (July 25), and Fitzgerald of 5/60th commanded, till Walker actually joined in August. On November 18 Walker was transferred to command the 7th Division, Barnes being appointed to II A November 20.

* Not the same man who commanded the 7th Division in 1812, but the 1st Earl of Hopetoun.

3rd Division. Pakenham was transferred to the 6th Division January 26, the division being under Colville who had returned before that date. Picton rejoined in May, Colville reverting to the command of his brigade. Picton was again absent from September 8, but returned just before the end of the year. Colville was in command at the Nivelle (November), but was transferred to command the 5th Division, when Picton came back in December.

The 11th Caçadores were posted to Power's brigade before April 26, taking the place of the 12th.

Brisbane, appointed to Staff of Army January 7, was given command of III A, *vice* Kempt, March 25.

Colville being given temporary command of the 6th Division on August 8, Keane commanded III B, as also when Colville came back to the division.

4th Division. By Orders of July 2 Skerrett was transferred to the Light Division, his brigade going to Ross of 20th.

By September 1 the Portuguese brigade was under Miller: at the Nivelle (November 10) Vasconcellos had it.

5th Division. While Hay commanded the division Greville of 38th had his brigade. In April Oswald took over the division and commanded it till Leith returned—August 30. Leith was wounded at San Sebastian on September 1, and Oswald again took command; but at the Bidassoa, (October 9) Hay was in command, Greville having V A. On March 9 Robinson was appointed to "Walker's brigade," *i.e.* V B.

On April 12 2/59th from Cadiz was added to V B; on May 10 the 4th Provisional Battalion was ordered to return home. On October 17 2/84th from Lord Aylmer's brigade was added to V B, 2/47th being transferred to V A. Robinson was wounded before Bayonne December 10, and his successor, Piper of 4th, being wounded next day the command passed to Tonson of 2/84th.

At the passage of the Bidassoa the Portuguese brigade was commanded by de Regoa and until the end of the year.

6th Division. On January 26 Pakenham was appointed to command the division in Clinton's absence. On June 25 he was appointed Adjutant-General, and Clinton returned and resumed command. By July 22 Clinton was again absent, Pack getting the division. At Sorauren (July 28) Pack was wounded, and Pakenham took over the division temporarily, giving it over to Colville before August 8, Colville seems to have still been in command at the passage of the Bidassoa (October 9), but Clinton then returned, Colville reverting to the 3rd Division.

Pack had been appointed to command VI A, *vice* Stirling, July 2, Lambert at the same time getting VI B, *vice* Hinde. Stirling commanded VI A when Pack got the division, but went home in October.

The Portuguese brigade was under the command of Madden till the autumn: Douglas of the 8th Line had it at the Nivelle.

7th Division. By April 16 de Bernewitz was no longer in command of his brigade, to which Inglis was appointed May 21, though at Vittoria Grant of 1/82nd commanded it, but Inglis took charge before the Pyrenees.

Le Cor received command of the Portuguese brigade on March 9. When he was promoted in November Doyle had it.

Dalhousie went home after the Bidassoa, October 9, and at the Nivelle (November 9) Le Cor was in command. On November 18 G. T. Walker was given command " in Dalhousie's absence." Le Cor would seem to have been transferred to command the Portuguese division formerly under Hamilton.

On Barnes returning to the 2nd Division November 20, his brigade seems to have gone to Gardiner.

Light Division. On March 23 Kempt was appointed to A. On July 2 Vandeleur was transferred to a cavalry brigade, Skerrett getting B. At the passage of the Bidassoa and to the end of the year Colborne of 52nd was in command of B, *vice* Skerrett, who went home in September.

The 20th Portuguese never joined the division: in place of them on April 26 the 17th Portuguese appear in its " State."

Portuguese. Hamilton had had to give up command of his Portuguese division in February, owing to ill-health, upon which it was under Silveira, the brigades being under Da Costa and Campbell during the battles of the Pyrenees.

By the passage of the Nivelle (November 9) Hamilton was
again in command, Buchan had Da Costa's brigade, but
during the fighting on the Nive (December 9—11), Le Cor
had the division and Buchan and Da Costa the brigades.
Buchan was ordered to transfer himself to the Portuguese
Brigade of the 7th Division on Nov. 9, but this move was
countermanded.

When Pack was moved to a British command (July 2) his
brigade went to Wilson, who commanded it at the Bidassoa,
but had been replaced by A. Campbell by the Nive (December
9), Wilson having been wounded November 18.

Bradford seems to have retained the other unattached
brigade all the year.

1814.

On January 1 the organization was as follows :—

Cavalry. G.O.C., Cotton. I [O'Loghlin], 1st and 2nd Life
Guards, R.H.G. ; F [W. Ponsonby], 5th Dragoon Guards,
3rd and 4th Dragoons ; C [Vandeleur], 12th and 16th Light
Dragoons ; D [Vivian], 13th and 14th Light Dragoons ;
E [V. Alten], 18th Hussars, 1st K.G.L. Hussars ; G [Bock],
1st and 2nd K.G.L. Dragoons ; B [Fane], 3rd Dragoon Guards,
1st Dragoons ; H [Somerset], 7th, 10th and 15th Hussars.

1st Division. G.O.C., Hope, with Howard as assistant ; A
[Maitland for Howard], 1/1st Guards, 3/1st Guards, 1 company
5/60th ; B [Stopford], 1st Coldstreams, 1st Scots, 1 company
5/60th ; C [Hinüber], 1st, 2nd and 5th Line, K.G.L. ; 1st
and 2nd Light Battalions, K.G.L. ; D [Aylmer], 2/62nd,
76th, 77th, 85th.

2nd Division. G.O.C., W. Stewart. A [Barnes], 1/50th, 1/71st,
1/92nd, 1 company 5/60th ; B [Byng], 1/3rd, 1/57th, 1st
Provisional Battalion (2/31st and 2/66th), 1 company 5/60th ;
C [Pringle], 1/28th, 2/34th, 1/39th, 1 company 5/60th ; also
Ashworth's Portuguese.

3rd Division. G.O.C., Picton. A [Brisbane], 1/45th, Headquarters 5/60th, 74th, 1/88th ; B [Keane], 1/5th, 2/83rd,
2/87th, 94th ; also Power's Portuguese.

4th Division. G.O.C., Cole. A [W. Anson], 3/27th, 1/40th,
1/48th, 2nd Provisional Battalion (2nd and 2/53rd), 1

company Brunswick Oels; B [Ross], 1/7th, 1/20th, 1/23rd, 1 company 5/60th; also Vasconcellos' Portuguese.

5th Division. G.O.C., Colville. A [Hay], 3/1st, 1/9th, 1/38th, 2/47th, 1 company Brunswick Oels; B [Robinson], 1/4th, 2/59th, 2/84th, 1 company Brunswick Oels; also de Regoa's Portuguese.

6th Division. G.O.C., Clinton. A [Pack], 1/42nd, 1/79th, 1/91st, 1 company 5/60th; B [Lambert], 1/11th, 1/32nd, 1/36th, 1/61st; also Douglas' Portuguese.

7th Division. G.O.C., Walker. A [Gardiner], 1/6th, 3rd Provisional Battalion (2/24th and 2/58th), Headquarters Brunswick Oels; B [Inglis], 51st, 68th, 1/82nd, Chasseurs Britanniques; also Doyle's Portuguese.

Light Division. G.O.C., C. Alten. A [Kempt], 1/43rd, 1/95th, 3/95th, 1st Caçadores; B [Colborne], 1/52nd, 2/95th, 3rd Caçadores, 17th Portuguese.

Portuguese. Le Cor's division, with Da Costa and Buchan commanding brigades. Unattached brigades under A. Campbell and Bradford.

Subsequent changes were :—

Cavalry. By January 16 several changes had taken place : V. Alten had gone and Vivian had been transferred to his brigade, Fane having transferred from B to D (late Vivian's). Bock also went (he was drowned off the coast of Brittany in February) about the same time.

From January 25 W. Ponsonby was absent, Lord C. Manners of 3rd Dragoons commanding his brigade.

By March 25 Arentschildt (of 1st K.G.L. Hussars) had been given Bock's old brigade : on Vivian being wounded (April 8) Arentschildt was transferred to E, and Bülow got the " German Heavy Brigade."

Fane's name appears in the "States" both as commanding B and D. According to the *Regimental History of the 14th Hussars* (by Col. H. B. Hamilton) he commanded both, working them practically as a division, the brigades being respectively commanded by Clifton of the Royals (B), and Doherty of the 13th Light Dragoons (D).

1st Division. 1/37th joined Aylmer's brigade before March 25. On April 14 Stopford was wounded at Bayonne and his division went to Guise.

2nd Division. On February 15 Pringle was wounded and O'Callaghan commanded the brigade.

It was arranged that when Lord Dalhousie rejoined, and resumed command of the 7th Division, Walker should revert to II A and Barnes take over III B, but Walker was wounded at Orthez and went home, so the arrangement was never carried out.

By January 16 Harding had replaced Ashworth in command of the 5th Portuguese brigade.

3rd Division. No changes : Brisbane was slightly wounded at Toulouse.

4th Division. Ross was wounded at Orthez (February 27) and the brigade was without a G.O.C.

5th Division. After February 1 Robinson was absent. Hay was killed before Bayonne April 14.

6th Division. Pack was wounded at Toulouse, as was also Douglas.

1/32nd missed Toulouse, being at San Jean de Luz refitting.

7th Division. Walker was wounded at Orthez and went home : Dalhousie arriving almost immediately after the battle and resuming command.

By January 16, the Portuguese brigade was under Doyle (he may have got it when Le Cor obtained command of the Portuguese division.)

Light Division. 1/43rd and 1/95th both missed Orthez, being away refitting.

Portuguese. Da Costa was ordered back to Portugal before March 15,

APPENDIX III.

PENINSULAR AUTOBIOGRAPHIES, JOURNALS, LETTERS, ETC.

THE subjoined list, which includes all the printed autobiographies, diaries, journals, and series of letters utilized in this volume, makes no pretensions to be exhaustive. It contains, however, all the more important original sources of this character, as opposed to formal histories, controversial monographs, and biographies of Peninsular officers written by authors who were not themselves engaged in the war. But I have added to the list those later biographies which contain a great proportion of original and contemporary letters or diaries, such as Delavoye's *Life of Lord Lynedoch*, Rait's *Life of Lord Gough*, Wrottesley's *Life of Sir John Burgoyne*, and C. Vivian's *Life of Lord Vivian*. Much valuable first-hand information is imbedded in such works.

The books are arranged under headings according to the position which the writer held in the Peninsular War, mainly by regiments, but partly under departmental sections [staff, commissariat, medical, etc.]. I trust that the list may be found useful for those wishing to compile regimental, brigade, or divisional annals of any part of the war.

I. STAFF.

[*Including the Diaries, Memoirs, Correspondence, etc., of General Officers, their Aides-de-Camp, and Officers attached to Head-Quarters.*]

Blayney (Lord). Narrative of a Forced Journey through Spain and France, by Major-General Lord Blayney [The Fuengirola Expedition, etc.]. London, 1814.

Burghersh (Lord). Memoir of the Early Campaign of the Duke of Wellington in Portugal and Spain [anon]. London, 1820.

Cotton, Sir S. Life and Correspondence of Field-Marshal Lord Combermere [Sir Stapleton Cotton], ed. by Viscountess Combermere and Capt. W. Knollys. London, 1866.

Douglas, Sir H. Life of General Sir Howard Douglas from his Notes, Conversation, and Letters [Campaigns of 1811–14]. London, 1863.

Fitzclarence, A. An Account of the British Campaign of 1809 under Sir A. Wellesley in Portugal and Spain by Lt.-Col. Fitzclarence [Earl of Munster]. London, 1831.

Graham, Sir T. Life and Letters of Sir Thomas Graham, Lord Lynedoch, by Captain A. M. Delavoye. London, 1868.

Gomm (Sir W.). His Letters and Journals from 1799 to Waterloo [1808–9 and 1810–14]. London, 1881.

Hill, Lord, Life and Letters of, by Rev. E. Sidney. London, 1845.

Larpent, F. S. The Private Journal of Judge-Advocate F. S. Larpent, attached to Lord Wellington's Headquarters, 1812–14. London, 1853.

Leith Hay, A. Narrative of the Peninsular War, by Sir Andrew Leith Hay [Aide-de-Camp to General Leith]. 2 vols. London, 1879.

Mackinnon, General Henry. Journal in Portugal and Spain, 1809–12 [Privately Printed]. 1812.

Moore, Sir J. The Diary of Sir John Moore, ed. by General Sir T. F. Maurice. 2 vols. London, 1904.

Picton, Sir T. Memoirs and Correspondence of General Sir T. Picton, by H. B. Robinson. 2 vols. London, 1836.

Porter, Sir R. K. Letters from Portugal and Spain written during the March of the British Troops [by Sir Robert Ker Porter], 1808–9. London, 1809.

Shaw-Kennedy, T. [Aide-de-Camp to General Craufurd]. Diary of 1810, printed in Lord Fitzclarence's *Manual of Outpost Duties*. London, 1849.

Sorell, T. S. Notes on the Campaign of 1808–9, by Lieut.-Col. T. S. Sorell, Aide-de-Camp to Sir D. Baird. London, 1828.

Stewart, Sir Chas. Lives and Correspondence of the Second and Third Marquesses of Londonderry [the third was Chas. Stewart, Adjutant-General to Wellington]. 3 vols. London, 1861.

Vere, C. B. Marches, Movements, and Operations of the 4th Division, in Spain and Portugal, 1810–12, by Chas. Brooke Vere, Assistant Quarter-Master General of the Division. Ipswich, 1841.

II. REGIMENTAL REMINISCENCES AND JOURNALS.

(a) CAVALRY.

7th Hussars. Vivian (Lord). Richard Hussey Vivian, First Baron Vivian, Memoir and Letters, by Hon. Claud Vivian [1808–9 and 1813–14]. London, 1897.

11th Light Dragoons. Farmer, G. " The Light Dragoon," the story of Geo. Farmer, 11th Light Dragoons, ed. Rev. G. R. Gleig [1811 and Waterloo]. London, 1844.

14th Light Dragoons. Hawker, Peter. Journal of the Campaign of 1809, by Lieut.-Col. Hawker, 14th Light Dragoons. London,1810.

——. Reminiscences of 1811–12 by Cornet Francis Hall. In *Journal United Service Institution* for 1912.

16th Light Dragoons. Hay, W. Reminiscences under Wellington, 1808–15, by Captain William Hay, 52nd Foot and 16th Light Dragoons. London, 1901.

——. Tomkinson, W. The Diary of a Cavalry Officer in the Peninsular and Waterloo Campaigns, 1809–15. London, 1894.

18th Hussars. Woodberry, G. Journal of Lieutenant Woodberry in the Campaigns of 1813–15. Paris, 1896.

20th Light Dragoons. Landsheit (N.). The Hussar: the story of Norbert Landsheit, Sergeant in the York Hussars and the 20th Light Dragoons, ed. Rev. G. R. Gleig. London, 1837.

Anonymous. Jottings from my Sabretache, by a Chelsea Pensioner [Campaigns of 1813–14]. London, 1847.

——. Personal Narrative of Adventures in the Peninsular War, 1812–13, by an Officer in the Staff Corps Cavalry. London, 1827.

(b) INFANTRY.

1st Foot Guards. Batty, R. The Campaign in the Pyrenees and Southern France, 1813–14, by Captain Robert Batty, 1st Foot Guards. *Illustrated.* London, 1823.

2nd Foot Guards. Stepney, S. C. Leaves from the Diary of an Officer of the Guard, Sketches of Campaigning Life, by Lieut.-Col. S. Cowell Stepney, K.H., Coldstream Guards [Campaigns of 1810–12]. London, 1854.

3rd Foot Guards. Stevenson, J. Twenty-One Years in the British Foot Guards, by John Stevenson, 3rd Foot Guards, sixteen years a non-commissioned officer, forty years a Wesleyan class-leader [Campaigns of 1809–11]. London, 1830.

3rd Foot Guards. Stothert, W. Journal of the Campaigns of 1809–11, by Captain William Stothert, 3rd Foot Guards. London, 1812.

3rd Foot (the Buffs). Reminiscences of a Veteran, being Personal and Military Adventures in the Peninsula, etc., by Lieut.-Gen. T. Bunbury [only 1808–9 in the Buffs]. London, 1861.

5th Foot. Morley, S. Memoirs of a Sergeant of the 5th Regiment, by Sergeant Stephen Morley, 5th Foot [Campaigns of 1808–11]. Ashford, 1842.

7th Foot. Cooper, J. S. Rough Notes of Seven Campaigns in Portugal, etc., by John Spenser Cooper, Sergeant 7th Royal Fusiliers. Carlisle, 1869.

——. Knowles, R. Letters of Lieut. Robert Knowles, 7th Fusiliers, during the Campaigns of 1811–13, ed. by Sir Lees Knowles, Bart. Bolton, 1909.

9th Foot. Hale, J. Journal of James Hale, late Sergeant 9th Foot [1808–14]. Cirencester, 1826.

20th Foot. Steevens, C. Reminiscences of Col. Chas. Steevens, 1795–1818 [Campaigns of 1808 and 1813–14]. Winchester, 1878.

24th Foot. Tidy, C. Recollections of an Old Soldier, a Biographical Sketch of the Late Col. Tidy, C.B., 24th Regt. [1808]. London, 1849.

28th Foot. Cadell, C. Narrative of the Campaigns of the 28th Regt. from 1802 to 1832, by Col. Chas. Cadell [1809–1814]. London, 1835.

——. Blakeney, R. Services, Adventures, and Experiences of Capt. Robert Blakeney, " A Boy in the Peninsular War," edited by Julian Sturgis [1808–14]. London, 1899.

29th Foot. Leslie. Journal during the Peninsular War, etc., of Colonel Leslie of Balquain [1809–14]. Aberdeen, 1887.

——. Leith-Hay, A. A Narrative of the Peninsular War, by Sir Andrew Leith Hay (personal adventures, first with the 29th, then as Aide-de-Camp to General Leith). London, 1839.

31st Foot. L'Estrange, G. Recollections of Sir George L'Estrange, 1812–14. London, 1873.

32nd Foot. Ross-Lewin, H. Life of a Soldier, a Narrative of 27 years' service in various parts of the World, by a Field Officer [Major H. Ross-Lewin] [1808–14]. 2 vols. London, 1834.

34th Foot. Bell, G. Rough Notes by an Old Soldier, during Fifty Years' Service, from Ensign to Major-General. 2 vols. [Campaigns of 1811–14]. London, 1867.

40th Foot. Lawrence, W. The Autobiography of Sergeant Wm. Lawrence, 40th Regt., ed. by G. N. Banks [Campaigns of 1808–14]. London, 1901.

42nd Foot. Anton, J. Retrospect of a Military Life, during the most Eventful Period of the late War, by James Anton, Quartermaster-Sergeant, 42nd Highlanders [1813–14]. Edinburgh, 1841.

——. Malcolm, J. Reminiscences of the Campaign in the Pyrenees and the South of France in 1813–14, by John Malcolm, Lieut. 42nd Foot: in Constable's *Memorials of the Late Wars.* Edinburgh, 1828.

——. Anon. Personal Narrative of a Private Soldier who served in the 42nd Highlanders for Twelve Years [1808–9 and 1811–14]. 1821.

43rd Foot. Cooke, J. H. Memoir of the late War, a Personal Narrative of Captain J. H. Cooke, 43rd Light Infantry [Campaigns of 1811–14]. London, 1831.

——. ——. A Narrative of Events in the South of France and America, 1814–15 [continuation of the above]. London, 1835.

——. Napier, Geo. The Early Military Life of Gen. Sir Geo. Napier, K.C.B., written by himself. London, 1886.

——. Anon. Memoirs of a Sergeant late of the 43rd Light Infantry, previously to and during the Peninsular War, including the account of his Conversion from Popery to the Protestant Religion. London, 1835.

47th Foot. Harley, J. The Veteran, or Forty Years in the British Service, by Capt. John Harley, late Paymaster 47th Regt. [Campaigns of 1811–14]. London, 1838.

48th Foot. Moyle Sherer, G. Recollections of the Peninsula, by Col. G. Moyle Sherer [Campaigns of 1809–13]. London, 1823.

50th Foot. MacCarthy, J. The Storm of Badajoz, with a Note on the Battle of Corunna, by J. MacCarthy, late 50th Regt. London, 1836.

——. Napier, Chas. Life and Opinions of Sir Charles James Napier, by Sir William Napier [First vol. for the 50th at Corunna, etc.]. London, 1857.

50th Foot. Patterson, J. Adventures of Captain John Patterson,
with Notices of the Officers of the 50th Queen's Regiment,
1807–21. London, 1837.
——. Patterson, J. Camp and Quarters, Scenes and Impressions
of Military Life by the same Author. London, 1843.
51st Foot. Wheeler, W. Journal from the year 1809 to 1816 by
William Wheeler, a Soldier of the 51st or King's Own Light
Infantry. Corfu, 1824.
52nd Foot. Hay, W. Reminiscences under Wellington, 1808–15,
by Captain William Hay, 52nd Foot and 16th Light Dragoons.
London, 1901.
——. Seaton (Lord). Life and Letters of Sir John Colborne
[Lord Seaton], ed. by G. C. Moore-Smith. London, 1903.
66th Foot. Henry, W. Events of a Military Life, being Recollections of the Service in the Peninsula, etc., of Walter Henry,
Surgeon, 66th Regt. [Campaign of 1812–14]. London,
1843.
68th Foot. Green, J. Vicissitudes of a Soldier's Life, by John
Green, late of the 68th Durham Light Infantry. Louth,
1827.
71st Foot. Anon. Vicissitudes in the Life of a Scottish Soldier,
1808 to 1815, including some particulars of the Battle of
Waterloo. London, 1827.
——. Anon, TS. Journal of T. S. of the 71st Highland Light
Infantry, in *Memorials of the Late Wars* [ed. Constable].
Edinburgh, 1828.
82nd Foot. Wood, G. The Subaltern Officer, a Narrative by
Captain Geo. Wood of the 82nd Prince of Wales's Volunteers
[1808 and 1813–14]. London, 1825.
85th Foot. Gleig, G. R. The Subaltern [Campaigns in the Pyrenees
and South of France, 1813–14], by G. R. Gleig, 85th Foot.
London, 1823.
87th Foot. Gough [Lord]. See Letters 1809–14 in R. S. Rait's *Life
of Lord Gough.*
88th Foot. Grattan, W. Adventures with the Connaught Rangers,
1804–14, by Lieut. Wm. Grattan. London, 1847.
——. ——. Second series of Reminiscences. London, 1853.
92nd Foot. Hope, J. Military Memoirs of an Infantry Officer,
1809–16 [Lieut. Jas. Hope, 92nd Highlanders]. London,
1833.

92nd Foot. Anon. Letters from Portugal, etc., during the Campaigns of 1811-14 by a British Officer [92nd Gordon Highlanders]. London, 1819.

——. Robertson, D. Journal of Sergeant D. Robertson, late 92nd Highlanders, during the Campaigns between 1797 and 1818. Perth, 1842.

94th Foot. Donaldson, J. Recollection of an Eventful Life, chiefly passed in the Army, by Joseph Donaldson, Sergeant 94th Scotch Brigade [1809-14]. London, 1825.

95th [Rifle Brigade]. Costello, E. Memoirs of Edward Costello of the Rifle Brigade, comprising narratives of Wellington's Campaigns in the Peninsula, etc. London, 1857.

——. Fernyhough, R. Military Memoirs of Four Brothers, by the survivor, Lieut. R. Fernyhough, Rifle Brigade. London, 1829.

——. Green, W. A brief Outline of the Travels and Adventures of Wm. Green, Bugler, Rifle Brigade, during a period of ten years, 1802-12. Coventry, 1857.

——. Harris. Recollections of Rifleman Harris, ed. by Capt. Curling [1808-09]. London, 1848.

——. Kincaid, J. Adventures in the Rifle Brigade, in the Peninsula, France, and the Netherlands, 1810-15, by Captain Sir John Kincaid. London, 1830.

——. ——. Random Shots from a Rifleman [Miscellaneous Anecdotes]. London, 1835.

——. Leach, J. Rough Sketches of the Life of an Old Soldier, during a service in the West Indies, the Peninsula, etc. [1808-14]. London, 1831.

——. ——. Rambles on the Banks of Styx [Peninsular Reminiscences], by the same author. London, 1847.

——. Simmons, G. A British Rifleman: Journals and Correspondence of Major Geo. Simmons (95th) during the Peninsular War, etc., ed. Col. Willoughby Verner. London, 1899.

——. Smith, H. The Autobiography of General Sir Harry Smith [vol. i. contains Peninsular Memoirs], ed. G. Moore Smith. London, 1901.

——. Surtees, W. Twenty-five Years in the Rifle Brigade, by Wm. Surtees, Quartermaster [1808, 1811-14]. London, 1833.

III. ARTILLERY.

Dickson, Alex. The Dickson Papers, Diaries and Correspondence of Major-General Sir Alexander Dickson, G.C.B.   Series 1809–18. ed. by Major John Leslie, R.A. 2 vols. Woolwich, 1908–12.

Frazer, A. S. Letters of Sir Augustus Simon Frazer, K.C.B., Commanding Royal Horse Artillery under Wellington, written during the Peninsular Campaigns. London, 1859.

[See also numerous short Journals and Series of Letters in the Journal of the Royal Artillery Institution, Woolwich, in recent years, Swabey, Ingilby, Downman, etc.]

IV. ENGINEERS.

Burgoyne, J. F. Life and Correspondence of Sir John Fox Burgoyne, ed. Hon. Geo. Wrottesley. London, 1873.

Boothby, C. Under England's Flag, 1804–9, Memoirs, Diary, and Correspondence of Captain C. Boothby, R.E. [Corunna Campaign]. London, 1900.

——. A Prisoner of France, by the same [Oporto and Talavera Campaigns]. London, 1898.

Landmann, G. T. Recollections of Military Life, 1806–8 [Vimeiro Campaign], by Colonel Geo. Landmann, R.E. London, 1854.

V. TRAIN AND COMMISSARIAT.

Dallas, A. Autobiography of the Rev. Alexander Dallas, including his service in the Peninsula [1811–14] in the Commissariat Department. London, 1870.

Chesterton, G. L. Peace, War, and Adventure, an Autobiography by George Laval Chesterton [vol. i. contains service in Catalonia 1812–14]. London, 1853.

Graham, W. Travels in Portugal and Spain, 1812–14, by William Graham of the Commissariat Department. London, 1820.

Head, F. Memoirs of an Assistant-Commissary-General (in the Peninsular War), by Gen. F. Head. London, 1840.

Hennegan, R. D. Seven Years in the Peninsula and the Netherlands, by Sir Richard D. Hennegan, of the Field Train [Campaigns of 1808–14]. London, 1846.

VI. MEDICAL DEPARTMENT.

Henry, W. Events of a Military Life, Recollections of the Peninsular War, etc., by Surgeon Walter Henry, 66th Regt. London, 1843.

McGrigor, J.   The Autobiography and Services of Sir Jas. McGrigor,
    Bart., late Director General of the Medical Department
    [1812–14].   London, 1861.
Neale, A.   Letters from Portugal and Spain [Vimeiro and Corunna),
    by Adam Neale, M.D.   London, 1809.

VII. WORKS BY CHAPLAINS.

Bradford, W.   Sketches of the Country, Character, and Costume in
    Portugal and Spain, 1808–9, by Rev. Wm. Bradford, Chaplain
    of Brigade.   40 coloured plates.   London, 1810.
Ormsby, J. W.   Operations of the British Army in Portugal and
    Spain, 1808–9, by Rev. Jas. Wilmot Ormsby, with appendices,
    etc.   London, 1809.

VIII. OFFICERS IN THE KING'S GERMAN LEGION.

Hartmann, Sir Julius, Ein Lebenskizze, 1808–15.   Berlin, 1901.
Ompteda, Baron, C.   Memoir and Letters of Baron Christian Ompteda,
    Colonel in the King's German Legion [Campaigns of 1812–14].
    London, 1894.
Anon.   Journal of an Officer of the King's German Legion, 1803–16.
    London, 1827.

IX. WORKS BY OFFICERS IN THE PORTUGUESE SERVICE.

Blakiston, J.   Twelve Years' Military Adventure, in three Quarters
    of the Globe [by Major John Blakiston], 1813–14, with the
    Portuguese Caçadores.   1829.
Bunbury, T.   Reminiscences of a Veteran, Personal and Military
    Adventures in the Peninsula, etc. [1810–14 with the 20th
    Portuguese Line].   1861.
Madden, G., Services of, 1809–13, by a Friend.   London, 1815.
Mayne, R., and Lillie, J. W.   The Loyal Lusitanian Legion, 1808–10.
    London, 1812.
Warre, G.   Letters, 1808–12, of Sir George Warre [of the Portuguese
    Staff], ed. by Rev. E. Warre, D.D.   London, 1909.

X. OFFICERS IN THE SPANISH SERVICE.

Whittingham, Sir S.   Memoir [and Correspondence] of Lieut.-Gen.
    Sir Samuel Ford Whittingham.   London, 1868.

INDEX

A.

THE END